ALSO BY PAUL SCHNEIDER

The Adirondacks

The Enduring Shore

The Enduring Shore

A History of
Cape Cod, Martha's Vineyard, and Nantucket

PAUL SCHNEIDER

A JOHN MACRAE BOOK

Henry Holt and Company • New York

Henry Holt and Company, LLC
Publishers since 1866
115 West 18th Street
New York, New York 10011

Henry Holt® is a registered trademark of
Henry Holt and Company, LLC.

Published in Canada by Fitzhenry & Whiteside Ltd.,
195 Allstate Parkway, Markham, Ontario L3R 4T8.

Library of Congress Cataloging-in-Publication Data
Schneider, Paul, date.
The enduring shore: a history of Cape Cod, Martha's Vineyard,
and Nantucket / Paul Schneider.—1st ed.
p.   cm.
"A John Macrae book."
Includes index.
ISBN 0-8050-5928-8 (hb)
1. Cape Cod (Mass.)—History.   2. Natural history—Massachusetts—
Cape Cod.   3. Nantucket Island (Mass.)—History.   4. Natural history—
Massachusetts—Nantucket Island.   5. Martha's Vineyard (Mass.)—History.
6. Natural history—Massachusetts—Martha's Vineyard.   I. Title.
F72.C3 S34 2000   99-048496
917.44'92—dc21

Henry Holt books are available for special
promotions and premiums. For details contact:
Director, Special Markets.

First Edition 2000

Designed by Paula Russell Szafranski

Cartography by Clifford Dorr

*Title page photograph of
Menemsha, Martha's Vineyard. Courtesy of Grant Smith/Corbis.*

Printed in the United States of America

3   5   7   9   10   8   6   4   2

For Nina

CONTENTS

ACKNOWLEDGMENTS

There are many people to whom I am grateful, foremost among them my wife, Nina Bramhall, without whose encouragement, support, insight, and above all patience there would be no book. Also in a league of her own is my mother, Pat Schneider, whose magnificent talent for teaching and editing and whose willingness to read and re-read, listen and re-listen, is superseded only by her own gift for writing. Others whose readings of early versions of all or part of the text were helpful include my father, Peter Schneider, who long ago taught me that every sentence has at least two meanings. And my sister and sometime paddling partner, (the Reverend Doctor) Laurel C. Schneider, who patiently reminds me that one meaning is relatively closer to absolute truth. My other siblings, Rebecca and Bethany, were not subjected this time to text, but got their usual periodic earfuls over the long-distance wires, as did Cindy Davenport. Kib Bramhall, Tess Bramhall, and Jeff Ciciora read all or part of the manuscript at various stages and made helpful comments. Kib also offered to rescue me in his Boston Whaler if I ever found myself drowning in the middle of Vineyard Sound, for which I am grateful.

Thanks are due to many, many previous writers and researchers, the most important of whom are mentioned in the notes section. And to the staffs of various museums and historical societies around the region, including: Bruce Andrews, Peter Van Tassel, and Jill Bouck at Martha's Vineyard Historical Society; Elizabeth Oldham at Nantucket Historical Association;

Mary Sicchio at the William Brewster Nickerson Memorial Room at Cape Cod Community College; Lynn Horton at the Sandwich Glass Museum; Janet Lexow at the Sturgis Library in Barnstable; Diane Shumway at the Truro Historical Society Museum; Rebecca Aaronson at the Society for the Preservation of New England Antiquities; and various anonymous employees of the New York and Boston public libraries. Thanks to Nat Benjamin and Emily Bramhall for clarifying various points of sailing, and to Book Den East, of Oak Bluffs, where I spent a significant portion of my advance with no regrets.

I'd like to thank my friend Anita Leclerc, who first gave me the opportunity to write for publication and then kindly took the time to teach me how to do it. And my friend Laura Marmor, who introduced me to my agent, Kim Witherspoon. Kim in turn introduced me to my editor Jack Macrae, whose very good idea this book was and without whose insight and guidance it would never have come to completion. Thanks as well to Katy Hope and Rachel Klauber-Speiden, also of Henry Holt.

Finally, I wish to acknowledge my son Nathaniel, whose patience is boundless as long as he's permitted to ask every ten minutes if the work is done for the day. The answer, at last, may be yes.

The Enduring Shore

CAPAWACK

It was too good to be true. But there he was, back among his friends and
family on Chappaquiddick. Back on Edgartown Harbor. Back on the island
of Martha's Vineyard in the indescribably exquisite month of July, with the
rest of his life stretched out before him.

Giant schools of striped bass crashed nightly along the beaches during
that month, gulping into flickering clouds of sand eels. Bluefish blitzed in
broad daylight in the outer harbor, under flocks of screaming and diving
terns and along the heaving rip out at Wasque Point. Up-island, all over the
woods, the small green nuggets that hung where the blueberry blossoms
had fallen off a month before were softening now, and darkening. The last
of the strawberries were ripe. The corn was waist high. How many times
had he thought about the last lobster he had eaten, the last clambake on the
beach before a warm fire, the sloppy hands and cool air? How many times
had he wondered when, or if ever, such perfect days would come again?

For three years, most of them spent in the miserable city of London, he
had worked hard for various bosses who occasionally tried to be polite but
always managed to say *no* when the right thing to say would have been *yes*.
Never was he away so far or for so long before. But despite all that, it now
felt as it always did whenever he got back on-island; he felt as if he had
never left.

Or maybe he didn't feel that way at all. Maybe he felt as if things could
never be the same again. Maybe it wasn't Edgartown Harbor, but up the

Lagoon Pond in Vineyard Haven. There's no way, really, to know. All that is known is that the year was 1614—twelve years since the first English attempt to establish a year-round presence in the neighborhood of Cape Cod and the Islands had failed, and six years before the Pilgrims would succeed. It was 1614, and Epenow, the prized Wampanoag slave of Sir Ferdinando Gorges, was back home. Back home, having swum with all his formidable might for shore with the sound of muskets firing over his head.

Out on the ship from which he had just escaped, the English tended to their injured. The captain, Nicholas Hobson, was struck by an arrow, as were "many of his company." They may additionally have been in a state of shock. Only the day before, the deck of their little vessel was crowded with friendly Wampanoag, many of them brothers and sisters of Epenow. "The principal inhabitants of the place came aboard," wrote Ferdinando Gorges (who wasn't actually there) in his memoir many years later. They "were kindly entertained by the Captain, [and] departed in their canoes promising the next morning to come aboard again and bring some trade with them."

When the roughly twenty dugout canoes arrived the next day at the appointed hour, the men who paddled them were standoffish, remaining "at a certain distance with their bows ready." They refused to come nearer no matter how much Captain Hobson talked and gestured. Hobson called Epenow up from the middle of the ship, where he was being held, to the forecastle, in order to have him speak some reason to his countrymen. He came forward immediately, leaving behind the two men who were supposed to guard him, and called out to his friends in the canoes. He spoke English, encouraging his old neighbors to come aboard in a language none of them understood. He also spoke in his native tongue, giving his relatives quite different instructions in a language that none of his captors understood. Then, according to Gorges, "in the interim [he] slips himself overboard, and although he was taken hold of by one of the company, yet being a strong, heavy man, could not be stayed." As soon as Epenow was in the water, his relatives let fly a "shower of arrows," under the cover of which he swam away from captivity. "Epenow privately (as it appeared) had contracted with his friends how he might make his escape without performing what he had undertaken," Gorges sulkily reported.

According to at least one informed source, Epenow had planned his dramatic return to the Vineyard long before the family reunion the day before on the deck of Captain Hobson's boat. Gorges's mention of Epenow not "performing what he had undertaken" is typically coy in regard to the purpose of the visit to the island. Even though he was writing thirty years after the event, Gorges wrote only obliquely about "my pretended designs," perhaps because he still harbored them. And he mentioned what Epenow "had contracted to do" without saying what that was particularly, and how Epenow was risking getting "his brains knocked out as soon as he came ashore" if his friends found out he had disclosed what Gorges called "the secrets of his country."

But Captain John Smith—of Virginia fame—had no motive to hold back what *he* knew. (Though he may have had his reasons for embarrassing Gorges, who had apparently decided that Smith was at least one of the causes of his spate of bad luck and had consequently stopped sending him on voyages to the New World.) According to Smith, Epenow laid the groundwork for his escape using the same strategy that another enslaved Native American used almost a century before on Coronado: he simply told the master what he wanted to hear. Hobson and his crew were "in search for a mine of Gold about an Isle called Capawick, Southwards of the shoals of Cape James (Cod), as they were informed by a savage called Epenow." Epenow, it turned out, had not been unobservant of the hopes and aspirations of Gorges and his colleagues during his years in London. He "deluded them," said Smith, "thus to get home."

In fairness to Sir Ferdinando Gorges, he was not a cold-blooded Pizarro. Nor was he, by historical standards, an abusive slave driver. He had no plantations, factories, or gold mines in which his human acquisitions toiled (though he was looking for the latter). In fact, it's not clear what work, if any, Epenow and the other Indians in Gorges's household actually performed; sources tend to describe them as "in his retinue," or even "in his family." Sir Ferdinando was, one might say, something of a collector of the New England natives who periodically showed up in Old England in the decades before the Pilgrims arrived at Provincetown.

A self-interested collector, to be sure. After Walter Raleigh's final fall from influence with the ascension of James VI of Scotland to the English throne in 1603, Gorges and his partners in the Plymouth Company acquired the "rights" to develop a vast tract of real estate stretching from Delaware to Maine. For them, owning Native Americans was a kind of industrial espionage, a cheaper way to find out about their theoretical holdings than blindly funding voyages. In Gorges's case, such voyages had a discouraging tendency to turn up nothing in the way of profits.

"While I was laboring by what means I might best continue life in my languishing hopes," he wrote, "there comes one Captain Henry Harley unto me, bringing with him a native of the island of Capawick, a place seated to the southward of Cape Cod, whose name was Epenowe." Gorges was a little fuzzy on the details of Epenow's capture and previous life, other than that some earlier master had used the Vineyarder as a sideshow attraction in London. "It is true," Gorges wrote, "he was a goodly man, of a brave aspect, stout, and sober in his demeanor, and had learned so much English as to bid those that wondered at him 'Welcome! Welcome!'"

Gorges put Epenow up in London with Assacumet, one of five "sachems of Pemaquid" that had been taken from the shores of Maine in 1605. Like the vast majority of native New Englanders, both men spoke languages from the Eastern Algonquian linguistic family, and Assacumet plied Epenow for information about Cape Cod and the Islands. Whether it was his experience of the Spanish slave market or of the London street carnivals that inspired Epenow's story of gold back home on Martha's Vineyard is unknown. There's some possibility it was Assacumet's suggestion, or that Gorges himself helped put the idea in Epenow's head by asking a little too anxiously about the copper that many New England natives had been observed wearing. In his roundabout way, however, Gorges implied that Harley already had gold fever when he brought Epenow to him. Gorges's usual partner, the earl of Southampton, agreed to invest one hundred pounds and introduced Gorges to Hobson, whose own willingness to put up one hundred pounds no doubt went a long way toward ensuring him the job as commander of the expedition.

When the ship sailed in June of 1614, Epenow wasn't the only Native American expatriate on board. Assacumet and Wenape ("another native of those parts, sent me [Gorges] out of the Isle of Wight for my better information") were included in the crew as well. For the most part, the three Indians did as they were asked, and Gorges reported that Captain Hobson was "piloted from place to place by the natives as well as their hearts could desire." Until, that is, they got to the Vineyard.

Gorges apparently was not entirely without his suspicions about Epenow's story.* His crew was specifically instructed to keep a good eye on the man: "I gave the Captain strict charge to endeavor by all means to prevent his escape," he wrote later, "and for the more surety, I gave order to have three gentlemen of my own kindred (two brothers of Sturton's and Master Matthews) to be ever at hand with him, clothing him with long garments fitly to be laid hold on if occasion should require." Captain Hobson

---

*There was similar talk of gold during the 1607 attempt to establish a colony at Sagahadoc, Maine, which had proved false.

and his crew had reason therefore to worry about what Sir Ferdinando would say if he found out that Epenow had escaped unharmed; Epenow was killed in the fracas, they agreed to tell him.

Near the guildhall in the city of London was a bar called the Mermaid. In the first decades of the 1600s it was the favorite gathering place for people interested in the New World. John Smith went there when he was in town, as did Captain Barlowe of Sir Walter Raleigh's 1584 expeditions to the coast of America. Many of the plans regarding the founding of the Virginia Colony were discussed at the bar, as were more than a few decisions regarding New England. Bartholomew Gosnold, Bartholomew Gilbert, and others from the 1602 voyage to Cape Cod and the Islands visited occasionally, as later did Miles Standish, John Winthrop, and, when he was in town, William Bradford. The earl of Southampton and his good friend William Shakespeare were known to drink occasionally at the Mermaid, as were Ben Jonson and the famous enslaved New England native Squanto.

In all likelihood Epenow spent some evenings there during his years as a professional curiosity. Bar owners loved the crowds that Indians inevitably brought. Trinculo complains in Shakespeare's *The Tempest* that in England, "when they will not give a doit to relieve a lame beggar, they will lay out ten to see a dead Indian." And if Epenow himself didn't actually get to the Mermaid, many who knew and remembered his cries of "Welcome! Welcome!" certainly did.

Some of the talk at the bar after Hobson's crew returned from Martha's Vineyard in 1614, with their battle scars and tales of volleys of arrows, was no doubt about how things were getting tougher in America, how it wasn't like in the old days when Bartholomew Gosnold returned from Cape Cod and the Islands with his market-crashing load of sassafras and his side-splitting stories about sitting around the campfire with Wampanoags, who screwed up their faces and howled at the taste of mustard and tried to buy the Englishmen's beards right off their faces.

By 1614, even good old Gosnold himself was dead and buried in Jamestown, along with nearly a thousand other unlucky colonists and Indians. With the news that Epenow, too, was dead, many probably agreed with Gorges's grim assessment of the situation in New England. Only a dozen years had passed since Gosnold's voyage, and yet there was, said Gorges, "a war now new begun between the inhabitants of those parts, and us."

Yet Epenow wasn't dead at all, as Thomas Dermer, another Englishman who crossed the Atlantic in the employ of Sir Ferdinando Gorges, would find out the hard way a few years later.

CHAPTER 2

CUTTYHUNK

The first Europeans to arrive on the coast of New England with the intention of founding a year-round colony were greeted by a Native American wearing imported shoes. "About twelve of the clock the same day, we came to an anchor, where eight Indians in a Basque shallop with mast and sail, an iron grapple and a kettle of copper, came boldly aboard of us," wrote John Brereton, one of the thirty-one members of Bartholomew Gosnold's 1602 expedition. They were north of their ultimate destination of Cape Cod and the Islands, probably near the mouth of the Penobscot River in southern Maine. "One of [the Indians was] appareled with a waistcoat and breeches of black serge, made after our sea fashion, hose and shoes on his feet."

The rest of the natives were dressed more as we typically imagine pre-colonial Americans, in little but sealskins tied at their waists, which reminded Brereton of a look he'd seen before in Ireland. They were all "of tall stature, broad and grim visage, of a black swart complexion, their eyebrows painted white; their weapons bows and arrows." But one Indian in a waistcoat is enough to show that though they may have been the first Europeans with plans to stay year-round in the region, Gosnold and his crew were not the first visitors from across the ocean.

There had been a century of contact between the Old and New Worlds. The vast majority of these voyages were unrecorded, which makes definitive statements about North America before and after colonization impossible. In 1498, only six years after Columbus's first crossing, John and Sebastian Cabot sailed from Nova Scotia to Hatteras. Four years later, Miguel Cortereal may or may not have washed up in Narragansett Bay, shipwrecked while looking for his brother Gaspar, who had disappeared along the coast the year before. He may or may not have carved M. CORTEREAL 1511 V. DEI DUX IND—king of the Indians—onto a rock in Dighton, Massachusetts. Verrazano visited in 1526, and his subsequent reports to the French government stirred the Spanish into sending Estevan Gomez in 1525. Gomez named Cape Cod "Cape James," presumably after the saint, and called Nantucket "Cape Shoals" after its treacherous waters.

The most unlikely pre-Pilgrim Europeans of all didn't come to the region in a ship, but supposedly walked through New England on their way from Mexico to Canada. In 1568, David Ingram and two companions were among the crew of a caravan of six English slavers waiting out a storm in a harbor near Vera Cruz, Mexico, when an armada of thirteen Spanish warships pulled into the same port. Slave traders in good standing with the pope were welcome in New Spain, but heretical English slavers were most definitely not, and the armada opened fire. Four of the slave smugglers' vessels were quickly sunk. One of the two that escaped, overloaded with more than three hundred survivors, was the *Judith*, under the command of a twenty-three-year-old novice named Francis Drake. For two weeks the badly damaged ship slunk around the Mexican coast looking for provisions without success before a hundred men agreed to try their luck ashore. Of the five known survivors, two escaped to England after serving as slaves to the Spanish for decades. The other three came out of the woods near today's U.S. border with Canada and were picked up by French fur traders, having walked, David Ingram later reported, up the entire coast of North America. It was an outrageous undertaking, made even harder to believe by Ingram's reports of having run into elephants in the vicinity of North Carolina.

In all likelihood, however, it wasn't from any of these Europeans that the Indian gentleman Gosnold and his crew met off the coast of Maine got his waistcoat, pants, and shoes. Brereton's account mentions that the boat the Indians met them in was a Basque shallop, and "by some words and signs they made" it became clear that the Indians had been trading with Basque fishermen. Depending on how the price of fish in late medieval Bilbao and Bristol is interpreted, there's evidence of anywhere from several hundred voyages total to hundreds of trips per year by Basque, Portuguese, French, and English fishermen and fur traders to Newfoundland, Nova Scotia, and

Maine, beginning before Columbus's 1492 voyage. There were fifty European ships off Newfoundland in 1517 alone. In 1534 Jacques Cartier saw what he thought were a thousand Basque fishing vessels off the Gaspé Peninsula. One French mariner named Savalet claimed in 1607 to have already made forty-two voyages to the Cape Breton area. And John Smith, in his 1614 description of New England, noted "800 sayle of ships a year" from Portugal and Biscay off Newfoundland.

It's not clear how many of these fishing voyages made it as far south as Cape Cod. Those that did probably returned: there's anecdotal evidence of temporary fishing camps at Provincetown in the decades before the *Mayflower*. Brereton wrote that he was "persuaded that there is upon this coast better fishing than in Newfoundland, wherefore we named the place 'Cape Cod.'"

But Gosnold didn't choose to stay at the Cape. A letter he wrote to his father implies that he may have been searching the region, then known to Europeans as Norumbega, in hopes of finding Refugio, a plentiful river valley that Verrazano had glowingly described. Also, given the smallness of his party, setting up his outpost on an island—preferably a deserted one—may have seemed to offer more security than a crowded peninsula. At several points on the Cape the *Concord* traded with locals who came out in canoes, but the English found them "more thievish" than those they met farther north. "The Coast is very full of people," wrote Gabriel Archer, an officer on the voyage. Specifically, the upper Cape, the Elizabeth Islands, and Martha's Vineyard were a part of the Wampanoag nation that stretched from the eastern reaches of Narragansett Bay to the Massachusett lands north of Plymouth. The lower Cape and most of Nantucket, meanwhile, were populated by Nausets, a semi-autonomous client state of the more powerful Wampanoag.

Whether out of fear of the locals or hope of finding richer grounds farther south, Gosnold ordered a course around Provincetown. They passed Monomoy, which they aptly called Point Care, and after almost a week successfully navigated the famously treacherous shoals of Nantucket Sound to the Vineyard.* There they spent two days sampling the local strawber-

---

*The exact location of virtually every early landing, whether Gosnold's or Thorwald's, is a matter of intense and periodic revision by local scholars. Some say Gosnold's descriptions are of Nomans Island, and that he named that island "Martha's Vineyard" and the Vineyard "Dover." Others say he didn't ultimately set up camp at Cuttyhunk but on Naushon. These are old and interesting debates that will not be settled by me.

ries, which they thought were bigger and sweeter than those back home. "There are also on this island great store of deer, which we saw, and other beasts, as appeared by their tracks; as also divers fowls . . . in great plenty; also great store of pease, which grow in certain plots all the island over," wrote Brereton.

The Vineyard, too, was rejected as a site for their trading post. Part of the reason may have been the thirteen "fast running savages" they met, possibly at Lambert's Cove. Archer, who called himself a "gentleman in the said voyage," described the Vineyarders as "armed with Bows and arrows without any fear." They were, according to Brereton, "tall big boned men, all naked, saving they cover their privy parts with a black tewed skin, much like a Black smith's apron, tied about their middle and betweene their legs behinde." They were perfectly friendly, bringing tobacco, deer skins, and cooked fish as gifts; also, "they came more rich in Copper than any before."

"This island is sound, and hath no danger about it," wrote Archer, but Gosnold nevertheless wanted to look further, perhaps for something more secluded. They sailed up-island toward Aquinnah (Gay Head), "which we called Dover Cliff," and spent the night in Vineyard Sound. The next morning, May 25, they rounded the Sow and Pigs reef, entering Buzzards Bay, which Archer described as "one of the stateliest sounds that ever I was in." They named it Gosnold's Hope, and after a few more days of exploring landed at Cuttyhunk, which they called Elizabeth's Island.*

According to Archer's and Brereton's accounts, it was a place of "high timbered oaks," along with beech, elm, walnut, hazelnut (hickory), witch hazel, sassafras, cedars, and various trees they didn't recognize. The middle story was "young sassafras, cherry trees, vines, eglantines, gooseberry bushes, hawthorn, honeysuckles, with others of like quality. The herbs and roots are strawberries, raspberries, ground-nuts, alexander, surrin, tansy, etc. without count." Also for the taking on Cuttyhunk and the nearby islands (at that time Cuttyhunk and Nashawena were a single island) were "scallops, mussels, cockles, lobsters, crabs, oysters and wilks, exceedingly good and very great."

The greatest of these was the sassafras, which was something of a rage in Europe as a cure for the "French Pox." But syphilis wasn't the only thing the root in root beer supposedly could fix. Not long after their arrival,

---

*Though not, in all likelihood, after the queen, who had previously instructed Raleigh not to name Virginia after her. Cuttyhunk would appear to be a Wampanoag word, but another native name for Gosnold's island was "Quawck."

when one of the crew "had taken a great surfeit by eating the bellies of dog fish, a very delicious meat," he was cured by powdered sassafras root.

Most important, though, given the smallness of the party, Cuttyhunk was "altogether unpeopled and disinhabited." Even better, at its western end they found a small freshwater lake in the middle of which lay a tiny island. Gosnold and his cocaptain, Bartholomew Gilbert, put one crew to work constructing a fort on that island. Others began cutting and stacking a cargo of sassafras. A few samples of European grains and vegetables were planted as a test. The commanders, meanwhile, went with the remaining men to nearby Penikese Island and stole a dugout canoe.*

This seems an odd first strategic move for a small group of uninvited strangers in a well-populated land, some of whom hoped to stay the winter—the more so since the English at that point didn't have any real idea of the strength of the neighboring Wampanoag owners of the place. Since leaving the Vineyard, the only locals Gosnold and his men had encountered were "an Indian and two women, the one we supposed to be his wife, the other his daughter, both clean and straight-bodied, with countenance sweet and pleasant."

Archer wrote that the women were very forward and friendly with the visitors, and that the Wampanoag man, therefore, kept a close eye on them. But, Archer added, the women "would not admit of any immodest touch." Someone among the English, perhaps in pursuit of a greater understanding of local cultural mores, was rebuffed.

The outer Elizabeths may have been unpopulated, but the islands were nonetheless used regularly for fishing and lobstering by a few families who lived on Naushon, as well as by a far more sizable population of Wampanoag from Woods Hole and Falmouth (Succonessitt). In all likelihood, the four Indians who left their canoe behind and fled into the woods as soon as they saw the strangers approaching Hill's Hap, as the English called Penikese, were from one or the other of those two places. They no doubt watched as the newcomers hefted their boat aboard the strange big vessel and sailed back across the half mile or so of water to Cuttyhunk. And they were presumably unhappy to be left without a paddle on an island the remoteness of which later induced the state of Massachusetts to use it as a leper colony.

"Now when a group of Indians have at great pains chopped down a

---

*Cape Cod and the Islands are south of the range of the canoe birch, so local boats were made from single logs.

huge tree with stone axes and, by dint of two or three weeks of firing and scraping, have hollowed it out to make a boat big enough to carry five or six men safely across the tide rips of Buzzards Bay, can anyone suppose that they should accept the theft of it lightly?" one historian of precolonial New England asked and then promptly answered: "The Indians obviously did not, for within three or four days they appeared in force with their sachem to investigate matters. . . ."

There is a more charitable explanation for the June 5 arrival on Cuttyhunk of a large contingent of armed Wampanoag. Immediately after the canoe caper, a party of English sailed across Buzzards Bay to the mainland, probably landing near New Bedford. There they met "men, women and children, who, with all courteous kindness, entertained [us], giving [Gosnold] certain skins of wild beasts, which may be rich furs, tobacco, turtles, hemp, artificial strings colored, chains and such like things as at the instant they had about them." It is likely that the large party of Indians were some of these, come for more trade, rather than a squad of canoe avengers. Brereton, at any rate, was later certain he recognized one of the visitors as a man he had made friends with on the mainland. But it is also clear that Gabriel Archer and the skeleton crew of eight men cutting sedge for the new building on Cuttyhunk were not at first overjoyed to see "fifty savages, stout and lusty men, with their bows and arrows . . . [who] . . . in a hasty manner came toward us." Gosnold and his cocaptain, Gilbert, were, as usual, off somewhere in the ship. This left Archer, as the presiding officer, to engage in a high-stakes game of charades.

He didn't want the Wampanoag to see the construction project, so he went toward them on the beach. He clapped himself on the head, and then again on his chest, in a gesture he described as an offer of peace. Then he struck up a tough pose: "presented my musket with a threatening countenance, thereby to signify to them either a choice of peace or war." It was a tense moment, but it passed quickly. Archer reported that when the leader of the visiting Wampanoag responded with "mine own signs of peace, I stepped forth and embraced him; his company then all sat down in a manner like greyhounds, upon their heels, with whom my company fell a bartering." At this point Gosnold came back ashore and gave the chief a straw hat and a pair of shiny knives; "thus our courtesy made them all in love with us."

This love-and-fur fest continued off and on for the better part of a week, with a break in the middle to allow the Wampanoag to return to the mainland for more "beavers, luzernes, martins, otters, wildcat skins, very large and deep fur; black foxes, coney skins of the color of our hares, deer skins, very large; seal skins and other beasts' skins to us unknown." Like their cousins on Martha's Vineyard, these people also had an abundance of copper, which they used primarily for jewelry—"none of them, but have chains, earrings or collars of this metal . . . four hundred pieces in a collar, very fine and evenly set together." They also had copper pipes and large copper drinking cups, and manufactured some of their arrowheads out of the metal.

Through sign language, one of the Wampanoag explained that the copper came from a hole in the ground on the mainland.* They also had a word for gold, *wessador*, which the Englishmen took as a very good sign. In the end, both sides seemed pleased with the prices, especially Brereton, who was surprised that the Indians traded "their fairest collars or chains for a knife or such like trifle."

When it was time to leave, the Wampanoag got in their dugouts and set off across the bay. A few dozen yards offshore they stopped paddling, Brereton remembered, and turned and raised a loud cheer. The English standing on the beach, in response, blew their trumpets and cornets, and "casting our caps up in the air, made them the best farewell we could." It felt, no doubt to both sides, like an auspicious beginning to a long relationship.

Within a few days, however, the English changed their minds about staying permanently on Cuttyhunk. Once again, Gosnold and the other senior officers were away in the ship when the conflict began, having gone to Penikese again, this time to harvest cedar logs. Back on Cuttyhunk, Gabriel Archer and nine others were left with three meals' worth of food, so when Gosnold didn't reappear the next day as promised, Archer sent four men "to seek out for crabs, lobsters, turtles, etc. for sustaining us till the ship returned, which was gone clean out of sight."

These four would-be hunter-gatherers divided themselves into two groups of two, one of which was shortly "assaulted by four Indians." Whether these were the same four seen running into the woods on Penikese the day their canoe was stolen by the English a week and a half

---

*As with almost every facet of precolonial history, there is a dispute with political overtones among historians about the origins of the copper that virtually every early explorer to the southern New England coast commented on. "The alternatives are these," wrote Howe. "First, that they imported native copper from the great Lake Superior lodes which Indians there are known to have mined; second, that they found enough nuggets in glacial gravel here and there locally to fulfill their needs for beads and pipestems; third, that European traders carrying copper had preceded Verrazano in Rhode Island."

before is not clear, though it seems plausible. Nobody was killed: one Englishman was hit by an arrow, the other ran up and cut the Indians' bowstrings, whereupon they ran off. The two Englishmen, however, had completely lost their bearings in the scuffle, and, after traipsing pointlessly around in circles for a few hours, they spent the night in the woods, "not knowing the way home through the thick rubbish."

Back at the camp they were sorely missed: "The want of these sorrowed us much, as not able to conjecture anything of them unless very evil," Archer later recalled. But by the time they stumbled into camp the next day, their fellow Cuttyhunk inmates were far too obsessed with the continued absence of the *Concord* to fully appreciate their safe return. The fact that Gosnold was not back, Archer said, "struck us in a dumpish terror for that he performed not the same in the space of almost three days." Contrary to the glowing reports of plenty later written for investors back home, the foraging was not overwhelmingly successful. They survived on salad and groundnuts. Their only comfort was that there was tobacco for after-dinner smokes.

Gosnold finally did sail back to Cuttyhunk. There was no explanation for the delay; nothing had gone wrong. But seventy-two hours of living off the land was enough for a critical majority of the aspiring Elizabeth Islanders. The men had invested three weeks collecting sedge for their abode; they had had mostly good times with the neighboring inhabitants. But the foretaste of the pioneer's life was enough, and several who were expected to stay behind announced that under no circumstances would they agree to be left behind when the *Concord* returned to England.

Brereton, for one, bitterly thought the faintheartedness had more to do with the price of sassafras than anything else. "After our bark had taken in so much sassafras, cedar, furs, skins and other commodities as were thought convenient, some of our company that had promised Captain Gosnold to stay, having nothing but a [profitable] voyage in their minds, made our company of inhabitants (which was small enough before) much smaller." There were still twelve men willing to winter over, but Gosnold overruled them. After a stay of only six weeks, he ordered the crew of the *Concord* to set their sails for England, "leaving this island (which he called Elizabeths Island) with as many true sorrowful eyes as were before desirous to see it."

CHAPTER 3

VINEYARD SOUND

Crossings make convenient starting points for American histories: Asiatic mammoth hunters crossing the Bering Strait twelve thousand years ago or thirty thousand years ago, or maybe both. Then crossing to fill the continent, arriving in New England by nine to twelve thousand years ago. Norsemen crossing to Greenland in 1000 and then (some people believe with as much circumstantial evidence as they can muster) passing all the way down the coast of North America to the "wonderstrands" of Cape Cod and the currents of Nantucket and Vineyard Sounds. Columbus across the Atlantic. Cortes across the Caribbean. Raleigh to Roanoke. Gosnold to Cuttyhunk. Pilgrims first to Provincetown and then across Cape Cod Bay to Plymouth, where their survival was largely assured by Squanto's reverse voyage of a few years before. Mayhews to the Vineyard in the 1640s; Thomas and Sarah Macy and their friends to Nantucket nearly two decades later. African, Portuguese, and Polynesian sailors on returning whalers and merchantmen in the eighteenth and nineteenth centuries. Slaves on slavers. Tourists and summer people by the millions over the canal to the Cape and over the water to the Islands. Most stories begin with a crossing.

In my case, in this instance, on a late May dawn, the beginning is a modest passage by plastic kayak. From the north shore of Martha's Vineyard, where due to unparalleled good fortune in the form of love and marriage I now live, I'm bound across Vineyard Sound to the Elizabeth Islands, which stretch from Woods Hole on the Cape's southwest corner like the disjointed backbone of some mythical sea monster out toward the mouth of Buzzards Bay.* The westernmost of them is Cuttyhunk, where Gosnold's hope of founding a colony faltered, and where I am headed.

From Cuttyhunk my thought is to paddle up the eastern coast of Buzzards Bay and through the Cape Cod Canal to Plymouth, where, as every New England schoolchild knows, the first successful New English colony was planted in 1620. Historically, and to a lesser degree geologically, Plymouth belongs with the Cape, which was converted from Indian to English under the jurisdiction of the "Old Colony" of the separatist Pilgrims at Plymouth, as opposed to the Massachusetts Bay Colony of the Puritans. But I may decide to skip Plymouth proper, since no one on the Cape or Islands today considers it a part of the region any more than New Bedford, which was founded by Nantucketers. Maybe I'll take a right at the mouth of the canal and head down the long inside arm of Cape Cod toward Provincetown, where the Pilgrims first landed. Or I may just turn around, come back home, and save those stretches of water and land for another trip. It's a relatively good job I have, if you don't think too long about the famously convoluted currents of Vineyard Sound.

I've never kayaked across the sound before. So even though I've spent many hours paddling up and down and around the local coast in all kinds of weather and water, I'm officially something of a novice among local paddlers. The distance where I'm crossing is not far, only about four and a half miles. In fact, just half a mile down the beach from where I plan to put in is Cedar Tree Neck, where the first signal corps cables were strung across the sound in 1885 because it is the closest spot between the Vineyard and the Elizabeth Islands, and from thence to the mainland. But a shorter passage is really only half a blessing; as with a pinched hose, constricted water tends to flow faster.

According to Charles Banks's three-volume 1916 history of Martha's Vineyard, the original residents called the island "Noe-pe," which he translated as "a compound term consisting of the radical *Noe*, signifying, middle of, midst, amid, and the generic *-pe*, which in all Algonquian dialects signifies 'water,'—and thus we have the full and free definition, 'amid the waters.'" Banks's command of the Wampanoag language wasn't what it might have been, which is unfortunate, because "amid the waters" evokes nicely the contortions of the local tides. The Vikings, say those who believe

---

*According to legend they are the laid-out bodies of the children of the patron giant of the Wampanoag, Moshup, slain by his midget enemies.

they actually sailed this far south, called the whole Buzzards Bay–Vineyard Sound area Straumfiord, or "Bay of Currents." During the age of sail, when the number of vessels traveling around Cape Cod and around or through Nantucket and Vineyard Sounds was second only to those in the English Channel,* the southern coast of the Elizabeth Islands was one of several places in the region called "the graveyard" because so many ships were piled up there by the confusing currents.

In 1854, George W. Eldridge pointed out in his first tide-and-pilot book that most of the sailing vessels that wound up in the Elizabethan graveyard probably got into trouble because they assumed the flooding tide flowed east throughout the length of the two sounds, which for the most part it does, and then reversed on the ebb. But Eldridge, an obsessive measurer who compiled intricate maps of the currents, discovered that at the western entrance to Vineyard Sound, during the first few hours of the incoming tide the water actually flows north, straight toward the rocky southern shores of the Elizabeths.

This current doesn't bother me. Where I'm starting is far enough "down-island"—which is to say east—to avoid the strong northerly push. More to the point, running aground on the Elizabeth Islands is precisely my goal: at Tarpaulin Cove on Naushon, I hope. What I'm more concerned about is an area approximately three-quarters of the way across, where when the tide is falling strongly from the east and the prevailing winds of summer are blowing even moderately from the southwest, the water can get piled up into rather messy waves. My brother-in-law calls the area simply "the zone," and I've seen it in action from various small fishing boats, including his. I'd sincerely like to avoid the zone.

Waves can actually be quite fun in a kayak, a lot more fun than flat water, in fact; I just prefer them closer to shore, and warmer. When my wife's father heard of my intention to paddle across the sound, he very nearly insisted on following me in his Boston Whaler. He has probably spent as much time exploring Vineyard Sound in small motorized boats as anyone alive; he knows it still occasionally claims lives. I took his opinion very seriously, but I declined the offer.

---

*In 1829, 11,653 vessels passed through Vineyard Sound; in 1830, 12,603 passed through. In 1851, in three months, 182 ships and 544 brigs, 4,991 schooners, 954 sloops, and 5 steamers passed Cuttyhunk, roughly 73 boats per day. Between 1854 and 1976, 207 ships wrecked in the Elizabeth Islands. Ninety-three wrecked on the shores of Cuttyhunk, and 43 on the Sow and Pigs reef off Cuttyhunk.

I did bring along my marine radio in its waterproof case, with which I can call out the Coast Guard from Woods Hole or Menemsha. If that fails, I've also got a cell phone, though I'm not optimistic about its ability to work underwater. I have an inflatable float that fits over the paddle to create a kind of pontoon to help me get back into the boat should I need to self-rescue. I've got a backup inflatable float in case I lose the first one trying to attach it to the paddle. I've got a pump to bail out the kayak, and a bailer if I lose the pump. I've got a spare paddle attached with a bungee cord to the deck, and I'm wearing a newfangled outfit that feels like lightweight polar fleece and keeps the body warm whether in or out of the water.

I've got my compass and maps, and if those fail and the fog rolls in, I've got a spray-can foghorn and a little electronic global positioning system that can lock onto twelve satellites at once and has a built-in map of the entire coastline of North and South America. With its software designed to correct for the United States Defense Department's efforts to keep the world safe from homemade homing missiles, this cigarette-pack-sized device should theoretically be able to guide me from Tierra del Fuego to within one hundred feet of the spot from which I'm shoving off. Assuming, of course, the batteries don't fail. I've got extra batteries. If they do fail, and the spray-can foghorn runs out, I have a whistle attached to my life preserver, which is firmly on. I have a waterproof strobe light attached to my life preserver, too.

It's worth pointing out that notwithstanding the zone and all this equipment, I'm not really about to embark on all that much of a kayaking challenge. There's a fellow who commutes across the sound in a kayak, all year long, three days a week, from Vineyard Haven to Woods Hole. It's my understanding that the writer and kayaker Paul Theroux periodically shows up unannounced at a friend's Vineyard Haven dock for a late literary breakfast, having paddled over from his Falmouth home on a whim. It's my further understanding that in recent seasons he has taken to doing this at night. And of course Epenow and countless other original locals made the trip in hollowed-out logs. Not only that, they paddled their logs to Nantucket, which is six miles across Muskeget Channel from the Vineyard and roughly seventeen miles across Nantucket Sound from the Cape.

If I paddle strongly straight across, these four fat miles should take me less than an hour. Particularly since (even more important than all the gadgets) I have picked a glass-flat sea at dead-low tide on a crystal-clear late-spring dawn before the wind has had a chance to pick itself up for the day.

All that was my plan, anyway. On the morning of my intended departure, I awoke in a fog. From the beach I could see water, but the Elizabeth Islands were invisible. The lobster buoys a few hundred yards offshore were invisible. Compass and global positioning system notwithstanding, I went back home to bed.

The following morning I awoke to a wind, an uncharacteristically howling one for that time of year. From the beach the Elizabeth Islands beckoned sweetly over a broad expanse of white and furious water. I went home again, sat at my desk for as long as I could, and then, out of frustration, began to cut brush in an area downhill from my house that has fallen prey to the voracious procreation of chokecherries and oaks.

Four hundred years ago the same land probably resembled Brereton's and Archer's descriptions from the voyage of the *Concord*: large trees, occasional open grassy areas, prodigious grapes. A hundred years ago the land was open pasture, kept that way, like most of the Vineyard (and Nantucket and parts of the upper Cape), by grazing animals, and tidily bounded by the ancient stone wall that still runs past it on through the woods to a place where it mysteriously ends.

Ten years ago the same area was covered in half-century-old oaks and maples, grown up in the wake of the overgrazing, the two world wars, and the one Great Depression that together spelled the demise of local agriculture. There was sassafras again, too, and grapes. This, too, could be said of most of the Vineyard and parts of the upper Cape and, with a slight change of species, Nantucket. Nine years ago it was newly cleared and brush-cut, like ever more of Cape Cod and the Islands, to make a place and a view for a new house. (Like nowhere else, our house.)

Having been left pretty much alone since then, the half-acre in question is now intermittently populated with remarkably dense dog patches of young trees the thickness of broom handles, and stands of towering, flowering poison ivy. Here and there are great standing armies of cat brier, with spiky thorns that will tear jeans and puncture mountain-bike tires. And after a long day—or what feels like a long day—at my desk, I periodically go there, "down below the wall," armed with loppers. In long sleeves and leather gloves I do battle with these intruders in defense of the high-bush blueberry, flowering viburnum, shadbush, and sweet pepperbush that were spared during the previous clearing.

I had the thought during one of these lopping sessions that by perpetually going to this same battleground but never really winning my war with the legions of scrub oak and chokecherry, I am preserving a moment,

West Tisbury as it appeared around 1900. The same area today is almost entirely covered with oaks, beeches, briars, and houses.

maintaining a little monument to that particular generation of Cape and Islanders who left seaside farms to go to war in Europe and didn't return. At least not as farmers, or not to a place where farming was a viable way to earn one's keep. At one point, perhaps in the 1930s and 1940s, great expanses of the now-wooded portions of the upper Cape and Martha's Vineyard must have had this scrubby, lost-meadow appearance. In the flowering month of June it's not unattractive. Perhaps this forever unfinished fight of mine is to keep this little piece of land safe for chokecherry, which loves the sun and will lose ground if the larger oak, maple, and beech are permitted to take over. I also realized—and it caused me to question the whole endeavor—that just about the only thing I may have in common with Ronald Reagan is this belief in the spiritual value of recreational brush cutting.

The wind blew hard for a week and a half. On the third day of it I rested my loppers and walked to the beach where my boat, fully loaded with what I thought I would need for my voyage of Elizabethan discovery, sat there with its cockpit slowly filling with sand. I looked at the waves and then at the boat again, then at the sky and at the boat and the waves again. There are times when you know what the smart thing to do would be, but the smart thing is not what you want to do. I stood in the wind and looked at the boat again and at the waves and at the sky.

For four thousand years or more, Cape and Islanders have looked and thought these thoughts hundreds of thousands, perhaps millions, of times. What will the weather do? Shall we go out to sea today, or wait? But wait for what? How bad could it be? How bad can it get? It could be worse. I turned the boat over so the sand would cease to accumulate and went back home.

An hour later I was back at the beach, this time with paddles in hand. If I couldn't cross (or, at least, *wouldn't* cross), at least I could try out the fully loaded boat to see how it handled in moderately rough conditions; take it out for a spin, so to speak, but, I hoped, not for a roll. If I could paddle up the coast six miles to the old fishing village of Menemsha—where the summer tourists in the past few years have adopted the bizarre practice of applauding after sunsets—if I could get there straight into both wind and tide, and back, then at least I would know I had the physical stamina to handle the sound once conditions improved.

It was a glorious push followed by a sliding, rubbery, and occasionally harrowing withdrawal. By the end of the former, where the high land of Prospect Hill gives way first to a house-strewn bluff and then to the short, sandy stretch of Menemsha Beach, I was barely moving. The wind seemed to have picked up in perfect pace with the rate of weakening in my arms and back, and I counted progress not against passing landmarks, which now were frozen in place, but from lobster buoy to lobster buoy. What began as songs sung lustily to no one but the waves decomposed first to vocal percussion and then to mere animal exhalations. On the shore to my left, an early season beachcomber easily walked past me as I huffed, puffed, and grunted mightily against the blow.

As always, the coffee at the Menemsha Texaco was bad to perfection, and two cups and three apples later I was back on the water, this time with the wind at my back, which would have been a fine thing if it didn't also mean the sea was following. With fresh arms and a friendly shore, a following sea is an opportunity to look for free rides. On the other hand, with a spent body and a boat riding low with gadgets I didn't want to lose, outsized pushes from behind that rolled right over the stern and tried to shove the boat broadside were less amusing. (Sailors call this being pooped, as in water over the poop deck.) A course directly parallel to shore was out of the

Menemsha Bight in the 1920s, from the silent movie Annabelle Lee. (COURTESY OF THE MARTHA'S VINEYARD HISTORICAL SOCIETY)

question, due to the incoming surf, so I tacked as far out as I felt like getting swamped and waited for a calm moment to come about. Then I worked my way along, watching warily over my shoulder for the next swell, either slowing down and letting it pass under me or speeding up to try to catch a little ride, until I got as near the breakers as was comfortable. Then it was time to turn back out to sea and repeat the process.

I took one extended rest at the Brickyard, a ruined factory—only the chimney and foundation remain—where nineteenth-century Vineyarders built strong arms and backs baking local dirt. Otherwise I made great time. When finally I did capsize, it was in six inches of water on my home beach, and none of my neighbors saw my involuntary kissing of the sand.

The Elizabeth Islands, once I had dragged my boat and myself up beyond the high-tide line, looked farther away than I remembered them.

CHAPTER 4

NAUSHON

To a quite remarkable degree, a visitor arriving by dugout today might very well think the shoreline of Naushon looked relatively unchanged from Gosnold's day. There are still, as he noted then, "many plane places of grass." And though the oaks aren't quite as "high timbered" as Brereton made them sound, nor would one necessarily describe the cedars as "straight and tall," there are more woods than anything else on Naushon. The only documented remnant of original forest left on Cape Cod and the Islands is on Naushon: a patch of old-growth beeches and black, white, and red oaks, along with a smattering of hickories, black and yellow birches, red and white cedars, and pitch pines. Too many generations of sheep and not enough forest fires have prevented a complete return of the islands to their pre-European ecology. Yet from the water, it is only the rare building and periodic stone wall that look undeniably human in origin; those and the regularly spaced, well-maintained signs that say PRIVATE PROPERTY, KEEP OFF.

Over the course of the past century and a half, all the Elizabeth Islands, with the exception of Cuttyhunk and Penikese, have become the property of a single family named Forbes.* As a result, there are only a handful of houses clustered at Hadley Harbor near Woods Hole, and a few more

---

*The Forbes family of Boston and Senator Kerry, not that of New York and Son of Malcolm.

scattered around the rest of the islands. The resulting wildness and beauty of the coast is more than just appearance: sometime in the late 1980s, coyotes returned to the Elizabeth Islands, apparently having swum both the Cape Cod Canal (or crossed the bridge) and the channel at Woods Hole. They are still there, and the sheep herd that once numbered in the hundreds is not.

Gosnold's men, for their part, "stood awhile like men ravished at the beauty and delicacy" of the land in the vicinity of Buzzards Bay. Though clearly accurate, it's an interesting word choice given the usual American image of settlers hewing small claim stakes, Honest Abe–like, out of some deep impenetrable forest or unforgiving prairie. Our usual image of colonists on the coast is of them huddled there with a continent of truly dangerous virginity before them (or in later interpretations, of lovely unspoilt forest primeval).

The disappearance of Raleigh's outpost at Roanoke probably started the trend, but the Pilgrim William Bradford was the first to articulate it: "What could they see but a hideous and desolate wilderness, full of wild beasts and wild men—and what multitudes there might be of them they knew not. Neither could they, as it were, go up to the top of Pisgah to view from this wilderness a more goodly country to feed their hopes; for which way soever they turned their eyes (save upward to the heavens) they could have little solace or content in respect of any outward objects. . . . If they looked behind them, there was the mighty ocean which they had passed and was now as a main bar and gulf to separate them from all the civil parts of the world."

In Bradford's defense, as he himself alluded, the Pilgrims arrived at the tip of Cape Cod in a snowy November. Gosnold and the crew of the *Concord*, on the other hand, came to the Islands at the end of May. As the late, great Vineyard writer (and "country editor") Henry Beetle Hough pointed out more than sixty years ago, this was "the proper time of year to be a summer visitor." There were "strawberries, red and white, as sweet and much bigger than ours in England; raspberries, gooseberries, whortleberries and such an incredible store of vines. . . . Also many springs of excellent, sweet water . . . running exceedingly pleasantly through the woody grounds," wrote Brereton.

But Gosnold's men were by no means alone in their good impressions of the countryside; most of the other explorers before and after them spoke favorably of the New England coast, taking particular note of the amount of land under cultivation by the locals. Verrazano's first attempt to explore

North America for King François I of France had been cut short when he encountered Cortes's initial shipments of Aztec gold, which naturally had to be confiscated and taken to France. In 1524, though, he got as far as Block Island, and possibly the Vineyard, which he refers to by the name "Louisa." He spent two weeks among the Indians of Narragansett Bay and traveled as far as fifteen or twenty miles inland through countryside he thought "as pleasant as it is possible to conceive," with "open plains as much as twenty or thirty leagues in length, entirely free from trees."

Similarly, Martin Pring, an English captain who on the basis of Gosnold's modest success spent six weeks in Plymouth Harbor in 1603, described Wampanoag gardens there as big as an acre apiece planted with corn, beans, squash, and tobacco. Again, there were the "faire, big, strawberries." Samuel de Champlain's 1605 map of Plymouth shows the land around the harbor largely free of trees. His map of Chatham, meanwhile, shows the harbor surrounded by Nauset villages. "All along the shore," he wrote of the Massachusetts coast in general, "there is a great deal of land cleared up and planted with Indian corn." The country, he said, was "very pleasant and agreeable." And Francis Higginson, writing in 1630, saw from a hill in Boston what he estimated to be thousands of acres with "not a tree in the same."

By the time the Europeans arrived on Cape Cod and the Islands, the Nauset and Wampanoag people who lived there had been agriculturists for somewhere between six hundred and one thousand years. The essential technology of corn and bean cultivation was first developed by Central Americans nearly nine thousand years ago, a time when the latitudes of New England were still too cold to farm, but it took millennia for the practice to spread to the Northeast. As important as know-how, locally viable strains of the primary crops needed to be perfected through centuries of selective planting and harvesting; by the beginning of the seventeenth century, there were between two and three hundred varieties of corn grown in the Americas, several of which grew well on the New England coast. Native American farmers were also the first to domesticate potatoes (thousands of varieties of both white and sweet) and tomatoes. They were the first to grow cocoa, peanuts, eggplants, peppers, avocado, sunflowers, pimento, and Jerusalem artichoke. They grew hundreds of varieties of beans—red, white, yellow, blue, and spotted—along with an equally wide array of pumpkins, squashes, gourds, and melons. And, of course, tobacco.

Tobacco was traditionally raised by men in ceremonial plots set off from the food crops, but the rest of the agricultural work was typically done by women using only stone and shell tools. In spring, when the white-oak leaves reached the size of a mouse's ear, or the shadbush leaves were as large as a squirrel's ear, or the Pleiades rose in the spring sky—in other words, after the danger of frost had passed—corn was planted in small hills or mounds, two or three seeds per hill. In late June or early July, the soil would be pushed up around the young plant, making the mound taller. Beans and squash were allowed to grow around the base of the corn so that the corn's stalks could serve as beanpoles and the big squash leaves would shade out late summer weeds. (By all accounts, Native American farmers were meticulous weeders.) The practice of growing bean crops among the corn also reduced the latter plant's propensity to destroy the fertility of soil, and local yields of around forty bushels of corn (with cobs) per acre were not uncommon.

Groundnuts—a long, whitish tuber—and the roots of Jerusalem arti-chokes were important local crops because of their resistance to frost, both when growing and when stored underground for the winter. There were watermelons, and gourds raised for their shells. Hemp may have been culti-vated in places for its fiber, though Champlain, at least, thought it was nat-urally abundant enough on the Cape that planting was unnecessary.

If herring had been used as fertilizer,* for the first two weeks the fields had to be guarded day and night from the depredations of raccoons and dogs. In some places, children watched the fields from raised platforms, a job that again became important later in the year when ripening crops brought birds and raccoons, and occasionally even bear. Marauding black-birds and passenger pigeons were killed if possible, but crows were believed by many traditions to have brought back the first corn seeds to the Indians and so were merely discouraged from overindulging. Occasionally, a domes-ticated hawk might help guard the crops.

A few students of Native American agriculture have suggested that even the water lily was cultivated for its edible roots. One seventeenth-century European thought they tasted like sheep's liver, which was meant to be a compliment. The best thing about lily roots, however, was probably that muskrats also like to collect them, which saved a lot of work at harvest time. The rodents politely made little stashes in their dens, which the women raided. Modern sources almost always point out that Native American women always took care to leave enough behind for sister muskrat to get

---

*Whether fish were actually used for fertilizer is yet another of the many contentious, if minor, fault lines among historians of early New England.

through the winter, though how exactly this surplus was calculated has apparently been lost to time.

There were also a wide range of wild and semiwild plants that were nonetheless managed to varying degrees. Verrazano observed that the Indians along the coast to the south of Cape Cod and the Islands pruned around many of their grape vines, presumably to let in more light and encourage the production of fruit. Champlain commented that nut-bearing trees appeared to be well tended, and went so far as to suggest that some of the oaks he saw appeared to have been planted for ornamental effect, though he may not have been aware of the importance of acorns in the local diet. The acorns of the red oak had to be boiled with the ashes from a rotten maple to remove their tannic acid before they could be eaten, but white-oak acorns, when boiled, render a butter that was used in baking nut and fruit breads.

Even if the local Indians didn't raise strawberries as a crop per se, the evidence is pretty good that they actively encouraged them through regular burning of nearby lands and probably by sowing them in their fallow fields. (John Smith, who was a careful observer and list maker, grouped strawberries with domesticated plants as opposed to other berries.) Blackberries and raspberries would also have benefited greatly from these annual burnings, as would the production of many different nuts.

Among the hundreds of wild plants collected (most often by women) for food and medicinal purposes were cranberries, bayberries, wild leeks, beach plums, various wild cherries, shadbush fruit, red cedar berries, and occasionally crab apples. The roots of arrowhead, sweet flag, Solomon's seal, jack-in-the-pulpit (good for colds), and Turk's-cap lily were collected. Various teas and other concoctions were made with smooth sumac, strawberry, and raspberry leaves, chokecherry and dogwood bark (good for colds), grape sap, black raspberry root (good for sore throats), wintergreen (for pain relief), spruce, and wild cherry. One wild food the natives of New England apparently did not make much use of was mushrooms. Also, there were not enough sugar maples on the coast for sugar, and, interestingly, there was apparently no word for dietary salt in the local languages.

Even where the fields and gardens stopped, most early European visitors to southern New England did not describe the vast (and still very much dominant) eastern mixed hardwood forest as a mythically impenetrable wilderness à la William Bradford. More often, they encountered woods and savannahs that were almost parklike in their openness. Any fallen branches in the immediate vicinity of a village were collected for fuel, and firewood availability may have been almost as important as game as a motive for seasonal migrations: "They use not to winter and summer in one place, for that would be a reason to make fuel scarce," reported one colonist in the 1620s. In Rhode Island, a Narragansett friend of Roger Williams asked him if the reason the English had come to America was because they had run out of wood at home.

Of even greater impact than firewood collection, however, was the Indian use of ground fires as a forestry management tool. "There is no underwood save in the swamps and low places," wrote William Wood in a typical description in 1634, "for it being the custom of the Indians to burn the woods in November when the grass is withered and the leaves dried it consumes all the underwood and rubbish." Fires intentionally set by the Narragansett and Wampanoag are what no doubt produced the woods around Narragansett Bay that Verrazano said could be easily traversed by a large army.

By removing underbrush, fallen leaves, and some smaller trees, the burning allowed more sunlight through to the forest floor, promoting the growth of little bluestem and other native grasses. This, in turn, profoundly affected the relative animal populations by creating a situation that more resembled an edge habitat between forest and grassland than it did a virgin forest. Brereton mentioned deer, bears, luzernes (lynx), black foxes, beavers, otters, wildcats, ("very large and great") dogs like foxes, black and sharp-nosed, and rabbits, along with "snakes foure foot in length, and sixe inches about, which the Indians eat for daintie meat, the skinnes whereof they use for girdles." Regular burning also dried the soil, favoring some tree species, such as the nut-bearing oaks and hickories, over others, such as the less useful maples.

As William Cronon pointed out in his brilliant ecological history of colonial New England, *Changes in the Land*, "Indian burning promoted the increase of exactly those species whose abundance so impressed English colonists: elk, deer, beaver, hare, porcupine, turkey, quail, ruffed grouse, and so on. When these populations increased, so did the carnivorous eagles, hawks, lynxes, foxes, and wolves." The Wampanoag, the Nausets, and other natives of southern New England, in other words, actively and no doubt consciously created a massive game park from which they satisfied their protein needs. "There has been no timeless wilderness in a state of perfect changelessness," Cronon wrote, "no climax forest in permanent stasis."

One reason for the consistent reports from early visitors and colonizers of a New England of incredible abundance of game was surely propaganda; hunting in Europe was by then already a restricted pleasure of the ruling classes, and it therefore served the purposes of those who were always keen for more immigrants from back home to talk up the wildlife. Furthermore, many of these accounts come from a period after the population of Indian hunters had declined significantly due to disease and removal but before the benefits of native land-management policies would have fully deteriorated due to forest regrowth and, later, widespread agricultural clearing. In other words, the abundance of large game animals in the 1630s and '40s may not have existed in quite the same fashion since time immemorial.

"Any notion, however, that moose, deer, and bear abounded every-where to be taken close at hand with bow and arrow, ignores the reality," wrote Howard Russell in *Indian New England before the Mayflower.* "We must not forget that for the most part the New England natives were agricultural. Of the large animals just named, deer and bear raise havoc in cornfields and gardens; so do raccoons, woodchucks, and rabbits. None of these was more to be tolerated close at hand than they are by gardeners today. Nor were bears wanted in the berry pastures that the Indians maintained near their villages. As a source of meat, therefore, every tribe had a hunting ground or deer pasture at a distance, which was kept open, and its herbage kept succu-lent, by seasonal fires. . . ."

Russell used this line of reasoning in part to defend the men of precolo-nial New England against the persistent European (and historical) accusa-tion of laziness, especially as compared to their wives and daughters. "The men employ their time wholly in hunting and other exercises of the bow," wrote Governor Edward Winslow of Plymouth in a typical description, "except that they sometimes take some pains at fishing. The women live a most slavish life: they carry all their burdens, set and dress their corn, gather it in, and seek out much of their food, beat and make ready the corn to eat and have all household care lying upon them." Likewise, though the men might help construct the frame of a dwelling, its ongoing care, mainte-nance, and seasonal moving were typically the work of women.

However, Russell, who by no means belittled the labor of women in Indian society, warned that hunting was not considered or approached as the recreational activity it had already become among many Europeans.

"The hunter's legs had to carry him to the deer run perhaps twenty miles distant; and he might return after several days with only a paltry bag of game, and half famished," wrote Russell. "Carefully prepared traps might be found empty. Yet on the brave's skills, wind, and endurance might depend both food, if the harvest had been poor, and clothing for his whole family. The notion that in the early times the woods were full of animals and birds waiting patiently for the hunter is a myth."

It must also be said that almost all but the earliest European descriptions of Indian work habits were colored by the need to justify the taking of land. And not surprisingly one of the most popular justifications was that the Indians didn't work the land enough to deserve keeping it. One of the first English to try to live in the Cape and Islands, John Brereton, didn't make any observations about Wampanoag labor policies. In fact, he met only three native women. But he noted that the men "were very dutiful towards them."

Whatever the relative workload of the sexes, taken together, the hard-earned products of their agriculture and the fruits of their hunting and fishing made the Wampanoag diet enviably diverse. The foundation was corn, which they called *weatchimin*, and when pounded into pieces, *msickquatash*, from which our word *succotash* is derived.

The most important corn preparation on Cape Cod and the Islands and elsewhere was *samp* or *newsamp*, a sort of porridge made of beaten boiled corn. This was usually eaten with meat, fish, fruit, vegetables, or, later, if you were an English colonist, milk and butter. There was also corn bread, corn chowders, corn fritters, hominy, hulled corn, Johnnycake dough wrapped in leaves and baked in ashes (*pone* or *apoon*), nut bread, berry breads, and squash breads. For travelers along the major routes through the forest, there were large boulders with bowls worn into them that could be used for grinding parched corn, a few ounces of which mixed with a little water would suffice for a day's walking. When a mother's milk gave out, infants were given a formula of fine cornmeal and ground hickory nuts.

There were, no doubt, many variations and recipes that are now lost. There's no recorded count of corn preparations specific to the Wampanoag, but a woman from one of the western Iroquois tribes "detailed to an inquiring anthropologist a hundred and fifty recipes of various kinds without exhausting her mental cookbook of maize dishes." And the inland Iroquois, unlike the people of Cape Cod and the Islands, generally cooked without the benefit of seafood ingredients.

The native New Englanders preferred their meat boiled rather than grilled or roasted—presumably to avoid the waste of juices—and well done. Virtually all animals, even skunk, were considered edible, though carnivores, in general, were avoided. Passenger pigeons came through twice a year and were so plentiful that at night they could simply be knocked off the trees with sticks. Sometimes birds were roasted whole, basted in bear grease or, more likely on Cape Cod and the Islands, in seal or whale oil. Families typically had four or five dogs, some of them trained to catch woodchucks and other small animals, but in times of great need even a pet might be eaten.

Fish were caught primarily with weirs and traps and then grilled on flat rocks, planked, added to chowder, or smoked. There were clambakes, of course, complete with corn on the cob, steamed lobsters, and roasted oysters. During the season for shell fishing, lobstering, and fishing, great numbers of relatives and allies from the interior might congregate at the coast to collect, smoke, and dry the catch. There are dozens of large shell heaps on Cape Cod and the Islands, built over generations of use. One such heap on the Connecticut coast covers twenty-four acres.

In all, it was a very healthy diet, which explains at least in part why the early explorers were so unanimous in their marveling at the strength, beauty, and health of the locals. Southern New England natives were invariably described as taller and stronger than the average European, and the whiteness of their teeth and the straightness of their postures were also frequently noted. They were not without health problems, of course—arthritis, rheumatism, neuralgia, chills and fever, pleurisy ("which all their remedies can't conquer"), and eye troubles from smoky homes were not uncommon. But most researchers think the life span for native New Englanders was likely longer than that of most contemporary Europeans—probably over sixty years, and some individuals lived much longer than that.

Like the Europeans who were soon to arrive and unlike some other Native American peoples, such as the Iroquois, the basic social unit of Wampanoag and Nauset culture was the nuclear family, each housed in its own house and tending its own fields. "Their dwellings are separate from each other according to the land which each one occupies," wrote Champlain, describing a Nauset village in Chatham. "They are large, of a circular shape, and covered with thatch."

The typical precolonial dwelling on the Cape and Islands was constructed from a frame of saplings lashed together and overlaid with woven mats and six- to nine-foot strips of elm, chestnut, birch, or oak bark sewn together with evergreen tree roots. There was a smoke hole in the center of the roof, with flaps that could be raised and lowered with a string from inside the building to deflect the wind, and various doors around the structure that could be opened as needed for ventilation. The largest of these, which served as the main entry, traditionally faced toward the southwest.

Interior walls were hung with dyed and decorated skins or embroidered mats, though not all homes were so well appointed, depending on class and social status within the tribe. Floors were dirt, but there were usually raised platforms surrounding the center fire on which lay more mats of grass and various soft skins of deer, seal, bear, otter, beaver, raccoon. Native New Englanders as a rule were gifted basket makers, and from the ceiling usually hung a variety of their creations. Some were watertight vessels; some were sieves for corn flour; some were decorated; some were from black ash or oak that had been pounded until the grains split; others were of rushes or reeds. Also hanging indoors were bows, arrows, dried foods, clothing, fired-clay ceramics, and other valuables. Wampanoag and Nauset homes were, by all accounts, very snug and comfortable, though they occasionally had to be moved to escape fleas.

When Captain John Smith came down the coast in 1614 he counted more than forty Indian towns between the mouth of the Penobscot River and Provincetown Harbor. Nobody, in fact, raved more than the ex-governor of Virginia about the settled nature of the Massachusetts coast, which he said "shows you all along large corn fields and great troups of well-proportioned people." And if he was vaguely unimpressed with Cape Cod proper, which he described as "only a headland of high hills of sand overgrown with shrubby pines, hurts, and such trash," it may have been because it was in his way. As an employee of Ferdinando Gorges, Smith naturally aimed to get around the Cape to the islands described by Epenow and Gosnold, to "Capawack and those abounding Countries of copper, corn, people, minerals." But he ran out of time.

On a particular morning in 1998, however, as on the day Gosnold and the *Concord* crossed Vineyard Sound four centuries before, there was not a sign of human life—ruddy-skinned, pale-skinned, or otherwise—on the visible shore of the Elizabeth Islands. There was only me, quite pink on the bridge of the nose by the feel of it, paddling in a plastic log the color of a thoroughly nonnative but nevertheless all-American dandelion.

CHAPTER 5

TARPAULIN COVE

The wind had finally died, 396 years almost to the day after Gosnold crossed Vineyard Sound in the *Concord*, and my own morning to face the zone had come. More worrisome than the water, really, given the look of the day, was where I might stay once I got wherever I ended up. In honor of Gosnold I planned to simply arrive without advance reservations. I'd have my boat, my plastic *Concord*, and minimal provisions. I was happy to be off at last, though my four-year-old son cried on the beach as I paddled away.

By the middle of the sound the water took on a different aspect. There was no change of weather or wave or tide conditions. But land is so imbricated with its past and future, both human and natural, that our mud- and time-bound brains cleave to it: the massive boulder poised to fall from an eroding cliff, the unfortunate new picture window going onto an otherwise perfect old shingled house, running children. Only when landscape recedes to the point of hazy indistinctness does one pass from merely "off the shore" to "on the water." Then the salty fluid that for ten thousand years has surrounded and held, whittled away and piled up Cape Cod and the Islands, has and holds you, too. You are at sea, where change is constant but nothing really changes.

For swimmers this transformation may happen almost immediately, just out where the lobster buoys lie on the relatively calm waters of bay or sound, or where the sand drops away from feet in strong surf on the ocean side. For larger and faster boats than a kayak, it may not happen until land is gone from view altogether, or until blue water is reached. And then, I think, only when the engine is killed, sails luffed, or in heavy weather. (In true Weather, a hurricane or a significant northeaster, Cape Cod and the Islands themselves can seem to go to sea.)

Today, in my tiny boat on this calm morning, the sea began just past the Lucas Shoals, about where the Vineyard became as indefinite behind me as Naushon was in front. I noticed it when I stopped paddling for a moment to watch the disappearing boil made by a fish that I heard, but did not see, leap. It didn't rise a second time, and after a moment the surface was again without form, and void. But even in its August calm, it was undeniably potent. The word that came to mind as I paused there was, inexplicably, *pregnant*, and though the morning was innocent I felt the urge to keep moving.

In *Cape Cod*, Thoreau noticed the shifting sameness of the sea and, as usual, described it as well as it could be described: "Though once there were more whales cast up here," he wrote of the ocean after a series of explorations along the great beach of the lower Cape during the 1850s, "I think it was never more wild than now." He went on:

> We do not associate the idea of antiquity with the ocean, nor wonder how it looked a thousand years ago, as we do of the land, for it was equally wild and unfathomable always. The Indians have left no traces on its surface, but it is the same to the civilized man and the savage. The aspect of the shore only has changed. The ocean is a wilderness reaching around the globe, wilder than a Bengal jungle, and fuller of monsters, washing the very wharves of our cities and the gardens of our seaside residences. Serpents, bears, hyenas, tigers, rapidly vanish as civilization advances, but the most populous and civilized city cannot scare a shark far from its wharves. It is no further advanced than Singapore, with its tigers, in this respect. The Boston papers had never told me that there were seals in the harbor. I had always associated these with Esquimaux and other outlandish people. Yet from the parlor windows all along the coast you may see families of them sporting on the flats. They were as strange to me as the merman would be. Ladies who never walk in the woods, sail over the sea. To go to sea! Why it is to have the experience of Noah,—to realize the deluge. Every vessel is an ark.

There is far too much, sadly, that Thoreau got wrong. He mentioned that there were fewer whales than there once were in the waters around Cape Cod and the Islands, but he didn't know or didn't point out that the good Quakers of Nantucket (and to a lesser degree the people of the

Vineyard, the Cape, and Buzzards Bay) had already, by the eve of the Civil War, fished the sperm and right whale not only out of the waters around home. Whales were gone from the Azores already, and the Brazil grounds. The whalers had rounded Cape Horn into the Pacific, where the onshore grounds near the coast of Chile were considered past their prime. Even the offshore grounds, more than a thousand miles out into the Pacific, were not where the most successful voyages were by then taking place. By the time Thoreau wrote *Cape Cod*, New England whalers were whaling off the coasts of Japan and Siberia and beginning to poke on through the Bering Strait into the Arctic.

Thoreau knew that native oysters were gone from Wellfleet before the American Revolution. But he couldn't have predicted the commercial extinction of the Atlantic halibut, which was not imagined possible until it happened suddenly a century ago. Or the recent collapse and partial closing of George's Bank, the Grand Banks, and the Gulf of Maine, once the world's most prolific producers of cod, flounder, haddock, and other flaky white fish. The virtual disappearance of inshore swordfish was more than a century away when the hermit of Walden Pond went to the beach and saw his permanent wilderness; likewise the 90 percent drop in giant bluefin tuna stocks—which took place in a single decade in the waters off Cape Cod and the Islands once it was discovered in the 1980s that the meat could be jetted to Tokyo and sold by the ounce—was as yet undreamed. Striped bass seem to be back from the brink, thanks to aggressive management by the federal government, but few local anglers would even recognize a *squeteague*, or weakfish, though less than one hundred years ago the Daggett family of Cedar Tree Neck on Martha's Vineyard were catching as many as sixty thousand of them annually in traps and taking them across Buzzards Bay to sell in New Bedford. With the closing of the scup fishery in June of 1999, for the first time in the history of the Vineyard not a single species of fish was abundant enough in local waters to support a commercial fishery on the island.

Yet out in the middle of the sound, particularly if you are in a self-propelled boat with the seat of your pants a few inches below the waterline and your head only a torso's length above it, Thoreau's observation holds: any obvious interrelation of geography and history is lost. The water below is roughly as deep—eighty to one hundred feet—as in Gosnold's day, though it might as well be one thousand. And give or take a degree or two it is as cold—fifty-five chilly degrees this spring day. The zone can be just as ugly, though today I have chosen well, and it is only visible as a slight nervousness on the water. Even that is enough of a reminder to keep me paddling.

What's more, despite the criminal devastation of virtually every so-called commercially viable marine species, these waters are still full of enough life to entrance anyone who cares to take the time to look. Once, while paddling through a massive bluefish blitz and wondering why I had left my rod and reel at home, a large fish came clear out of the water, presumably in pursuit of a terrorized silverside, and smashed head first into the bow of my kayak, surprising me as much as itself. I have paddled through an acre of shimmering bait fish, and near enough to giant ocean sunfish to touch them. I've slicked up close enough to seals to see their breath and trade exclamations. Off Menemsha, a friend and I crossed wakes with a leatherback turtle whose head, I think, was bigger than my own and whose butterfly stroke was, I know, better than mine. And once, in a small aluminum boat off Cape Poge on Martha's Vineyard, I saw what I think was a small pilot whale lolling around in the swell. There are again enough whales on Stellwagen Bank and elsewhere in the vicinity to support a fleet of hunters out of Provincetown and Nantucket, though armed this time around with cameras and suntan lotion.*

The ocean is still full of death, as well, for unwary and unfortunate land creatures. People I know have seen deer come swimming ashore, apparently from the Elizabeth Islands, but I myself have only seen the sodden remains of those that failed to make the crossing. I spent an hour once ferrying to the beach waterlogged but still living monarch butterflies that had run into trouble, with the wind I suppose, early in their fall migration. They refused to stay below decks long enough for their wings to dry, crawling prematurely up my legs toward the kayak cockpit, efforts I rebuffed with gentle firmness until back on shore. In biological terms, as far as monarchs are concerned, it was a futile, syrupy exercise. But as one profoundly afraid of drowning, it gave me comfort to see them at last launch themselves successfully. They headed up over the dune grass and beach plums, out of sight above the scrubby oaks toward Mexico, in the general direction that Epenow and other Algonquians thought the souls of the dead traveled.

---

*What might Thoreau have thought of the return of bass and whales and birds of prey? That "that government is best which governs least," or "in wildness is the preservation of the world"?

Back toward the land from which corn originally came, back toward "the great south west God," Kiehtan.

Another time, while I fished from shore in the dark, unbeknown to me a fifteen-year-old boy drifted from somewhere to my left where he had fallen out of his canoe at dusk, past my lures, to the spot down the beach to my right where the next morning his body was found face down in the water still clutching his life preserver. He was, I read in the paper later, well loved.

So no matter how many houses are built on Cape Cod and the Islands—in one recent year the population of Nantucket grew by 24 percent, faster than any other county's in the state, and the Cape and Vineyard weren't far behind—the sea around them remains somehow aloof. Not invulnerable, as the demise of so many fishes attests, but aloof. And wild. All the dry places hereabouts remain islands, even the Cape.

For my purposes, somewhat contrary to Thoreau's observations, I'm hoping to recover some sense of history on the water. Or to distill the story out of it. Vineyarders I know often speak with pride of never having set foot on Nantucket, a place known to be populated by pink-trousered probable Republicans from Connecticut and Westchester. Nantucketers, for their part, are equally leery of "the other island," where live the kind of good liberal Democrats who wouldn't think of lending their private beach keys to their own first born (or, for that matter, to the first family). Their leeriness is an old tradition: in the 1770s, Nantucketer Kezia Coffin Fanning wrote in her journal that "One Allen of the Vineyard dined here. Very polite for the Vineyard."

Meanwhile, residents of both islands tend to look at the Cape, with all its malls and rotaries and drive-up Starbucks, as something of a lost cause. This, too, has deep roots: when in 1761 the British government enticed thirteen Cape Cod families and thirty-five Nantucket families to move to Nova Scotia to found a whaling industry there, a line was drawn in the new town, and all the islanders settled to the south of it while all the Cape families lived to the north. And Cape Cod gazes down its armpit at the pretensions of both islands. "Here's what Cape Cod doesn't have," wrote lifelong summer visitor and novelist Peter Smith in a 1999 issue of *Travel & Leisure Family*, "tons of celebrities. There's no $40-a-pound lobster salad. No cell phones (or very few) on the beach, no Humvees clogging the supermarket parking lots, not a lot of entertainment lawyers."

But if there is a unified story to be told of Cape Cod and the Islands, it must be the story of the two sounds, two bays, and one ocean that surround them. Cape Cod Bay, Nantucket Sound, Vineyard Sound, Buzzards Bay, the Atlantic Ocean. I'm betting on salt water as the great unifier of the region, the corroder of provincialism, both temporal and geographical. The link. The "realization of the deluge" that connects Epenow the Wampanoag with Ahab the whale killer with Bradford the Pilgrim with Clinton the tourist, with the Nantucket Nectar "juice guys," with the Black Dog. With me.

The truth is I've been looking for an excuse to paddle across Vineyard Sound to the Elizabeth Islands for some time.

There was a minor blitz of small bass going on at the western end of Tarpaulin Cove when I arrived, maybe a dozen terns diving and screeching above forty or fifty boiling fish. It was a congratulatory gift of sorts for having reached the other side of the sound, or so it seemed to me, and I quickly put together my rod and reel and caught two on a white Lefty's Deceiver made of chicken feathers and deer fur. Even a relatively small fish can tow a kayak around, and while I was getting the second of my ersatz Nantucket sleigh rides, two loud but not grotesquely outsized boats motored up from the direction of Woods Hole. They stopped long enough to throw some plugs at the fish before heading farther west, probably aiming for the potentially larger—i.e., big enough to keep—stripers of Quicks Hole.

Tarpaulin Light is a tiny, one-and-a-half-story thing, almost toylike in appearance, that was built in 1759 in an effort to stem the deluge of wrecks in Vineyard Sound. Surprisingly, given Naushon's relative obscurity today, it is the second oldest lighthouse on Cape Cod and the Islands. Only Nantucket's Brant Point Light of 1746 predates it, and only the Boston Light (1716) is older than that. By contrast, Highland Light, which was the first on the Cape, wasn't built until 1797, and Gay Head was dark until 1799. Both Tarpaulin and Brant Lights were built and initially maintained by private citizens of Nantucket, whose ships traveled regularly between their home port and Dartmouth and Fairhaven in Buzzards Bay. In those days, Tarpaulin was a popular stopping place for ships coming around the Cape and down the sound. There was a lively inn and tavern, which still stands.

I beached right below the lighthouse—"Tarps" is one of five places on the private islands of the Elizabeths where uninvited visitors are welcome to come ashore—and climbed up along an old stone wall to the lighthouse. I stopped there long enough to add the light as a waypoint on my hand-

Tarpaulin Light and Cove, Elizabeth Islands, circa 1880. (COURTESY OF THE
MARTHA'S VINEYARD HISTORICAL SOCIETY)

held electronic map of the western hemisphere, and then wandered around
to the graveyard behind it.

Cemeteries are where ordinary people put things they want remembered by history, such as themselves, and the one at the Tarpaulin Lighthouse is even more diminutive than the beacon itself. It's no bigger than a
bedroom in an old house, and the two graves and a geographical-marker
stone standing in a line through its middle fill it to capacity, suggesting a
story but not quite giving it up. On the right is a fading slab of white mar-
ble on which it's possible with effort to make out an intricately carved
image of a weeping willow overhanging a crypt. The inscription reads, IN
MEMORY OF JUDITH, WIFE OF JOSEPH GAME, WHO DIED SEPTEMBER 10, 1811.
On the left is a very simple stone with only the initials J G, presumably for
Joseph Game, but with no date. Between the two lies a tiny cube with the
initials of the United States Light House Service.

It is possible that J.G. died first and Judith put this unadorned slab over
his grave, saving her money for the much nicer monument to herself. That's
a better story in some ways than the more likely one: that Joseph wanted to
remember Judith in a manner befitting some contentment they shared on
this exposed point, and then, with her gone, there was no one left to do
much for him other than have his initials carved in an unremarkable slab of

soft stone. The day I was there, as if to accentuate the difference between his memory and hers, a large dry cow turd lay directly over the final resting place of J.G.'s rib cage. The dead, as John Muir wrote of another cemetery, do not reign here alone.

What we think we are leaving behind is not always what endures, and when both these graves are finished wearing away and perhaps the lighthouse is gone, too, what will remain here is the stone wall that someone—maybe the two of them together along with a team of oxen, or he grieving alone, or even some respectful member of a later generation—built to surround the little graveyard. Immense slabs and sizable boulders of granite tugged from their first too certain hold in the glacial till, loaded on a stone boat and hauled and stacked here one at a time.

The land behind the lighthouse rolls up a bit and then down again into a swale, so that if you stand next to Judith's headstone, only the light of the lighthouse is visible, as if resting on the green grass. It's a forlorn place, though beautiful, and there was a strong odor of honey in the air coming from an ancient chokecherry not far away.

Back at the kayak, I packed up to push on. Then I discovered that I had left my wallet on the seat of my car back on the Vineyard. I cursed; I kicked the boat and hurt my foot; I sat down on a rock and fumed at my pathetic self. But there was nothing to do except recross to the Vineyard. I could not go on to Cuttyhunk and beyond. I had no trinkets to offer the natives.

CHAPTER 6

CHATHAM

Whether or not Sir Ferdinando Gorges ever actually directly requested the taking of native slaves from the coast of New England is uncertain. Many of his Indians, Epenow included, seem to have come to him second- or thirdhand. And as a practical matter, he definitely worried (albeit somewhat after the fact) that the kidnapping done by various explorers of the North American coast was going to make his life's dream of planting "Christian colonies on that continent" more difficult to achieve. "An act much tending to our prejudice," he called it.

Nevertheless, with or without his explicit approval, the fact remains that more than one ship sailing under the auspices of Gorges and/or his partners returned to Europe from New England with unwilling natives on board. The pattern began much earlier with Columbus and Vespucci, continued with Verrazano's generation, and really didn't end in New England until at least the conclusion of King Philip's War in 1675.

Gorges got his first Indians shortly after the Gosnold expedition. In 1605 he, the earl of Southampton, and a few others sent out the ship *Archangel* under the command of George Waymouth. The ship left Dartmouth at the end of March, and on the fourteenth of May sighted a "whitish sandy cliffe" that was most likely Sankaty Head on Nantucket.*

---

*As usual, there is debate among sources over which sandy white cliff in a region of sandy white cliffs it was.

Waymouth appears to have been aiming for Plymouth Harbor, probably because a ship funded by Southampton and commanded by Martin Pring had collected a moderately profitable cargo of sassafras there in 1603. Waymouth may have been after more than the cure for syphilis, however. Ironically, given the future religious history of Plymouth, there is some evidence to suggest the *Archangel* may have been seeking a suitable location for what one writer described as "a colonial refuge for oppressed English papists." They landed too far north for sassafras, however, and returned home with a cargo that consisted primarily of five natives of the Maine coast, along with two canoes and all their bows and arrows. Three of these men wound up, as Epenow later would, in Gorges's "retinue." One, a man named Skidwares, escaped in 1607 when Gorges sent him back to Maine in a disastrous second attempt to establish a year-round colony in New England, this time at Sagahadoc (Kennebec). Another, the already mentioned Assacumet, became the translator for Epenow's tales of island gold.

The ship that took Epenow prisoner in 1611 was under the command of Edward Harlow, who had been part of the failure at Sagahadoc, which may explain why the earl of Southampton and Gorges didn't send him back to Maine. More likely, though, the memory of Gosnold and Pring's moderate financial success is the reason Harlow was specifically sent "to discover an Isle supposed to be about Cape Cod." Still another possibility is that he was seeking an uninhabited island from which the English could carry on seasonal trade in relative safety, the way they already did in Maine.

What Harlow spent most of his time doing, however, was picking fights with Indians all around Cape Cod and the Islands. According to John Smith, the main source of information on the voyage, Harlow's charts "much abused them, for . . . they found only Cape Cod, no Isle but the Maine, there they detained three Salvages aboard them, called Pechmo, Monopet, and Pekenimne." The wording implies that these three Indians, who were most likely Nausets from Chatham, were caught in the usual way: lured aboard with promises of friendship and trade, then detained.

Pechmo, for one, apparently saw what was coming and "leapt over board and got away." He wasn't gone long, though. With a few friends he later swam silently up to the ship and cut away its small boat and "got her on shore and so filled her with sand and guarded her with Bowes and Arrowes, [that] the English lost her." Shortly thereafter, either in a failed effort to recover the boat or in some other action nearby, three members of Harlow's crew were "sorely wounded with Arrowes."

Their next stop was "the Ile of Nohono," which was either Nantucket or one of the small islands—Nauset, Webb's, Ram, Slut's Bush—that have long since disappeared from the coast near Chatham. Here "the Salvages in their Canowes assaulted the Ship till the English Guns made them retire." The reason may have been that Harlow had just taken aboard another local. His name was Sakaweston, and he became the first American to intervene in a European war. After living for many years in England he went off to fight in "the warres of Bohemia," from which he never returned.

In Harlow's defense, it may not have been his own actions that drove the people of Chatham or Nantucket to arms. A half dozen summers before, in 1606, the French navigator Samuel de Champlain had come down for the summer from his frozen and half-dead outpost in Canada and pretty well shot the place up with his harquebus. Champlain, in fact, had the dubious distinction of helping preside over not only the first documented killing of a European by a native of Cape Cod and the Islands, but in a separate voyage the following year, also the first regional slaying of natives by Europeans.

In June of 1605, after a calamitous winter during which thirty-five out of seventy-nine settlers in a small Canadian outpost died of starvation, disease, and exposure, Champlain and his commander, the Sieur de Monts, sailed south in search of a more hospitable location. By mid-July they reached Cape Anne, where the locals danced on the beach until Champlain went ashore and distributed knives and biscuits. This, he said, "caused them to dance again better than before." He asked them to draw an outline of the coast to the south, which they did.

Though quite good, the map didn't prevent their ship from running aground a few days later in Plymouth Harbor, which the French named St. Louis and which the locals called Patuxet. The people there were also friendly. They no doubt remembered Martin Pring's visit of two years before, when a young crew member who played the guitar created a sensation among the people of Patuxet, a young Squanto perhaps among them. "In [his] homely Musicke they took great delight, and would give him many things, as Tobacco, Tobacco-pipes, Snakes skinnes of six foot long, which they use for Girdles, Fawnes skinnes, and such-like," reported Pring. "And [they] danced twenty in a ring, and the guitar in the middle of them, using many Savage gestures, singing Lo, la, lo, la, la, lo: him that first brake the ring, the rest would knocke and cry out upon." They were good times, from the sound of it: Pring recalled that more than one hundred Wampanoag gathered on shore to trade and dance. Good times, that is, until the English apparently overstayed their welcome, and Squanto's cousins and uncles felt obliged to light the woods on fire to hasten their departure. Like Gosnold the year before, Pring and his men apparently took an unpaid-for canoe along as a souvenir. *

For his part, Champlain admired the gardens of Plymouth and the way the locals twisted fishing line out of local hemp, which seemed to grow everywhere. But he didn't remain long—perhaps, some have argued, because the place was far too well populated with healthy locals to consider planting a colony there. It also could be that Champlain, whose countrymen had carried on a profitable fur trade for nearly a century with the interior of Canada, saw immediately what the Pilgrims only discovered after they were committed to the place: that without a major river, Plymouth was a poor spot to conduct business. At any rate, after a day spent getting their ship unstuck, the French sailed up the inside of Cape Cod, narrowly avoiding the rocks at the mouth of Wellfleet Harbor, and on the twentieth of July rounded Provincetown. Champlain named it "Cap Blanc."

"It was almost low tide when we entered," he later wrote of their arrival at Nauset Harbor in Eastham, "and there were only four feet of water in the northern passage; at high tide there are two fathoms. After we had entered, we found the place very spacious, being perhaps three or four leagues in circuit, entirely surrounded by little houses around each one of which there was so much land as the occupant needed for his support. . . . It would be a very fine place if the harbor were good." Because of the complicated approach, they named the place "Port de Mallebarre."

Relations with the resident Nausets went well enough at first, and many of the Indians paddled out in canoes and went aboard the French ships to trade for the usual trinkets, but trouble began almost as soon as four or five Europeans went ashore to collect fresh water. A Nauset tried to steal a kettle, Champlain later explained, and though a Frenchman gave chase, he was no match for the thief. The other sailors immediately ran to the beach and swam for the ship, calling for it to fire its guns, while at the same time the Indians on board the French ship dove off and swam for shore, presumably also yelling to their friends. One Indian was captured by Champlain's crew and held on board as a hostage. At some point during the fracas Champlain's gun exploded in his face, which was apparently the nearest any of the French firearms came to killing anybody.

---

*As with every story we have from the period, this is the European interpretation of events. As mentioned earlier, burning the woods was a relatively common undertaking, and Pring's fire may have had nothing to do with the presence of the English.

Champlain's Map of Nauset Harbor ("Mallebarre"), which he visited in 1605. (COURTESY OF THE NICKERSON MEMORIAL COLLECTION, CAPE COD COMMUNITY COLLEGE)

Meanwhile, back on the beach, when the Nausets realized that the French were not going to stay onshore and fight for their cookware, they "returned straight to the sailor from whom they had taken the kettle, hurled several arrows at him from behind, and brought him down. Seeing this, they ran at once to him and dispatched him with their knives."

Then, in a remarkably restrained settlement, the French commander, Sieur de Monts, released the hostage; the Nauset leadership apologized for the behavior of the thief; and the dead sailor was given a Christian burial. Two days later, low on supplies and fearing the arrival of heavy weather, the French headed back to St. Croix for another long Canadian winter.

Unfortunately, the following year's visit did not end in nearly so diplomatic a fashion. With a new governor, Jean de Poutrincourt, on board, Champlain arrived at Wellfleet Harbor on the morning of October 1, 1606, and apparently spent the day eating oysters; they named the place "port aux Huistres." The surf was too high the next morning for them to safely enter Nauset Harbor as they had the year before, but after several canoes came out over the breakers to tell them of the opening around to the south and west, they managed to make it around the bottom of Cape Cod's elbow into what is now called Stage Harbor in Chatham. There they were greeted by 150 Nausets singing and dancing onshore.

For ten days, while a repair crew worked on their ship's rudder, which had broken somewhere near the Pollock Rip, the French and the Indians exchanged bracelets, fish, raisins, and other goods. De Poutrincourt, meanwhile, spent the time out rambling around the country with a dozen or so harquebusiers. Such a band of armed men prowling around the interior may have been what made the people of Chatham anxious for the visitors to finish up their work and move on. Or perhaps the Nausets were alarmed or annoyed by the strangers' decision to plant a cross on the beach, before which they then naturally engaged in some rather suspicious-looking genuflections.

Something, at any rate, caused the women and children of Chatham to begin disappearing from the vicinity of the harbor. The French who were exploring back from the beach noticed that the women were also taking down their cabins. "This made us suspect some evil intention and that they purposed to attack those of our company who were working on shore," wrote Champlain later.

On the issue of Nauset intentions, it's interesting to note that once the corn was harvested and buried, October was, in all likelihood, a traditional time for taking down the cabins and moving to the fall hunting grounds. If an unprovoked attack were imminent, as the French believed, it also seems odd that any locals would continue to accompany them to their ship, where they would no doubt become hostages as soon as violence broke out. But, assuming Champlain's version of the story is accurate, French fears were not entirely unfounded. As a precaution, everything and everyone was ordered to return to the ship. Among those on the beach were three men baking bread, however, who simply refused to leave until the crust was browned to perfection. What's more, the prospect of steaming cakes just about to come out of the fire convinced two more sailors, who had been sent from the ship at dusk to round them up, to go AWOL as well. The next morning, the fifteenth of October, four hundred Nausets surrounded the sleeping gastronomes and "sent them such a volley of arrows that to rise up was death." Four were killed outright.

Fifteen Frenchmen with guns immediately rowed ashore and scared off the attackers. "To pursue them was fruitless, for they are marvelously swift," Champlain wrote. "All we could do was to carry away the dead bodies and bury them near a cross which had been set up the day before." Three hours later, the Europeans watched from their ship as a group of Indians came back down onto the beach and "in mockery" beat down the cross, disinterred the dead, and scattered the corpses around on the dune grass. All of this, said Champlain, "displeased us greatly."

Back to shore went the French and reburied their dead. The next day, October 16, they sailed away from "Port Fortune, to which we had given this name on account of the misfortune which happened to us there." They got as far as Woods Hole or thereabouts before the wind came around and drove them back to Chatham, where, out of apparent boredom due to the weather, they decided to seek revenge. "Being unable to put to sea," says Champlain, "we resolved meanwhile to get possession of some savages of this place, and taking them to our settlement, put them to grinding corn at the hand mill, as punishment for the deadly assault which they had committed on five or six of our company."

There was no way to capture them outright, so the French attempted to look peaceful, endeavoring to "coax them by showing them beads and other gewgaws, and assure them repeatedly of our good faith," as Champlain put it. The plan was for the strongest men to go ashore with a rope. This they hoped would not arouse the suspicions of the locals, as it was customary in the New World to carry a long piece of cord, smoldering at one end, to use as a pipe lighter. Then, when the Indians were lured near enough, the French planned to feign putting strings of beads around their quarry's neck while slipping the rope over them instead.

Suffice it to say there were no Nauset kitchen slaves grinding the polenta at the little outpost at Port Royal the following winter. The French did succeed in killing "a number" of Nausets, apparently seven, whose scalps they gave to an Indian from Maine who was traveling with them. Champlain never returned to Cape Cod and the Islands, and the French never again attempted to settle the New England coast. But they were no doubt still remembered by the people of Chatham in 1611, when Edward Harlow arrived in the neighborhood on his own slaving voyage. As late as 1614, when John Smith explored the lower Cape, the Nausets did not repeat their mistake of piloting foreign sailors into their harbor: "the Salvages say there is no channel," wrote Smith, though he seemed to suspect there was.

Even over on the Vineyard, by the time Harlow appeared in 1611 Epenow and the other resident Wampanoag could not have been unaware of the bloodshed connected with recent visits by Europeans to the Cape. In addition to regular trade among villages, there were annual meetings of the Indian leadership, at which such momentous events would doubtless have been major topics of conversation. It's even possible that the Vineyarders had already heard of Harlow's abductions and failed abductions in Chatham and Nantucket of the previous few weeks, though this seems less likely. All that is known, unfortunately, is a single sentence from John Smith: "At Capawe they took Coneconam and Epenow . . . and so with five Salvages they returned for England."

CHAPTER 7

NASHAWENA

Almost nowhere looks its best in the noonday sun, Cuttyhunk included. I didn't get there until August. Not because of wind or fog, or forgotten money, or even my ceaseless lukewarm war against the cat brier and chokecherry below my stone wall. It was just the usual seasonal disturbances on the Cape and Islands that kept me mostly close to home: houseguests; whole weeks that seemed to pass in a day or two; offspring that will only catch their first striped bass once in their lives and are therefore worth observing closely. July departed without warning. And with it, though I didn't know it at the time, went my plans for a grand circumnavigation of the Cape.

Early one August morning I finally shoved off from the beach to paddle across to Tarpaulin Cove. Again I ate breakfast on the beach below the lighthouse, but this time instead of returning home I poked along the shore toward the westernmost isle.

Paddling the south coast of Naushon Island, the intermittent cliffs and low rocky beaches look so much like places opposite them on the north shore of Martha's Vineyard that it's easy to imagine the two high grounds connected, as they once were by a low valley of the same rolling, forest-covered land, rather than separated by five or more miles of salty waves. The Vineyard rises to nearly twice the elevation of the Elizabeths—320 feet on the Vineyard's Prospect Hill versus less than 150 on the highest point on the Elizabeths—and there are, of course, many houses on the bigger island

and almost none on the smaller. But the shoreline on both sides of Vineyard Sound alternates between pleasant stretches like Naushon's "French Watering Place," where small ponds and wetlands conspire with the sound to build and maintain slim rock or sand beaches between them, and places where the wet and dry worlds are obviously engaged in a long-term test of will.

The struggle between land and sea manifests itself in the eroding cliffs that are a common feature of most nonbarrier beaches on the Cape and Islands, including those near the western tip of Naushon, where I was paddling. There are falling-down bulwarks of land like this at Falmouth Heights and Succonesset Point on the Cape's southern shore, along much of its bay-side coast, and to a lesser or greater degree along most of the national seashore north of Nauset Light. At Nantucket Cliffs and Sankaty Head on Nantucket, at Squibnocket Point and Cape Poge and most of the north shore of the Vineyard, on the south side of Nomans, and here and there all over the Elizabeths, the land is falling into the sea. The hodgepodge of gravel, sand, clay, and boulders is generally not sturdy enough to maintain a truly vertical front against the nearly constant undermining of the sea, so they are more accurately called "scarps" than "cliffs": unlike almost all the rest of the New England coast, there is no exposed bedrock on the Cape and Islands. But where there is enough clay, they can rise spectacularly, as at Truro's Clay Pounds and, most famous of all, at Aquinnah (Gay Head) on the Vineyard.

The naked substrate of the scarps is exquisite in soft light; early and late it typically transmutes from bleached gray into gold and red—rich and warm as a luminist painting. At Aquinnah the cliffs go further still: gold, red, yellow, black, white, and green. Along the modest coast of Naushon where I was paddling, not long after leaving Tarpaulin Cove I saw a young deer, still in her spots. She worked her way slowly along the top of a golden wall in light almost too romantic even for a Disney movie.

In places, the cliffs calve great boulders out of themselves, which seem to have been hurled down as if to form a front-line defense against the sea. This works after a fashion; wherever more than the usual number of such immovable objects drop out of the land, a point forms, behind which a crescent of beach may find shelter. But it's only temporary: the physics of waves are such that their erosive energy is concentrated on points. For every big rock still standing guard at a corner of land, lying just offshore are a dozen or more of its predecessors that the sea has already undermined, rolled off shore, and drowned. The Devil's Bridge off Aquinnah is a string of boulders that presumably was built of what one geologist described as "stolen cliff materials." The bridge goes out a mile past where the cliffs now stand.

Because they bear no relationship to any underlying bedrock, the boulders are called erratics, which is sort of a geological version of an off-islander. Along with all manner of other debris scraped up from the surface of the mainland, erratics were carried here and dumped between ten and thirty thousand years ago by the glaciers that built the underpinnings of Cape Cod and the Islands. Some erratics originally came from the sides of the White Mountains of New Hampshire; gouges were left by the glacial ice in the granite near the summits of those mile-high peaks that point this way. Other Cape and Island rocks are from Katahdin or elsewhere in Maine, and an unlikely few may even have come from farther still. But because it typically requires only ten miles or so of travel in glacial ice to demolish all but the toughest rocks, most of the larger ones are probably just over from northern Rhode Island and eastern Massachusetts. *

Of all the cliffs and eroding hills on Cape Cod and the Islands, only the famously colorful ones at Gay Head are not predominantly built of rocks and rubble collected by the ice from somewhere off-island. Ice still did much of the lifting at Aquinnah, but perhaps because of the elasticity of the underlying soil, at the western end of Martha's Vineyard the once-flat land lying in front of the glacier crumpled and buckled and bulged up like the hood of a car in a head-on collision. It did not give way, however, and, more importantly, was not entirely overrun and removed by the ice or its meltwater. Nowhere else on Cape Cod and the Islands, or for that matter in all of New England, is the preglacial past so clearly on display. One hundred million years of preglacial history is what gives the cliffs their wild variety of pigments. It makes the cliffs "gay" and the local geologists cheerful.

The cliffs of Aquinnah are a tangled mess of sedimentary layers laid down over the eons and overlain in places with glacial debris and outwash. They continuously fall down on themselves, further confusing matters. But they are a gold mine of information to those who know how to look at them. The black coaly remains of a great swampy forest, which 100 million

---

*Not all the erratics have fallen into the sea, of course. Among the more well known, i.e., larger, landed erratics are the "great rock" a mile southeast of Bourne Village, the thirty-foot-long "Enos Rock" in Eastham, and Wiscossom's rock in Chilmark. Patches of great erratic boulders are called "bear dens" and can be found in Falmouth, West Tisbury, Pocasset, and elsewhere.

Early tourists to the cliffs of Aquinnah (Gay Head), circa 1870. (COURTESY OF
THE MARTHA'S VINEYARD HISTORICAL SOCIETY)

years ago stretched past the current locations of Nantucket and Provincetown almost to the continental shelf, are visible. Then, when the sea rose
and flooded the forest, for 30 million years light-colored Cretaceous clays
from the continent to the west piled up. The sea fell again, and for another
40 million years forest again grew in the vicinity of Cape Cod and the
Islands. The dinosaurs, meanwhile, died. The Rocky Mountains rose.

So it went, with the sea claiming and retreating from a great coastal plain
as if on some galactic tidal cycle. The third time the ocean crept back over
the region in the period visible in the Gay Head cliffs, it deposited a layer of
green sands loaded with more marine fossils than are found anywhere else
on the New England coast. Crabs, scallops, mussels, quahogs, long-necks,
cockles, and razor clams have turned up, along with the bones of whales,
seals, and walruses and the teeth of the immense sharks that hunted them.
Astonishing things have been deduced from the green-sand fossils of
Aquinnah: from a stone worn smooth in the belly of a seal that died in the
clays, it is thought that the animal probably traveled to and from Hudson
Bay, where the particular type of flint occurs. The tooth of an early, mud-
loving rhinoceros was found in the green sand, and the tooth of a crocodile
as well.

Lying on top of all the clay is a layer of gravelly material called the
Aquinnah Conglomerate, which is the last visible deposit before the com-

ing of the ice. Though it's only about a foot and a half thick at the most, there are so many bones and teeth in the Aquinnah Conglomerate that it was once called the Osseous Conglomerate. There are jaws, teeth, ribs, skulls, and paddle bones of whales and other marine mammals, along with the four-inch-long teeth of gigantic Pleistocene sharks that were probably sixty feet long. These gave way in the usual pattern to land animals as the water receded. A camel that roamed the rolling dry savanna that would become the Cape and Islands left its bones in the middle of the Aquinnah Conglomerate. Then the climate cooled until it was unfit for camels, and small ancestral horses moved to the greener grasses; the bones of one of these was found at a higher, more-recent level in the conglomerate. Then it became too cold for horses.

In the far north, the process of glacier building may already have been well under way, which is to say more snow was falling each winter than melted in the warmer seasons. When snowfields reach roughly two hundred feet deep, the pressure on the old snow at the bottom is great enough to transform it from six-rayed snowflakes to "mosaically interlocked ice." When the weight gets even heavier—the pack over Greenland today, for instance, is eleven thousand feet thick—what seems solid begins to ooze out the bottom of the snowfield.

At least four times in the last million and a half years the earth chilled and glaciers crept out from the poles, only to withdraw again. At the beginning of each expansion, up on the Labrador Peninsula and other high-latitude centers of glacial activity, the ice may have moved as much as five feet per day. But as it progressed south and spread laterally, it slowed. By the time the great ice sheet was a mile deep over almost half of the North American continent, it gained only a few inches per year at best. Finally, though, it reached a latitude where the sun's warmth melted it back just as fast as the northern snowfalls pushed it forward, and the ice was stopped. In New England, that place was in the vicinity of what ultimately became Cape Cod and the Islands. Then, after a brief pause of maybe a few thousand years, the climate rewarmed and the ice began to melt back again. The sea, in turn, which had fallen as much as 450 feet with so much of the globe's water tied up in 8 million cubic miles of ice, began to rise again.

As glaciers advanced first around, then up and over, annoying obstacles like the Appalachian Mountains, they picked up and carried virtually every loose thing in their path. This is how the future United States got most of the good soil that had built up over the previous million centuries in the future Canada. During the long, slow trip south, much of the smaller material was ground first to gravel, then to sand, and finally to "rock flour" and clay, a large proportion of which eventually made its way to the bottom of the ice, where it was spread into a relatively even veneer called "ground moraine" that was left behind when the ice margin retreated north.

Likewise, as seas advance toward a retreating ice front, they lay down layers of clay and marine sediment. Great, sediment-rich lakes formed between the retreating ice and the moraine long enough for thick bands of clay, like those in the cliffs at the Clay Pounds, to settle out. Layers upon layers slowly raised the land to a cold, sandy coastal plain punctuated by vaguely scallop-shaped ridges.

There are some visible remnants of the first advances, primarily in the lower layers of ancient outwash and ground moraine visible in scarps around the region. But it is the nature of glaciers and dinner guests alike that the last one to leave is the most conspicuous. Their memory can obscure or even erase all that came before. It was the final substage advance of the final glacial period—the Wisconsin glaciation, which arrived in New England roughly 25,000 years ago and retreated again 6,000 years later—that left behind the underpinnings of Cape Cod and the Islands.

Not all of the solid material picked up by the ice became ground moraine. An immense amount of rock and rubble flowed forward until it reached the leading edge of a glacier. There, when the ice that had held it for so long melted or evaporated, the rubble was unceremoniously piled up into a long snaking ridge called a terminal moraine. The terminal moraine of the most recent glacial advance in North America runs from Nantucket Shoals to the high(ish) lands along the north(ish) edge of Nantucket. After Tuckernuck and Muskeget it drops underwater for a few miles and comes up again at Chappaquiddick to run roughly along the northeast and north-west shores of the Vineyard. West of the Vineyard it continues underwater to Block Island and Rhode Island, then dips and rises out of the water again at Montauk Point to form the south fork of Long Island. On it goes across northern Pennsylvania, then down across the Midwest almost as far south as St. Louis, then up and across the continent.

For thousands of years water off the glaciers' leading edge eventually warmed, evaporated, traveled north, and precipitated out as snow, which in turn pushed more ice south, which accumulated more wreckage of the previous eons along the way. The great watery conveyor belt carried on like this until in places the moraine was hundreds of feet high. According to the calculations of Nathaniel Shaler, an eminent nineteenth-century Harvard geologist who summered on the north shore of the Vineyard, the total mass

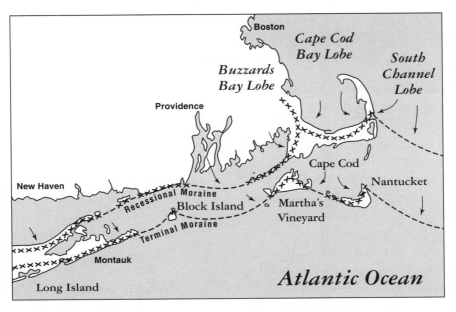

Approximate locations of the terminal and recessional moraines that are the foundations of Cape Cod and the Islands, and the three principal glacial lobes that created them.

of the moraine on that island alone is about the same as that of New Hampshire's Mount Monadnock.

When the final advance of the Wisconsin glaciation ended roughly eighteen thousand years ago and the backbones of the outer islands were in place, the ice didn't give up unconditionally to the warming world. Several times, for periods of hundreds or even thousands of years, the ice stopped, or even pushed forward again, though it never regained all its lost ground. The recessional moraines thus formed created the parallel lines of shoals in Nantucket and Vineyard Sounds that appear on nautical charts: Squash Meadow, Hedge Fence, L'Hommedieu, Lucas, Middle Ground. All the well-named rocky trouble spots around Cape Cod and the Islands—Rose and Crown, Hen and Chickens, Bishop and Clerks, and the like—are places where the glacier paused.

Far more important than any of the shoals, however, are the massive recessional moraines that provide the backbones of Cape Cod and the Elizabeth Islands. Just as the terminal moraine of Nantucket and Martha's Vineyard continues east and west, the recessional moraine of the Elizabeths reappears in New York as the north fork of Long Island.

For all its destructive and creative power, ice doesn't present a unified front. When the advancing glacial sheet hit the White Mountains in New Hampshire and Mount Katahdin in Maine, it split into three fat fingers, or lobes, each with a rounded leading edge. And though the glacier eventually covered the mountains completely and joined with itself again, the ice maintained its scalloped leading edge all the way to what would become Cape Cod and the Islands. The uneven advance is what ultimately determined the shape of the landscape: if it weren't for Mount Washington and its neighbors, the Vineyard wouldn't have its distinctive triangular shape. If not for Thoreau's "Ktaadn . . . made out of chaos and Old Night," then Cape Cod would not fit his even more famous description as "the bared and bended arm of Massachusetts: the shoulder is at Buzzard's Bay; the elbow, or crazy-bone, at Cape Mallebarre [Monomoy]; the wrist at Truro; and the sandy fist at Provincetown,—behind which the State stands on her guard, with her back to the Green Mountains, and her feet planted on the floor of the ocean, like an athlete protecting her Bay,—boxing with northeast storms, and, ever and anon, heaving up her Atlantic adversary from the lap of earth,—ready to thrust forward her other fist, which keeps guard the while upon her breast at Cape Ann." But for the lobes, there would be no elbow.

Farthest west of the three fingers of ice was the Buzzards Bay Lobe. At its extreme southern position it laid down the high ground of the Vineyard's northwest shore—from Tashmoo to Gay Head—before receding to create the Elizabeth Islands and the ridge of highland along the western shore of Buzzards Bay now occupied by the road to Woods Hole. Because it advanced over some of the rocky heart of northern and central New England, the lands created by the Buzzards Bay Lobe are richer in erratics (and, later, stone walls) than the rest of the region.

Between the White Mountains and Katahdin lay the Cape Cod Lobe, the terminal moraine of which forms the basis of the far-less-prominent northeast ridge of the Vineyard—from Tashmoo to Chappaquiddick. There it drops below the water to form the Wasque Shoal before reappearing five miles farther west to form Tuckernuck, Muskeget, and the central ridge of Nantucket. At Sankaty Head, the moraine again drops below the surface to form the famous Nantucket Shoals, which begin thirty-odd miles southeast of the island.

This lobe also created the main ridge of the lower Cape, the Sandwich Moraine that runs from Sandwich to Chatham and is currently crested for the most part by the Mid-Cape Highway. The lovely islets in Pleasant Bay are the final petering out of the Sandwich Moraine. Because the Cape Cod Lobe traveled across the old coastal plain beneath what is now Massachusetts Bay, Nantucket and the mid-Cape received somewhat less in the way of rocks than points west. (What rocks did make it to Nantucket—mostly from the Boston area—were long ago pried up and put to use in wharves and other construction projects.)

There is no unsubmerged evidence of the terminal moraine of the massive South Channel Lobe, which advanced east of Katahdin and rearranged the previously laid-down glacial outwash of George's Bank. Coming across the gulf of Maine, it carried the least rock of the three lobes. But the lobe left its mark on the land nonetheless. Wherever two receding lobes met, a third kind of moraine formed in the crotch. Such an interlobate moraine forms the north-south ridge from Orleans to High Head in Truro. There it disappears below the ocean-built lands of Provincetown, though farther out it forms the basis for the area of shallow water known as Stellwagen Bank.

Even before the moraines were fully constructed, enormous rivers of meltwater pouring off the glaciers carried lighter materials away and spread them out in relatively flat alluvial plains to the south. In fact, the moraines typically sit on top of earlier outwash plains. Such outwash eventually filled the triangles made by the Buzzards Bay and Cape Cod Lobe moraines on the Vineyard and Cape, and built the misnamed "moors" to the south of the moraine on Nantucket. In places, the gravel and sand is five stories deep or more. Once the glaciers were in full retreat, the fans joined together into a single outwash plain crisscrossed by a network of sediment-rich streams, which carried the meltwater down to the then-distant sea.

On the Vineyard and Nantucket, broad lowlands where great outwash rivers once flowed bisect the last unsubmerged remnants of that plain. The great ponds of the Vineyard's south shore were once the estuaries of such rivers, as were Hummock, Long, and Miacomet Ponds on Nantucket. Torrents of glacial water carved out the great ponds of Falmouth as well, and the lowlands of the Bass River. Because they were created when the sea lay far to the south and west, their bottoms are often below today's sea level. Similarly, the "holes" between the Elizabeth Islands are where the meltwater that backed up behind the recessional moraine broke through.

The smaller Buzzards Bay glacier retreated first, which allowed the waters from the Cape Cod glacier to excavate the valley that a group of private entrepreneurs widened in 1913–1914 to form Cape Cod Canal.*
Likewise, the smaller Cape Cod glacier retreated more rapidly than the

---

*The canal, which had been talked about since at least 1676, was later taken over and expanded by the Army Corps of Engineers.

massive South Channel glacier, and the waters pouring off the latter dug the east-west "hollows"—Dyers, Newcomb's, Pearce's, Cahoon, Snow's, et cetera—that slope down from east to west across the Nauset Plain on the lower Cape. Spectacular waterfalls, also from the South Channel Lobe, piled up the hillocks—or kames—that are scattered around Eastham.

Unlike the outwash plains on the Islands, which were never covered with ice, the outwash areas of Cape Cod lay under the glacier while Nantucket and Martha's Vineyard were being built. During the period of recession, even before the Cape's moraines were built, immense pieces of the glacier broke off and melted in place, creating the nearly five hundred kettle hole ponds that perforate the Cape. The largest is Long Pond at 743 acres and 66 feet deep. Mashpee is half the size and 2 feet deeper. Some are ringed with erratics, boulders still being slowly pushed around by ice, though now the far less dramatic ice of ten thousand normal winters inches them up the bank.

In the hundred centuries since the big ice left, more than a few kettle holes have seen their walls crumble, boulders and all, into the sea. The sweet little high-walled harbor of Quissett in Woods Hole was a kettle hole that lost its grip. So was Chatham's Stage Harbor.

Before the ocean rose to near its current level some six to eight thousand years ago, the Cape and Islands were just relatively nondescript ridges in an immense plain that stretched all the way out to George's Bank. The first pioneer plants were probably various cold-weather berries, along with golden heather, poverty grass, and water lobelia. Mastodon and caribou wandered in, followed by the sturdy humans who made a living hunting them. Many of the smaller species of wildlife that now inhabit the various islands arrived by land as well, only to be isolated when the water rose, and ate away at both moraine and outwash plain. Nantucket and Martha's Vineyard each has its own particular subspecies of short-tailed shrew, both of which differ from the short-tailed shrew of the mainland. The Vineyard also has a unique version of the white-footed deer mouse. And Muskeget Island off Nantucket is the only home of the beach vole.

It occurred to me as I slipped along the water below the cliffs of Nashawena on my way to Cuttyhunk that our status as relatively short-lived dirt dwellers no doubt skews our view of the battle being played out on the scarps of Cape Cod and the Islands. What appears from the receding precipice to be a struggle between sea and land—particularly if your personal piece of paradise in the form of a house is at the edge of the abyss—might just as well be seen as the swings of a violent personality disorder of water. In this the Cape and Islands play the tragic role of malleable spouse. Ice in a brooding ten-thousand-year funk piled up the backbones of the region without regard for order. Rock and dirt and clay and whatever else could be scraped from the continent in the glacier's long-frigid binge were simply dumped in a heap and left behind when the cold finally lifted.

And now, for nearly four million mornings, the same substance, in a more fluid mood, has scurried around attempting to make sense of the mess. For all its eternal wildness, the ocean is, like all water, a maniacal sorter and classifier of the junk that falls into it from the land. Even in the most memorable storms, each object is moved according to its weight and size; as the energy drains out of a given wave, tide, or storm, any nugget of formerly overpriced real estate will likely end up with others of its kind. Sand will be put with sand, pea gravel with pea gravel, pebbles with pebbles, rocks with rocks, cobbles with cobbles. True sediment, meanwhile, might waft around in suspension for years, or even decades, before winding up in a marsh or over a barrier beach into a pond or onto an oozy bayside clam flat.*

The ocean is so reliably temperamental that one day's effort is often piled on top of the previous day's, which can mask the organization somewhat; at least compared with the steadier work of rivers. But even on the beach, objects of similar sizes will sometimes be sorted further, according to heft or hydrodynamic shape: skippers here, rounds there. So it is that there may be driftwood and other flotsam at the top of the last storm surge, then a perfect strand of sand for beach towels, then slightly coarser sand at water's edge, then, maddeningly, ankle-breaking rocks just below the waterline where you want to wade or swim. Only in and around the boulders that collect on a rocky point is the ocean usually forced to allow rocks and sand and crab legs of various sizes to coexist in a relatively heterogeneous fashion, though even there the sorting takes place on a smaller scale. Only an erratic is self-confident enough to demand from the ocean a diverse society of neighbors.

---

*The work was actually begun by the meltwater, which sorted the outwash according to weight and size so that, generally speaking, the farther from the moraine, the smaller the particles of till.

· · ·

I arrived at Cuttyhunk around two in the afternoon to find that it was not exactly the little gem of a long-lost salt-born New England village that I remembered from a previous visit. In the bright light of an August weekend it had more the feel of a campers' canteen and supply store at some upscale Winnebago park in Canada—the kind of place where the patrons talk on about what kind of supplies and additional gear they might need for a big trip to Alaska but never quite get around to hitting the Al-Can Highway.

The yachts, both motorized and wind-driven, bobbing cheek by jowl in every available corner of the harbor, were pretty and well maintained. Many looked capable of long voyages to exotic and deserted destinations. But although their aspirations may have included the far-flung isles of the Pacific or the Caribbean or even the Carolinas, from the profusion of caps that said BLOCK ISLAND, anchor-embossed shirts that said NANTUCKET, and accents that said Boston, I had the distinct impression that most of the sailors in line on the dock for seafood-salad sandwiches and ice cream were, like me, strictly three-day Ahabs.

Meanwhile, there was something I didn't like about the look of the golf carts—there are very few cars on Cuttyhunk. The assorted rusting tanks and whatnot lying around waiting, seemingly indefinitely, to be taken off-island looked more like common junk than quaint artifacts. Doubtless Cuttyhunk's scruffiness is a more authentic picture of Ye Olde New England than the progressive prettification that occurs as one travels east along the outer arc of the terminal moraine—Gay Head to Chilmark to Edgartown to Nantucket Town to the clipped privets of 'Sconset, which caused me to worry about the implications of my distaste as I walked the low road around the island to the venerable Cuttyhunk Bass Club. Worry that my decade of life spent largely in the middle of that arc had infected me with a terminal case of creeping bourgeoisification. I should be happy to have found a little piece of a less-fussy yesterday only a day's paddle away. Rusting junk is good. Cheap bad '70s architecture is better than expensive bad '90s architecture. I didn't paddle all the way over here in order to poke easy fun at the locals.

The Bass Club, which is now one of two lodging places on the island, was perfect in every way, except that they had no room available at the last minute on a Saturday afternoon in August. It was founded by a group of gentlemen anglers who arrived in 1865 in a yacht called *Theresa* and bought "the larger part of the island." In its heyday in the late 1800s there was a lot-

*The Pasque Island Clubhouse (Elizabeth Islands) with Robinson's Hole behind it,
as shown in a 1931 prospectus offering the entire island for sale for $60,000.*
(COURTESY OF THE MARTHA'S VINEYARD HISTORICAL SOCIETY)

tery every evening to determine who would fish the next morning at each
of the twenty-six bass stands the club constructed all around the island.
Members were the first anglers to use the term *chum*, and it referred not to
the fish scattered on the water but to the local teenager who was paid the
astronomical amount of one dollar to throw lobster tails into the water
around the stands. Menhaden were preferred as the actual bait, though,
because, as Teddy's uncle Robert Roosevelt complained, lobster tails
wouldn't stay on the hook. There was a similar club on nearby Pasque
Island that was arguably even more posh.

I wandered in and looked at the fishing memorabilia, then wandered
back out and peered over the edge of the cliff to search in vain for any remnant of the bass stands. It looked like good water, though the prevailing
west wind would make it tough for right-handed fly fishermen. "The
Elizabeth Islands offer the condiments of existence to season the dry hurry-
scurry and commonplaceism of the business world on the main lands of
America," wrote an angler who visited in the 1840s. "We arrived before
lunch time, and, having examined the trout preserve, the black bass and
white perch ponds, and taken each a couple of striped bass from that
incomparable stand, Bass Rock, we adjourned to dinner, where we were
regaled with choice viands, wines, and the recital of angling exploits by the
members of the club. . . ."

I began to think more highly of Cuttyhunk; even what appeared from the road to be the dessicated carcass of a large dog lying in the yard of a house on the way back to the waterfront didn't dispel my improving mood. (The jaws and skull were half-exposed, and after a classic movie double take, I looked up to a pretty but listless young woman on a second-floor porch who stared back in a way that dissuaded me from saying, "Your dog looks thirsty," which I later wished I had done.) The sun was lower in the sky now, improving the color of things immeasurably, and back at the dock the charter boats arrived loaded with happy sports. A man cleaned an immense bass at the public fillet stand on the dock, to the great amusement of assembled children and seagulls. People who earlier seemed to be wondering what to do with themselves now knew that cocktails on the aft deck were not long off, and were notably happier for it.

At the Cuttyhunk Historical Society, a lovely couple closing it up for the day were suitably impressed to hear that I had paddled all the way from West Tisbury that morning to let me look around briefly. They offered to call the only other place they thought I might find a bed, which sounded from their description suspiciously like the house with the dead dog. I thanked them and said I'd stop by and ask in person.

Which, of course, I did not. I had another plan and paddled around to the entrance of West End Pond. The tercentennial monument that was erected in 1902 on the island where Gosnold and company set up their little outpost is appropriately defensive in character, a medieval-looking turret of cement and beach stone with no entrance. There are windowsills and lintels, but the implied openings are also solidly mortared in with large stones. The island itself is about the size of a two-car garage, and I paddled around to the back side, out of sight of the one house that overlooks the pond, and scrambled up the steep bank. It was devoid of trees, covered entirely with waist-high brambles and poison ivy. It did not take long to decide that not even the fear of wild Wampanoag would persuade me to sleep there.

So after a decent fried meal at Bart's, where a taped medley of Carly Simon and James Taylor tunes emanated from outdoor speakers made to look like rocks, and where the foursome at the table next to me debated whether they did or did not actually see a particular celebrity the week before in Oak Bluffs, I paddled off into the sunset. Somewhere beyond where the Cuttyhunk floating raw bar was delivering oysters to the assembled yachts, I found a spot on the beach to spread out my sleeping pad and wait until it was light enough to continue.

Whether this was strictly legal I can't (or won't) say. I will say that in the middle of the night three loud and evidently drunken fishermen in a boat motored close to shore and shined a very bright light on me. I'd heard them yipping and swearing their way up the coast in my direction for half an hour.

"Hey there's people up there, shine that light there. *There*," said one.

"Are they naked?" asked another.

CHAPTER 8

GOLGOTHA

The year 1614, when Epenow escaped from the deck of Nicholas Hobson's ship and swam ashore to Martha's Vineyard, was a busy one for European contact with Cape Cod and the Islands. The Dutch navigator and fur trader Adriaen Block sailed by in the little yacht *Onrust* (*Restless*), which he and his men had built in New York Harbor. Block apparently thought he was the first from his country to identify Nantucket, which he transcribed as Petockenock. But his remark to a director of the Dutch West India Company that the Vineyard was "commonly called by our Dutch captains, Texel [after one of the West Friesian Islands off the Netherlands]; and by others Cape Ack," suggests that there were other, now-forgotten visits to the region from the low countries. Block generously bestowed Dutch names almost everywhere he went: Buzzards Bay was the Zuyder Zee, Monomoy was Vlacke Hoeck, and Chatham, perhaps because he had heard of Champlain's misfortune there, was Ungeluckige Haven.

As mentioned previously, John Smith also visited the region that year. He arrived with two ships in April on the Maine coast, where he aimed "to take whales . . . and also to make trialls of a Mine of Gold and Copper." As for the whales, "we saw many, and spent much time in chasing them; but could not kill any." As for the gold, it was a ruse, more a "device to get a voyage" than a real possibility. So they headed south in search of fish and furs. Unlike many other explorers, Smith made a sincere and remarkably systematic effort to get the local names for places; his famous map of the region, published in 1618, lists twenty-eight of them.

Like virtually every other official explorer, however, Smith was dependent on the largess of more powerful persons than himself. Ferdinando Gorges was running out of both cash and faith. So after his next Gorges-funded voyage ended abruptly when he was taken prisoner by French pirates, Smith began actively shopping for a new patron. This may be why he dedicated his map and accompanying description of New England to the sixteen-year-old prince of the realm, Charles.

The royal teenager made a few helpful suggestions. Charles thought, for instance, that a more mellifluous name for the river that Smith identified as the Massachusetts might be Charles. Trabigzanda became Cape Anne after his mother, while Cape Cod was renamed Cape James after his father, the king. Some of the prince's names stuck, like Plymouth, which he apparently liked better than Accomack. Twenty others, such as Cape James, did not. Prince Charles, even when he became king, never did produce a ship for John Smith.

Various Smithophiles through the centuries have argued that although his swashbuckling in Virginia is more often remembered today, Smith's persistent promotion of New England as a place for English expansion means that he, not Gorges or anyone else, should carry the deeply dubious title of Father of English Colonization in the area. In some of his more populist moments, his arguments sound astonishingly like the rhetoric of later centuries: "Here are no hard Landlords to rack us with high rents, or extorted fines to consume us; no tedious pleas in law to consume us with their many years disputations for Justice. . . . Here every man may be master and owner of his own labour and land. . . . If he have nothing but his hands, he may set up his trade; and by industry quickly grow rich; spending but half that time well, which in England we abuse in idleness."

But of a more immediate impact on the future history of the Cape and Islands than any of Smith's writings were the actions of his fellow traveler Thomas Hunt. When Smith went off exploring the coast to the south, he left Hunt, then in command of the larger of the two vessels, the *Long Robert*, with orders to continue catching and drying fish. As soon as his hold was full, Hunt was supposed to proceed to Spain to sell the cargo and make a profit for Gorges and the other investors. On his way home, though, Hunt apparently figured he could improve his own purse by picking up another cargo then in demand in Spain: slaves. And he stopped at Cape Cod to do it.

Smith, as he often did, took it personally:

> One Thomas Hunt, the Master of this ship (when I was gone), thinking to prevent the intent I had to make there a Plantation, thereby to keepe this abounding Countrey still in obscuritie, that onely he and some few Merchants might enjoy wholly the Trade and profit of this Countrey, betraied four and twenty of those poore Salvages aboord his ship; and most dishonestly and inhumanely, for their kinde usage of me and all our men, carried them with him to Maligo, and there for a little private gaine sold those silly Salvages for Rialls of eight; but this vilde act kept him ever after from any more imployment in those parts.

Smith reported elsewhere in his text that there were "twenty seven of these poore innocent soules," and that their abduction served to "moove their hate against our Nation." The anonymous writer of *Mourt's Relation*, the earliest published report from the Pilgrims at Plymouth, also used the larger number and added that Hunt "deceived the people, and got them under color of trucking with them, twenty out of this very place where we inhabit, and seven men from the Nausets [at Eastham]." The exact number is relatively unimportant. Likewise, Increase Mather's tidbit that some of the captives were confiscated by friars in Malaga in order to "nurture them in the Popish Religion" is interesting but inconsequential. And the same goes for the possibility that Hunt, in a bit of rare historical justice, was himself enslaved by Turkish pirates on his way home to England.

What makes Hunt's crime not simply another in the long line of native abductions from the New England coast is the fact that one of the men he took from Plymouth was Tisquantum, better known as "Squanto, friend of the Pilgrims." Squanto was taken only a few weeks before Epenow jumped ship, and Increase Mather, for one, later attributed some of Nicholas Hobson's difficulties on the Vineyard to the locals' presumed knowledge of Hunt's slaving spree. It's possible that the news traveled that fast, though John Smith didn't believe it. He clearly abhorred Hunt's behavior but scoffed at the possibility that the loss of Epenow was due to anything other than ineptitude.

In every important way, the Wampanoag and Nauset world of Cape Cod and the Islands, from which Squanto was taken and to which Epenow returned, was in 1614 the same as it had ever been. The regional politics were intact, with the strong Wampanoag nation and their client state, the Nauset, in relative balance with the nearby Massachusett and Narragansett peoples. Internal politics, as well, were stable, with the essentially monarchical local sachems, or chiefs, in place. These were hereditary positions that usually passed through the maternal line and were typically but not exclusively held by men. On the Vineyard there were four sachems: those of Chappaquiddick, Aquinnah, Nunnepog, and Takemmy. On Nantucket there were two districts, one of Nauset descent and a smaller western group of Wampanoag, who may have migrated back and forth from Chappaquiddick. On the Cape there were more than a half-dozen identifiable groups: the Manomets at Sandwich, the Succonessits at Falmouth, the Mattakees at Barnstable, the Cummaquids at Yarmouth, the Monomoyicks at Chatham, the Nausets at Eastham, and the Pamets at Truro. And presiding over it all was the sachem of Pokanoket, residing at Mount Hope (Bristol, Rhode Island), who was perhaps already Massasoit himself or one of his uncles.

More basic than politics were the rhythms of corn and strawberries, game and shellfish, planting and hunting, loving and playing. There were ball games, one village against the other, that ranged over miles of beach and could last for days. The losers, typically, were forced to go home virtually naked. Another fun way to lose your loincloth was to gamble it away in any number of games at special outdoor casinos in the fat season after the harvest. In Put-tuck-qua-quock, an arbor was ceremonially built of poles sixteen to twenty feet tall, on which players and their backers hung various items of value—wampum, skins, strings of dried clams, and whatnot—that they wished to wager. Then the players rolled the dice, usually made of painted plum pits, into a special tray. Whole towns played against each other, and it was traditional to swear loudly. An even louder pastime was called "Hubbub." According to Russell, "two small bones or beans, black on one side, were put in a smooth wooden tray. When the player lifted the tray and then thumped it hard on the ground, the bones jumped and changed colors and positions. Meanwhile, the players whipped their hands back and forth, smiting themselves on the Breast and Thigh, crying out 'Hub, Hub, Hub' so as to be heard for a quarter mile." There were also various spear- and stone-throwing competitions, dart games, dice games, swimming matches.

Dancing, both ceremonial and recreational, was popular. Storytelling of all sorts was also part of life on the Cape and Islands. Many tales were creative myths starring Moshup, the friendly giant. Nantucket had its own version of the Montagues and Capulets: two forbidden lovers—he a royal Tomkaud (from the west), she a Kaud princess (from the east)—brought lasting peace to the island. Their Romeo and Juliet came to a happier ending: the young couple survived the ordeal.

Occasional visits by people from across the sea were no longer astounding novelties. Given the behavior of Champlain, Hunt, and Harlow, they were no doubt still events to be feared. By 1614 in Maine, where the natives had more experience with strangers, Indians were reportedly trading only with baskets let down from cliffs to boats below. But the Wampanoag-Nauset order of life was firmly in place, and who could imagine it changing?

The years Squanto was away and Epenow was newly home were relatively quiet in terms of contact with Europeans. There were the usual visits by fishermen and fur traders, the most notable of these a French ship that wrecked off the Cape in 1616. William Bradford reported in *Of Plymouth Plantation* that after the men came ashore and salvaged much of their food and goods, the local Nauset people all gathered "and never left watching and dogging [the castaways] till they got advantage and killed them all but three or four which they kept, and sent from one sachem to another to make sport with, and used them worse than slaves." Whether the captives learned enough Algonquian to say "Welcome, Native Americans," is not remembered. But the absence of recorded visits by Europeans to the region that includes Cape Cod and the Islands is ironically cruel. The years of Squanto's wanderings were in fact among the most momentous in Wampanoag history, when the impact of European contact was near or at its pre-settlement apex. They were the years of plague.

Exactly which disease did the killing along the New England coast has long been a matter of debate among historians. Yellow fever, smallpox, chicken pox, flu, and bubonic plague have at various times been contenders, either singularly or in overlapping waves. What is certain, however, is that the disease was devastatingly fatal and the few Europeans who witnessed it were largely immune. In 1615, the plague was at its height in Saco, Maine, where an agent of Sir Ferdinando Gorges named Richard Vines spent the winter and reported that "the country was in a manner left void of inhabitants" by the malady, and though he and other Europeans "lay in the cabins" with the sick, they themselves never fell ill.

During the following two years the disease spread south toward Cape Cod and the Islands, consuming along the way the powerful tribes of Massachusetts Bay and the main Wampanoag populations of Plymouth and Buzzards Bay. It abated before reaching the Nausets and the islanders, however, and the Narragansett to the west were also spared the worst of it—for the time being, at least.

Other than Vines's, there are almost no surviving eyewitness reports of the disease in action. Europeans did, however, witness and record the pathogen's progress several decades later when it, like they, spread farther inland to the valley of the Connecticut River. "This spring also, those Indians that lived about their trading house there, fell sick with the small pox and died most miserably," wrote William Bradford:

> For want of bedding and linen and other helps they fall into a lamentable condition as they lie on their hard mats, the pox breaking and mattering and running one into another, their skin cleaving by reason thereof to the mats they lie on. When they turn them, a whole side will flay off at once as it were, and they will be all a gore of blood, most fearful to behold. And then being very sore, what with cold and other distempers, they die like rotten sheep. The condition of this people was so lamentable and they fell down so generally of this disease as they were in the end not able to help one another, no not to make a fire nor to fetch a little water to drink, nor any to bury the dead. But would strive as long as they could, and when they could procure no other means to make fire, they would burn the wooden trays and dishes they ate their meat in, and their very bows and arrows. And some would crawl out on all fours to get a little water, and sometimes die by the way and not be able to get in again.

As did Vines, Bradford reported that the Europeans were spared:

> But those of the English house, though at first they were afraid of the infection, yet seeing their woeful and sad condition and hearing their pitiful cries and lamentations, they had compassion of them, and daily fetched them wood and water and made them fires, got them victuals whilst they lived; and buried them when they died. For very few of them escaped, notwithstanding they did what they could for them to hazard of themselves. The chief sachem himself now died and almost all his friends and kindred. But by the marvelous goodness and providence of God, not one of the English was so much as sick or in the least measure tainted with this disease, though they daily did these offices for them for many weeks together.

The estimated population of the Americas before and after European conquest and the degree to which disease did the grisly work of native removal has long been fraught with politicized implications for professional historians. It is, in fact, a sort of touchstone around which takes place the academic process of new interpretations continually replacing old, of "modern unbiased" replacing "old apologist," of presently correct replacing formerly correct. Generally speaking, high initial population estimates are usually meant to imply a more advanced native culture and therefore a greater subsequent genocide (without, of course, implying that advancement changes an entitlement to existence). Likewise, a low estimate of deaths by disease implies a higher direct moral responsibility for the later elimination of native culture by Europeans.

It is an important debate that will not end soon. But there is little doubt that with its plentiful supplies of shellfish and other seafood to augment produce and game, southern coastal New England was one of the most densely populated areas in native America. There may have been as few as one thousand or as many as three or four thousand people living on Nantucket. The same range is reasonable for the Vineyard, and double or triple that for Cape Cod.

Whatever the actual numbers, a startling change is evident in the surviving reports of visitors to New England beginning a year after John Smith reported seeing the "great troups" up and down the New England coast. Just as consistently as the earlier travelers found well-populated towns, the English later found abandoned villages and fields. When the Pilgrims first traveled to Pokanoket (Mount Hope) to visit Massasoit, they passed places where "thousands of men have lived . . . which died in a great plague not long since." Likewise when they sent a diplomatic mission to the north to the land of the Massachusetts, they found "many, yea, most of the islands have been inhabited, some being cleared from end to end, but the people are all dead, or removed." And they found bones. It was generally believed among the Algonquian peoples that the souls of the dead went southwest, and skeletons were typically buried seated and facing in that direction. At the beginning of the plague, the Indians no doubt tried to keep up with the appropriate ceremonies. But as with the later plague in the Connecticut Valley, at some point the mortality became too high to keep up with.

"They found [Massasoit's] place to be forty miles from hence, the soil good and the people not many, being dead and abundantly wasted in the late great mortality, which fell in all these parts about three years before the coming of the English, wherein thousands of them died," wrote Bradford. "They not being able to bury one another, their skulls and bones were found in many places lying still above the ground where their houses and dwellings had been, a very sad spectacle to behold."

Thomas Morton, who attempted to settle in the mid-1620s at Merry Mount, near Quincy, wrote that "they died on heapes, as they lay in their houses; and the living that were able to shift for themselves would run away & let them die and let their carcasses lie above the ground without burial.

For in a place where many inhabited, there hath been but one left alive, to tell what became of the rest, the living being (as it seems) not able to bury the dead, they were left for Crows, Kites and vermin to prey upon. And the bones and skulls upon the several places of their habitations made such a spectacle after my coming into these parts that as I traveled in that Forrest, near the Massachusetts, it seemed to me a new-found Golgotha."

Whole towns disappeared, or were disbanded when the population became too small to support them. The most famous of these was at Plymouth, where the Pilgrims found "about four years ago all the inhabitants died of an extraordinary plague, and there is neither man, woman, nor child remaining." Eight towns in the plague region that John Smith identified on his generally accurate map seem to have vanished by the time the Pilgrims arrived. There were no doubt others as well.

So it was that when Thomas Dermer sailed down the coast from Maine in May of 1619 and discovered that his old acquaintance Epenow was in fact alive and well on Martha's Vineyard, he found a very different New England than his predecessors had. Instead of the great troups and corn fields of Smith, Dermer wrote of passing "ancient Plantations, not long since populous now utterly void." At the harbor that would become Plymouth, where hundreds had danced to Pring's man's guitar only a decade before, Dermer had to travel almost a day's journey inland before finding anyone alive at all.* And he knew where to look. Guiding him was a local named Tisquantum, or Squanto.

Nobody knows for certain the exact peregrinations of Squanto in the six years between his capture by Hunt and his reappearance at the Pilgrim's fledgling colony at Plymouth in 1620. He may have spent some time enslaved in Spain, but it's more likely he was one of the captives passed over by the buyers. William Bradford, who was probably as good a friend of Squanto as any European, says he escaped directly from Hunt and got to England, where he was "entertained by a merchant," John Slany. Slany was involved with the colonization of Newfoundland, and Squanto soon made his way there, where a few years later he met Dermer.

Dermer, in turn, contacted Gorges with the news that he had a potential guide to the region that included the suspected goldfields of Capawack.†

---

*At Nummastaquyt (Middleboro).
†If Squanto went with Dermer back to England to discuss the voyage with Gorges, which seems likely, he crossed the Atlantic four times between his capture and his return to his recently extinct village at the foot of Cape Cod Bay.

Gorges, whose optimism always exceeded his luck, wanted to know more but ultimately approved the project. According to a letter Dermer later wrote from Virginia, among the Indians he and Squanto met inland from Plymouth Harbor were two Wampanoag "kings," one of whom was probably Massasoit. There was a moment of tension, which Squanto managed to diffuse, and then, wrote Dermer, "I redeemed a Frenchman and afterwards another at Mastachusit, who three years since escaped shipwrecke at the North-east of Cape Cod." Dermer also sought to verify some "former relations," which some have argued refers to information about the locations of Nantucket and Martha's Vineyard and the possibility of navigating between them.

Squanto, perhaps in shock at the disappearance of his hometown, elected not to accompany Dermer around the Cape to the islands. He was sorely missed. "We had not now that faire quarter amongst the Savages as before, which I take it was by reason of [Squanto's] absence—for now almost everywhere where they were of any strength they sought to betray us," wrote Dermer. "At Manamock [somewhere in the vicinity of Pleasant Bay and Monomoy] I was unawares taken prisoner, when they sought to kill my men, which I left to man the Pinnace; but missing their purpose, they demanded a ransom." A quantity of hatchets were left at an undisclosed location, but still Dermer was not released. Then, in some inadequately explained way, the tables turned, and "it pleased God at last, after a strange manner to deliver me, with three of them into my hands." The hatchets were returned along with a canoe full of corn, and everyone went on his way, which, for Dermer, was over to the Vineyard.

Epenow presumably hadn't spoken with a European since jumping from the deck of Hobson's boat six years before. As a result, Dermer reported as news the fact that Epenow was indeed alive. "I met with Epenow a Savage that had lived in England, and speaks indifferent good English, who four years since being carried home, was reported to have been slain, with divers of his countrymen, by Saylors, which was false."

It sounds peaceable enough: a meeting between two men with many English acquaintances in common. It's even possible that they themselves had met before, at Gorges's home, or over a drink at the Mermaid in London. When it was over, Dermer, seemingly satisfied, left in his little open boat and sailed on down Long Island Sound, past Manhattan and on to Jamestown, "searching every harbor" all the way to Virginia.

The following summer, though, when Dermer returned to Capawack, Epenow very nearly killed him; Epenow, at any rate, is the Vineyarder who often gets the credit for the fracas that William Bradford reported left "all

[Dermer's] men slain, but one that kept the boat. But [Dermer] got aboard very sore wounded, and they had cut off his head upon the cuddy of the boat, had not the man rescued him with a sword. And so they got away and made shift to get into Virginia where he died, whether of his wounds or the diseases of the country, or both together, is uncertain."

Bradford's account is virtually all that is known of the incident. We don't know if it started, as Gorges thought, because Dermer tried a little too hard to encourage Epenow to revisit the old country; or, as Gorges also thought possible, out of revenge for Hunt's slaving voyage. Or if, as Bradford suggested, the Wampanoag were afraid that this latest English visitor was seeking revenge for the French captives he redeemed the year before. Or if the rising tension of a century of European contact with Cape Cod and the Islands simply simmered over, as it had more often than not in the past.

Maybe Epenow just decided the time had come to take action. It's not out of the realm of possibility that Epenow, who had presumably seen various poxes while in Europe, may have sensed some vague connection between the English and the general death that had squandered so many of his compatriots on the mainland.* But an understanding of biological causation wasn't necessary for him to know that the pace of change on Cape Cod and the Islands was more likely to accelerate than slow. He had lived among England's colonial enthusiasts. He knew Gorges well enough to fool him, and the earl of Southampton, too, and perhaps John Smith. He almost certainly knew of the settlement at Virginia and of the attempted colony in Maine. Maybe Epenow, who had seen more of the strangers' world than they had seen of his, was simply tired of the thought of more and more of them coming to his homeland, loaded down with all their trinkets and fancy clothes and oversized boats.

All that is certain is that he or some other Vineyarder won the skirmish and drove the Englishmen from the shores of the island, and that the Indians of Cape Cod and the Islands maintained a fearsome reputation for decades afterward, though probably more for the simple fact that they were alive and relatively healthy by regional postplague standards than for any specific actions they took.

What is also known is that less than two months after the incident with Dermer, a sixty-foot ship called the *Mayflower* set sail from Plymouth, England, and that she was headed, though no one on board knew it at the time, for Cape Cod.

---

*Squanto, as we shall see, later made explicit use of just such a suspicion.

CHAPTER 9

PROVINCETOWN

In 1622, two years after Dermer was expelled from Martha's Vineyard, the supreme sachem of the Wampanoag nation sent a diplomatic envoy over to his new ally, Governor William Bradford of Plymouth Plantation. The messengers carried with them a knife, some beaver skins, and a request: would the governor please use this blade, which was Massasoit's own, to sever the head and hands of the Indian known to the English as Squanto? Knife, hands, and head should then all be sent back to Pokanoket, on Mount Hope Bay, where Massasoit made his royal home. For their trouble, Massasoit's messengers added, the English could keep the beaver.

Bradford hesitated. For nearly two years Squanto had been pivotal in securing with the Wampanoag relations that were better than the Pilgrims ever dared hope to achieve. He pleaded: didn't Massasoit understand how difficult the loss of their translator might make future relations between the two peoples? He prevaricated, which merely infuriated the Wampanoag representatives.

It must have been an awful and unexpected turn of events for the little community of separatists. Before leaving Europe, the more nervous among them had predicted they would face violence in America, but it was always more along the lines of bloodthirsty aborigines "flaying some alive with shells of fishes, cutting off the members and joints of others by piecemeal and broiling on the coals [and eating] the collops of their flesh in their sight whilst they live."* No one foresaw this polite, political sort of violence, supposedly to be carried out by themselves at the formal request of a neighboring sovereign. As if that weren't enough, the capital charge was being leveled against Squanto, who was their "special instrument sent of God for their good beyond their expectation."

In southeastern New England, however, where the recent plague had drastically rearranged the relative power structure of the various native nations, the arrival of a new tribe from across the ocean was bound to be a highly political occurrence. As a result, the two years since the Pilgrim arrival had been marked by far more intrigue and diplomacy than outright confrontation. Massasoit was right, Bradford finally announced, Squanto must die. What's more, the Pilgrim governor said, he too thought the perfidious diplomat deserved to lose his life for what he had done to their good friend Massasoit. The English could not, however, accept the bonus beaver.

Back in Leyden, Holland, there had been seemingly endless debates within the little community of English exiles over whether and where to emigrate. (Emigrate *again*, that is, for only twelve years before they had fled from England the first time.) In addition to their paramount fear of Indian violence already mentioned, some worried about drowning during the crossing. Others, pointing to what they knew about the attempts to colonize Virginia, cautioned about malignant American air and deadly diseases. They would surely starve.

Those in favor of crossing over to America invariably answered the timid with questions of their own: could the American Indians really be all that much more barbaric than the Spanish, who were, after all, Roman Catholic, and were about to invade Holland? A twelve-year truce between Spain and Holland was due to expire in 1621, "and there was nothing but beating of drums and preparing for war." Wouldn't war bring famine and pestilence to them in Holland, too?

Unfortunately, Holland hadn't turned into the permanent sanctuary some had hoped for when they had departed their little village of Scrooby, England, about 150 miles north of London, under rather unpleasant circumstances in 1608. Whereas most Puritans held out hope for the possibility

---

*In its gruesome particulars, their fear shows that some of them had read or heard of early Jesuit accounts of Canada.

of reform from within the existing religion—principally through the elimination of bishops—more-radical separatists like the Scrooby congregation
knew in their hearts that the "false church" of England was corrupted
beyond repair. The only hope for salvation, then, was to separate from it
entirely, to be particular, and to seek a personal covenant with each other
and with God. Anyone who thought differently, said William Bradford, was
clearly "unacquainted with the Bible."

The king and the archbishop of Canterbury, perhaps not surprisingly, fit
into that category. "No Bishop, No King," is how James the First summed
up his own evolving faith. Evolving because when he first ascended to the
throne of England in 1603, religious reformers hoped that because he was
Scottish he might have certain Presbyterian leanings; he might, in other
words, reduce the power of the bishops in favor of committees of clergy.
Instead he said of the Puritans, "I will harry them out of the land."

In the case of the relatively obscure Scrooby congregation, at least, he
succeeded. According to Bradford, during the last years in England before
moving to Holland, they "were hunted and persecuted on every side . . .
some were taken and clapped up in prison, others had their houses beset
and watched night and day, and hardly escaped their hands." They tried to
get permission to leave the country legally in 1607, but were denied the
necessary papers. "Though they could not stay," said Bradford, "yet they
were not suffered to go."

Mariners promised to secret them out of the country, then either didn't
show up or turned them in. "But when he had them and their goods
aboard," Bradford wrote of one captain, "he betrayed them, having beforehand complotted with the searchers and other officers to do; who took
them, and put them into open boats, and there rifled and ransacked them,
searching to their shirts for money, yea even the women further than
became modesty; and then carried them back into the town and made
them a spectacle and wonder to the multitude which came flocking on all
sides to behold them. . . ."

Another time, a group of separatist men were on board a Dutch ship and
were waiting for their families, who came by a different route. When the
captain saw a mob of armed townspeople approaching on horse and foot,
he raised anchor and sailed off. At around the same time, the latecomers
arrived on the beach, but the men on board could do nothing but squint at
the receding land from the deck as the mob rounded up their wives and
children and marched them off. "It drew tears from their eyes, and anything

they had they would have given to have been ashore again; but all in vain. . . ." Eventually, though, 125 Scrooby Puritans "got over" to Holland, where life was only marginally better. They weren't harassed for their beliefs, but they didn't know the language and couldn't afford land on which to practice the only trade they knew, farming. They took whatever jobs they could find but barely got by. Bradford, for instance, lost his inheritance in an attempt to become a weaver. And like countless generations of immigrant parents, they worried continually about the influence of the local culture on their children, who began to think potentially heretical thoughts, like, "What's wrong with a nice Sunday dinner? All the Dutch kids have it." The Pilgrims were not nearly as dour as their later reputation made them out to be, but they did firmly believe the Lord's day was meant to be one of solemn rest, not, as the Dutch treated it, a time to enjoy the goodness of life. Not surprisingly, perhaps, no one from England seemed eager to follow the Scroobyites over, and as the original elders got ever older, they began to wonder if their community of saints would simply wither away.*

The final reason Bradford gave for the decision to move has the ring of an afterthought: the possibility of proselytizing in "those remote parts of the world. . . ." So, bloodthirsty Indians notwithstanding, the Scrooby cum Leyden separatists at length decided to cross the blue ocean. Then commenced the protracted arguments over where in the New World to go. One faction thought that Guyana would be a good place for a commune of true believers—warm all the time, green and generous. No, said others, too full of disease. Too full of Spaniards! But the Guyana advocates came back with the sensible point that one doesn't need as many clothes there as one might farther north. The selection of a location was further complicated by the need for both a charter and, even more importantly, investors. Going to America required at least as much money as courage, and the Leyden separatists had only the latter. Nor did they have much leverage with which to negotiate. Investors were leery: as Ferdinando Gorges could attest, plenty of money had already been lost in America. Ultimately, though, a group of roughly seventy merchant adventurers was lined up under the leadership of a "citizen and ironmonger of London" named Thomas Weston. Weston agitated for a New England destination, but Gorges and his partners were

---

*They were right to be worried; by 1660, the small English community that remained behind in Holland when the rest went to America was completely assimilated.

in the process of renegotiating their own charter with the Crown and were temporarily unable to provide any subsidiary charters.

"After many other particular things answered and alleged on both sides," wrote Bradford, the majority decided that the best option was to "live as a distinct body by themselves under the general Government of Virginia; and by their friends to sue to His Majesty that he would be pleased to grant them freedom of religion." The contract was signed July 1, 1620. Three weeks later the separatists left Leyden for England, from which they would sail for America. "So they left that goodly and pleasant city which had been their resting place near twelve years, but they knew they were Pilgrims," wrote Bradford, using for the first time the term that became forever associated with the colonists.

According to Bradford, the mood was excited: "That night was spent with little sleep by the most, but with friendly entertainment and Christian discourse." And it was sorrowful: more than half the Leyden congregation, including their minister John Robinson, were staying behind, though they intended to follow eventually. Those who would remain accompanied their neighbors and relatives to the dock at the nearby town of Delftshaven to see them off in the *Speedwell*, a small ship they intended to keep with them in America. Still other sympathizers came down from Amsterdam to wish them well. "Truly doleful was the sight of that sad and mournful parting," wrote Bradford. "What sighs and sobs and prayers did sound amongst them, what tears did gush from every eye, and pithy speeches pierced each heart; that sundry of the Dutch strangers that stood on the quay as spectators could not refrain from tears." Many never saw each other again.

The passage to Southampton, where the *Mayflower* and the rest of the emigrants were waiting, was uneventful. Once the friendly greetings and reacquaintances were over, however, they fell to arguing among themselves over who was at fault for the terms of their final agreement with Weston and the other investors. Under the contract, no colonist could personally own any output, tools, houses, or real estate for seven years, after which there would be a division based on shares—not what the Leyden group thought they had agreed to. But when Weston couldn't secure a royal monopoly for fishing off New England, he had demanded last-minute changes. One of the Pilgrims' negotiators, John Carver, claimed to have been out of town at the time the deal was struck, and the other, Robert Cushman, said he had no choice. He hadn't consulted with the emigrants back in Holland out of fear of postponing their departure, when they were "already delayed overlong in regard of the season of the year, which he feared they would find to their cost."* They argued as well over whether too much had been paid for the beer supply, and the particulars of other decisions regarding provisions. "To speak the truth," wrote Cushman in a letter to another member of the congregation who was not going to America, "there is fallen already amongst us a flat schism, and we are readier to go to dispute than to set forward a voyage."

They finally set sail on August 5, 1620, after unloading and selling four thousand pounds of their butter supply in order to pay the port taxes, which Weston refused to do. They were barely out of sight of land, however, before turning back and putting in at Dartmouth. The *Speedwell,* which was supposed to become the Pilgrims' primary fishing vessel in America, leaked so badly that her captain refused to go farther. After weeks in port plugging leaks, they set off again and made it one hundred leagues to sea before the *Speedwell* began taking on water. During this time, Cushman, and no doubt many others whose sentiments were not recorded, found their frustration with events and each other rising to the point of outright pessimism about the entire undertaking. "If ever we make a plantation, God works a miracle, especially considering how scant we shall be of victuals, and of all un-united amongst ourselves," wrote Cushman to a friend. "Violence will break all. . . . If I should write you of all things which promiscuously forerun our ruin, I should over-charge my weak head and grieve your tender heart. Only this, I pray you prepare for evil tiding of us every day . . ."

This time, though they searched the entire *Speedwell* for several days, no leaks of any significance were found, and the problem was determined to be "the general weakness of the ship." Bradford later suspected that the real problem with the *Speedwell* was that the sailors had lost their nerve at the prospect of staying in America for a year as contracted, and so deliberately put up too much sail in order to force open her seams and thus sabotage the crossing. If that were the case, it worked; the *Mayflower* set out alone with as many of the emigrants as she could carry. Perhaps not surprisingly, Cushman was one who stayed behind. "And thus," wrote Bradford, "like Gideon's Army, this small number was divided, as if the Lord by this work of His providence thought these few too many for the great work He had to do."

On September 6, 1620, for the third time the Pilgrims put to sea, and

---

*This is the only mention of the seemingly foolish idea of starting a colony at the beginning of winter.

"all being compact together in one ship," they were unequivocally on their way. Their intended landfall was the mouth of the Hudson River, which they optimistically imagined to be "some of those vast and unpeopled countries of America, which are fruitful and fit for habitation, being devoid of all civil inhabitants, where there are only savage and brutish men which range up and down, little otherwise than the wild beasts of the same." Their actual destination would be Cape Cod, where the Nausets were currently gathering in the sheaves of the corn harvest and putting it in baskets and burying it to protect it from winter rot and the depredations of marauding animals.

Though the crossing wasn't extraordinarily long for a ship of the period, the crowded conditions made the nine weeks on board a severe trial. The unintended lateness of their departure meant that throughout the voyage fall storms tossed them mercilessly. For days at a time they drifted, hove to, with almost no sails up at all, while the tempests blew over. During one such storm a young man named John Howland fell overboard but miraculously managed to hold both a halyard and his breath until he was pulled up.

Nor were the crew particularly friendly: one sailor, "a proud and very profane young man," according to Bradford, "of a lusty, able body, which made him the more haughty," was particularly scornful of the seasick Pilgrims. He couldn't wait to toss their corpses overboard and confiscate their possessions, he told them. But then, Bradford reported almost with glee, "it pleased God before they came half seas over, to smite this young man with a grievous disease, of which he died in a desperate manner, and so was himself the first that was thrown overboard." Bradford, for one, thought this piece of divine justice caused the rest of the crew to be a little nicer.

Not long after, it also pleased God to send a howling gale to break the main beam amidships of the *Mayflower*. With the frame of the ship "bowed and cracked," for the third time the crew and separatist leadership discussed turning back to England. The Pilgrims for the most part were not averse to returning rather than "cast[ing] themselves into a desperate and inevitable peril," but the captain pointed out that because they were in the middle of the ocean, going back was just as dangerous as going on. With a post set under the cracked beam, the *Mayflower* continued west until at dawn on November 19 someone in the crow's nest sighted the highlands of Cape Cod. "They were not a little joyful," reported Bradford, master of the deadpan understatement.

For half a day the captain and crew of the *Mayflower* tried to sail her around the Cape to the south, in keeping with the Pilgrims' charter to settle within the northern boundary of the Virginia Company's theoretical domain. But the roaring breakers of the Nantucket Shoals apparently put the fear of God more deeply into all of them than had any of their previous tribulations at sea, and according to Bradford, after the usual heated deliberations, "they resolved to bear up again for the Cape and thought themselves happy to get out of those dangers before night overtook them, as by God's good providence they did. And the next day they got into the Cape Harbor where they rid in safety . . ."

The author of *Mourt's Relation*, which was published in 1622, described Provincetown as "a good harbor and pleasant bay, circled round, except in the entrance . . . compassed about to the very sea with oaks, pines, juniper, sassafras, and other sweet wood." When at last they got to shore, some by wading and others in the captain's small boat, Bradford wrote famously, the Pilgrims "fell upon their knees and blessed the God of Heaven who had brought them over the vast and furious ocean. . . ."

They did not, as the old saw goes, fall "first upon their knees and then upon the aborigines"—at least not immediately, anyway. They were closer to coming to blows with some of their fellow passengers than with anyone else. Not all the emigrants on the *Mayflower* were "saints," as the members of the Leyden congregation humbly called themselves. There were also the "strangers," most of whom were recruited by the merchant adventurers as a way to look after their interests in the project—and some of whom were indentured servants. Many were Anglicans. And though the most famous of the strangers, Captain Miles Standish, remained a loyal ally of the Pilgrim leadership, there were some who by the end of the long trial by water had begun to chafe at the thought of living under the authority of religious fanatics.

They were apparently not afraid to say so. There were "discontented and mutinous speeches" on board the *Mayflower*, Bradford wrote. Most alarming of all, when it became clear that the ship was going to land on Cape Cod rather than in territory belonging to Virginia as planned, some went so far as to say that the Pilgrims' charter was entirely void and they would simply go their own way on land. To prevent such a potentially disastrous disintegration and to give themselves some semblance of official authority, someone drafted a short paragraph for the leadership to sign. The resulting Mayflower Compact may or may not have been, as John Quincy Adams later said, a sort of Magna Carta of American democracy. Certainly the society the Pilgrims later formed was less than democratic by current standards. But the saints and strangers (that is, the leading males among them) had formed a government based on a written contract of the governed.

The other famous line about the landing of the Pilgrims—Will Rogers's quip, "My forefathers didn't come over on the *Mayflower*, but they met the boat"—was also not quite an accurate portrayal of the immediate events in Provincetown Harbor. Though the women of the *Mayflower* may have been observed going ashore that following Monday morning to do the laundry, supposedly establishing that day as the regional washing day for generations to come, neither they nor their menfolk, who marched around importantly with muskets on their shoulders, nor anyone on the ship, saw any sign of the Nauset owners of the place. Nor were there any of the Wampanoag around; no Squanto, no Epenow, no Samoset, no Massasoit. There was no one.

A century and a quarter of intermittent contact between the people of Europe and those of Cape Cod was over. For the first time, whole families from the former had come to the latter to stay. And for those first few days, anyway, they had the entire beach to themselves.

CHAPTER 10

LONG POINT

I doubted the moon. It was a weak moment, perhaps, but I was out at the Long Point Lighthouse, out at the very tip of Cape Cod, having paddled a mile and a half across Provincetown Harbor in order to be there when the sun set and the full October moon rose. The sun had now done its part, going down commendably red behind the Wood End Light. A few high clouds still hung onto a slight blush, as if they too were straining from their lofty perspective to see the last bit of sun drop below some more distant horizon than mine. I turned away from the extravagance and scanned the eastern horizon for the other orb.

Various whale-watching boats were returning from their sunset cruises up to Stellwagen Bank. It was now dark enough to see clearly the red flash every ten seconds of the Wood End Lighthouse to the west, the occulting green every four seconds of Long Point Light right above me, and the white flash every five seconds of the regal Highland Light across the harbor and across the Cape. I was counting on the moon to provide me with light for the paddle back across the harbor. Judging from the day before, I expected it within half an hour of sunset. But where was it?

Some might argue that Race Point rather than Long Point deserves the title of end of the Cape, that it is where the land turns definitively back in on itself and away from the open water. At Race Point, not at Long Point, is where great currents collide. Others might point out that at the Highland Light, although there is really no point at all in the geographical sense, there is an undeniable end-of-the-earth feeling: Race Point points nearly due west to Plymouth on the horizon; Long Point points nearly straight north to the center of Provincetown; but from the Highland Light you face directly northeast, out to sea.

If Highland qualifies as the end of Cape Cod, then what about Chatham, farthest east of all, at Thoreau's elbow and Henry Beston's Outermost House? Off Chatham, the tables report, the "tides divide and run in opposite directions." Surely, though, the end of the Cape cannot be smack in its middle. So Long Point it is, I decide, humbly tucked up into Provincetown Harbor though it may be. Here is where the geographical pen leaves the paper and land is squeezed down from an arm to a finger, then even thinner, and then finally to nothing but that omnipresent "other thing" in Cape Cod and the Islands: brine.

The geographical pen in this case is not the glaciers of twelve thousand years ago but the ocean that took up their meltwater and crept back up the sandy outwash plain. The last stand of the moraine is easily visible from here, even in the fading light: High Head runs like a rampart directly across the peninsula approximately two miles to the northeast. From there all the way out here to Cape Cod's wispy conclusion, however, are roughly ten square miles of rolling dune land; land that is not just sanded—it is sand. Land built by the ocean itself, with help from winds and plants.

When at last some four to six thousand years ago the water began to achieve a level recognizably close to its current one, the coastline looked very little like it does today. Where today there are long, smooth lines of beach, the coastline was then full of bays and inlets. Before the Atlantic rasped the points and laid down barrier beaches across the inlets, and tombolos between some of the minor islets, the coastline everywhere on Cape Cod and the Islands looked more like that of Buzzards Bay, with myriad harbors and outcroppings. Or like the interior coast of Pleasant Bay, which remains relatively unchanged since the ice's retreat. There was, in other words, no Monomoy or Nauset Beach on Cape Cod, no Cape Poge, South Beach, or Katama Bay on the Vineyard. No Lobsterville Beach. No Wasque. And on Nantucket, there was no Coatue Beach. Eel and Smith Points—which come and go to this day—were not yet built either. No Coskata Beach, no Galls, no Great Point. And, of course, no sandy hook at the very end of the Cape on which to stand, watching the spring tide hurtle quietly past while waiting for a truant moon.

Even on a calm evening, there is something disconcerting about this thin spot. Though there are miles of shallow clam flats inside the arm of

Cape Cod, the water becomes deep startlingly near the tip. Unlike the fine sand of the great outer beaches, the sand at the tip of Long Point is uniformly coarse, about the size of rock salt, suggesting strong currents. And it drops off at the water's edge at a rate seemingly greater than its likely angle of repose, leaving one with the distinct (and correct) impression that the grains are not really in repose at all but are in the process of moving around this corner—from wherever the ocean picked them up to wherever the ocean will at last forget them.

The presence of the lighthouse and a little bit of grass are comforting in their illusion of permanence. And on a nearby pile of rubble there is a post with an American flag nailed to it, along with the remnants of several previous flags that presumably blew to shreds before this banner took up its residence. Still, though, Long Point was not a spot at which I cared to linger in the dark. The intersecting curves have the perfection of a curling wave or a periwinkle shell, but the feeling at the tip is not of being on an artistic and engineering masterpiece. The place feels more like a hangnail that might fall off at any time. The moon be damned; I got back in my boat.

Like virtually all the ocean-built lands of Cape Cod and the Islands, the foundations of this hook were built by the steady corrosive power of wind-driven waves and the constant sorting and rearranging of the various longshore currents they generate. Put most simply, waves striking a beach at an oblique angle produce a current that moves sand (and swimmers) steadily along the shore. When the old coast bends sharply away, as at High Head or into Chatham Harbor or Pleasant Bay, the sand is apt to keep going straight. The current dissipates into deeper water, dropping the sand, which forms first a bar, then a curving spit, and, finally, a hook. At Provincetown the process has repeated itself several times, with successive bars forming where the previous ones curl back; the Peaked Hill Bars, off Truro, may one day rise from the sea and attach themselves to the tip of Cape Cod.

The first materials to collect at what would become the Provincelands may have tumbled off of High Head itself, which was once a headland. But the majority of the sand comes east along the beach from farther up the moraine, from the cliffs of Wellfleet and Truro. Much of the heavier sands are deposited at Race Point, which is growing. The lighter clays and silts, meanwhile, swirl all the way into the harbor and gradually settle in the calmer waters there, creating the great tidal flats of Cape Cod Bay.

Not all the sand from the lower Cape ends up at Provincetown or in the bay—not by a long stretch. Past Truro the forearm of land trends more north–south than it does east–west, so the winter northeasters typically push the sand from there in the direction of Nauset Beach and Monomoy. Monomoy grows even faster than Race Point, and has been known to grow by as much as 175 feet in a year. Sometimes Monomoy is one island, sometimes it's two or more. Sometimes it's connected to the Chatham strip. In the 1850s there was a harbor on Monomoy, called the Powder Hole, big enough to shelter forty ships. The sand closed it off from the sea, and it is now a lake.

Once sand is above sea level, the construction work is continued by the equally restless currents of air. Except in truly memorable events, winds do not carry particles of sand larger than $\frac{1}{25}$ of an inch in diameter and do not lift them more than six feet off the ground. And virtually any obstruction—a blade of grass or a piece of driftwood—can slow the blow enough to force it to drop its load. As the pile of sand accumulates, it in turn begins to slow the wind, harvesting more grains. Sand then blows up from the base of the adolescent dune to its crest, then slips over the top down the back side, which is steeper than the windward side. Unless they run up against a significant cliff, like the eroding moraine, and as long as there is a continuous supply of sand from wind and water, row after row of wavelike foredunes develop and roll over themselves inland.

Eventually plants—beach grass, poverty grass, dusty miller, beach plum, bayberry, wild roses, goldenrod, beach pea, poison ivy—take root and hold the dunes in place, allowing them to grow higher still. Mount Arrarat, the tallest of the great parabolic dunes in Provincetown, is more than one hundred feet tall. Only when a dune is far enough inland to be somewhat sheltered from the wind that created it does humus begin to accumulate, and the trees the Pilgrims saw growing down to the waterline can eventually colonize. When the trees and grass are removed by axes and livestock, as they were by the time Thoreau arrived, the dunes can go on the move again; he visited an abandoned school where the sand was up to the desks.

It is a kind gesture of the ocean to construct new lands like these; above all, beaches are what lure today's visitors to Cape Cod and the Islands. There are beaches enough here to string from New York to Washington, D.C. But the price of sand in terms of clay and rock has been, as the scarps attest, quite steep. When the water began its renovation of the moraines that underlie the region, the lower Cape was probably two miles wider than it is today. Nor has all the erosion taken place on the ocean side: ground has also been lost on the inside of the arm.

Likewise, Martha's Vineyard and Nantucket have lost a mile or more from their respective southern shores. Nantucket's seaward edge, in fact, is thought to be a picture of the Vineyard's future: both famed beaches started as barrier strands lying offshore from a series of estuaries left over from the melting glacier. Within historical memory it was possible to ice skate from Edgartown to Tisbury's Great Pond. Now the barrier beach has rolled back far enough to reach the longer necks of land on the Vineyard, segmenting what was once a single, truly great pond into a series of lesser (though still technically "great") ponds. On Nantucket the retreat of the beach has already eliminated the lion's share of the pond water, leaving only a few deep coves at the top of what were once large, multifingered ponds.

Erosion is a constant of life on the Cape and Islands and has been a regular topic of resigned dinner conversation for at least a century and a half. In the 1850s Thoreau and the septuagenarian keeper of the Highland Light calculated together that according to their observations, the old man would likely outlive the Cape (or, at least, the land as a cape rather than an island). In 1889, the federal government estimated that the volume of land lost between Chatham and Truro during the previous forty years would cover the fifty-five acres of the Capitol grounds in Washington, D.C., to a depth of 375 feet: "In other words, the statue of Freedom on the dome of the Capitol would be buried to a depth of 67 feet."

The process usually goes along at a general pace that is alarming enough, but sometimes in localized events erosion can accelerate wildly, so that people living safely back from the shore make grim jokes about their grandchildren inheriting valuable oceanfront property. During one week in 1961, 450 feet of Madaket, on Nantucket, washed away. During one decade, the 1870s, the Chatham Twin Lights went from being a healthy 228 feet back from the cliff to 27 inches from the precipice, until finally one went over the brink. By the time the second light went over in 1881, a new light was in place farther back from the edge and the erosion had slowed, at least temporarily. A new opening through Chatham's barrier beach forms roughly every 140 years and then slowly migrates south, until finally the passage of waters out of Pleasant Bay becomes too constricted and the process begins anew. In 1987 the ocean again opened a small breach in the barrier beach, which soon widened to more than a mile; since then, more than a dozen houses that were once on sheltered Pleasant Bay have been lost to the sea.

The phrase *washing away* doesn't quite capture the process: during the most violent storms the cliffs can quite literally explode into the ocean. The

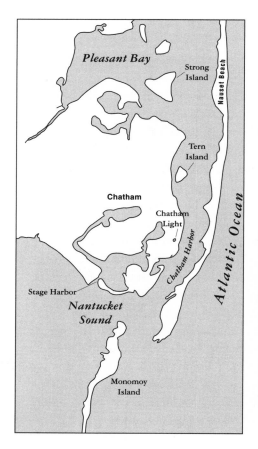

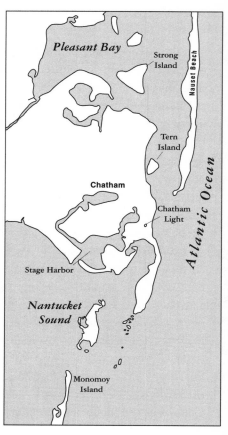

Chatham Harbor and the opening to Pleasant Bay as it existed prior to the northeaster of January 2, 1987.

Chatham Harbor and the opening to Pleasant Bay, 1999. (Both maps based on USGS topographical maps and NOAA nautical charts.)

pressure exerted on the land by a wave only ten feet high and a hundred long has been estimated to be more than sixteen hundred tons per square foot of land. A storm wave can smash against a wall of land with such force that it compresses the empty spaces within the cliff. "This air struggles to free itself with explosive might, causing entire sections of cliff material to burst loose and fall." The same process on a smaller scale slowly widens the cracks in great boulders lying in the surf, until at last they split.

The Chatham Twins were not the only lights forced into retreat. One of the more peripatetic is the Cape Poge Light on Chappaquiddick, which was first constructed in 1801. It was moved in 1838, replaced in 1844, moved again in 1893, again in 1907, and yet another time in 1960. There's small consolation, perhaps, in the knowledge that the job is getting easier: the light was moved in 1986 by a giant helicopter. Even in the seemingly protected waters of the bays and sounds, the erosion is ongoing. Billingsgate Island Light, off Wellfleet, operated from 1822 until the island, which was sixty acres when the Pilgrims landed, dwindled down to nothing but a sandbar in the 1940s. Nor is Billingsgate alone. Ram, or Scotchpenacot, Island used to lie off Chatham until 1851, when the Minot Gale washed all thirteen acres of it into the sea. Nauset Island, opposite Eastham, where Leif Ericson supposedly stopped in 1003, was called Slut's Bush for a while, though it's not clear why. It's on Champlain's map of 1605, but was entirely gone by 1900. Where there were once four islands worthy of the name off Nantucket in the seventeenth century, there are now only two, Tuckernuck and Muskeget. A concrete bunker on South Beach that Vineyarders currently in their mid-sixties remember as "up in the dunes" is now one hundred yards offshore.

Beaches occasionally build back out: Henry C. Kittredge, in his classic 1930 history of the Cape, quotes one seventy-year-old who remembered the sea eating away at the base of scarp below the Highland Light, though at the time he spoke the beach there was one hundred yards wide. Squibnocket Pond on Martha's Vineyard, where Jackie Onassis summered in seclusion throughout the '70s and '80s, was once open to the sea; in the 1690s casks were rolled over the ridge from boats in Menemsha Pond on one side to ships moored on the other. Then the opening closed, and the dunes between pond and sea built themselves into the largest on the Vineyard. Today, though, the Squibby Dunes are again in retreat. Everything is in flux on Cape Cod and the Islands.

Yet there is only one long-term direction. The moraines never regenerate, and they are the source of sand for Nauset Beach, which is the source of sand for Monomoy, which hemorrhages grit off its southern tip just as Nantucket's Great Point spills sand off its northern end. And so Truro must fall into the sea for the sake of Chatham and Provincetown: if the cliffs were artificially hardened with seawalls, cutting off the supply of new sand, coastal geologists predict the entire Great Beach would be gone in eighty years. For every five acres lost to erosion, the sea gives back only two in dunes, barrier beaches, and marshes. Some predict that the Cape will be unrecognizable by the year 4000, gone by 6000. Nantucket may last only

The forever falling down scarps of North Truro, near the Highland Light. (GRANT SMITH/CORBIS)

another six hundred years, though another island of sand may rise out of the rubble in the middle of Nantucket Sound. It will all happen much faster, say others, when global warming raises the ocean levels. Some pray for ice.

So, just as the old Cape and Islands were built from the glacier-wrecked slopes of the rest of New England, today's hooks and spits and glorious dunes come from the wreckage of the glacier's handiwork. "No joy but lacks salt that is not dashed with pain," wrote Robert Frost.

Even if the sea takes far more than it will ever return and Long Point is all that remains of untold acres of lost wooded highland, this ocean-built hook is not to be disparaged. Generations of sailors have seen the trade-off as a bargain: Provincetown Harbor has sheltered as many as one thousand ships at a time from the very storms at work undermining the moraine around the corner and down the way. As Thoreau said of the offerings of the sea when he waded into the cold fall surf on Nauset Beach to collect a scrap of drifting rope, it "seemed ungracious to refuse the least gift which so great a personage offered you."

. . .

The moon did finally come up, so oversized and egg-shaped at first that I laughed out loud with pleasure and surprise. And I was happy, as it turned out, to be afloat in the harbor at the moment when every living thing seemed to come to a stop to wait and watch its arrival. When I stood on land in the dark near the tip of Long Point, the currents had seemed furtive and anxious, as if hurrying to finish the preparations for their queen's arrival. I confess; I got spooked. For the first quarter mile after shoving off the steep inside bank of sand, I paddled strongly, glancing regularly over my shoulder for wakes from the incoming working boats. Paddling at night is exhilarating under any circumstances, and in a canoe or rowboat on a quiet lake somewhere it can be an exquisitely peaceful endeavor. On a flowing body of water with past history of rearranging major landforms, on the other hand, I prefer to hug the shore after hours.

With the moon above the horizon everything relaxed, particularly me. The water flowed and rose in obeisance to a benevolent being, and I, sitting on top of it, in it, rose too. I was no longer in a rush once I got across the harbor and was drifting among the moored boats. Bass sometimes seem to shun the full moon, but there were hordes of adolescent stripers scooting around under the floodlights at the Coast Guard dock, and I put together my fly rod and caught and released a half dozen in about as many minutes. But there was no sport in it, other than to momentarily feel their electric slipperiness, and I went back to watching the moon. I drifted until I got cold, then dragged my boat over the disappearing mudflat and tied it to a bit of fence next to someone else's dinghy.

A man in a newsstand off Tremont Street looked at me closely when I asked if there was anywhere in Provincetown to get a burger and a beer and maybe see the baseball game on television. "No," was all he said.

Next door, though, at a place called Stormy Harbor, a tall black man was preparing to dress up like a tall black woman and lip synch "What's Love Got to Do with It," along with various other Tina Turner hits. I resolved, like Ishmael at the Spouter, to be a spectator. The food was excellent, the show was decent, the bartenders were friendly, and the next morning, as the sun came up, I paddled down the coast and up the Pamet River to Truro.

CHAPTER 11

TRURO

The Pilgrims didn't begin to die immediately, though the author of *Mourt's Relation*, for one, later believed that their troubles had started in those late November weeks in Provincetown Harbor. Many passengers were impatient to get off the ship, which was understandable enough. But, as was typical with transatlantic voyages in those days, the ship's shallop, a large longboat that could be either rowed or sailed, had been partially disassembled and stowed below-decks for the crossing. Reassembling the *Mayflower's* shallop was made more complicated than normal by the fact that passengers had used its pieces as beds. It took sixteen days for the carpenters to make it seaworthy again, which was ten days longer than expected.

There was another small boat on board, but it was generally employed for official business, like collecting wood and water, and wouldn't hold more than a few people. So Pilgrims and strangers started wading ashore through chest-deep water that was probably in the neighborhood of fifty degrees cold. "Some did it necessarily," reported *Mourt*, "and some for their own pleasure, but it brought to the most, if not to all, coughs and colds, the weather proving suddenly cold and stormy, which afterwards turned to the scurvy, whereof many died." The "scurvy" was more likely pneumonia.

As soon as it became clear that the shallop wouldn't be ready soon, some began to argue that they should at least look around where they were; perhaps go down to the river they saw on their way into the harbor and determine if it was a possible spot to colonize. This was not a unanimous action. But then, nothing ever was. "The willingness of the persons was liked, but the thing itself, in regard of the danger, was rather permitted than approved." So sixteen men went out on Wednesday the fifteenth, armed with muskets and swords and dressed in corselets. Miles Standish, who got the job of military coordinator for the colony after John Smith's application had been rejected, was in charge. William Bradford, Stephen Hopkins, and several other men of authority within the community were along as well. They marched off in single file, and after a mile they saw their first Indians.

At first they thought the "five or six people with a dog, coming towards them" were Captain Jones of the *Mayflower* and some of his men, who were also ashore. But just about the time the Pilgrims figured out that they were looking at Native Americans, the Nausets themselves realized they were approaching possible kidnappers and "ran into the wood and whistled the dog after them."

For about ten miles, until it got too dark to see clearly, the English hustled along after the Americans, "but they soon lost both them and themselves." So they built a fire, posted sentries, and went to sleep. As soon as there was enough light to see, they started following the tracks again. But at a salt creek the Indians managed to lose them altogether. "They took into another wood, and we after them," reported *Mourt*, "supposing to find some of their dwellings, but we . . . could meet with none of them, nor their houses . . ."

By this point the Pilgrim fathers were "sore athirst." All they had thought to bring with them to drink was a bottle of hard liquor. And though none of the saints, presumably, drank more than his share, when one was chasing Indians "through boughs and bushes, and under hills and valleys, which tore our very armor in pieces," one "small bottle" of aqua vitae didn't go very far. "We brought neither beer nor water with us," lamented *Mourt* in hindsight, "and our victuals was only biscuit and Holland cheese." Finally, though, around ten o'clock in the morning, they came into one of the valleys that carve across the great moraine of the Cape and found a spring of fresh water. They "were heartily glad, and sat us down and drunk our first New England water with as much delight as ever we drunk drink in all our lives."

More walking brought them to a place where there were "certain heaps of sand, one whereof was covered with old mats, and had a wooden thing like a mortar" turned over on it. They dug it up and found a rotten bow and arrows. "We supposed there were many other things, but because we deemed them graves, we put in the bow again and made it up as it was, and left the rest untouched, because we thought it would be odious unto them to ransack their sepulchres." As it turned out, this particular common-sensical inhibition didn't last long.

Everyone kept an eye out for sassafras, which was still a popular commodity back home in England and a possible cargo for the *Mayflower*. They seemed to be moving into a more-populated area, passing one fifty-acre meadow, probably near Village Pond in Truro, that had at one time been planted with corn. Farther on they found another field, this one more recent, "and many walnut trees full of nuts, and great store of strawberries, and some vines." Then a few more fields, and finally the remains of a house. "Also we found a great kettle which had been some ship's kettle and brought out of Europe."

This was Truro's Corn Hill, where they found and stole their first batch of Indian maize. "There was also a heap of sand, made like the former—but it was newly done, we might see how they had paddled it with their hands—which we digged up, and in it we found a little old basket full of fair Indian corn, and digged further and found a fine great new basket full of very fair corn of this year, with some thirty-six goodly ears of corn, some yellow, and some red, and others mixed with blue, which was a goodly sight. The basket was round, and narrow at the top; it held about three or four bushels, which was as much as two of us could lift up from the ground, and was very handsomely and cunningly made." They discussed what to do and decided to take the kettle with as much of the corn as they could carry in it. "And when our shallop came, if we could find any of the people, and come to parley with them, we would give them the kettle again, and satisfy them for their corn." But over the course of that rainy night it became both "our kettle" and too heavy to lug back to the *Mayflower*. So, for reasons unexplained, they sunk it in Village Pond in Truro.

A funny thing happened on the way to the *Mayflower*. The men at the front of the column discovered a deer snare made out of a bent-over sapling, and while they were inspecting it, William Bradford walked right into it and was strung up. "It was a very pretty device, made with a rope of their own making and having a noose as artificially made as any roper in England can make, and as like ours as can be." As they had the corn and kettle, they took it with them.

Finally, around the first of December, the shallop was gotten in working order, and twenty-four men were chosen to go off in search of a place to settle. The day they left it was too windy for all to travel in the boat, however, so some of the men waded ashore and walked ahead. "We marched six or seven miles further, and appointed the shallop to come to us as soon as they could. It blowed and did snow all that day and night, and froze withal," reported *Mourt*, reiterating the theory that "some of our people that are dead took the original of their death here." The next day it cleared a bit, and "the wind being good, we sailed to the river we formerly discovered, which we named Cold Harbor." They had planned to sail up the river, which was the Pamet, but decided against it, since it wasn't big enough to be a serviceable harbor. They did, however, send a party on foot back up to Corn Hill, where they used their swords to dig up another ten bushels of Indian corn, a "bottle of oil," and a bag of beans.

The pious and seemingly blind-eyed justifications for this thievish behavior in early Pilgrim accounts have been easy pickings for later historians and other hypocrisy hunters. For instance, *Mourt* reported that "it was God's good providence that we found this corn, for else we know not how we should have done, for we knew not how we should find or meet with any Indians, except it be to do us a mischief," without even a nod at the mischief entailed in appropriating for God or for anyone else's purposes a good supply of someone else's winter food.

The way the English looked at things—or at least the way William Bradford and the author of *Mourt* later reported it—they didn't steal the corn and beans so much as buy them on credit. Without prior permission, albeit, but in good faith. "The corn and beans they brought away, purposing to give them full satisfaction when they should meet with any of them," Bradford explained several decades later. And in fairness to their explanation, one of the first requests they later made to Massasoit through Squanto was that he arrange a just payment to the Nausets for them.

Perhaps because he had no intention of staying in America and founding a civilization of corn borrowers, Captain Jones of the *Mayflower* was not as impressed with routing around in the half-foot of snow. He had been put in charge of the expedition in part, it seems, to shut him up: "We thought it best herein to gratify his kindness and forwardness." Or maybe Jones was nervous for his health; of the twenty-four members of the expedition, who were no doubt chosen from among the healthiest aboard the *Mayflower*, five were already too ill to go forward. Whatever the reason, Jones went back to the *Mayflower* in the shallop, taking along all the sick and the stash of corn. He promised to send the shallop back immediately with spades and tools more fit for digging than the swords they were using.

The eighteen who remained behind spent the next morning following paths through the woods, marching, according to their own estimates, about five or six miles altogether. It was nerve-wracking. At one point they were so certain they were nearing a village that they lit the wicks on their matchlock muskets, only to find out they were on a deer-driving path that led nowhere in particular.

The mood was eerie. On the way back to the Pamet, they came upon another grave, this one much larger than the one they found on the earlier reconnaissance. The Pilgrims, evidently, were getting the feel of the place, or getting the hang of the colonial process, and quickly "resolved to dig it up." What if there was corn underneath? someone may have asked. And what's the real harm if it's just a heathen grave? any among them who retained the previous week's inhibitions about disturbing the dead were no doubt told. And so they began to remove the sandy soil. First they came to a mat, beneath which was a bow, then another mat, and a board about three-quarters of a yard long, which was "finely carved and painted, with three tines, or broaches, on the top, like a crown." There were also bowls, trays, and other dishes "and such like trinkets." Then another mat, and under that two bundles, one bigger than the other. The smaller bundle contained the body of a young child. The larger they found full of "fine and perfect red powder" and the bones of a man; a man, it appeared from the skull, who had possessed "fine yellow hair."

The blond corpse was an Indian king, someone announced. Others insisted there were no blond Indians, probably pointing to the sailor's cassock and cloth pants that were also in the bundle. Then it was a Christian who had been buried with honors, some said, and others said it was a Christian who had been killed. Christian or no, they took "sundry of the prettiest things away with us, and covered the corpse back up again," and went to work on a few more nearby graves.

At around the same time, however, some of the others found some abandoned houses nearby, and everyone left off the archeology and went to look at what *Mourt* later described:

> The houses were made with long young sapling trees, bended and both ends stuck into the ground. They were made round, like unto an arbor, and covered down to the ground with thick and well-wrought mats, and the door was not over a yard high, made of a mat to open. The chimney was a wide open hole in the top, for which they had a mat to cover it close when they pleased. One might stand and go upright in them. In the midst of them were four little [stakes] knocked into the ground, and small sticks laid

over, on which they hung their pots, and what they had to [cook].
Round about the fire they lay on mats, which are their beds. The
houses were double matted, for as they were matted without, so
were they within, with newer and fairer mats. In the houses we
found wooden bowls, trays and dishes, earthen pots, handbaskets
made of crabshells wrought together, also an English pail or
bucket; it wanted a bail, but it had two iron ears. There was also
baskets of sundry sorts, bigger and some lesser, finer and some
coarser; some were curiously wrought in black and white in pretty
works, and sundry other of their household stuff. We found also
two or three deer's heads, one whereof had been newly killed, for
it was still fresh. There was also a company of deer's feet stuck up in
the houses, harts' horns, and eagles' claws, and sundry like things
there was, also two or three baskets full of parched acorns, pieces of
fish, and a piece of a broiled herring. We found also a little silk
grass, and a little tobacco seed, with some other seeds which we
knew not. Without was sundry bundles of flags, and sedge, bul-
rushes, and other stuff to make mats. There was thrust into a hollow tree two or three pieces of venison, but we thought it fitter for
the dogs than for us.

It is obvious from the description of the place that the inhabitants were
probably not far off. But with three hundred years of hindsight, there is
something exquisitely bittersweet about the mysterious emptiness of the
place. No, not sweet at all. Just inexpressibly sorrowful. "Some of the best
things we took away with us, and left the houses standing still as they were."

Once again, say the Pilgrim sources, they fully meant to pay fairly for
what they took. They wanted to leave a token of peace or of commerce.
But, regrettably, someone forgot to bring the beads.

CHAPTER 12

PLYMOUTH

The Pilgrims were not the only impatient people on board the *Mayflower* as she lay at anchor in Provincetown Harbor. Not many days after their arrival, the officers and crew began to grumble audibly that the settlers better find somewhere they wanted to stay soon or the ship might just leave them there on the beach. There was some beer and butter and meat left, but everyone knew that the ship would depart before that got so low as to threaten the rations for the return voyage. What's more, according to *Mourt*, "scarce any of us were free from vehement coughs." Time was running thin. And so commenced another debate.

Some among them thought the mouth of the Pamet River near Corn Hill was where they should set up the colony. They argued that the harbor, though not great, was good enough, and obviously the ground was fertile. The bay, they pointed out, was well known as a good fishing spot, and "we saw daily great whales of the best kind for oil and bone, come close aboard our ship, and in fair weather swim and play about us." One day, in fact, a whale lolled so near the ship for so long they thought it was dead. One man took a shot at it, but his musket blew up in his face—both stock and barrel "flew in pieces." Neither human nor whale was hurt, but the leviathan left.

Others wanted to go up to Ipswich, above Cape Anne, which they called Angoum, because they heard there was a good harbor there for ships. They worried about the summer water supply on the Cape, and they didn't like the idea that all year long it would have to be carried up a steep hill from the pond to the probable building site.

Plymouth emerged as something of a compromise solution. The ship's pilot, a man named Robert Coppin, seemed familiar with a good harbor and navigable river across the bay, but not as far as Ipswich. He called it Thievish Harbor, for reasons that are not entirely clear. They decided they would look for that, so on the sixth of December the shallop went forth again, with Miles Standish, William Bradford, and about a dozen others on board. "We set out, being very cold and hard weather," reported *Mourt*. The water was relatively smooth, but the spray eventually froze on their clothing until it became "many times like coats of iron."

Near Wellfleet they saw a dozen or so Indians on shore cutting up a pilot whale that had come aground, and decided to make camp a few miles up from them. They built themselves a small windbreak out of driftwood, and a fire, around which they huddled, trying to get warm without the aid of a decent meal. They had only been out a day, but two of them were by now "very sick"; Edward Tilley, in particular, seemed almost ready to expire from cold and fever. As darkness fell, they periodically looked over at the yellow speck of a similar fire down the beach. They wondered and spoke, no doubt, about the people squatting around it, and about whether their first meeting would be friendly. And those down the beach, with bellies full of whale meat, were no doubt wondering back.

As it turned out, the first real exchange between "saints" and "savages" was of arrows and bullets. The following day the English split up—eight in the boat and the rest on shore—to explore the harbor, which turned out to have no sizable river coming into it. They found another dead pilot whale, which they called a grampus, and cut it open to see how much fat it had. The shallop, too, found some stranded whales, so they later called the place Grampus Bay.

Where the Nauset had been butchering grampus the day before there were a few pieces of carefully cut meat lying around, which the English interpreted as evidence that the Indians had left in haste. They followed the footprints, which they noted were bare despite the cold, to the edge of the beach, and then along a trail "a great way into the woods." But once again, all they found were graves, cornfields, and abandoned houses, none of which they disturbed. They camped again on the beach, again building a driftwood barricade and having little to eat.

Around midnight, the sentinel heard a "great and hideous cry" and yelled at the top of his lungs, "Arm! Arm!" Everyone was instantly awake, and they quickly lit the fuses on their guns. It was just a wolf, said one of the crew members (probably the pilot, Coppin), adding that he had heard the same noise in Newfoundland. Someone fired a few shots into the darkness just for good measure. They went back to bed. At dawn they woke, tested their guns, and prayed.

It turned out not to be a wolf. They were loading the boat when they heard another "great and strange cry," and someone yelled, "They are men! Indians! Indians!" Then a volley of arrows "came flying amongst us." Some who had already taken their guns down to the beach from the campsite now ran down to get them. Miles Standish, however, had his flintlock musket ready and fired off a shot, as did another man. Two more were ready to shoot, but Standish told them to wait till they had something at which to aim.

Soon enough they had a target: "There was a lusty man and no whit less valiant, who was thought to be their captain, stood behind a tree within half a musket shot of us, and there let his arrows fly at us," remembered the author of *Mourt*. The English shot and missed. The Indian in turn sent another arrow their way, but its intended target ducked, and it also missed. Then they exchanged fire again, and both sides missed, and so it went three times. Finally a piece of lead seems to have found its mark, for "he gave an extraordinary cry and away they all went." The enraged saints gave chase, following the locals for about a quarter of a mile before ending the pursuit with a couple of fierce shouts "all together" and a handful of musket balls sent into the leafless trees. The intended message was that the English "were not afraid of them nor discouraged." This was the "First Encounter," and the beach at Eastham still bears that name. The English collected a dozen and a half arrows to send back to England. They prayed again and boarded the shallop and carried on looking for Thievish Harbor, where they hoped to make their new home.

All day they sailed and saw nothing, about fifteen leagues in all. After an hour or two it began to snow, which is probably the reason they passed right by Wellfleet Harbor without noticing it. The wind picked up; the sea got quite rough. In the middle of the afternoon the rudder broke, "so that we could steer no longer with it, but two men with much ado were fain to serve with a couple of oars." The wind increased still more. The sun set. It grew dark. They were afraid.

Finally Coppin, the pilot who had first told them about Thievish Harbor, said he could make it out in the dim. "Be of good cheer," he said. And they were, until the mast self-destructed, splitting into three pieces—in their eagerness to get into Plymouth they had piled on too much sail. The boat was very nearly lost, and no doubt all on board would have been as well. "Yet, by God's mercy, recovering ourselves, we had the flood with us," reported *Mourt*.

And so the first permanent Europeans arrived at Plymouth, rudderless and without a mast, rowing hard but virtually adrift. They almost ran aground in large breaking surf because it wasn't the harbor the pilot thought he knew after all, and they could not, in fact, head north as he remembered. But in the end, covered with snow and ice, they came into the lea of a rocky island "where our shallop did ride safe and secure all that night." They spent the next day exploring the island, which they found uninhabited. Sunday they rested, and Monday they explored the harbor and found it good. Or good enough: Bradford, perhaps because he wrote his history during a period when better ports like Boston and Gloucester had already eclipsed Plymouth, recalled that "at least it was the best they could find."

On Saturday, December 16, the *Mayflower* sailed into Plymouth, and after several days of exploring and evenings engaged in the usual heated debates, the moment came to make a final decision, "for we could not now take time for further search or consideration, our victuals being much spent, especially our beer." By a voice vote, they chose the mainland over the small island, "on a high ground, where there is a great deal of land cleared, and hath been planted with corn three or four years ago, and there is a very sweet brook runs under the hill side, and many delicate springs of as good water as can be drunk, and where we may harbor our shallops and boats exceeding well, and in this brook much good fish in their seasons; on the further side of the river also much corn-ground cleared." There was so much cleared land, in fact, that they worried about the distance they would have to carry their wood.

What should have been an optimistic time—at last they had found their new home and now all that was needed was that they build it—was instead quite desperate. For days at a time the weather was so bad that they couldn't travel between ship and shore, leaving some stranded on the beach without supplies. They repeatedly convinced themselves that sounds they heard in the nearby woods were those of hostile Indians on the way to attack them. This happened on both Christmas Eve (when they did no work, for it was a Sunday) and again on Christmas day (on which they did work, for it was a pagan holiday). Their common-house roof burned up almost as soon as it was finished, and the same thing happened a few weeks later to the shed that was housing the sick, though luckily no one was injured in either accident. Goodwife Allerton went into labor during those weeks, but the first European son delivered in Plymouth was born dead.* And William Bradford's wife, Dorothy, apparently committed suicide by jumping overboard.

The general sickness affected everything. At the end of December, when they began the process of formally appropriating Wampanoag real estate, casting lots to determine where each of the nineteen families should build, they kept lot sizes to a minimum. A strip only 8¼ feet by 49½ feet per family member was "large enough at the first for houses and gardens, to impale them round, considering the weakness of our people, many of them growing ill with cold . . . which increased so every day more and more, and after was the cause of many of their deaths," remembered *Mourt's* author. Even the first marriage in the new colony was a somewhat grim union; Edward Winslow, a recent widower, married Susannah White, a new widow.

During January and February, days when two or three colonists died and were buried were not uncommon. Of the 102 passengers who reached Cape Cod, 4 died during the month in Provincetown. Another 46 gave out in the first months in Plymouth, so that by summer, says Bradford, "scarce fifty" were alive. It was, he wrote in a letter to Thomas Weston, "so general a disease that the living were scarce able to bury the dead, and the well not in any measure sufficient to tend the sick." (Some historians have interpreted the fact that they buried the dead at all as a sign that the winter, though deadly, was not overly severe.) At times only a handful were in full health.

For the most part the crew of the *Mayflower* was unsympathetic, and Bradford wanted it remembered that when he himself was at his lowest ebb and thought himself near death, the sailors denied him even "a small can of beer." Later, when they too fell ill and started dying, Bradford, as usual, interpreted it as divine retribution for their earlier hardheartedness.

Not that some days weren't better than others, as when the shallop finally had some luck, "returning with three great seals and an excellent good cod, which did assure us that we should have plenty of fish shortly" (though the experience caused them to worry that they had brought the wrong size hooks). Or when John Goodman and Peter Brown turned out not to have been killed by vicious natives but only to have gotten themselves lost in the woods trying to chase down a deer with a dog. (Goodman's

---

*Peregrine White was born in Provincetown Harbor in 1620.

boots did, however, have to be cut off his frozen feet.)* Or the several more times they were not, after all, attacked by Indians. Best of all, there was a brief January thaw in the middle of the month that brought a few "very fair sunshiny days, as if it had been in April, and our people, so many as were in health, wrought cheerfully."

During this fleeting foreshadow of summer, the first Indian visitors arrived at the plantation. The English were in the midst of a meeting to organize themselves militarily: a hunter had seen a dozen natives the day before, and several tools that Miles Standish had left out in the woods were missing. "Two savages presented themselves upon the top of a hill, over against our plantation, about a quarter of a mile and less, and made signs unto us to come unto them." The English signed back, trying to get the visitors to come to them, to no avail.

Ultimately Captain Standish and Stephen Hopkins were chosen as emissaries and headed across the brook with one musket. This they laid on the ground "in their sight, in a sign of peace . . . but the savages would not tarry their coming" and disappeared into the woods. All that came of the incident was that the Pilgrims brought two cannons and two large guns from the *Mayflower* and planted them "in places most convenient."

They didn't see another native until a month later, when they were once again trying to finish the job of organizing themselves into defensive units and a man walked out of the woods, up the hill, into the middle of the "rendezvous," and said, in plain English, "Welcome." This was not Squanto but Samoset, a native of Pemaquid, Maine. He had learned the language from the fishermen who frequented that place. "You from England? I know some Englishmen," he apparently said, "maybe you know them too," and rattled off the names of most of the captains of the English cod fleet.

"He was a man free in speech, so far as he could express his mind, and of a seemly carriage," wrote the author of *Mourt*. They talked all afternoon, and Samoset apparently filled them in on the sizes of and relationships between the various neighboring Indian groups. Massasoit's village, he said, was about sixty strong. The Nausets numbered around one hundred, and were still leery of the English because of Hunt's slaving voyage. Samoset

---

*Goodman's dog was not, it seems, his best friend. A few days later, when he decided to try out his recovering feet, man and dog again went for a walk in the woods. This time instead of deer the dog attracted the attention of two large wolves, which chased it back to Goodman. There the pet took up a brave stand between his master's lame legs. Goodman took up a fence post, "and they sat both on their tails, grinning at him a good while, and went their way and left him."

also told them the place they were settling was called Patuxet, and explained that "about four years ago all the inhabitants died of an extraordinary plague, and there is neither man, woman, nor child remaining, as indeed we have found none, so as there is none to hinder our possession, or to lay claim unto it."

Samoset stayed for dinner. "The wind beginning to rise a little, we cast a horseman's coat about him, for he was stark naked, only a leather about his waist, with a fringe about a span long, or little more; he had a bow and two arrows, the one headed, and the other unheaded. He was a tall straight man, the hair of his head black, long behind, only short before, none on his face at all; he asked some beer, but we gave him strong water and biscuit, and butter, and cheese, and pudding, and a piece of mallard, all which he liked well and had been acquainted with such amongst the English."

Then he invited himself over for the night: "We would gladly have been rid of him," recalled *Mourt*, "but he was not willing to go." Presumably to keep a better eye on him they offered him a berth on the *Mayflower*, which was fine with him. But as so often happened in Plymouth Harbor, the tide and wind prevented the shallop from making the mile-and-a-half trip out to where the ship was moored. So Samoset stayed at the home of Stephen Hopkins and was watched all night. Finally, the next morning, after they had given him a knife, a bracelet, and a ring, he left, promising to return with someone from Massasoit's village and some furs for trade.

A few days later Samoset and five other "tall proper men" appeared. Massasoit's emissaries were notably better dressed than Samoset; "every man [had] a deer's skin on him, and the principal of them had a wild cat's skin, or such like on the one arm." Some painted their faces black, "from the forehead to the chin, four or five fingers broad; others after other fashions as they liked."

Once again, it was an entirely amicable day. The visiting Indians sang, danced, and ate "liberally of our English victuals." They had brought with them the tools Miles Standish had left behind in the woods, which they returned. What they didn't have, though, were many furs. Perhaps out of fear of setting too high an initial price, the Pilgrims insisted on seeing more before they would begin to trade. So the natives went home, promising to bring more furs the next day.

All except Samoset, that is, who wanted to stay the night again. According to *Mourt*, he "either was sick, or feigned himself so." The next morning, with a new pair of stockings, shoes, shirt, and "a piece of cloth to tie about his waist," he felt good enough to go back to Mount Hope Bay and find out why Massasoit's men had not returned.

On March 22, the residents of New Plymouth* were yet again meeting to try to organize themselves militarily when they were interrupted by Native American visitors. It was Samoset and several others, as was becoming usual. Only this time there was a difference; with Samoset was another English-speaking native. This, at last, was Squanto, who had been taken from Plymouth in 1614 by Thomas Hunt and returned to America in 1618 or 1619 with Thomas Dermer. Squanto told them that he was the last surviving member of the Patuxet group of Wampanoag who had cleared and maintained these fields the Pilgrims were just beginning to plant. He told them that the "great sagamore," Massasoit, his brother Quadequina, and all the men of Mount Hope Bay were nearby and ready to treat with the Pilgrims.

One hour later, just as Squanto promised, Massasoit appeared at the crest of a nearby hill. With him were sixty or so of his men. But he would not come down to the collection of barely finished thatched cabins and mud huts that had appeared on the site of yet another of his extinct villages. Nor, presumably for the same reasons of protocol and fear, would the English send their governor, John Carver, up from New Plymouth to him. So Squanto engaged in a round of shuttle diplomacy and ultimately arranged for Edward Winslow to go up alone with the appropriate gifts. For Massasoit himself, Winslow brought a pair of knives and a necklace. For his powerful brother Quadequina, there was one knife and an earring. He brought "a pot full of hard water" as a general lubricant, and some crackers.

"In his person he is a very lusty man, in his best years, an able body, grave of countenance, and spare of speech," *Mourt's* author later wrote of the Wampanoag leader. "In his attire little or nothing differing from the rest of his followers, only in a great chain of white bone beads about his neck, and at it behind his neck hangs a little bag of tobacco, which he drank and gave us to drink; his face was painted with a sad red like [mulberry], and oiled both head and face, that he looked greasily. All his followers likewise, were in their faces, in part or in whole painted, some black, some red, some yellow, and some white, some with crosses, and other antic

---

*Spelling was a creative art form in those days: *Mourt's Relation* alone spells Plymouth six different ways: Plimoth, New Plimoth, Plimouth, Plimmouth, New Plimmouth, and New Plymouth.

works; some had skins on them, and some naked, all strong, tall, all men in appearance."

Winslow told Massasoit that King James of England saluted him and that the English came in peace and that they desired trade. Though Winslow didn't think much of his speech was clearly translated, it was apparently good enough, and Massasoit ate and drank of the English gifts. Then, leaving Winslow behind as a hostage with Quadequina, he took twenty unarmed men over to the Pilgrim village.

After they had secured five or six hostages of their own, the Pilgrims did their best to entertain the visiting sovereign in a manner befitting his rank. "Captain Standish and Master [Williams] met the king at the brook, with half a dozen musketeers. They saluted him and he them, [and then] one on the one side, and the other on the other, conducted him to a house then in the building, where we placed a green rug and three or four cushions."

The English also endeavored to give themselves an aura of respectability, perhaps hoping to offset the poverty- and disease-ridden reality of their own battle for survival.* "Then instantly came our governor with drum and trumpet after him, and some few musketeers." Massasoit loved the trumpet, and some of his men later attempted to play it. "After salutations, our governor kissing his hand, the king kissed him, and so they sat down." Governor Carver called for some more strong water and raised a glass to Massasoit. The Wampanoag sagamore then took a "great draught" himself, which "made him sweat all the while after." Carver called for a little fresh meat, "which the king did eat willingly, and did give his followers. Then they treated of peace."

The peace to which both sides agreed was fairly straightforward: none of Massasoit's people would harm the colony, and if any did, he would send them to Plymouth to be punished. Similarly, if the Pilgrims did any harm to the Indians they would also receive punishment, though notably, they would not be delivered to the Wampanoag for the administration of such justice, but would receive it at home. Tools would not be taken, and weapons would not be brought into each other's villages. And finally, Massasoit promised to inform the other neighboring tribes that the English and Wampanoag had formed a defensive alliance against any potential enemies. This agreement was not just theoretical. *Mourt* mentions that Massasoit was

---

*Winslow, at least, was aware that they lived a precarious existence, even given the recent plague. In *Good Newes from New England*, he notes that had God not possessed "the hearts of the salvages with astonishment and fear of us, they might easily have swallowed us up."

currently at war with the Narragansett, "against whom he thinks we may be some strength to him, for our pieces are terrible unto them."

Massasoit's peace held for fifty-five years, during which time almost all the major English towns on Cape Cod were established. Likewise, though the first permanent English residents of Nantucket and Martha's Vineyard were not technically under the jurisdiction of Plymouth Plantation, the natives who lived in those places were certainly under Massasoit's governance. The English presence on both islands was established during the period of amity with the Wampanoag.

The peace wouldn't last everywhere. When Massasoit, Bradford, Squanto, Massasoit's son Wamsutta, Winslow, Standish, and Samoset were all dead—when the whole generation had passed away—Massasoit's younger son Metacomet (King Philip) and the Pilgrim grandchildren fell into one of the bloodiest wars in Euro-American history. The heirs to the "saints" of the *Mayflower* sold Massasoit's nine-year-old grandson into sugar slavery in the Caribbean. But even when all that had come to pass, Cape Cod and the Islands largely escaped the violence.

CHAPTER 13

BARNSTABLE

Massasoit's peace notwithstanding, the process of the English coming in, pushing out, and taking over the lion's share of Wampanoag and Nauset land during the decades after their arrival was not achieved without bloodshed—far from it. There were attempted coups against Massasoit, threats of attempted coups against Massasoit, and surgical military actions by the Pilgrims against various rumored threats of attempted coups and against rumors of attacks on Plymouth itself. Many of these involved the neighbors of Massasoit and the Wampanoag, the Narragansett and the Massachusetts peoples. Some involved his own citizens, particularly those of Cape Cod and the Islands, who may have resented his growing interest in the international whale-oil trade. Some conflicts deeply involved Squanto, which is what ultimately sent him to the executioner's doorstep.

The first few months after the treaty, at least, were something of a honeymoon between the saints and savages—a very hungry honeymoon, from the Pilgrims' perspective, and one for which they were generally supplying the provisions. Approximately three months after Massasoit's initial visit to Plymouth, Edward Winslow and another emissary went for the first time to visit him at his home at Pokanoket. One reason for their visit was that they wanted to know where to find the sachem if they needed him. They wanted to "make satisfaction for some conceived injuries to be done on our parts, and to continue the league of peace and friendship between them and us." But they were also interested in conducting a little friendly reconnaissance; it would be nice to know his true strength. The main reason for Winslow's visit to Pokanoket, however, was to ask Massasoit to stop his people from hanging around Plymouth so much.

They spent the first night at Namasket (Middleborough), where Squanto had been with Thomas Dermer only a few years before and where they were entertained by a relatively healthy village, feasting on shad roe and cornbread with a side of boiled acorns. But as they neared Pokanoket they began to see the usual signs of the plague's devastation. They crossed a river (presumably the Taunton) at a village where only two old men were still alive, but who nevertheless came out to defend their homes with bows drawn until Squanto informed them they were all friends of Massasoit. Elsewhere, there was no one left: "and pity it was and is to see so many goodly fields, and so well seated, without men to dress and manure the same."

Massasoit wasn't at home when they arrived and had to be summoned from his summer place. When he met them, he apologized for not being able to offer them more in the way of a formal greeting, or even food. For their part, they presented him with a nice red coat they had brought along as a token of their good will and, at Squanto's suggestion, fired off a salute when he first appeared. Then, when the required formalities were concluded, and after a suitable preamble about maintaining the peace, they came to the point: "But whereas his people came very often, and very many together unto us, bringing for the most part their wives and children with them, they were welcome; yet we being but strangers as yet at Patuxet, alias New Plymouth, and not knowing how our corn might prosper, we could no longer give them such entertainment as we had done, and as we desired still to do."

Massasoit himself, of course, was more than welcome, as were any representatives of his. They presented him with a special copper chain, which anyone on official business was to bring with him so that the colonists would know he was there at the behest of Massasoit. And anyone who had skins to trade could by all means come at any hour. But, they added, if the honored sagamore could possibly "hinder the multitude from oppressing us."

Massasoit understood perfectly and promised to take care of the problem. He gave a great speech to his assembled people about the importance of peace with the colonists, calling out individually the names of thirty towns in his jurisdiction. After each name was announced, representatives from those villages replied in a sort of call and response: Yes, Massasoit was their leader, yes, they would be friends to the English, and yes, they would only trade at Plymouth. "It was delightful," according to *Mourt*, but "it was tedious." Later, they smoked some of Massasoit's tobacco and talked into the evening. The Wampanoag monarch found it outrageous that the recently widowed King James did not have a wife, and he wondered if the English could do something about the French who were frequently visiting Narragansett Bay (and no doubt fraternizing with the pesky Narragansetts who lived there).

When it was time to sleep, Winslow and Hopkins could not convince their host that he needn't honor them by sharing his bed with them. So the two Pilgrims took off their hats and crawled in with Massasoit and his wife. Later in the night, two more of his chief men also joined them on the small mat-covered platform. "We were worse weary of our lodging than of our journey," Winslow remembered. "What with . . . the savages' barbarous singing (for they use to sing themselves asleep), lice and fleas within doors, and mosquitoes without, we could hardly sleep all the time of our being there."

There was one more piece of business, and it was somewhat related to the issue of feeding too many native visitors. The English had survived the winter diseases, but just barely, and now they were facing the prospect of starving before any of their first crops grew to maturity.* They wanted to pay for the corn they had found earlier at "Paomet (called by us Cape Cod)," perhaps because they were already considering traveling down there to buy more. Could Massasoit please facilitate this? And could he, if possible, spare a little more corn himself? Yes, said the king of the "savage and brutish men which range up and down, little otherwise than the wild beasts of the same," he could sell a bit of seed corn, and yes, he would talk to the Nausets.

As it turned out, though, an opportunity came to repay the Cape Indians before Massasoit had a chance to use his good offices. Not long after Winslow's return from Massasoit's home, the oldest son of John Billington got lost in the woods somewhere in the general direction of the Cape. This was not the first or last time a Billington boy caused trouble: one had almost blown up the *Mayflower* back in December by firing off a gun next to a barrel of gunpowder. Billington Sr., meanwhile, who spent time in the stocks for swearing at Miles Standish, later became the first person executed by the

---

*In all likelihood, they didn't quite reveal the true extent of their deprivation to Massasoit, but spoke of their uncertainty in regard to yields in the new land.

colony for murder. The Billingtons were, said Bradford, "the profanest" people in Plymouth. But nonetheless, Standish and some others went off in the shallop to try to find young John.

The day started nicely enough, but a squall came up "with much lightning and thunder, insomuch that a spout arose not far from us." Standish and the others barely managed to put into Barnstable Harbor, which they called Cummaquid, and spent the night in their boat. The next morning they saw some people down the beach collecting lobsters and sent Squanto out to question them. The boy was fine, they said, and living in Nauset (Eastham), and they invited the men to stay for dinner. The Pilgrims accepted and dined on lobsters with the sachem of Barnstable, a young man named Iyanough (Hyannis).

There was a moment of embarrassing irony, given that they were on a mission to rescue a child: an old woman, "no less than a hundred years old," appeared at some point during the occasion. Though she had never before seen English people, she couldn't look at the strangers "without breaking forth into great passion, weeping and crying excessively." When the guests asked the reason for her grief, they were told that all three of her sons were among those who went aboard Hunt's ship to trade and were never seen again, "by which means she was deprived of the comfort of her children in her old age."

"We told them we were sorry any Englishman should give them that offense," wrote the author of *Mourt's Relation*, "and that all the English that heard of it condemned him for the same; but for us, we would not offer them any such injury though it would gain us all the skins in the country. So we gave her some small trifles, which somewhat appeased her." At least they hoped it did.

After the meal, Iyanough and two of his deputies accompanied them on the sail down to Nauset. Standish was worried about the lower Cape, because they had been attacked there the year before and it was where they had stolen the corn. But all went well, thanks to Aspinet, the sachem of the Nausets. He and about one hundred of his people delivered the boy "behung with beads" and in good health. The person whose corn they had taken (or at least the husband of the woman who likely owned the corn) was among the crowd, and the English invited him to Plymouth, or promised to bring him corn back, whichever he wanted. He said he'd come to Plymouth. It was a wonderfully successful voyage.

Successful until that night, anyway, when they heard the alarming news that Massasoit himself had been taken captive, or possibly even killed, by the Narragansett. This was a horrific development under any circumstances, but particularly since the majority of the colonial defense force was far down the Cape, rounding up the wayward Billington boy.

CHAPTER 14

MANOMOYIK

The leader of the supposed coup against Massasoit was the sachem of the Pocasset band of Indians, a man named Corbitant, who resided in Namasket (Swansea). Though technically subservient to Massasoit, Corbitant, the Pilgrims learned, disapproved of the alliance with the English and now conspired with the Narragansett to remove Massasoit from the leadership of the Wampanoag nation. (The Namasket band were apparently suspicious of the English from very early on; they almost killed Thomas Dermer before the Pilgrims' arrival.) When Squanto and Hobomok, another Wampanoag friend of the colonists, showed up in Namasket from Plymouth to find out for William Bradford and the English if there was any truth to the rumored attack on Massasoit, they were immediately arrested.

In the scuffle that broke out, Corbitant threatened—or "offered," to use *Mourt's* phrase—to stab Hobomok, but somehow he managed to escape and ran the fourteen miles back to Plymouth to tell the English that there was indeed trouble and that their translator was most surely dead. The last thing he saw, he said, was Corbitant holding a knife at Squanto's chest.

The colonists decided to send ten armed men to Namasket, with Hobomok as a guide, in order "to revenge the supposed death of Squanto on Corbitant our bitter enemy, and to retain Nepeof, another sachem or governor, who was of this confederacy, till we heard what was become of our friend Massasoit." If Squanto was indeed dead, they were instructed to return with Corbitant's head but not his body.

The Pilgrims left in the rain the next morning, August 14, and spent that evening hiding in the woods about three miles from Namasket. The plan was to storm Corbitant's house at midnight. They were understandably quite nervous, and though each had been given specific jobs by Miles Standish—you guard the women and children, I'll decapitate Corbitant, et cetera—they tried to keep spirits up by "encouraging one another to the utmost of their power." But it didn't help morale that they had gotten lost. Finally, they reached the outskirts of the village, ate all their food, hid their knapsacks, and charged the main house.

Nobody move! cried the Pilgrim raiders. *We only want Corbitant, and whoever else helped him kill Squanto.* It took a while for the confused residents of Namasket to figure out what in the world the mad Englishmen were talking about. But when they did, they replied by saying something to the effect that *Corbitant isn't here, Squanto isn't dead, and maybe you would feel better if you had a smoke, or some food, perhaps?*

A few moments of mayhem followed. Someone began firing guns into the air: "In this hurly-burly we discharged two pieces at random, which much terrified all the inhabitants . . ." Hobomok climbed up on the roof and began yelling Squanto's name. The English ordered a fire built in order to search Corbitant's house, which from the descriptions was bigger than most Wampanoag residences. Whether it was the gunfire or Hobomok's yells that brought Squanto and Tokamahamon is unclear, but *Mourt* reported that even the two prisoners, who were under guard, were unsure why the English had come and had to assure the villagers that everything would be all right and that the midnight raiders wouldn't hurt them.

The next morning the English had breakfast with Squanto, "but all Corbitant's faction were fled away." So they made some tough pronouncements about not resting till they found him, and how Massasoit had better be all right, and then they went home, taking the three Indians wounded in the scuffle along with them for medical attention.

The exaggerated report of Squanto's death (and the Pilgrims' tough response to it) is one of the many maddeningly unfinished stories of that early period of contact. It is incomplete because the only sources are scanty reports from English observers who didn't speak the local language and didn't understand the culture of the other side. The conflict blew over when Massasoit reappeared unharmed—perhaps never having been attacked at all—mediating for the English to forgive the misunderstood Corbitant.

For their part, the English interpreted the outcome as evidence that a reputation for quickness to anger was well worth cultivating as a counterbalance to their otherwise weak position in the strategic scheme of things in New England. After the revenge of Squanto, "they had many gratulations from divers sachems, and much firmer peace," wrote Bradford. Even the hitherto famously anti-English Vineyarders, whose reputation for fierceness was cemented by the attack on Dermer, softened up a bit: "Yea, those of the Isles of Capawack sent to make friendship." One of these was named Appanow, and though it would have made sense to send along someone who spoke English, whether or not this was in fact Epenow is unknown.

The Narragansett, however, were not impressed. Not long after the conflict, their leader Canonicus sent Plymouth a bundle of arrows wrapped in a snakeskin. After consulting Squanto, they sent it back with a bag of bullets.

The first Thanksgiving came and went, with Massasoit and ninety of his people bringing the venison and staying for three days of feasting. The second Christmas came and went with the separatists working—it was, after all, a pagan holiday. The "strangers" claimed it was against their conscience to work on Christ's birthday, which Bradford allowed, but when he found them playing with a ball he took it away and sent them all home. With the arrival of thirty-three more colonists, everyone was again put on half-rations. All winter they worked on an eight-foot-high stockade around the town, and on their little houses. The best of these were still not much more than cabins with oiled-paper windows, wooden chimneys, and thatched roofs. The least of them were merely mud and sticks. By now the colony was fairly well militarized, with all the men and older boys organized into four squadrons, which drilled with some regularity.

Then, in March and April, there was another serious scare. The previous fall, when the Pilgrims visited the Massachusetts Indians in the Boston area for the first time, they promised to return the following spring to buy furs. Just as they were getting ready to leave, however, Hobomok started talking about a vast conspiracy between the Massachusetts and the Narragansett. In a simultaneous action, he said, the Massachusetts were going to attack the English trading party and the Narragansett were going to lay to waste the town. What's more, Hobomok said, even Squanto was involved; it was his job to make sure the residents of Plymouth were outside the fortifications at the time of the raid. *Under no circumstances*, Hobomok told Standish, *should you go to the Massachusetts right now.*

But Standish, who was by no means immune to seeing conspiracies directed at both himself and the colony—indeed, reading Winslow gives one the distinct impression that he was a bit paranoid—set out for Boston anyway. As usual, the strategic thinking was that the English couldn't afford to look scared. But he took the precaution of bringing both Hobomok and Squanto along with him in the shallop, as well as the usual eight or so men of the colony.

As soon as they were out of sight, "an Indian of Tisquantum's family" came running up to Plymouth with blood on his face. (Interestingly, the description implies that his relatives were not all as dead as had been supposed.) The Narragansett, this man said, were mustering about fifteen miles away in Namasket. And this time Corbitant had even convinced Massasoit to join in the attack on Plymouth, he added ominously. If the English didn't believe it, *Look at this blood on my head*, he said. Hadn't he barely escaped with his life after defending the Pilgrims? Bradford fired off the cannons, which brought the trading party back around the point and into the harbor as fast as they could row and sail.

Hobomok was outraged at the absurdity of the accusation, and his reasoning is particularly interesting in that it gives some insight into the democratic nature of Massasoit's power and the importance of process in Wampanoag governance. Hobomok told the alarmed Pilgrims that even if Massasoit wanted to attack the English, which he did not, he simply couldn't have done it without a council of the leading *pinse,* or warriors, of the nation, of which Hobomok was a principal.

Hobomok's wife, whose name was not recorded, went back to Pokanoket as an undercover agent to spy on the goings on there and report back to Plymouth. She found no sign of any activity out of the ordinary and promptly told the Wampanoag leader everything that had recently transpired. She took care to add, somewhat obsequiously, that of course Bradford and the others never really suspected him of any treachery.

Needless to say, the great sachem of the Wampanoag "was much offended at the carriage of Tisquantum." He lectured the English on the legal terms of their treaty together. Even if he had wished to take action to redress some wrong, which he had not, in accordance with the treaty he was required to "send word and give warning."

It became apparent that Squanto was not, after all, one of God's simpler gifts. Telling the English that Massasoit was about to attack was, according to Bradford, just a variation on his usual game of telling other Indians that the English were just about to arrive and start shooting up the wigwams. Squanto didn't have to convince his countrymen that such an attack was possible; everyone knew the newcomers were hot-blooded, even crazy. But there was a chance they could be stopped, he would say, if he, Squanto, were to intercede. Of course, Squanto would be much more likely to talk to the bloodthirsty newcomers if a few presents came his way. A particularly cruel twist on this game, given the still-visible bone fields surrounding Pokanoket, was Squanto's assertion that the English kept the plague buried in the ground under their storehouse and could call it out at will.*

"Thus by degrees we began to discover that Tisquantum['s] ends were only to make himself great in the eyes of his countrymen, by means of his nearness and favor with us; not caring who fell, so he stood," wrote Edward Winslow. And for a while it worked as Squanto hoped; both William Bradford and Winslow reported that Wampanoag who previously "were wont to rely on Massassowat for protection, and resort to his abode, now . . . began to leave him and seek after Tisquantum." But as long as there was peace between Plymouth and Massasoit, Squanto couldn't really produce anything for his followers that the traditional leadership of the Wampanoag wasn't already providing. "He therefore raised this false alarm; hoping, whilst things were hot in the heat of blood, to provoke us to march into his country against him, whereby he hoped to kindle such a flame as would not easily be quenched; and hoping if that block were once removed, there were not other between him and honor, which he loved as his life, and preferred before his peace."

Bradford bawled him out and got on with the plans for a trading trip to Boston. But Squanto had finally overplayed his hand with Massasoit. The leader of the Wampanoag demanded his death under the terms of the peace.

After trying in vain to convince Massasoit to spare the translator's life, Bradford sent for Squanto, who immediately "accused Hobomok as the author and worker of his overthrow, yielding himself to the Governor to be sent or not according as he thought meet."

The moment arrived to decide. Unlike virtually all other colonists in the Americas, the various Puritans who came pushing their way into Algonquian New England in the seventeenth century did periodically execute or

---

*The English didn't entirely discredit this idea: when Hobomok asked about a suspicious bag of gunpowder buried in the storehouse, he was told that of course it was not the plague. But the Pilgrims said that their God did have a power over the plague and could use it against their "enemies."

otherwise punish European offenders for crimes perpetrated against Indians.* And to this degree, at least, they were making a sincere effort to find a morally justifiable method of appropriating a continent. But perhaps because they sincerely believed their own talk about creating saints like themselves out of the Native Americans, at least in the early decades, they always found it much more difficult to deliver partially assimilated Indians back to the traditional authorities. In the case of Squanto, however, Bradford decided that he must be delivered to Massasoit.

"But at the instant when our Governor was ready to deliver him into the hands of his executioners, a boat was seen at sea to cross before our town, and fall behind a headland [Manomet Point], not far off." In the excitement—It might be the French!—Squanto's extradition was put off indefinitely. Massasoit, however, continued to seek his revenge (or justice) "both privately and openly, which caused [Squanto] to stick close to the English, and never durst go from them till he died."

Which, as it turned out, wasn't very long in coming.

The boat that appeared out of the blue and saved Squanto's life was not French. It was a shallop from an English ship full of new colonists sent by the principal financial backer of the colony. This wasn't the first time Thomas Weston had sent uninvited (and nonseparatist) additions to Plymouth, or the last. And, as usual, these came without any provisions of their own, but with a letter from Weston saying, in effect, "Please feed." During the summer of 1622, when sixty extra men showed up and expected to be housed and victualed, there was semistarvation; "famine began now to pinch them sore."

The Pilgrims were constantly having trouble with Weston, and he with them. In his first letter to Plymouth, though he knew that half the colonists had died, he couldn't help letting them know how disappointed he was that the *Mayflower* was not full of furs and fish when it returned: "I know your weakness was the cause of it, and I believe more weakness of judgment than weakness of hands. A quarter of the time you spent in discoursing, arguing and consulting would have done much more."

---

*Alden T. Vaughan: "For example, in 1638 Plymouth Colony hanged three Englishmen for murdering an Indian. That same year, Connecticut's general court rejected the protest of Wethersfield inhabitants who demanded revenge on a local chief for conspiracy in the killing of several English settlers; the colonial magistrates decided that an earlier though lesser violation of Indian rights by the settlers justified the lethal retaliation. And even in 1675, when wartime passions generated virulent animosities, Massachusetts executed two colonists for murdering Indian non-combatants."

At times the intrigues between the Pilgrims and their London backers seem humorous: letters were secretly sewn into shoes with details of planned coups. There was the minister sent uninvited from England whose premarital counseling to young virgins turned out to include a fairly complete course in sexual education—he "meddled with the maids."* The next minister, who turned out to be "crazed in his brain," was also sent packing. There was the salt maker who couldn't make salt, and a botched fur theft, and the time Weston himself arrived in the New World disguised as a blacksmith only to have every stitch of his clothing stolen by the natives. There were immigrants who arrived at the starving colony and then complained about the mosquitoes: "We would wish such to keep at home till at least they be mosquito-proof," Bradford wrote with a sniff.

At other times, though, the outcome of their intrigues was less than amusing, as when Weston's brother Andrew kidnapped the son of a local sachem (though he was forced to return him by Gorges's Council for New England). Or when Massasoit, out of gratitude for having been cured of a potentially lethal case of constipation by Edward Winslow's chicken soup,†

---

*The troublesome minister's sidekick reappeared after the two were expelled and received the following punishment: "They committed him till he was tamer, and then appointed a guard of musketeers which he was to pass through, and every one was ordered to give him a thump on the breech with the butt end of his musket, and then was conveyed to the waterside where a boat was ready to carry him away. Then they bid him go and mend his manners." The minister himself, meanwhile, ended up preaching out his days in Virginia, where they were apparently less scandalized by his past.

†Winslow's account is touching and amusing enough to include: "When we came thither, we found the house so full of men, as we could scarce get in, though they used their best diligence to make way for us. There were they in the midst of their charms for him, making such a hellish noise, as it distempered us that were well, and therefore unlike to ease him that was sick. When they had made an end of their charming, one told him that his friends, the English, were come to see him. Having understanding left, but his sight was wholly gone, he asked, Who was come? They told him Winsnow, for they cannot pronounce the letter *l*, but ordinarily *n* in place thereof. He desired to speak with me. When I came to him, and they told him of it, he put forth his hand to me, which I took. Then he said twice, though very inwardly, Keen Winsnow? which is to say, 'art thou Winslow?' I answered, 'Ahhe,' that is, 'Yes.' Then he doubled these words; 'Matta neen wonckanet namen, Winsnow!' that is to say, 'O Winslow, I shall never see thee again.' After apologizing that Bradford himself could not come, Winslow cooked up and gave him "a confection of many comfortable conserves, & etc. . . .

"Then I desired to see his mouth, which was exceedingly furred, and his tongue swelled in such a manner, as it was not possible for him to eat such meat as they had, his passage being stopped up. Then I washed his mouth, and scraped his tongue, and got abundance of corruption out of the same. After which I gave him more of the confection, which he told the Pilgrims that the Massachusetts were about to attack the ill-fed, ill-bred, all-male rival colony that Weston had set up at Wessagusset (Weymouth). After they finished off Wessagusset, Massasoit hinted, the Massachusetts would turn their attention to Plymouth. What's more, he said, even the Wampanoag and Nauset peoples of the lower Cape and Martha's Vineyard were allied with the Massachusetts, and that he, too, had been approached for his support against the English.

After a long and emotional town meeting in Plymouth, Miles Standish and eight armed men went up to Boston, and without asking many questions, brought back the severed heads of the suspected Massachusett leadership to stick on poles over the fortifications at Plymouth. "And instead of an Ancient [flag], we have a piece of linen cloth died in the same Indian's blood, which was hung out upon the fort when Massasoit was here."

The wisdom and motives behind that particular action, and others both more and less violent, have been debated by historians ever since. Explanations range from justifiable self-defense to conscious and unconscionable genocide. The Pilgrims' own minister, John Robinson, who had not come over from Europe, said of the Wessagusset raid that he wished they had managed to convert some Indians before they killed any. But fortunately for this book, perhaps, most of the military actions of the various New English colonies took place off-island and off the Cape.

There were, however, repercussions in the region. According to Edward Winslow, the Indians of the peninsula who had been allied with the Massachusetts became convinced that they were going to be the next targets of English action. As a defense, he reported, they moved out of their villages and moved into the "swamps and other desert places, and so brought manifold diseases amongst themselves, whereof very many are dead; as Canacum, the sachem of Manomet, Aspinet, the sachem of Nauset, and Iyanough,

---

swallowed with more readiness. Then he desiring to drink, I dissolved some of it in water, and gave him thereof. Within half an hour this wrought a great alteration in him, in the eyes of all that beheld him. Presently after his sight began to come to him, which gave him and us good encouragement. In the mean time I inquired how he slept, and when he went to stool. They said he slept not in two days before, and had not had a stool in five. They gave him some root beer and tea like concoctions.

"That morning he caused me to spend in going from one to another amongst those that were sick in the town, requesting me to wash their mouths also, and give to each of them some of the same I gave him, saying they were good folk. This pains I took with willingness, though it were much offensive to me, not being accustomed with such poisonous savours." But Massasoit wouldn't stay on his prescription of clear chicken soup. As soon as he was well enough, he ate too much goose fat and had a relapse.

sachem of Mattachiest."* It is difficult to know whether Winslow's interpretation of the origins of the sickness is accurate, or if the usual string of European maladies had finally worked its own way to the previously spared Nausets. Nonetheless, Winslow reported that a spiral of disruption was under way. "Neither is there any likelihood [the sickness and death] will easily cease; because through fear they set little or no corn, which is the staff of life, and without which they cannot long preserve health and strength." This, in turn, wasn't good for the English, who continued to rely in the early years on the Indians of Cape Cod to produce a surplus of corn. After the Indians moved into the swamps, however, the trade fell off.

It was apparently the starving men of Weston's Wessagusset colony who approached the starving families of Plymouth after the disappointing 1622 harvest and suggested they use their ship, the *Swan*, and the Pilgrims' beads to go on a food-finding cruise of the Cape and Islands. The failure of the *Speedwell* to make the crossing left the Pilgrims without a vessel of their own until the arrival the following year of the *Little James*, which they promptly wrecked on a rock in Maine. In the meantime, the shallop was used round the clock: "No sooner was the boat discharged of what she brought, but the next company took her and went out with her. Neither did they return till they had caught something, though it were five or six days before, for they knew there was nothing at home, and to go home empty would be a great discouragement to the rest." The Pilgrims lived for the most part on clams, and even Massasoit began to disdain them, they were so weak.

Hunger remained a constant feature of life for years, particularly in spring and early summer before the crops came in. After Bradford was able to purchase some additional bread from a fishing vessel, rations were raised to a quarter of a pound of bread a day, which the governor personally doled out; "otherwise, had it been in their own custody, they would have ate it up and then starved." There were numerous public whippings for settlers caught stealing and eating young corn before it had a chance to mature. There were some in Plymouth with distended bellies and others who looked like walking dead, and it was not unusual for new arrivals getting off the ships that followed the *Mayflower* to burst into tears when they saw their own futures reflected in the emaciated welcoming committee.

---

*Iyanough's body was found 240 years later in a field grave, buried under a kettle in a sitting position. Near the Cummaquid post office is a stone: ON THIS SPOT WAS BURIED THE SACHEM IYANOUGH, THE FRIEND AND ENTERTAINER OF THE PILGRIMS, JULY 1621.

So despite their distaste for the Wessagusset men, the leadership of Plymouth was inclined to take them up on the offer of a joint venture. In the fall of 1622, Bradford and Squanto (Standish was sick) and a few others set off. "The chief places aimed at were to the southward of Cape Cod; and the more, because Tisquantum, whose peace before this time was wrought with Massassowat, undertook to discover unto us that supposed, and still hoped, passage within the shoals."

Squanto told them he had been through the Nantucket shoals twice, once with an English captain (perhaps Dermer) and once with the French. Nevertheless, once again the Pilgrims were unable to find the mysterious route through the shoals into Nantucket Sound. Squanto was, however, able to tell them about a harbor called "Manomoyik," or Chatham, "which they found, and sounding it with their shallop, found the channel, though but narrow and crooked; where at length they harboured the ship."

The good Nauset people of Chatham were understandably leery of this latest batch of strange-looking men in a large boat to come winding up into their neighborhood. Perhaps remembering the depredations of Harlow and Champlain, they remained out of sight. Only after Squanto went ashore and made a few introductions did they come "to them, welcoming our Governor according to their savage manner; refreshing them very well with store of venison and other victuals, which they brought them in great abundance; promising to trade with them, with a seeming gladness of the occasion." They weren't about to be taken for fools, however, so when the English insisted on staying overnight on shore, they hid everything they owned.

The party from Plymouth was about to make another attempt to get through the shoals, armed perhaps with some piloting tips from the locals, when disaster struck in the form of a nosebleed. "In this place Squanto fell sick of an Indian fever, bleeding much at the nose (which the Indians take for a symptom of death) and within a few days died there; desiring the Governor to pray for him that he might go to the Englishmen's God in Heaven." Bradford doesn't say what he thought Tisquantum's chances were, but he doubtless prayed for him.

CHAPTER 15

SANDWICH

Twenty years after the death of his friend Squanto, William Bradford found himself praying in earnest for the soul of his own community of saints and strangers. They had survived those terrible first years of starvation and disease. (After burying Squanto's remains in Chatham, they purchased nearly thirty hogshead of corn and beans from Wampanoag and Nauset farmers at various stops along the bay side of the Cape.) The Pilgrims had, in fact, thrived beyond what they could have dared expect during the lean first years.

In addition to Plymouth, there were now towns at Sandwich, Barnstable, Yarmouth, Scituate, Marshfield, and Duxbury. Though not a part of the colony of Plymouth, both Nantucket and Martha's Vineyard, along with the Elizabeth Islands, had recently been "purchased" from Ferdinando Gorges by Thomas Mayhew, who had also previously taken the precaution of purchasing them from a rival English claimant, the earl of Sterling. Both islands would soon also have English outposts.

But hand in hand with prosperity and expansion had naturally come the dispersion of the original community. Far worse than that, though, as far as the governor was concerned, all manner of ungodly sin had lately appeared in the old colony.

From almost the beginning there was the usual run of moral lapses in the colony. There were adulterers, who after being whipped twice—once in Plymouth and once again for the home-town crowd—actually did wear *A*s on their chests. Fines were regularly levied for premarital sex, too, though these were typically reduced if the dalliance wasn't discovered until a baby arrived to a newlywed couple a few months early. There were foolish people who sold both guns and alcohol to the Native Americans, and others who took up the native way of life beyond what the law allowed. In 1646, the whole town of Plymouth was taken over by a pirate named Thomas Cromwell and his eighty drunken sailors, who stayed for a month and, wrote Bradford, "spente and scattered a great deale of money among the people, and yet more sine than money."

The summer of 1642 was by far the worst. That year there was, in Bradford's words, a "breaking out of sundry notorious sins." The usual "drunkenness and uncleanness" were only the beginning. There was also widespread "incontinency between persons unmarried, and married people were doing the same with others than their spouses." All that was bad enough, to be sure. But what really dissipated any lingering hope among the community of saints that they might have a chance of creating a paradise on earth was the little Pilgrim boy who was found that summer to have been fornicating with a turkey.

No one actually saw Thomas Granger, a teenaged servant to an upstanding citizen of Duxbury, engaged in his fowl pleasure, but he was observed consummating his forbidden passion with his master's mare. It was only later under questioning, after initial denials, that he admitted not only being with this horse "sundry times before," but also that the animal was not the only object of his affection. "Horrible it is to mention," wrote Bradford almost in the manner of a tabloid, "but the truth of the history requires it." Granger was indicted for buggery with "a cow, two goats, five sheep, two calves and a turkey." His only defense was that he'd heard about the practice from an older newcomer, someone who had supposedly perfected the technique back in England.

About cases like this the Bible was clear: both animals and boy were to be put to death. The application of justice, however, was often more complicated. Though the Pilgrim authorities were in possession of the horse in question, and the other animals were apparently identifiable from young Granger's description, only he could really tell the various sheep from one another. So the entire flock of suspects was brought before the prisoner and, saying something along the lines of *Yes . . . yes . . . no . . . yes,* "he declared which were they and which were not."

"A very sad spectacle it was," wrote Bradford of the executions. "For first the mare and then the cow and the rest of the lesser cattle were killed before his face, according to the law, Leviticus XX.15; and then he himself was executed. The cattle were all cast into a great and large pit that was digged of purpose for them, and no use made of any part of them."

How in God's creation, Bradford must have wondered, did we get here? How in the world, Pilgrim parents must have wondered aloud after the children were asleep, do we explain why little Tommy's been locked up and killed?

It had taken five years of hardship for the colony to find its feet. They "never felt the sweetness of the country till this year," wrote Bradford in a letter dated June 1625. That fall, for the first time, the English sold corn to the Native Americans in exchange for beaver, rather than having to buy corn from them with beads. Bradford attributed their agricultural progress to the abandonment of their experiment in communal living in favor of private property. By 1626, in fact, the English had essentially given up on fishing as a commercial venture in favor of expanded agriculture and fur trading. To facilitate the latter and eliminate the need to sail around the Cape, they opened a trading post on Buzzards Bay at Aptucxet (in Bourne).

Then, starting in 1629, the "great migration" of Puritans to the land of the Massachusetts Indians around Boston Bay began. Bradford was obviously a bit dismayed at the rapidity with which the Massachusetts Bay Colony surpassed Plymouth; by the end of the first year, Massachusetts Bay had five times as many English settlers as Plymouth. Plymouth went almost overnight from being larger than all other English communities combined to being not even the second largest in New England. But the short-term effect of the Puritan influx to the north was a dramatic rise in the price of food, which brought prosperity to the more-established farmers of the "Old Colony," as it became known.

Unfortunately, money hadn't bought happiness for the governor. Bradford's nostalgia for the good old, bad old days of the Old Comers—a nostalgia that by the end of his history becomes almost overbearing—first appears in his account of the 1640s. "And yet in other regards this benefit turned to their hurt, and this accession of strength to their weakness. For now as their stocks increased and the increase vendible, there was no longer any holding them together," he wrote. "By which means they were scattered all over the Bay quickly and the town in which they lived compactly till now was left very thin and in a short time almost desolate."

The first split came in 1632, when Miles Standish, John and Priscilla Alden, Jonathan Brewster, and a few others set up across the harbor from Plymouth in Duxbury. Then those at Scituate desired a church of their own. Between 1636 and 1639, the Old Colony grew from these three towns to seven, with three of the new ones on the Cape. Sandwich, only sixteen miles from Plymouth, became the first English town on the Cape when "ten men from Saugus" (Lynn) got permission from the colony in the spring of 1637 to look for land for sixty families. Bradford, "acting in association with the Old Comers" paid the Indians sixteen pounds, nineteen shillings in goods for the land around Sandwich, and by 1638 the town was fairly well established.

What attracted the English to Sandwich, and to many of the other earliest settlements on the Cape and Islands, was the vast supply of free hay. The thousands of acres of salt marsh were called the "hay grounds," and their presence meant that new farmers need only clear enough land (or appropriate enough already-cleared Indian land) for a small corn and vegetable patch to sustain themselves. With "snowshoes" for both humans and horses, enough grass could be harvested from marshes to supply roofing and winter feed for animals.

The availability of native fields, salt hay, and the high price of corn were not the only attractions of the Old Colony, however. From quite early on Plymouth developed a reputation for religious tolerance, at least when compared to Massachusetts Bay. And the new towns on the Cape were typically even looser than Plymouth proper. Most of the people who settled the Cape (and later the Islands) were not technically separatists like the Pilgrims, but various splinter groups from Massachusetts Bay Colony.

Both Barnstable and Yarmouth were first "settled" by certified religious rebels from the colony to the north. The exact problem with Reverend Stephen Bachelor's doctrine is unclear, but in the winter of 1637 the seventy-five-year-old cleric was instructed by the authorities in Lynn not to accept any new parishioners. They generously allowed that he could, if he wished, continue to lead his current flock. This he did, leading them right out of town on a righteous exodus to the south; he and his small band of followers walked out of Lynn and didn't stop until they got to what is now Yarmouth. They had planned to stay, but a single freezing winter, during which they were presumably kept alive by the resident Wampanoag, was enough, and they walked back out of local history. Within the year, however, another batch of malcontents from the larger colony to the north

Salt marshes at Barnstable, circa 1885. (COURTESY OF THE STURGIS PUBLIC LIBRARY, BARNSTABLE)

arrived—though not under any unified leadership and not as clearly motivated by religion—to take their place.

The settlement of Barnstable grew in part out of a fight in Scituate over when was the right time to baptize believers: the Anabaptists argued for adult baptism by total immersion, while the rest of the congregation, including the minister, John Lothrop, were confirmed infant sprinklers. Both sprinklers and dunkers seemed to agree on only one point: that the outrageous suggestion by a misguided dunker named William Vassall that they all simply tolerate each other's differences in a spirit of Christian love and doctrinal humility was foolish in the extreme. So after two years of looking for a suitable location, Lothrop and about twenty families moved in 1639 to Barnstable. Not that Lothrop's flock stopped arguing about the right road to paradise once they arrived on Cape Cod. Another minister, this one a part-time cattle trader named Joseph Hull, who was previously run out of Weymouth for being "contentious," was already there with his own small band of like-minded worshipers. Unlike in Scituate, however, this time Reverend Lothrop and his sprinklers were in the clear majority. And though it was all very cordial at first, Reverend Hull soon felt obliged to try spreading his message next door in Yarmouth. Hull apparently drew enough parishioners from both towns to warrant his arrest and eventual banishment. A few of his followers, meanwhile, responded to his tribulations by following the "official" Yarmouth pastor, the Reverend Marmaduke Matthews, around the street. "Fye fye! For shame!" they are remembered to have yelled. They too were shortly given six months to get out of town. Hull died somewhere off-Cape.

The Islands were not part of Plymouth Colony, having remained in the theoretical domain of the Council for New England until that ineffectual entity was broken up in 1635 and split between its principals, primarily Sir Ferdinando Gorges and Alexander, earl of Sterling. But the Islands' remoteness gave them an aura of tolerance, nonetheless, which was only partly offset by the fierce reputation of the local natives. By the 1640s Martha's Vineyard and Nantucket began to attract the attention of persons who for various reasons had dropped out of Massachusetts Bay Colony's Puritan culture.

In October of 1641, Thomas Mayhew sold his holdings in Watertown and gained from Lord Sterling's agent the right to settle both Martha's Vineyard and Nantucket in exchange for the payment of an annual rent to be determined later. Not long after, he purchased the exact same rights from an agent for Ferdinando Gorges, who also claimed the Islands.* Mayhew's religious standing was never in question. But his employer—he managed the American holdings of Matthew Craddock, one of the London speculators who founded the Massachusetts Bay Company—had begun to complain about certain perceived irregularities in his bookkeeping. Mayhew may have begun thinking then about getting out of the colony: when the previous holder of his job ran afoul of the local power structure, apparently for something he said, he was whipped, his ears were cut off, and he was banished.

Also, Mayhew had recently at his own expense built the first bridge over the Charles River, only to have it taken away by eminent domain before he had an opportunity to collect much in the way of tolls. His mill, which for a time had been profitable, now had a lien on it from Craddock. With money troubles mounting, he evidently saw the Vineyard as a chance to begin building virtually his own colony—or rather, as he later styled it, his

---

*Gorges's was the stronger claim. But the power of the Duke of York, who took over Sterling's holdings in 1663, resulted in a de facto recognition of New York's claim to the islands from then until 1692, when the crown reorganized its North American holdings and incorporated both islands and Plymouth and Cape Cod into Massachusetts. The last vestige of New York's brief influence is the name "Dukes County," which was a companion to Queens, Dutchess, and Kings Counties.

own fiefdom called "Tisbury Manor." His son, Thomas Jr., went to the Islands first, arriving in Great Harbor (Edgartown) around the beginning of 1643, probably joining a small community of English who had been squatting on the island without official sanction since 1635.* Mayhew himself followed in 1646.

None of this should be taken to imply that Plymouth Colony or the Islands had anything resembling religious or civil freedom by current standards, or even by the contemporary standards of Roger Williams's colony in Rhode Island. Church attendance was everywhere mandatory, and the senior Billington was by no means the only person to be put in the stocks for the heinous crime of swearing. Anyone who questioned the Bible was whipped. But witches, for instance, were generally released on their own personal recognizance.†

Quakers, on the other hand, were recognized as highly dangerous. The first two, Anne Austin and Mary Fisher, arrived in Boston in July 1656 and were immediately banned. Eight more landed a few weeks later and were promptly thrown in jail. When out of some misguided sense of Christian charity a Dorchester innkeeper named Nicholas Upsall bribed a jailer to let him bring the prisoners some food—and then went so far as to speak out against the new anti-Quaker laws—he was fined, his property was confiscated, and he, too, was sent packing. He turned up in Plymouth in October, where he was given permission to spend the winter in Sandwich. It was a bit of leniency the authorities learned to regret: from then on Sandwich was a hotbed of Quakerism, eventually having the first meeting house of that faith in America.

Throughout the remainder of the 1650s, Plymouth tried unsuccessfully to eradicate the sect from Cape Cod. Beginning in 1657 they required an oath of allegiance to the colony, under penalty of a fine and deportation. Taking oaths of any kind was against the tenets of the Quaker sect, and about a dozen Sandwich believers were fined, but they weren't deported. And, of course, Quakers, along with "drunkards, liars, and swearers," were not allowed to vote.

Interestingly, women weren't required to make the oath, which made

---

*The first English to settle on the Islands were probably four men who got off a disease-ridden ship en route to Virginia at Edgartown in 1635. Over the centuries since, various Peases, Nortons, and Athearns have squabbled with sundry Mayhews over who actually has been on the Vineyard longer, inaugurating a tradition still carried on by many Islanders.
†There were only two accusations of witchcraft in Plymouth Colony, and both were dismissed for lack of evidence.

the Quakers among them somewhat more difficult to ferret out. But as Quakers believed in the truly blasphemous idea that the sexes were equal in the eyes of the Divine and seemed to place nonconformity next to Godliness, a fair number of Quaker women took it upon themselves not to miss out on the oppression. Quite early, Sarah Kirby and her sister Jane Landers took to disrupting the official Sandwich church service and were hauled before the general court; Sarah was whipped.

Quakers on the Cape were fined for attending meetings, for not taking their hats off in the presence of colonial officials, for failing to serve on juries (an oath was required to do so). They were fined until, by the end of the decade, they were generating roughly one-third of the colonial budget. But nothing seemed to have much effect on the number of believers. The colonial government sent a special marshal down to Buzzards Bay to try to head off the arrival of new troublemakers from Rhode Island. They instituted a relocation program whereby they promised not to fine any Quaker who would move to Rhode Island within six months, and even offered financial aid for the needy. Not even jail could make them leave: when a certain undesirable named Wenlock Christoferson tried to tell the court that he couldn't depart because his God had not yet instructed him to, the separatists' God told *them* to tie him "neck and heels" and whip him soundly.

Plymouth's reputation for tolerance was by now wearing thin among the authorities, and though they never did follow Massachusetts Bay Colony's lead and actually hang Quakers, they made an effort to crack down. In June 1660, the general court ordered that cages be built in every town for the imprisonment of Quaker women and children who could not afford to pay fines. Also around that time, a special under marshal was appointed to keep an eye on Sandwich, Barnstable, and Yarmouth. His name was George Barlow and he came from Massachusetts Bay Colony, which meant he was tough.

Barlow's mandate was broad in the extreme: his authority to search Quaker homes and assess the value of their contents jibed well with his authority to both levy and collect fines. He could not grant immunity in exchange for testimony, but he could and did fine non-Quakers who refused to assist him in his duties. What's more, he tended to sue anyone who complained for defamation of character. Barlow enjoyed his job. He once broke into William Newland's house in the middle of the night. When the cow he confiscated from John Jenkins and Peter Gaunt died, he simply came by and took another. He confiscated Ralph Allen's shirt, though whether it was off his back was not recorded.

Whereas the previous laws against Quakers were simply ineffective, the tactics of Barlow downright backfired. Even non-Quakers began to complain about his tactics, including members of the founding families of Sandwich. Almost no one would help him, despite the threat of fines. But the colony didn't back down in its fight to rid the Cape of the scourge of Quakerism. Ironically enough, it was only the end of the Glorious Revolution and the restoration of the king in England that brought a measure of religious tolerance back to the colonies of the formerly oppressed Puritans and separatists. After Charles II made it clear that repression of Quakers was to stop, the Plymouth government concentrated its efforts on the somewhat more benign policy of taxing everyone to support the official church. This, in turn, infuriated the residents of Yarmouth, who, though certainly not Quakers, were not interested in paying taxes to support a minister.

The original English settlement on Nantucket may have grown indirectly out of the oppression of Quakers, though probably not to the degree that some later histories of the island imply. In 1658, Thomas Macy, a "merchant and clothier" who lived in Salisbury in Massachusetts Bay Colony, let a few passing Quakers come inside out of the rain. The authorities were not amused and demanded an explanation for such an outrageous act of Christian charity. There is evidence that Macy never personally suffered significant consequences from his act of mercy, and his own Puritan credentials were not in doubt: he had served in Oliver Cromwell's army before emigrating to America. But it wasn't long after the incident that he and Tristram Coffin met with Thomas Mayhew on the Vineyard to discuss buying Nantucket.

In October of 1659, Macy, along with Edward Starbuck, a friend, and his family, traveled in an open boat down the coast of Massachusetts Bay to Cape Cod. Rather than face a trip around the hook with its dangers, they crossed the Cape at Boat Meadow River in Eastham and made their way to Edgartown. There, they were joined by a pilot named Daggett, who would take them across Muskeget Channel from the Vineyard to Nantucket. For the previous eighteen years, Peter Folger had been the Mayhews' primary assistant in their efforts to convert the local Wampanoag, but his growing Baptist convictions had brought him into conflict with the more-Puritan Mayhew. He went along as a translator to the Indians.

The presence of healthy native populations on the Cape and Islands presented a quandary. For though it never stopped them or their heirs from appropriating virtually the entire continent, the English did sincerely worry at the beginning of settlement about the correctness of their colonizing activities. "But some will say, what right have I to go live in the heathens' country?" wrote the separatist Robert Cushman in his 1622 pamphlet entitled, somewhat self-defensively, "Reasons and Considerations Touching the Lawfulness of Removing out of England into the Parts of America."

The first reason Cushman gave was evangelical: that it was impractical to bring all the Indians to England in order to convert them. "To us they cannot come, our land is full; to them we may go, their land is empty." (He had already dispensed with the option of staying home to pray and trust that "God's extraordinary work from heaven" alone would save the souls of the Indians.) This wasn't entirely disingenuous. By the time Macy, Coffin, and company bought the rights to Nantucket in 1658, the Mayhews had established at least two, and possibly three, congregations of "praying Indians" on Martha's Vineyard, each served by native ministers. There was a Christian school with at least thirty Wampanoag children taught by Folger, and at least three "Indian schoolmasters." All this was supported monetarily by donations from congregations in England, and somewhere in the neighborhood of one-fifth of the island's native population had given up the old religion for the new.

For five generations, various members of the Mayhew clan devoted almost as much energy to spreading the Gospel to the natives as they did to maintaining their control over the English settlement and purchasing Indian land. Foremost among missionary Mayhews was the first to arrive, Thomas Mayhew Jr. (One of his earliest converts, Towanquatick, may have been the son of Epenow.) Before he disappeared at sea on his way to England in 1657, the thirty-five-year-old was the second most famous missionary to the Indians in America, after John Eliot. Stories of miraculous Vineyard conversions appeared so regularly in the religious press in England that the current dean of Vineyard historians, Arthur Railton, has written that more is actually known of the early Christian Indians than of the early English settlers on the island—other than the Mayhews themselves, that is.

Thomas Mayhew's brand of conversion was far more lenient than Eliot's; one didn't have to change one's name and eating habits and become English, one just had to pray to the one true God. Some have suggested that this explains why the congregations Mayhew established lasted long after his death, while the many more "Christiantowns" of Eliot withered as soon as the missionary had gone on to his final judgment.

On the Cape, meanwhile, an equally charismatic Richard Bourne began proselytizing to the local Indians in the 1650s. By 1660, he was already concerned enough about the English infiltration that he secured a grant of 10,500 acres in Mashpee as a sort of reservation (the first in the country) for the Indians. "No part or parcel of those lands might be bought by, or sold to, any white person or persons, without the consent of all the Indians, not even with the consent of the general court." The general court in Plymouth reaffirmed the promise in 1670, but of course much of the land was in fact later sold with no such consent. By 1674 Bourne reported that there were 22 "places where the praying Indians met." There were, he said, about 500 praying Indians on the Cape, 142 of whom could read their own language, 72 of whom could write it, and 9 who could read English.

But if the primary purpose of the English program in America was, as Cushman tried to argue in the 1620s, conversion, an obvious question arises: Why not just send missionaries? Why take the land? Cushman himself attempted to close the obvious loophole with a position that became a staple of English justification of expansion throughout the period of New England colonization. Basically, he argued, because they did not clear the land and fence it in, the Indians did not have a justifiable claim to it. Never mind that the Wampanoag and other natives of southern New England made significant use of the woodlands surrounding them, or that they actively managed them with fire to improve their productivity.

"This then is a sufficient reason to prove our going thither to live lawful," explained Cushman. "Their land is spacious and void, and there are few and do but run over the grass, as do also the foxes and wild beasts. They are not industrious, neither have art, science, skill or faculty to use either the land or the commodities of it, but all spoils, rots, and is marred for want of manuring, gathering, ordering, etc. As the ancient patriarchs therefore removed from straiter places into more roomy, where the land lay idle and waste, and none used it, though there dwelt inhabitants by them . . . so it is lawful now to take a land which none useth, and make use of it. . . ." The English were, in other words, unable to see the forest management program for the trees. Conveniently for the newcomers, the appearance of emptiness and, even more importantly, of wildness was seen as an abdication of long-term rights. The colonists therefore made somewhat greater efforts to pay fairly for the corn fields they coveted than they did for the minimally altered seasonal areas, like hunting and shell-fishing grounds. These were more often simply appropriated (though some native or other was generally paid something in exchange, even if after the fact).

One often hears, in the way one often hears vaguely patronizing simplifications, that the Native American had no concept of private land ownership in any European sense and was therefore ill-equipped to resist the purchases made by the incoming Europeans. To what degree this was true no doubt varied among Indian societies. (There were at least five hundred different tribes in North America when the Pilgrims arrived.) It varied as well from individual to individual, and from generation to generation. Roger Williams, the founder of Rhode Island and one of the most sympathetic of early Englishmen to the rights of Native Americans, was of the opinion that they were very sophisticated about boundaries and privileges.* Certainly by the time Massasoit's son Metacomet (a.k.a. King Philip) ascended to the leadership of the Wampanoag nation and found himself at war against his father's old allies, he, at least, understood the permanent and ultimately destructive nature of the English program.

Likewise, despite generations of vitriolic debate among professional historians of every political stripe, the English attempts both to satisfy their own consciences and to compensate native owners doubtless ran the gamut from sincere to craven. It is a debate that will probably never end and probably never should.

Thoreau had his own take on the process:

> When the committee from Plymouth had purchased the territory of Eastham of the Indians, "it was demanded, who laid claim to Billingsgate?" which was understood to be all that part of the Cape north of what they had purchased. The answer was, "there was not any who owned it." "Then," said the committee, "that land is ours." The Indians answered, that it was. This was a remarkable assertion and admission. The Pilgrims appear to have regarded themselves as Not Any's representatives. Perhaps this was the first instance of that quiet way of "speaking for" a place not yet occupied, or at least not improved as much as it may be, which their descendants have practiced, and are still practicing so extensively. Not Any seems to have been the sole proprietor of all America before the Yankees. But history says, that when the Pilgrims had held the lands of Billingsgate for many years, at length "appeared an Indian, who styled himself Lieutenant Anthony," who laid claim to them, and of him they bought them. Who knows but a Lieutenant Anthony may be knocking at the door of the White House some day? At any rate, I know that if you hold a thing unjustly, there will surely be the devil to pay at last.

---

*Williams, who was a pioneer of both religious freedom and Indian respect, said that "the natives are very exact and punctual in the bounds of their lands, belonging to this or that prince or people, even to a river, brook, etc."

Officially, only the colonial government at Plymouth could purchase land from the Indians, and for the most part it made a sincere effort to enforce the rule. When William Nickerson persisted in buying up large amounts of land in what would become Chatham, he was repeatedly fined and his holdings reduced to one hundred acres. But the intent of the law was less to protect the natives from unscrupulous buyers than it was to preserve control over the incoming population. The remainder of Nickerson's land claims were notably not returned to the Nausets, but distributed to nine prominent English residents of Cape Cod. Similarly, as it expanded toward "the southern sea," as Nantucket Sound was known, Barnstable had numerous disputes with the Indians about what rights exactly had been purchased. The colonial government stepped in on several occasions, and though it tried for the most part to find the truth, not surprisingly Barnstable generally grew each time rather than shrank.

One justification for appropriating land that was not used by the English on Cape Cod and the Islands was racial. Until at least 1675, it was the generally held belief of the Europeans in New England that the Native Americans were not of another race. They were born white, most believed, and gained their slightly darker color through exposure to the sun and the various dyes and paints ceremonially applied throughout their lives. Most of the first English settlers to Cape Cod and the Islands had reason to believe that the Indians they encountered were the lost tribe of Israel. Why else, they reasoned among themselves, would Indian women have such little trouble giving birth? Also, some argued, didn't Algonquian sound a little like ancient Hebrew? Only after King Philip's War did the language referring to the original New Englanders begin to become overtly racialized. "It was the historian, not the Puritan or the aborigine, who insisted on making racial division the focal point of Puritan-Indian relations in New England" is how historian Alden Vaughn summed up the point in his classic (though perhaps at times a bit too apologetic) history of Puritan-Indian relations, *New England Frontier.*

Once land was gotten from the Indians, legitimately or otherwise, it had to be divided among the English. This was usually handled in a way modeled after the workings of grants from England to Plymouth Colony itself: the governor's council made grants to committees of grantees, who in turn subdivided their new holdings among the new residents. This process left a lot of room for trouble. Equality was not even a goal, and the holders of the original grants generally ended up with the best land, even if they were outsiders. In Sandwich, for instance, the ten original grantees from Saugus received more than half the total land, while the remainder was split among more than forty others who were primarily from Plymouth. Even after the Plymouth contingent complained that not only were they the home-town crowd but had actually arrived in Sandwich first, the general court only remarked that land was to be distributed "fairly according to the rank, estate, and quality of the recipient." It scolded the Saugus grantees for their absentee status but did not revoke either the grant or their distribution of it.

As more and more persons from Massachusetts Bay moved out to the Cape, some among the Old Comers grew concerned that all the good real-estate opportunities were slipping away. After twenty years of effort, it was clear that Plymouth was one of the less-attractive spots to settle. The abandoned fields that seemed so inviting in 1620 had not proved sufficient to support a growing population, and the rocky hills behind—part of the same interlobate moraine that runs down the east coast of Buzzards Bay—meant that clearing new fields wasn't an attractive option. What's more, the harbor was substandard. Not only did goods have to be ferried ashore due to shallowness, but it was also directly to windward of Cape Cod, which often made it tough to enter. So beginning in the early 1640s, there was an effort on the part of some of the members of the Plymouth congregation to move the entire town to Nauset.

It was an emotional debate, the likes of which had not occurred since the earliest days of the colony. The town was torn, voting at first to go, then, on second thought, to stay. Those who wanted to leave were determined, however, and in 1644 seven families of Plymouth received a grant to settle in Nauset. Included in the group were some of the most prominent citizens of the Old Colony, including Thomas Prence, who had been and would again become governor. The move took place in the spring or summer of 1645, and in June of 1651 Nauset was incorporated as the town of Eastham.*

Out of four towns—Sandwich, Yarmouth, Barnstable, and Eastham—came virtually all the others on the Cape.† The exception was Provincetown.

---

*Which should never, by the way, be pronounced *Eastum*, but always *EastHam*.
†The towns of Plymouth Colony (and the Islands) include Plymouth, 1620; Scituate, 1636; Duxbury, 1637; Barnstable, 1639; Taunton, 1639; Sandwich, 1639; Yarmouth, 1639; Marshfield, 1641; Rehoboth, 1645; Eastham, 1646; Bridgewater, 1656; Dartmouth, 1664; Swansea, 1667; Middleborough, 1669; Edgartown, 1671; Tisbury, 1671; Little Compton, 1682; Freetown, 1683; Falmouth, 1686; Nantucket, 1687; Truro (Pamet, then Dangerfield), 1700; Wellfleet, 1763. Harwich was incorporated in 1694, Bourne in 1884.

In all likelihood the hook periodically sheltered temporary populations of European fishermen, pirates, castaways, and others, even before the arrival of the Pilgrims in 1620. The modern settlement of the town didn't begin until 1727, however, and even then the land remained the property of the royal province and commonwealth of Massachusetts. Hence the name "Province-Land," or Provincetown. Only in 1893 by special act of the legislature did it become an actual town.

The attempt by many of the original Pilgrims to abandon Plymouth for Nauset seems to have been the unkindest cut of all for William Bradford. The outbreak of sin, after all, could be explained as the work of Satan. Perhaps the Prince of Darkness just hated the Pilgrims more than most because of their general goodness. (They had, after all, established a beachhead of Christianity in the Prince of Darkness's private continent.) At least this explanation was far preferable to the thought that the Pilgrims were actually more under Satan's sway than those in the old country, as Bradford was self-critical enough to consider. Or perhaps the unrighteousness of the 1640s was the result of overzealous efforts by the saints to control sin. "As it is with waters when their streams are stopped or dammed up," reasoned Bradford, so it is with sins. "When they get passage they flow with more violence and make more noise and disturbance than when they are suffered to run quietly in their own channels."

The main reason for the outbreak of sin, Bradford decided, was probably that the separatists were just better than others at finding out the secret doings of the people among them. There were turkey lovers like Thomas Granger all over the place in Massachusetts and England, he implied. Plymouth would survive these trials. They had, after all, successfully dealt with Thomas Granger's forbidden passions according to God's law.

Granger's sin could be atoned with blood. But the effort to remove from Plymouth to Cape Cod was indicative of something else entirely—something that wasn't quite sin, Bradford thought, but was potentially more dangerous. It showed a failure by the current generation to understand what the whole idea of living in this corner of the New World was supposed to be about.

The newcomers and children of the Old Comers were dissatisfied with the size of their houses and the quality of their lives. They simply wanted more, after their parents had made do with so much, much less. "And others still, as they conceived themselves straitened or to want accommodation, broke away under one pretence or other, thinking their own conceived necessity and the example of others a warrant sufficient for them." Because someone else had a bigger house, they thought they needed one, too.

Over the years Bradford and his council attempted to rein in the building frenzy on the Cape. Towns were warned to be careful to whom they gave land. All newcomers were required to apply to the court for permission to settle in the colony, bringing with them a letter of recommendation from a previous congregation. There were architectural restrictions as well, intended to prevent the proliferation of the new, showy homes. Clapboard on more sides than the front was unlawful ostentation, and the town of Barnstable retained the right of first refusal on the sale of houses. But humility and taste are difficult to legislate, and a significant portion of the Plymouth congregation itself wanted to trade up while there were still better lands to be had on Cape Cod. For Bradford, this was a dishonor to the dead of 1620 who had crossed over with nothing but faith (and muskets). "Stay and make a pause, and stand half amazed at this poor people's . . . condition," he instructed his readers. "Being thus passed the vast ocean, and a sea of troubles before in their preparation . . . they had now no friends to welcome them nor inns to entertain or refresh their weather-beaten bodies; no houses or much less town to repair to, to seek succour."

The governor, along with some others, continued to argue against joining the rush for new opportunities on the Cape. "Men might here live if they would be content with their condition," he said sullenly, but to no avail. By 1645 nearly half the town of Plymouth had left for Cape Cod without him. "It was not for want or necessity so much that they removed," wrote Bradford after they were gone. They went "for the enriching of themselves."

It is as time-honored a tradition on Cape Cod and the Islands as Thanksgiving: having presided over the subdivision of the land next door William Bradford was mortified by the outcome. Of the phenomenon in general, he said, "This I fear will be the ruin of New England."

CHAPTER 16

THE SOUTH SHORE

On a cloudless afternoon I landed at ACK. Through the alchemy of tourism and group-identity dynamics, ACK, the decidedly unmellifluous three-letter airport code printed on luggage tags bound for Nantucket, has in recent years become a totem of sorts for the entire island. I say *totem* rather than *nickname* because few people actually refer to Nantucket as ACK in conversation; they display the brand instead on baseball caps, T-shirts, coffee cups, and the like. Most of all, ACK appears on the bumpers of cars, on small oval stickers made to look like a European country code. There are stickers like this emanating from the Vineyard, too, that read MV, and they are annoying enough with their underlying message of "I'd rather be richer than you and I probably am." But ACK goes even further: it seems to say, "I'd rather be richer than you and I probably am. Plus, I know what ACK means."*

I should say that it's quite possible the stickers on both islands are purely innocent expressions of pride of place, and that I had thought about them for too long. It's possible I let my general distrust of stickers as a form of

---

*Once upon a time, the airport was called Ackerly Field. The Cape has its own rather perverse version: stickers made to look like some kind of resident tunnel permit for a tunnel under the Cape Cod Canal that doesn't exist. (I am indebted to Richard Todd's pioneering research into the semiotics of bumper stickers published many years ago in *New England Monthly*.)

personal expression carry me away. Walking a beach gives you time to think, and by the time I was thinking about the imbedded meanings of ACK, I had plodded through soft sand for more than three hours on my way from the airport to Siasconset. I had walked, in other words, long enough to be pondering relative obscurities, which is to say, not yet long enough to be released from the momentum of thought in general.

That release would come, though, I hoped. There were several specific things I wanted to see on this trip to Nantucket that I hadn't seen before, like the base of Sankaty Head and Altar Rock. But mostly, as it was undeniably spring, I went to the "far-away island"—the most seaward place in a seaward region—to walk until my feet and legs spoke to me at least as loudly as my brain. With that in mind, I stayed at ACK, the airport, only long enough to enter it into the memory of my little global positioning system and then struck out for the south shore. When I reached the water, I turned left.

Along most of the beach heading east the usual signs of erosion are obvious in the fifteen- to twenty-foot bluff where the sand stops and the remnant outwash plain begins. Once in a while a broken pipe or some other piece of human history sticks out of the exposed ledge. Elsewhere, wooden stairs built when the cliff was higher have been hauled back with its retreat, until now they rise eerily four or five feet above the top of the bluff. At the old military installation just past Forked Pond Valley, a pathetic layer of blacktop is crumbling over the edge; it looks like one of those charts of geological time that shows the entire span of human existence as a thin veneer sitting atop a massive accumulation of millennia.

But the usual signs of erosion can wear thin on a person; most of the time I kept my attention on the sea to my right. There were birds, mostly terns working over what I imagined might be early bluefish. At one point a group of excited all-black ducks, some kind of scoter, swam along about forty yards off. The birds were surprisingly good company, and while they remained in the vicinity I found I didn't think about how far I'd come or how far I still had to go before resting. Even better companions were a group of semipalmated sandpipers—"sand-peeps"—who ran along the surf line in front of me for quite a good distance, stopping occasionally to rest on one leg. Most of the time, though, I was alone.

'Sconset finally appeared as I rounded the corner at Tom Nevers Head. The village was still high enough to catch the setting sun, though the beach was already growing chilly in the shade. With its perfectly preserved antique cottages huddled together on a bluff overlooking the entire North Atlantic,

Sankaty Head Light, Nantucket, circa 1870. (COURTESY OF THE MARTHA'S VINEYARD HISTORICAL SOCIETY)

its tiny streets and climbing roses, its reliable fog, little 'Sconset is in many ways as pretty and English as New England gets. But from that distance it looked momentarily Moorish, gleaming white and flat like stucco between the two darkening blues of sea and sky. And thanks to the sudden wideness of Low Beach, I had the sensation that my steps were no longer bringing me appreciably closer to anything. Or farther from anything. All the grains of sand were moving west with the wind, everything moving west but me. I stumbled across a desert toward what was likely to turn out to be a mirage.

Of course it wasn't. I spent the night in a prearranged bed in 'Sconset from which I could hear the sea, and in the early morning walked up Baxter Road past the perfectly trimmed privets to the lighthouse and then back down around to the base of the Sankaty Head cliffs under the lighthouse. There the high tide had recently been working on a small outcropping of vertical clay. Every six inches or so in its smooth black face a small washed pebble protruded, perfectly set and gleaming in the rising sun, like uncut gems in some immense ceremonial door.

I wonder now if the base of Sankaty was a place where during Nantucket's century-and-a-half-long heyday as the capital of the global whaling industry youths might have come to say good-bye before one or the other of them went off to sea, possibly forever. It's where I would go, I think. But on the morning I was there, I merely sat with my back to the jeweled wall and enjoyed the morning light at the leading edge of the day on land. Until I noticed that even the slight spring breeze was sending down onto me and into my granola a constant mist of grit and sand from the cliffs behind, whereupon I left the beach and walked on dirt roads across the rolling "moors" that used to constitute the collectively owned "middle pasture" and "north pasture." I walked past the cranberry bogs and the sand pits used to treat them. Past Altar Rock, which turns out to be a place with a great view, but no rock worthy of such a name. Past a mother goose and six hatchlings who peeped and honked in a mighty fit of outrage until I was out of sight.

I walked into Nantucket Town, by a route I later figured to be around thirteen miles, where I had lunch and bought more water, and then walked out again. I took the north shore this time, under Nantucket Cliffs and along Dionis Beach. I clambered over a series of rock beach reinforcements and passed the rotting ribs of one good-sized old vessel. At the end of Eel Point, in late afternoon, I took out my GPS. The isle of Tuckernuck lay across a stretch of shallows and flats like a promised land. I thought I could even see Cape Poge on the Vineyard: two tiny hummocks of green so far off to the northwest that they appeared to levitate on a thin cushion of white haze. I wondered, as I often have, about kayaking from there to here, and squatted down to look from the paddler's view. When I did, the levitating hummocks disappeared altogether.

Which was why I took out the GPS. I wanted to know how far it was to Cape Poge, whose location I had long ago saved in the computer's memory. I was also curious to know how far it was back to Sankaty Head, from which I had come that morning. And finally, I wanted to store the coordinates of Eel Point for future reference. But I must have pushed the wrong button, for I erased them all.

It wasn't a simple error. The machine gave me some kind of warning, and then asked for confirmation. But I didn't read it closely enough. I looked down and they were all gone: Home, Cedar Tree Neck, Cape Higgon, the Brickyard, Menemsha, the Herring Creek, Gay Head, Squibby, Stonewall, the opening, Norton Point, Wasque, the Narrows, Cape Poge, the Gut, Edgartown Light, East Chop, West Chop, Paul's Point, the Steamship Authority in Vineyard Haven and Woods Hole, the Steamship Authority in Hyannis and Nantucket, Tarpaulin, Naushon, Quick's Hole, Robinson's Hole, Pasque, Cuttyhunk, Penikese, Uncatena, Quissett, Woods Hole, Nobska Light, Chatham Light, Nauset Light, Highland Light, Race Point Light, Wood End Light, Long Point Light, the mouth of the Pamet River, Truro Post Office, First Encounter Beach, Scorton Creek, Blish Point, the Nantucket Airport. There were, I think, more than 120 way-points altogether—120 times I had stopped, unpacked the high-tech device, and pushed its buttons to "save" the place for some hypothetical future reference—and in an instant all were lost. Except for one, Eel Point, where I presently stood, surrounded on three sides by water. I put the machine away.

The next morning at dawn I walked east along the south shore from Smith Point. It was one of those days when long parabolic rollers rise out of an otherwise glass-flat sea. Not big waves, but flawless nonetheless. For what was probably an hour I watched as I walked to see if I could tell where a wave began and where it ended. The crash, of course, seems like a mea-surable waypoint in the life of a wave, as does the place where the water reaches its highest elevation on the sand and turns back toward the base of the next big ripple in line. But even then, a wave is not finished rolling things back down the beach, and the next merely carries what its predeces-sors have loosened and lifted. There are waves within waves, only some of them discernable. Even the tide, according to marine geologist Orin Pilkey Jr., is best thought of as a great wave "whose length is half the circumfer-ence of the earth."

The day warmed. It was a Saturday in May. I removed my shoes. I began to see a few people: a woman threw a stick for a dog; a balding, wet-suited surfer paddled his board up and down the beach to keep his midriff in line, even though there were no waves big enough to ride. A man stood beside a bicycle; another held a child.

At one point during that clarion morning on Nantucket's south shore, a cold wave slipped farther onshore than those that preceded it, up over my ankles and cold enough to constrict the veins and send the synapses firing up my calves to my head with the message "There is a dull, aching pain down here." Houses and swing sets lost over eroding cliffs are not the only intersection between human history and natural history, my feet announced. There is also this moment, this irreplaceable instant. This animal moment.

I moved closer to the water until every wave washed over my ankles. Then even a little closer to the sea. Onward I sloshed with no fixed bearings until at last I got back to where I had started two and a half days earlier, back to ACK.

CHAPTER 17

NANTUCKET

There was nothing particularly unusual about a significant portion of the population of Nantucket turning out to welcome home the whaling bark *Two Brothers*. All over Cape Cod and the Islands, the people who stayed behind to tend the sheep and children, grind the grain, dry the fish, make the bricks and build the ships and blow the glass, were gladdened at the sight of homebound sails in their harbors. It hadn't happened overnight, but in the two centuries since the English arrival at Provincetown, the people of Cape Cod and the Islands had become the most ocean-faring members of a maritime nation. Which is to say, they had learned enough about the sea to give thanks when a ship returned.

And on Nantucket—an island overwhelmingly dominated by whaling and, in 1821, at the apex of its dominance of that industry—gathering along the wharves, and maybe even atop the ubiquitous roof platforms that were never, ever called "widows' walks," to welcome home oil-laden schooners and barks was a high and treasured ritual. As soon as the ship was identified, which was always long before the name could be read on the stern, children raced through sandy streets to the house of the returning captain's family, and there are semi-apocryphal tales of the first to arrive there with the good news being rewarded by the woman of the house with a whole dollar. That is, if the woman of the house had chosen not to accompany her husband on the voyage, or if she was not downtown running a business, which more than a few did in a community where so

View of Nantucket Harbor from the crow's nest. (COURTESY NANTUCKET HISTORICAL ASSOCIATION)

many men and boys were at sea that, according to one estimate, females outnumbered males by four to one.

So it would have been extraordinary if the good people had not gathered on the Sunday morning of August 5, 1821, when word sped through town that the ship *Two Brothers* was in sight after a voyage to the Pacific under the command of George Worth. There was something quite different about this particular returning ship, however, and everyone on Nantucket knew it. On board, not as commander but as a convalescent passenger, was Captain George Pollard. He had left the island almost exactly two years before, on August 12, 1819, in command of the whaler *Essex*.

In the previous century and a half of whaling on Nantucket, there had been plenty of wrecks, lives lost, ships that simply disappeared, and attacks by pirates. There were deaths by whales—many, many deaths by whales—and mutinies, massacres, outbreaks of disease. There were instances of incompetence by captains and crews, of desertions, of tragic maimings, and of wars. And there would be more of all those after 1820.

Tales can be told as well of the thousands of ships that sailed under captains and crews from Cape Cod and Martha's Vineyard, not all of them whalers. Tales of hundreds of merchant mariners enslaved by the dey of

Algiers, or impressed into the English Navy; of rival clippers commanded by neighbors from Brewster racing all the way home from China; of local boys who became minor potentates on obscure Pacific islands. More than a few times, entire crews climbed into the rigging and froze to death when in winter gales their ships struck sand within sight of the home shore. There are stories of vessels that narrowly escaped the depredations of Confederate warships, vessels that didn't escape, and one that escaped once, but not twice.

Finally, there are the countless forgotten successful voyages during the maritime centuries. For both those at sea and those left behind they represent tens of thousands of human years of loneliness punctuated by fearfulness and exhilaration. The stories of all the ships that sailed from Cape Cod and the Islands are, in that way, fundamentally alike. And in any one of them, in all likelihood, could be found the story of the era.

But nothing on Cape Cod and the Islands either before or after the wreck of the *Essex* resembled the horror and moral ambiguity of Pollard's voyage. He was not the sole survivor; six other members of his crew had already returned to Nantucket two months before, on the ship *Eagle*. Even before the return of the first survivors, rumors and facts had filtered back to Nantucket by the usual route, ship to ship, mouth to mouth, around Cape Horn and up. By best guess, on the same day that the *Dauphin*, under Captain Zimri Coffin of Nantucket, rescued Pollard at sea, she "spoke" the *Diana*, under Aaron Paddack of New York. Two weeks later *Diana*, in turn, spoke the *Triton*, under Captain Zephaniah Wood, and *Triton* brought the grim news home to Nantucket via New Bedford.

Pollard was the captain, however, the man who made the fateful decisions in the middle of the Pacific. Nantucketers knew this, so the crowds that lined the street to see him disembark and walk up to his home on Center Street were larger than usual. There were fifteen hundred spectators on the wharves alone, by one estimate. They were stone silent as he passed up to his house.

From the very beginning of their contact with Cape Cod and the Islands, Europeans looked upon the wealth of whales and fish in the nearby waters as a bonanza waiting to be reaped by anyone equipped with enough skill and courage to do so. When John Smith came to New England in 1614, his stated "plot was there to take Whales." But the newcomers weren't immediately successful at killing the leviathan, and Smith added that though "we saw many, and spent much time in chasing them, [we] could not kill any."

Likewise, the author of *Mourt's Relation* remembered that when the *Mayflower* first arrived in the bay, "every day we saw whales playing hard by us." But again: "If we had instruments and means to take them, we might have made a very rich return, which to our great grief we wanted."

Nor were the Pilgrims, it turned out, very successful fishermen. In their original business plan, cod was expected to be the principal money maker. But the colonists virtually gave up on fishing as a revenue generator by 1630, and almost a century passed before the people of Cape Cod and the Islands began taking to the sea in earnest. There's virtually no record of boats of any size being built in the region before the 1670s, and no one made a business of it until eighty years later, when Thomas Agrey opened a boatyard at Barnstable.

The failure at fishing was partly due to the failure of the *Speedwell* to make the crossing with the *Mayflower; Speedwell* was supposed to become the Pilgrims' primary fishing vessel. Early sickness also cut sharply into the colonists' labor supply. Nor did it help that they really didn't know a thing about fishing. And it didn't help the curing process that the master salt maker sent over from England turned out not to know how to make the stuff after all. But the main reason several generations passed before the English New Englanders began to look in earnest to the sea for their livelihood was that farming took virtually all their energy: "They had to be farmers or starve" is how Henry C. Kittredge described the situation in his classic 1930 history of Cape Cod.

In the first years, whatever energy remained after the clearing, planting, and building was better spent trading with the local natives for furs. The fur and agriculture strategy made perfect sense in the early days of settlement. As mentioned earlier, the Cape was a low-cost producer of salt hay, and thus cattle and horses, for the growing population in Massachusetts. Once predators were eliminated, fences were not needed on Nantucket and the smaller islands, making them natural places to maintain large herds of sheep and chickens. "Here they have neither wolves nor foxes," wrote J. Hector St. John de Crevecoeur in his *Letters from an American Farmer* in 1782. "Those inhabitants therefore who live out of town, raise with all security as much poultry as they want; their turkeys are very large and excellent."

But neither fur trading nor farming was ultimately sustainable, at least by the methods the English employed. The passengers of the *Mayflower* were happy to see "so goodly a land, and wooded to the brink of the seas," and

Picnic lunch at Gardner's Farm, Quaise, Nantucket, after sheep shearing, circa 1889.

named the final curl of the Cape "Wood End," presumably because the forest ended there.

By the first decades of the 1700s, however, so much vegetation had been removed from the dunes that make up Provincetown that the sand there went on the move. The colonial government felt constrained to regulate the cutting of trees to prevent Provincetown Harbor from being entirely filled in with sand, but to little effect. At the beginning of the 1800s, the big dunes were moving toward town at a rate of ninety feet per year; houses were built on pilings to let sand, not water, pass beneath. In 1825, the first organized attempts to plant beach grass and pitch pines began. The town had a beach-grass committee from 1838 to 1893, and the state and federal governments have also planted grass. By the 1890s, the progress of the dunes slowed to fifteen feet per year.

Wherever the English went the trees disappeared. Nantucket was already importing logs by the 1670s, having run through the "rich forests of oak and pine" of early reports. All over Cape Cod and the Islands, whatever grass and other vegetation took hold after the forests were gone was generally kept well cropped by grazing animals or rooted up by wandering pigs.

On Nantucket, the fear of overgrazing of the common land was such that by 1668—only a decade after the purchase from Mayhew—the proprietors were forced to limit each full-share proprietor to forty sheep and forty cattle. "Vineyard men," in particular, were told to remove their horses from the island. The limits were hardly conservative, however: in 1763 Crevecoeur estimated that there were more than fifteen thousand sheep on Nantucket, along with five hundred cows and two hundred horses.

On the upper Cape and the Vineyard, the process of forest removal and soil depletion took somewhat longer. Thirty vessels in Sandwich were still exporting timber to Boston from the area around Shootflying Hill as late as the 1820s, and the forests there were part of what convinced Deming Jarves to found his glass works in that town. There was enough timber in Wellfleet to support a ship-building industry until the middle of that century. But the outcome of excessive plowing and overgrazing was ultimately the same everywhere.

According to one estimate, the yield of an acre of Nantucket farmland fell from a reported 250 bushels of corn (husks included) in the 1720s to a mere 20 bushels by the time of the American Revolution. They went to sea, observed Crevecoeur, because "were they to stay at home, what could they do?" On the Vineyard, where Crevecoeur had guessed there were 20,000 sheep in 1763, the Harvard geologist Nathaniel Shaler estimated that by 1888 there were 33,000 acres "east of Tisbury" that had gone from forested to fertile to essentially unusable. As for the Cape, Thoreau in 1857 saw a cow tied to a rope 120 feet long to give the animal a better chance at finding something to eat: "Tethered in the desert for fear that she would get into Arabia Felix!" he commented.

The fur trade was exhausted even faster than the topsoil. In 1643 the colony sent back more than twelve thousand pounds of beaver pelts and eleven hundred of otter, but by as early as 1688, a commissioner from the king of England sent to look over the finances of the new colonies reported back "now beaver and peltry fail us." Local supplies of beaver and other fur bearers were doubtless exhausted much earlier than that. It was the loss to rival colonies of control of their trading posts on the Kennebec and Connecticut Rivers that put the Pilgrims essentially out of the skin trade by the time Massachusetts took over the Old Colony in 1691. There was one wild resource about which the king's emissary was optimistic, however. There could be "great profit by whale killing," he predicted. "It will be one of our best returns."

. . .

Just as it had always done for the Indians, throughout the period of English expansion and appropriation the ocean periodically gave itself freely in the form of "drift whales." In particular, blackfish, or grampus, as pilot whales were called, sometimes came ashore by the hundreds. (The largest school of blackfish ever recorded to have come ashore was in Truro in 1874, when 1,405 were driven ashore by men in boats.) Large whales, too, came ashore, either dead or soon to be.

To what degree the coastal Indians of New England hunted live whales with stone-tipped harpoons is unclear. (Waymouth in 1605 reported Indians going after whales with floats and harpoons. Brereton, in 1602, reported the north shore of the Vineyard covered with large whale bones.) But it is certain that long before the arrival of Europeans, Native Americans harvested meat and blubber from drift whales. In many places on Cape Cod and the Islands they maintained most of the rights to do so throughout the seventeenth century, perhaps even increasing their efforts once the English began buying whale products. One sachem on the Vineyard, for instance, included as a condition of sale of his land the perpetual right to harvest the amount of blubber equal to four spans of his arms from the middle of every drift whale that might wash up.

Whenever a whale came ashore during the colonial period, both native and newcomer alike rushed to the beach to get in on the action of cutting off the blubber and boiling it down for oil. The problem never was finding enough help for the work; more often it was sorting through the overlapping claims to the bounty. At various times different means of dividing the spoils were attempted: in 1653 Sandwich decided that everyone in town should share equally in any drift whales, as the beach was public. When that failed to produce either enough oil or harmony, four townspeople were granted a monopoly, with the stipulation that they give half the oil to the town. Eastham and Truro gave part to the local minister, a policy that amused Thoreau for several paragraphs.* The colonial government at

---

*"In 1662, the town agreed that a part of every whale cast on shore be appropriated for the support of the ministry. No doubt there seemed to be some propriety in thus leaving the support of the ministers to Providence, whose servants they are, and who alone rules the storms; for, when few whales were cast up, they might suspect that their worship was not acceptable. The ministers must have sat upon the cliffs in every storm, and watched the shore

Plymouth, meanwhile, constantly tried to get a piece of the action on the Cape, usually collecting a hogshead of oil per whale. Likewise the colonial authorities in New York and Massachusetts squabbled over the right to tax the Islands. Massasoit, too, from his residence in Mount Hope, had a finger in the whaling operations on Nantucket and Martha's Vineyard. In general, though, by the nineteenth century the initial finder was his blubber's keeper: in 1850 Daniel Rich cut his mark into seventy-five black-fish beached between Wellfleet and Truro and then promptly sold them for $1,900.

The disputes of the early decades were made more rather than less com-plicated by the innovation of placing permanent lookouts along the beach and then rowing out and attempting to herd the animals toward the surf. The general court in Plymouth eventually extended the definition of drift whales belonging to the towns on Cape Cod out to a mile offshore. Beyond that, however, whales were fair game to anyone willing to row or sail up to one, stick it with a harpoon, stab it with a lance, and tow it back home. And increasingly, as the seventeenth century wore on, Cape Codders were doing just that.

Nantucket, near which almost every migrating North Atlantic whale must pass every spring and fall, was a slow starter in the transition from drift whaling to whale hunting. (Though not as slow as the Vineyard.*) It wasn't for lack of trying. In 1672 a small whale made the mistake of hanging around in Nantucket Harbor for three days, giving the locals enough time to bang out a primitive harpoon and go get it. That same year, apparently inspired by the excitement of this "scrag" hunt, the leading citizens of Nantucket sent to eastern Long Island (which was colonized by New Englanders in the 1640s) in search of an expert. They offered a certain James Lopar ten acres of land and the right to graze some animals—what

---

with anxiety. And, for my part, if I were a minister, I would rather trust to the bowels of the billows, on the back-side of Cape Cod, to cast up a whale for me, than to the generosity of many a country parish that I know. You cannot say of a country minister's salary, commonly, that it is 'very like a whale.' . . . Nevertheless, the minister who depended on whales cast up must have had a trying time of it. I would rather have gone to the Falkland Isles with a har-poon, and done with it. Think of a whale having the breath of life beaten out of him by a storm, and dragging in over the bars and guzzles, for the support of the ministry! What a consolation it must have been to him!"

*In 1738 Captain Benjamin Chase, successful Nantucket whaler, moved to Edgartown, bought twenty acres on the harbor, built a wharf and a try works, and went broke. From 1738 to 1744 three others tried the same move and also failed. Eventually, though, whaling caught on in Edgartown.

Beached pilot whales in Wellfleet. (Courtesy of the Sturgis Public Library, Barnstable)

was called a "half-share"—if he would "follow the trade of whaling on the island two years in all the season thereof."

This wasn't particularly unusual: proprietors of new towns often tried to tempt craftspeople with sweetheart deals. In 1677, when the residents of Succonessitt (Falmouth) divided the land at Woods Hole among themselves, they reserved twelve acres as an incentive for a blacksmith to come. But Lopar was evidently that perennially mysterious type who actually preferred the Hamptons; he turned the Nantucket offer down.

Eighteen years later, in 1690, the island successfully lured a twenty-eight-year-old professional whaler from Yarmouth named Ichabod Paddock. Paddock, who some suspected was romancing mermaids in the bellies of whales while out of sight of land, stayed on Nantucket until 1710 before returning home to the Cape. But that was plenty of time to get the island on its single-minded way to whaling dominance. In 1694, a local regulation made it a crime to use cedar trees for any purpose other than "whale bots or the like." As on the Cape, regular beats were set up along the beach with teams constantly on the lookout for whales.

By 1700, according to writer Nathaniel Philbrick, "anyone who could hold an oar—English and Indian alike—was involved in the whale fishery, which in those days lasted from November into late March and early April, dovetailing nicely with the seasonal demands of farming and sheep graz-ing." There were, he estimates, approximately 60 English and 160 Indians involved in shore whaling on Nantucket.

In most histories and memoirs of American whaling—and whole libraries could be filled with the genre—the presence of generous numbers of Native Americans on early whaling voyages is pointed out as evidence of a certain degree of tolerance and good feeling between the races. And there was no doubt some truth to the sentiment in individual cases, particularly in the earliest decades of the industry. Crevecoeur noticed that as late as the mid-1700s most English islanders were able to speak a rough form of the native language.

But more recent research by the historian Daniel Vickers suggests that the vast majority of Native American whalers were little more than slaves, assigned by the English courts to specific captains for years on end as pun-ishment for relatively minor infractions. Because he apparently stole a sheep, a native named Moab was indentured to John Macy for three years. To atone for liberating a supply of beer and rum, a man named Alewife was sentenced to seven years' labor for Nathaniel Starbuck and Peter Coffin.

It wasn't always necessary to commit a crime to lose one's liberty, par-ticularly not when the Starbucks were more than happy to extend credit at their store. Debt, in fact, was the most common way to become attached to a whaling voyage, and Vickers estimates that three-quarters of the native whalers between 1725 and 1733 were debt slaves. "To virtually every Indian with whom they dealt, the Starbucks advanced enough cloth and other supplies (although never more than £10 worth) to oblige him to continue bringing in his produce," Vickers concluded. "We know that the same tech-niques were also used by other settlers. Hardly a session passed in the Nan-tucket courts during the seventeenth century without a Swain, Hussey, or Gardner launching an action against some native debtor who was refusing to continue this exchange."

The rights to Indian debt labor could be sold, and the court would occasionally hold auctions in cases where there wasn't an obvious plaintiff. What's more, native laborers were regularly handed down from generation to generation, Vickers discovered, virtually always connected with the fam-ily whaling gear: when Stephen Coffin Jr. died in 1725, he left "the one half of my fishing and whaling craft with the half of all my indian debts" to his two sons, and the other half to his wife.

The system was so insidious and so widespread that in 1716 a Nantucket Indian named John Punker optimistically appealed to the Massachusetts legislature to provide an off-island court where Nantucket Indians might get some justice. A committee of three was sent to investigate, and to its credit the colonial government ordered that off-island judges be appointed to hear all matters relating to Indians. "A great wrong and injury happens to said Indians, natives of this country," said the preamble to the resulting legislation. "Drawn in by small gifts, or for small debts, when they are in drink, and out of capacity for trade, to sign unreasonable bills or bonds for debts, which are soon sued, and great charge brought upon them . . . they have no way to pay the same but by servitude."

Native Americans were by no means the only indentured laborers on Cape Cod and the Islands. As early as 1646 Plymouth colony offered to sell troublesome Indians to plantations in the Caribbean "or exchange them for Negroes." This it proceeded to do most notably after King Philip's War in the 1670s. Europeans were also indentured; their labor could be bought and sold for periods of years. Beginning in the 1640s, orphans and fatherless children were periodically shipped to Massachusetts Bay Colony as "apprentices," and some no doubt found their way to the Cape with emigrants from that colony. Peter Folger of Martha's Vineyard and Nantucket bought his wife, Mary Morrill—Ben Franklin's grandmother—as an indentured servant for twenty pounds. Typically, though, indentured Europeans eventually earned their freedom. And there were Africans. "From 1640 until well after the Revolution, slaves were common in all parts of the Old Colony," wrote Kittredge, "and if there were fewer on the Cape than elsewhere, it was only because there were fewer rich men or extensive landowners." In the 1750s a Truro man known only as Pomp, who was stolen from the Congo by a whaler from that town, hanged himself from a tree. Slave trading wasn't officially banned in Boston until 1788.

As a result, small communities of Americans of African descent existed on Cape Cod and the Islands from the earliest days of European contact. Possibly the first reference to an African in New England was of a "lost blackamoor" reported by William Wood in the 1630s. More typical of the region as a whole are seventeenth-century references to "a Negro woman, valued at 20 pounds" or "my molato servant, Ishmael Lobb" in early Vineyard wills. There were undoubtedly also free African Americans in the region early on; in 1723, a dark-skinned weaver named Africa owned land on Nantucket, and several decades after that there was a black neighborhood there known as "New Guinea." A colonial government officer in 1765 counted forty-six blacks on Martha's Vineyard, which would have been about 2 percent of the population at that time, and the proportion may have been similar on Cape Cod and Nantucket. For the most part, though, it is extremely difficult to know how extensive the African-American population was in any given year.

Further complicating matters, African Americans in the eighteenth and nineteenth centuries intermingled extensively with the declining and equally marginalized—though still much larger—native population. There were a lot of reasons for this, including true love between individuals and greater racial enlightenment on the part of both groups. Before the abolition of slavery there was also the benefit for African men, at least, of knowing their offspring with native women would remain free, which could not be said of their children by spouses of African origin.

What is known is that there were enough people of African origin on Nantucket by the 1720s for them to be specifically discriminated against; in 1723 the town set a curfew for "Indians, Negroes, and other suspected persons . . . If they shall be found upon the wharf and about town after nine of the clock at night, they shall be taken up and carried before a Justice."

Not all was oppression, however. There is some circumstantial evidence that "at least one all-black whaling ship may have sailed from Nantucket" as early as 1788. And in 1822—two years after the *Essex* sailed—a crew of African Americans set off from that island in the *Industry* under Captain Absalom Boston. Boston's mother, Thankful Micah, was Native American. His father, known only as Seneca, was a former slave of William Swain. The voyage apparently was not a great success, and the experiment was not repeated, though Boston remained a person of some influence on the island. Among other things, he led a successful effort to desegregate the local schools.

Similarly, Paul Cuffe's mother, Ruth Moses, was a Vineyard Wampanoag. His father, Kofi, was from the Akan nation of Ghana, from which he was taken and sold around 1720 to the Slocums of Dartmouth, Massachusetts. Being Quakers, the Slocum family eventually saw the light and freed Kofi in the 1740s. They offered him the job of managing their lands on Cuttyhunk, which he accepted. After nearly twenty years in the Elizabeth Islands, Kofi and Moses had ten children and enough wealth from various entrepreneurial undertakings to buy a 116-acre farm back in Dartmouth.

From there, their young son Paul embarked on a truly remarkable life that began with running goods across Vineyard and Nantucket Sounds in defiance of the British blockade during the Revolution. He became a shipbuilder and a commander of whalers and coastal traders. He took on the legal and educational systems of the state of Massachusetts, arguing against being forced to pay taxes without representation. He dabbled in foreign policy. And he ended up quite wealthy, especially considering the racist circumstances in which he operated. If he had chosen to return to the island of his birth instead of living his life on the far side of Buzzards Bay, there would be much more to say about Paul Cuffe in this book.

Despite the few exceptions, like Boston and Cuffe, however, there's no escaping the unsurprising conclusion that real opportunity to command the vessels of Cape Cod and the Islands—and to profit therefrom—was reserved for persons of English origin. Male persons of English origin, to be more specific.

Judging from the number of complaints that came into the general court from all over the state, the 1718 effort to reform the Indian indenture system failed. But by the time the legislature again addressed the issue in 1725, the whaling interests were strong enough to win for Cape Cod, Martha's Vineyard, and Nantucket an exemption from the prohibition on indenturing Indian householders. Under the new law for the Cape and Islands, Indian servitude was regularized at two-year intervals, with employers supposedly helping to provide housing for their workforce. Furthermore, just in case someone had the idea of working off his debt, Indians were required to buy all supplies from the company store of whomever owned their initial debts. As Vickers summed it up, "Fraud had been prohibited, but servitude was now institutionalized."

By 1819, when the owner of the ill-fated *Essex*, Paul Macy, and his chosen captain, George Pollard, were looking for a crew, Nantucket Indians no longer made up a significant portion of the labor force of Nantucket whalers. Sadly, the reason was not that the natives had been emancipated from their debt servitude or had risen with experience to positions of authority in the industry. The reason was that they were virtually extinct as a viable community. From an estimated precolonial population possibly as high as 3,000—as dense as most parts of Europe at the time—the native population of Nantucket dropped to 1,500 by 1675, and then halved again to 750 by 1730. As in Plymouth a century and a half before, the final agent was disease: in 1763 yellow fever killed 222 of the remaining 358 island Indians.

After that, the Native American community on Nantucket slowly dissipated. Some members ended up off-island, on the Vineyard or the mainland. Others simply disappeared into the rich genetic soup that made up the underclass on Cape Cod and the Islands; from the English perspective, if Indians could be reclassified as blacks, one didn't have to spend as much effort justifying how all the land ended up in the hands of non-Indians. The last official Indian on Nantucket—though doubtless not the last on the island with Wampanoag blood—was Abram Quarry, who died in 1854.

Sadly, the decline in the native population of Martha's Vineyard and Cape Cod was almost as severe. There was never open warfare between English and Indians in the region: all native peoples on Cape Cod and the Islands chose not to support Massasoit's son King Philip (Metacomet) during the 1675 war that bears his name. But the familiar cycle of disease and displacement went on as elsewhere. As on Nantucket, there may have been some three thousand Native Americans living on the Vineyard at the time Epenow was born, but by 1680 the number had fallen to one thousand. On the Cape the decline probably began earlier: by 1792, according to one estimate, there were only fifty "pure blood" Indians at Mashpee (at least seventy native Mashpee men died fighting with the First Regiment of Massachusetts in the Revolution).

On neither the Cape nor Martha's Vineyard, however, did the population and culture of the native peoples entirely disappear. The survival of remnant but strong communities of Native Americans on Cape Cod (primarily though not exclusively at Mashpee) and on Martha's Vineyard (primarily though not exclusively at Aquinnah) has many roots. Foremost, of course, is the courage and creativity of the Wampanoag themselves in the face of nearly four centuries of overwhelming pressure to conform, sell out, and conveniently disappear. As early as 1681 a sachem of Aquinnah announced: "Know ye all People that I, Mattack and my principal men, my children and people, are owners of this—this, our land forever . . . no person shall sell any land." And he sold no more, though his children later did.

Perhaps ironically, two crucial early factors favoring the survival of the Wampanoag—when so many other native cultures of New England were eventually diluted and destroyed beyond recognition, even by themselves—appear on the surface to be evidence of assimilation. Most historians of colonial New England note a distinct hardening of English attitudes toward Native Americans after King Philip's War, which, per capita, was the bloodiest in the history of the country. The English came close to losing the war in its early phases, and it took fifty years for them to expand again to the prewar frontier. When they did, they showed far less sympathy for the rights of the original inhabitants. The decision on the part of the Indians of Cape Cod and the Islands not to participate in King Philip's War, and in some cases to fight on the English side, doubtless softened the vengeful instincts of the English in the region.

Amos Smalley and his wife, Lydia, shown here in Gay Head in 1969, were among the last Vineyard Wampanoag to live at Christiantown. Amos was the only whaler known to have killed a white sperm whale. (PHOTOGRAPH BY KATHARINE TWEED, COURTESY OF THE MARTHA'S VINEYARD HISTORICAL SOCIETY)

Of greater significance in the long run was the relative success of Christian missionaries. After his death, the story of Richard Bourne's Mashpee grant for the Indians became a familiar one of hypocrisy and corruption by individuals of all involved races. The upshot has been centuries of disappointment: in 1770, a Wampanoag named Reuben Cognehew went to London to complain to King George III that the Indians of Mashpee were not allowed to govern themselves and came home empty-handed; two hundred years later the Mashpee Wampanoag appealed to the United States government for federal recognition and were denied. Likewise, the history of land appropriation on Martha's Vineyard is as filled with dubious transactions as that of anywhere else in America.* The mixed motives of the European missionaries are easily and justifiably lampooned. But the fact remains that the lands of Aquinnah that were stolen out from under unwilling Wampanoag descendants of the defiant and farsighted Mattack were ultimately bought back for them in 1711 by the London Society for the Propagation of the Gospel, and Bourne's Mashpee grant was the grain of sand around which survival for the Wampanoag of the Cape coalesced.

As Indian populations on both islands fell into the low hundreds and below, native participation in the whaling industry declined precipitously. The year of the last major epidemic on Nantucket was precisely when Crevecoeur visited, and though he reported that there were still some Indians at the oars on the Vineyard, he noted that the days were gone when "it often happened that whale vessels were manned with none but Indians and the master." Native influence remained primarily in the masthead of the ships, where rather than "thar she blows" the traditional cry from the lookout was still *Awaite pawana*, or "Here is a whale." Then, said Crevecoeur, "they all remain still and silent until he repeats *PAWANA*, a whale."

That Crevecoeur put the lookouts in the masthead rather than on a pole planted in the sand of the beach is indicative of another change in the business of whaling that took place by the time of his visit to the islands. There were two hundred seasonal shore whalers in Barnstable in 1715, and the peak year for shore whaling on Nantucket was 1726, when twenty-eight boats "saved" eighty-six whales. But even by then, the most serious whalers were making month-long voyages out to the edge of the Gulf Stream in sloops ranging from fifteen to forty tons. These were built back in the island's remaining woods, a mile from shore, and dragged down to the water on sled by teams of one hundred yoke of oxen.

On the Cape, the progression from salvaging drift whales to going offshore in small boats, and eventually to sea voyages, was driven by the same process of extinguishing the local wild resources and moving on that had driven the whalers' grandparents to establish fur outposts in Maine and Connecticut. By the middle of the eighteenth century, the whales that for millennia came to shallow Cape Cod Bay waters to rear their young came no more. In 1739 only six whales were taken by shore whalers in Provincetown, hardly enough to support even a part-time industry. A decade later, Yarmouth was virtually impoverished by failure of local whale stocks. Forty

---

*Or, for that matter, Canada, Australia, New Zealand, South Africa, and the Caribbean.

men who had made a living from shore whaling left Harwich in 1760 and crossed the sound to Nantucket, presumably to take part in the deep-sea whaling industry that was by then centered on that island.

It was at sea that Nantucket really established and maintained its overwhelming dominance of the whaling industry, a dominance that lasted until the rise of New Bedford and Fairhaven in the mid-1800s. In 1714 there were nine sloops in the whaling fishery out of Nantucket, six of them outfitted for deep water. Fifteen years later there were twenty-five whalers, and Nantucketers began building their own ships. By the 1770s, according to a report to Congress by then–Secretary of State Thomas Jefferson, there were some 150 whaling ships in the Nantucket fleet. They employed 2,025 men and took 26,000 barrels of sperm oil and 4,000 of whale oil. At that time Wellfleet, by contrast, had some thirty whale ships employing 420 sailors. The Vineyard fleet was a dozen ships, Falmouth had 4, and Barnstable, 2.

There were towns on the Cape that helped to pioneer the move to ocean whaling—particularly Truro, Wellfleet, and Provincetown—but, as the eighteenth century rolled into the nineteenth, Cape Cod became better known as the home for crews and captains of great merchant vessels and trans-Atlantic packet ships operating out of Boston and other mainland ports. Many more sailors, still, turned to fishing. By the outbreak of the American Revolution, there were probably in the neighborhood of ten thousand people employed in fishing and processing the catch. On "the other cape," Cape Anne, Gloucester fishermen in their new schooners began in the 1820s to debunk the myth that George's Bank was too dangerous to fish, and the fishermen of Provincetown and other Cape Cod ports followed suit. In the first years they fished with hand lines from the sides of their schooners. Then they set out from their larger ship in small dories and hoped the notorious fog didn't roll in.

Those who didn't fish the banks for cod and other ground fish chased smaller, in-shore game, such as mackerel. When Thoreau was walking along the outer beach he saw the Provincetown and Truro fleet come around the Cape chasing mackerel. It was a thrilling sight: "countless numbers, schooner after schooner, till they made a city on the water. They were so thick that many appeared to be afoul of one another; now all standing on this tack, now on that."

Although Nantucket, like the Cape, eventually experienced a decline in prey along its shore, it wasn't scarcity alone that first drove their whalers to deeper waters; it was a howling gale. In 1712, Christopher Hussey, probably the son of one of the twenty original purchasers of Nantucket, went out in a small boat whaling on the Nantucket South Shoals and was blown to sea by a winter storm. When the storm had quieted enough to allow the crew to look around, they found themselves in the middle of a school of spouting spermaceti whales.

Sperm whales are creatures of the deep ocean and rarely come near enough to land to be hunted by shore whalers, so the usual prey of whalers up to that point had been right whales. They were the "right" whales to hunt primarily because their carcasses floated, allowing them to be towed back to shore. For a long time, a right whale meant any whale with baleen and oil; eventually, though, the Cape and Islanders learned to differentiate between the humpbacks, bowheads, and true Atlantic right whales.

The whales Hussey found himself surrounded by were different, however. Sperm and right whales can look similar if seen together at sea; both are black (unless they are white), both grow to about eighty feet. But only the sperm whale has the boxy head of cartoon cetaceans; the lower jaw is long and slender. What's more, a sperm whale has one bushy spout that shoots distinctly forward from near the front of its head, while a right whale produces two vapory jets that rise somewhat farther back on the beast. Of more interest to nineteenth-century whalers than spouts and profiles, sperm whales have forty to sixty teeth on their lower jaws instead of the right whale's valuable baleen on its upper jaw. But in the eyes of commerce, the quality of sperm oil more than made up for the loss of whalebone.

Hussey may or may not have known the implications of where he had stuck his iron. At least one sperm whale had drifted ashore within living memory on Nantucket. And in all likelihood, other lone cachalot, as they were also called, had occasionally been encountered. The oil rendered from those rare sperm whales was far superior to the usual right-whale oil. Even more valuable than the oil was the spermaceti, or head matter, stored in a tubular cavity in the sperm whale's head. This spermaceti was literally worth its weight in silver, as it could be crafted into the finest candles in the world. Finally, occasionally the bowels of a sperm whale yielded a lump of that waxy and odoriferous substance called ambergris, which was literally worth its weight in gold to makers of perfumes.*

---

*The first industrial revolution would have been quite different without the myriad whale products: oil was its lubricant and much of its light, bone was its plastic. In his book *Whales*,

If Hussey didn't know he had struck gold when he and his crew stuck a harpoon into one of the strange, square-nosed whales, he certainly found out not long after getting the prize back to Nantucket.

The realization that spermaceti whales were neither as rare nor as solitary as previously imagined first caused whaling cruises to creep in length to over a month, then even longer, as the technology improved. Beginning around the 1720s, portable try works were carried on board. This enabled ships to boil the oil out of blubber on any convenient shore, often to the

---

poet Heathcoat Williams attempted a nearly complete list: "For fuel;/For lamps/And candle-wax, to turn night into day;/For whale-oil appliances for sweat-shops,/And factories;/For domestic lighting;/For street lighting;/For shop lighting;/For flexible baleen filaments for watch-springs, umbrellas, toys and upholstery,/Even the springs in the first typewriter . . . //Millions and millions and millions died in a marine holocaust, /Generating the implacable human appetite for electricity,/petroleum and plastic.//For soap, to be returned, mixed with dirt, into the sea;/For margarine;/For glycerol for lipstick, and the idle fantasy world of beauticians;/For detergents, from whose froth modern advertising was spawned;/For glycerine for nitro-glycerine, to blow a hole in the human herd;/For brushes and brooms;/For linoleum;/For medical trusses;/For oilcloth;/For sausage skins;/For drum-skins;/For sword-hilts and scabbards;/For laces;/For surgical stitches;/For tennis racket strings;/For varnishes;/For parchment;/For printing inks;/For insecticide;/For calcium for Blanco, and military purification;/For calcium for fertilizer, to speed up the gestation of the earth;/For the jute industry/For the wool industry;/For the cotton industry;/For tempering steel . . . //Without the blood-letting of the whale:/Prime source of light and lubrication,/The industrial revolution would have been scantily equipped./A spectral colossus haunts the inflated myth of progress,/So keen to brush aside its hidden costs,/In the cause of pure profit;/So forgetful in the bright name of novelty./For paint;/For skin cream;/For stock-cubes;/For cattle fencing;/For mah-jongg counters;/For iodine;/For endocrinal hormones for those stiffened by arthritis;/For liver-oil and vitamins to treat those who are flagging;/For insulin from the pancreas to treat those whose blood is too sweet;/For gelatin for the coating of photographic film,/With which we see ourselves as we see ourselves, incessantly;/For gelatin for the transparent capsules of pills;/For gelatin for jelly;/For gelatin for glue;/For stays, and gussets, and busks, and bodices,/And statuesque corsetry, emphasizing the breasts and hips:/The aesthetic apparatus, the sensual sustenance/of empire building . . . //For fish-bait;/For cattle-meal;/For the food supplies to fur-farms;/For dog-food;/For cat-food;/For the fermentation process in the manufacture of antibiotics;/For oiling the automatic transmission systems of automobiles;/For anti-freeze;/For low-calorie cooking fat;/For shortening for bread, and pastry, and cakes;/For hair treatments;/For bath essence;/For steaks: sashimi slices and marinated yamotami,/For kujira nabe and obayuki soup,/For whale-meat rissoles;/For whale-meat stew;/For pipes, for piano keys, for ear-rings, for brooches, for cuff-links;/For cigarette holders;/For shoe-horns;/For car-wax;/For shoe-polish;/For plasticiser;/For fishing-rods;/For machine oil . . . //For ambergris, burned in religious ceremonies/To put you in good odour with the Almighty;/For cosmetics, to put you in good odour with each other."

chagrin of local populations, who more than once rebelled at the resulting stench. In the 1740s ships began carrying try pots and brick furnaces installed right on deck so that blubber could be boiled down to oil at sea rather than having to be taken ashore. These "factory ships" opened the door to the extraordinary multiyear voyages of the century that followed.

The whalers of Nantucket and elsewhere never stopped hunting the right whale, or for that matter virtually any other animal that could be boiled down for oil. Only the right and other baleen whales produced whalebone, about ten pounds of it for each barrel of oil. (The sperm whale feeds primarily on giant squid and so doesn't need the baleen used by the other great whales to strain plankton and small fish and shrimp out of immense mouthfuls of seawater.) As the industrial revolution picked up steam, the light, flexible whalebone came to rival oil as a salable commodity, fetching a higher price per pound even than spermaceti. No whaler on any sea was unhappy to find a shoal of right whales. But sperm whales were the trophy species, the whales that could make a lucky captain or even an officer rich in a single voyage; they made fabulous fortunes for various Macys, Starbucks, Coffins, and others. Prices varied according to supply and demand, but sperm oil typically brought twice the price of the darker, more odoriferous oil of the right whale.

Whalers followed the whales first to the edge of the Gulf Stream, which, according to Ben Franklin, they were the first to really understand. The Gulf Stream, in turn, led them south to the Hatteras grounds, then on to the coast of Cuba, north to the Banks of Newfoundland, and then east to the Azores and Madeira. From there it was just a jump over to the coastal waters of Africa, which whalers may have heard were full of game from slavers out of Rhode Island. (Though it was apparently rare, a few whalers sidelined in the slave trade.)

Sperm whales were what Captain David Smith and Captain Gamaliel Collins of Truro were after in the south Atlantic when they became the first to hunt whales at the Falkland (Malvinas) Islands in 1774. Sperm whales made the "Brazeel grounds," discovered that same year, famous, until they were fished thin. The resulting absence of whales off Brazil lured the Nantucket whaler *Beaver* around Cape Horn in 1791 to the west coast of South America and the "onshore grounds" there. James Shields of Nantucket had done the same the year before with great success. But the inevitable demise of whales there a few decades later tempted George W. Gardner to turn west in 1818.

Twenty-six months later, Gardner was back in Nantucket with the first two-thousand-barrel cargo of sperm oil ever, which he quickly sold for more than sixty thousand dollars. Gardner had found what became known as the "offshore grounds," one of the richest whaling areas of all. And it was there, one thousand miles off the coast of Peru, that Captain Pollard and the crew of the *Essex* hoped to get rich themselves.

CHAPTER 18

OVER THE BAR

George Pollard Jr. was twenty-eight years old when Paul Macy and his partners considered giving him the opportunity to command the three-masted ship *Essex* on a whaling voyage around the horn to the Pacific. It would be something of a risk for Macy, who owned the ship along with several partners, in that the young man had never before commanded a vessel. But Pollard had already proven his mettle in the usual manner, working his way up through the ranks on a series of earlier whaling cruises. He had served as the first mate on the previous voyage of the *Essex*, which was a great success. After only two years at sea, the ship had returned to Nantucket with more than 1,200 barrels of sperm oil and 160 barrels of whale oil in the hold. That was what was known as a "greasy" voyage; greasy enough to convince the previous captain, Daniel Russell, to retire from the sea. So Pollard, as one member of his crew later said, was "considered fully competent to command any ship in the whaling service."

What's more, Paul Macy no doubt knew that Pollard was related to the Coffin family. In the 1650s Coffins and Macys founded the English settlement on Nantucket together. In all likelihood it was originally Thomas and Sarah Macy's idea, but their neighbors on the Merrimack River, Tristram and Dionis Coffin, were in on the plan from the beginning. The Coffins put up much of the money and ultimately controlled five of the twenty shares in "the propriety," as the common land on the island was called.

A generation later, it was Mary Coffin Starbuck who, beginning around

1701, spearheaded the rise of Quakerism among the old-guard families on Nantucket. According to the visiting evangelist responsible for her conversion, after listening to him for an hour "she submitted to the Power of Truth and the doctrines thereof and lifted up her voice and wept: Oh! Then the universal cry and brokenness of heart and tears was wonderful!" Nantucket lore traditionally has it that her influence—she was fifty-six years old at the time and known as the "great woman"—was such that the entire island followed her into the Society of Friends shortly thereafter. There is no doubt that the daughter of old Tristram Coffin was a doyen of sorts among the powerful families on the island.

But both the speed with which Quakerism caught fire on the island and the degree to which it ultimately dominated have often been exaggerated. The Christianized native population, in particular, was steadfastly Congregational thanks in part to the efforts of the Mayhews and other missionaries in the decades before and after the sale of the island to the Macy-Coffin partners. What's more, it wasn't really until a grandson of Thomas Macy married a Quaker and the leading Macy families left their small group of Baptist worshipers to become Quakers in 1712 that the Society of Friends cemented its position as more than the Starbuck family religion. From that point on it grew rapidly; the meeting house was expanded in 1716 to hold more than three hundred people. By 1764, two thousand Friends could gather in the great meeting house. It was never the universal faith, but it was, essentially, the official religion of the Nantucket oligarchy.

Not that all members of the Macy and Coffin clans always saw eye to eye over the intervening generations. Far from it. During the big half-share revolt of the 1670s, various tradesmen and newcomers under the leadership of the Gardner family questioned the privileges of the old, full-share proprietors. In that dispute, various Macys were among the only fully vested Nantucketers to inexplicably side for a time with the half-share men rather than with their traditional peers, who were led by the now aged and infuriated Tristram Coffin. What's more, Mary Coffin Starbuck notwithstanding, not all the Coffins became Quakers. And not all the Quaker Coffins were considered by the Society to be good Friends. The best known of these was Kezia Coffin, a loyalist cousin of Ben Franklin's, who used her connections with the British government to turn her smuggling operation into a virtual monopoly on off-island products during the American Revolution. There were many reasons her neighbors didn't like Kezia Coffin— her house was too fancy, her prices too exorbitant—but the official reason she was "set aside" by a Quaker meeting in 1774 was her refusal to give up her new spinet. Other members were regularly disowned for marrying non-Quakers.

Only two dozen years before the final voyage of the *Essex*, an all-out feud erupted between the powerful Silvanus Macy, a Quaker, and the equally patriarchal William Coffin, a Congregationalist, over who exactly had masterminded the great bank heist of 1795. On a June night, three men with keys made from old spoons got away with twenty thousand dollars in gold from the vault of the brand-new Nantucket Bank, apparently loading the loot onto a sloop and sailing away. Macy, who was a bank director (and an early owner of the *Essex*), led a faction that accused Coffin, the bank president, of being in on the burglary. "The scandal pitted not only Quaker against Congregationalist, Democrat against Federalist," wrote Philbrick, "it also put members of the same family at each other's throats."

Ultimately Coffin was neither convicted nor, in the minds of most island Quakers, entirely exonerated. But he had apparently had enough of the old ways on the island. In 1810, he and several other powerful Nantucketers did the previously unthinkable and petitioned to have their shares of the common land—which was the vast majority of the island—converted into private property. The old-guard opposition was again led by Coffin's nemesis Silvanus Macy, but this time Coffin won. At first, only the "Great Set-Off" demanded by Coffin and his allies was split from the common land, but it was only a matter of time before the old proprietary was fragmented beyond recognition.

But by the time Paul Macy was looking for a replacement captain for the *Essex*, all of that was in the past, if not yet entirely healed. Besides, the differences between the various leading families of Nantucket had rarely if ever been allowed to interfere with the true passion of the island, which was whaling. If a Macy with a ship couldn't find another Macy or a Starbuck or perhaps a Folger to put at the helm, then a Coffin or a Swain or a Worth was just as good. And as for Pollard never having commanded a vessel before, people averse to risk were not in the shipping business in general, and not in the whaling business in particular. It was unusual but not rare that men were given command after only two previous voyages.

So Macy offered Pollard the *Essex*, and he accepted the job at the beginning of April, 1819. Presumably, he got right to work helping to assemble a crew, though he, like Melville's Ahab, may have left all such preliminary duties to the owners. During his brief months on shore, Pollard found time to woo and marry Mary Riddell.

Whoever actually hired the *Essex* crew, he didn't have far to look for a first mate. Just as Pollard himself was promoted from mate to captain, one of the boatsteerers from the previous voyage, Owen Chase, got Pollard's old job of first mate. The twenty-two-year-old Chase was five feet ten inches tall, had dark hair, and, like the new captain, was connected to several of the founding English families of Nantucket. On his mother's side, his lineage went back to Peter Folger, who came to Nantucket from Martha's Vineyard to act as the original Coffins' and Macys' intermediary with the native population.

Along with the Folgers on Chase's maternal side of the family tree are a generous sprinkling of another original Nantucket family, the Swains. And like Pollard, Chase was newly married to a woman from yet another old-guard lineage, the Gardners. On his father's side, meanwhile, First Mate Chase's roots went back to the founding of Yarmouth. His great-great-great-great-great-grandparents William and Mary Chase settled there in 1638 after living for eight years in the Massachusetts Bay Colony. What induced Owen Chase's grandparents to move from the ancestral turf of Cape Cod to Nantucket in the middle of the 1700s is not clear, though it may have been related to an out-of-wedlock pregnancy that resulted in the birth of Owen's father, Judah Chase. It apparently did not have anything to do with the collapse of shore whaling on the Cape around that time, which prompted the removal to Nantucket of more than a few other coofs, as off-islanders were scornfully called. Owen's father was a farmer.

Owen Chase is arguably the most famous of the *Essex* survivors, though not because of his later successes at the helm of more fortunate whaling vessels. In 1821, only eight months after his rescue, he completed and published what became the standard narrative of the ship's disaster.* The little book was passed among the literate members of later whaling crews and read with horror. On one such whaler in the middle of the Pacific, the *Acushnet*, under the command of a Captain Valentine Pease of the Vineyard, a young mariner with literary aspirations borrowed a copy of the narrative from Owen Chase's own son. "The reading of this wondrous story upon

---

*There is unanimity among historians and whaling buffs that Chase had the help of a local ghostwriter; who exactly it was, however, is still grist for pages. Chase rather admirably, at least from the perspective of the age of Oprah, confessed his motives up front: "The hope of obtaining something of a remuneration, by giving a short history of my sufferings to the world, must therefore constitute my claim to public attention."

the landless sea, & close to the very latitude of the shipwreck had a surprising effect on me," Herman Melville later recalled. Later, when Melville was nearly finished writing *Moby-Dick*, his father-in-law sent him a copy of the narrative. The novelist filled the margins with checks and x-marks and squiggly lines at passages that particularly appealed to him. He wrote a dozen or so pages of additional thoughts and notes on blank pages bound into the book before and after the text.

Interestingly, First Mate Chase wasn't the only one on the *Essex* with roots stretching back to the establishment of an early Cape Cod town. Fourteen-year-old Thomas Nickerson, who signed on as ship's boy, was a direct descendant of the William Nickerson who in 1641 was run out of Yarmouth by the local hierarchy (possibly including the patriarchal William Chase) for being a "Scoffer and jeerer of religion." The ancestral Nickerson went on to make numerous unauthorized purchases of land from the Nausets, purchases that eventually became the nucleus of the town of Chatham.

The Nickersons were a prolific bunch. In the multivolume Nickerson family genealogy, housed in the Nickerson Room of the Cape Cod Community College Library in Barnstable, are listed Nickersons in almost every corner of the Cape and Islands. One Nickerson grandfather paid seventy-one pounds for the privilege of sitting in the pew next to the door in church. Another was assessed for taxes on 4,400 feet of salt-making vats in Chatham. There are Nickersons in every possible profession, but most conspicuous are the number of Cape Cod Nickersons who went to sea: Captain Alexander, Captain Augustus, and Captains James, Moses, and Nathan Nickerson, Captains S. S., Warren, William, and Zenas Nickerson, and many more.

A Nickerson cousin, also named Thomas, was mysteriously murdered at sea in 1746 on his ship *Abigail*. Another cousin, Sparrow Nickerson, and a brother-in-law were also found on the deck of the *Abigail* in a mess of gore and blood. The sole survivor, Ansell Nickerson, was tried twice for murder but acquitted both times. Pirates came aboard, he told the juries, and killed the others while he hid himself in the water, hanging on to a line off the stern.

There was also a certain Captain David Nickerson who, local rumor had it, was rearing the lost dauphin of France in Brewster. Apparently a distraught woman with a veil approached him in the streets of Paris during the French Revolution and gave him an infant. The babe's name, she said, was Rene Rousseau. How exactly the captain's neighbors back on Cape Cod became convinced that this Rene Rousseau was in fact the heir to the throne of the Sun King is unexplained, but he clearly grew up to be a Nickerson. The lost dauphin went to sea, became a captain, and at twenty-five years old was lost again—this time at sea, and this time for good.

David Nickerson wasn't the only Cape Codder caught up in the French Revolution. (Nor, for that matter, was Rousseau the only suspected lost dauphin on the Cape. There was also the glass blower Gaffer Bonique.) David Nickerson's former captain, Elijah Cobb of Barnstable, went to sea to help support his widowed mother at the unbelievable age of six. At thirteen he was back home with a hernia, but again signed up for a voyage one year later. By twenty-four he was, like his lost-at-sea father, a merchant captain. He sailed several times to the West Indies, presumably to make the usual exchange of the salt cod fed to African slaves for the molasses produced by African slaves. And then, in 1794, he made his first trans-Atlantic voyage in a brig named *Jane*, bound for Cadiz. Because America was then at war with the dey of Algiers—a North African of ill repute who persisted in enslaving obviously white American sailors caught passing into the Mediterranean—Cobb headed first to the northern Spanish port of Corunna to ask about conditions through the Strait of Gibraltar. On his way in, he was captured by a French frigate flying the relatively new flag of Liberté, Egalité, Fraternité, and was taken to Brest.

Presumably in the name of those ideals, Cobb's papers were promptly confiscated and his cargo of rice and wheat distributed among the half-starved population of the town. "All was anarchy & confusion," Cobb later wrote in his memoirs, "the galliotine [was] in continual operation, & their streets & public squares, drenched with human blood—I minuted down 1,000 persons that I saw beheaded by that infernal machine; and probably saw as many more that I did not note down, men, women, priests & laymen of all ages." It was, Cobb said, "a very unpleasant predicerment" in which to find himself. Yet even with heads rolling all around him, Cobb's sense of fair play led him to hold out hope that if he could only recover his papers, he might get paid for his cargo, which after all didn't belong to him but to the owners of his ship. The problem was that no one could tell him who exactly had his papers. Finally, after six weeks of pestering local officials, he was informed that without his knowledge of any proceedings he had been duly tried and a verdict had been found. The good news was that he was innocent and would naturally be reimbursed.

The bad news was, it was illegal to take currency out of the country. It was illegal to take gold. "Goods, also, were out of the question, as was foreign currency." Government bills payable in England or America? Not possible, he was told. But, since he was very insistent, a solution was offered. If he would leave France and go to Germany, the French agents in Hamburg would surely pay him in sixty days. "I finally agreed," Cobb later recalled. But after another month of waiting he still had no paperwork to take to Germany. He sent the *Jane* home under the command of the first mate and decided to go to Paris.

"Many difficulties were to be surmounted, in order to attain this object," he later recalled. Because all horses had been requisitioned by the revolutionary government, his only hope was to get a ride with one of the "national dispatches," though it was technically illegal for them to take passengers. But his "mind was fixed upon going," he said, and so armed with multiple copies of his recorded efforts thus far—"as I had learned, that losing a man's papers was one of their methods of procrastination"—he went to the local power broker. The man hemmed and hawed, and repeatedly rubbed his neck, which Cobb surmised was "to see how it would bear the knife."

Ultimately the necessary permits were produced, and two days later Cobb and the mailman set off together in a bulletproof carriage surrounded by five to nine armed horsemen. There was also "a blunderbuss, loaded, in front." For 684 miles they sat in back, each with a pair of loaded pistols and neither capable of speaking the other's language.

On the second morning, they passed the remains of the previous courier, "laying in the road, the Master, the Postilion, & five horses laying dead, & mangled by it, & the mail mutilated and scattered in all directions." Some papers, it seemed, *were* legitimately lost. Cobb was made to understand that the unfortunate mail carrier had come to the spot where he was supposed to meet his evening guard—at night the security detail increased to as many as twenty-four riders—but there was no guard present. The penalty for not delivering the mail was the guillotine, though, so he went on and was ambushed.

It was not a happy moment when the next night the evening guard for Cobb and his companion failed to materialize. Like their predecessor, they elected to go forward. "Thus we drove on, Jehu like, without stopping," Cobb wrote later, "taking occasionally, as we run, a mouthful of bread, and washing it down, with some low priced, red Burgundy wine."

Their luck held, and finally after seventy-four sleepless hours they arrived in Paris at four A.M. on what Cobb remembered as "a beautiful June

morning." The only English the Cape Codder had heard en route was in
the village of Alançon, where a man in a tattered uniform approached him
as they were changing horses and said out of the blue, "For the love of
God, my dear Sir, do permit me to shake hands with one who comes from
that country where the great and beloved Washington resides."

At the office that was supposed to have received his complaint from
Brest, Cobb was told that they had never heard of him, never heard of his
boat, never heard of a problem like this before. So Cobb produced his
copies, which were notarized, and was told to return the following day.
When he did, the copies were mysteriously gone, and no one could recall
very well what had happened the day before. No one remembered putting
them away. No one remembered passing them along. No one remembered
receiving them. "And finally, after a long French jabber, it was concluded,
that they must have been left upon the counter, brushed off, & burned,
among the [loose] papers," Cobb later wrote in his memoirs.

It's hard to imagine that young Captain Cobb wasn't disheartened as
he made his way back to his hotel. Once there, as he drafted a request to
Brest for yet another set of papers, the man who was staying in the room
next door invited himself in for a visit. He was French, and he had some
advice. The only thing to do, he told the American, was to go to Robespierre himself.

Cobb was incredulous.

Mais, non, said his neighbor. *You must know that the Sea Green Incorruptible,*
as Robespierre was known, *is famously fond of Americans.* All Cobb had to do
was take care to write his note "in the republican style" and send it by hotel
courier. So he did: "An American citizen, captured by a French Frigate on
the high seas, requests a personal interview; & to lay his grievances before
citizen Roberspiere. Very Respectfully, E. Cobb." An hour later, a message
arrived written in Robespierre's own hand: "I will grant Citizen Cobb an
interview to morrow at 10 A.M."

Citizen Cobb was not late. Robespierre said nothing when the Cape
Codder was shown into the room but merely pointed to a chair. Robespierre waved the interpreter out of the room so that the two men were
alone. His English, Cobb thought, was very good. He wanted more details
on a few parts of the story, particularly about the business of lost papers.
He must simply go to an office in Rue St. Honoré, the office of the Second
Department, and demand his papers, the revolutionary leader advised. Cobb
explained that he had been to that office so many times that he now was
formally banned from the premises.

Sacra coquin, Cobb remembered citizen Robespierre exclaiming. The Sea Green Incorruptible then said he hated using his personal influence in a merely commercial situation, but he had no choice. "Go . . . to that office, & tell citizen F.T. that you came from Robespierre, and if he does not produce your papers, & finish your business immediately, he will hear from me again, in a way not so pleasing to him." He made Cobb promise to let him know the outcome.

Whether citizen F.T., like his colleague back in Brest, had a nervous habit of rubbing his neck, Cobb doesn't say. But F.T. did happily report that the missing papers had been found—or weren't actually necessary—and he was sorry for citizen Cobb's inconvenience. Cobb did have to go to Germany to collect his money, but he was eventually paid. He never got to report back to his new friend citizen Robespierre, though. Before he left Paris, "the great man, who had so essentially befriended me, was beheaded by the Galliotine." Cobb's description of those dramatic final moments of the Reign of Terror on the Ninth Thermidore are a study in classic Cape Cod reticence. There is no mention of the angry crowds, the women clutching dead babies, or of Robespierre's mangled jaw from his botched last-minute suicide attempt. Cobb says only: "Before I left the country; I saw Robertspiers head taken off, by the same Machine—But to return to my individual, and embarrassed affairs . . ."

When he finally returned to New England, the owners of the *Jane* were not disappointed with his efforts. After a four-day visit to Barnstable, where his daughter—who was a day old when he left—was now talking, he went back to France with another load of flour. Again the cargo was taken by the government, again it took him ten months of wrangling to get paid, and this time he only got his money out by sewing three thousand gold pieces into a pair of belts. He spent a few days home in Barnstable, and then he was off again, to Germany, where an attack of "the brain fever" caused all his hair to fall out.

Years went by this way for Cape Cod families like the Cobbs and the Nickersons. Cobb spent the better part of his adulthood smuggling rum to Ireland, and wheat to France, and bribing his way through Gibraltar, with only occasional visits home to see the beloved Mrs. Cobb and the children born while he was away.

"After discharging my cargo in Boston, I visited my dear family, at the Cape where I found an additional pledge of affection, in a little black-eyed daughter, which we called Mary P, then 69 days old," Cobb wrote. "It being in the night & no light in the house, I hauled her out of Bed, and held her up to the window to look at her by moonlight."

That was in 1805 or 1806, just about the time the young Thomas Nickerson, who sailed as ship's boy on the *Essex*, was born in Harwich. Nickerson spent only the first six months of his life on the Cape before moving with his parents to North Water Street on Nantucket. Both parents died within a year of the move, and young Thomas was raised by his grandfather, Captain Robert Gibson.

Like First Mate Owen Chase, Nickerson ultimately survived the *Essex* and became a successful whaling captain in his own right. He, too, wrote an extended account of the voyage and its aftermath, though not until he was an old man long retired from the waves. He wrote his version in 1876 at the request of a novelist of significantly lesser stature than Melville named Leon Lewis. Lewis never got around to turning it into anything before he died; all that remained of the narrative for generations of Melville scholars and whaling buffs was a tantalizing mention of the project in Nickerson's obituary. Finally, though, almost a century later, the manuscript turned up. It was found in the attic of the home that once belonged to the forgotten novelist's Connecticut neighbors by a couple with the good sense to send it to the Nantucket Historical Association.

Thomas Nickerson, as ship's boy, was the youngest member of the crew, but he wasn't the only Nantucket teenager to sign up. Barzillai Ray was seventeen, and Owen Coffin and Charles Ramsdell were both sixteen at the time of the disaster. Most of the rest of the crew of the *Essex* were fairly typical for the period in Nantucket, which is to say both officers and officers-in-training were locals. The second mate was twenty-six-year-old Matthew Joy, an islander who had been married for two years when he left. Two of the boatsteerers, twenty-year-old Obed Hendricks and twenty-one-year-old Benjamin Lawrence, were from Nantucket as well.

Only one officer, the lowly third boatsteerer, was not from Nantucket. He was a prankster named Thomas Chapple, from Plymouth, England; he also left behind a brief account of the voyage. Also from off-island were two young buddies from Barnstable named Seth Weeks and William Wright. They sailed before the mast, as did Isaac Cole, from Rochester, Massachusetts, Joseph West, and one other sailor whose name is not remembered in any of the accounts.

The *Essex* herself was older than a fair number of her crew. Built in 1799 in Amesbury, Massachusetts, the ship was originally meant for use in the China trade that was centered in Salem, but perhaps because the Far East traders were already beginning to look for faster, more glamorous vessels, after only five years her original owners sold the ship to Silvanus Macy of Nantucket. At some point she made a voyage to hunt seals, but ultimately Macy and his partners converted the *Essex* into a whaler.

When Nickerson and the other new crew members from Nantucket reported to the wharf for duty, they found waiting for them a black hull virtually devoid of all rigging. She was eighty-seven feet seven inches long, with two decks, three masts, a square stern, no gallery, and no figurehead— which is to say, not pretty. The *Essex* looked, Nickerson later recalled, "very much like the picture I have seen of Noah's Ark and from which one accustomed to the more modern ship would have turned in disgust."

In the opinion of a sailor or officer in the merchant marine at that time, or at any time, really, whalers were ugly vessels as a rule. "A 'spouter' we knew her to be as soon as we saw her, by her cranes and boats, and by her stump top-gallant mast, and a certain slovenly look to the sails, rigging, spars, and hull," wrote Richard Henry Dana Jr. in his classic sea memoir, *Two Years before the Mast*. "And when we got aboard we found everything to correspond in spouter fashion." He went on, "her rigging was slack and turning white, paint worn off the spars and blocks, clumsy seizing, straps without courses, and 'homeward bound' splices in every direction."

Nor were the men who sailed on "blubber boilers" ever up to the standards of the merchant ships: "the men looked more like fishermen and farmers than they did like sailors," recalled Dana with a snort. It took thirty whalers half an hour to go aloft and furl the sails, a job Dana thought his own crew of eighteen could do in half the time. The rivalry took on strong regional overtones on Cape Cod and the Islands, particularly because during the same century and a half that Nantucket outclassed its neighbors at whaling, dozens of Cape Cod captains like Elijah Cobb and David Nickerson earned that place a reputation as the foremost breeding ground for merchant commanders. Presumably, *Two Years before the Mast* was not a particularly popular book in Nantucket and Edgartown.

As for the ships themselves, not even the most die-hard whaler from the Islands could make the case that a whaler was more beautiful than the vessels commanded by his neighbors on the Cape. This was true even before the latter's transition to exquisitely sharp-lined, gilt-edged clippers in the middle decades of the 1800s. Whalers, one writer reported, were as a rule "heavy, bluf-bowed and stubby crafts that were designed with fine contempt for speed, comfort, and appearance." The masts were never raked glamorously back, as on a clipper, nor were they endowed with skysails and other extravagances of speed. Likewise, rather than carrying massive spars capable of supporting acres of sail, whalers were designed to be short-sparred so that the ships could be handled by as few as three men when the rest were out spearing leviathans.

Even converted merchant vessels such as the *Essex* looked like the factory ships they were. There was a crow's nest on every mast, sometimes just a barrel lashed to the top. There was the great pile of bricks and kettles—the try works—amidships. There were davits along both sides for the whaleboats, at least five, and the spare whaleboats lashed on deck. And worst of all, perhaps, there was a superstition among some whalers that cleaning away the dirt and grime that accumulated on the masts of a ship would bring bad luck, so the ships were left even fouler than they needed to be.

But whalers, including Owen Chase in his narrative, were quick to defend "the character and standing of a captain of a whale-ship, which those of the merchant service affect so much to undervalue."* If the whaling ship at sea occasionally looked threadbare and paint-peeled, it was precisely because no one stayed at sea as long or poked into more obscure corners of the salty world than a whaler. The clippers built at East Dennis by Asa Shiverick may have been fast and beautiful, but whaling crews knew looks and speed were never as important as luck. And after her first voyages, the *Essex* was considered a lucky ship.

Though the green hands who came aboard sometime during the beginning of August 1819 may have grumbled about working without "any compensation save the privilege of going to sea in the ship," they nonetheless spent a week thoroughly refitting the *Essex*. When they were finished, according to Chase, she was "in all respects a sound, substantial vessel." All that remained to do was get her over the bar and provisioned.

The bar: it was Nantucket's bane, and one of several reasons the island eventually lost control of the industry it helped to create. It was a belt of

---

*Not all whalers-turned-writers agreed: in *Typee*, Melville wrote of his fellow crew members on the *Acushnet*: "With a very few exceptions our crew was composed of a parcel of dastardly and mean-spirited wretches, divided among themselves and only united in enduring without resistance the unmitigated tyranny of the captain."

New Bedford's whaling docks with barrels of oil, circa 1890. (CORBIS/BETTMANN)

sand that stretched across the mouth of the harbor from Madaket to Great Point, leaving only six feet of water at low tide. This was plenty of clearance in the early days of shore whaling in small schooners. But for any vessel over 100 tons, which is to say almost all the ships used in the Pacific, the bar was a potential problem. The *Essex*, according to her first register, had a displacement of 238 tons ("and seventy two ninety fifths") and a depth of twelve feet two inches.

The only way such a vessel could be gotten out of Nantucket Harbor was to take it over the bar virtually empty at high tide, then ferry the cargo out to it in smaller boats. Likewise, when brought in, "lighters" would have to be sent out to bring casks of whale oil and tons of whalebone off. In 1839 the Nantucketers built "the camel," a sort of floating dry dock that could pick up a loaded ship and carry it across the bar. But like the lighters, it was not only expensive but also impractical in bad weather. Foul weather was, of course, precisely when a ship most needed to be able to get into a harbor. The innkeepers and tavern owners of Edgartown and New Bedford loved Nantucket's bar. As the nineteenth century progressed, they did a good business in all weather: Edgartown, wrote Henry Beetle Hough, was for many years a port of Nantucket.

Only when a ship was in the deeper water could it be laded with enough salt pork and fresh water for, in the *Essex*'s case, two and a half years—not to mention the harpoons, ropes, spare sails, clothing, tools for cutting blubber and cleaning whalebone, staves and hoops for oil casks, timber for repairs, trade goods for all manner of natives, and rum for sailors.

Even after the cargo was carefully stowed away and the lists were checked and rechecked, the *Essex* wasn't quite ready to sail. The fifteen men and boys already mentioned were not the ship's entire complement. The remainder of the crew consisted of a half dozen African Americans who were hired in Boston, presumably through a recruiting agent. They came by packet and, according to Nickerson's account, didn't arrive until the day after the *Essex* was fully loaded.

One of these six men, William Bond, served as the ship's steward. Another, a New Yorker named Richard Peterson, was about sixty years old and thus relatively aged to be shipping out. Of the other four, Samuel Reed, Charles Shorter, Isaiah Shepherd, and Lawson Thomas, little is known but their names. Little, that is, but the fact that like William Bond, Richard Peterson, Owen Coffin, Joseph West, Matthew Joy, Isaac Cole, Obed Hendricks, and Barzillai Ray, they would not live to see Nantucket again.

CHAPTER 19

SANKATY HEAD

On August 12, 1819, when Captain Pollard at last gave the order to weigh anchor and set sail, the crew of the *Essex* did not exactly snap to their stations. Not that they weren't anxious to go: after weeks of scraping, painting, splicing, and loading, the order to get under way was one "that all were overjoyed to hear," wrote Nickerson. The problem was rather that most members of "the cheerful crew" didn't know their spritsails from their topgallants.

"It would certainly have been very amusing to Seaman to have watched our motions whilst getting the ship under way," Nickerson recalled. "In fact all was bustle, Confusion and awkwardness, that is, on part of the crew. The officers were smart, active men and were no doubt something piqued at having such a display of awkwardness in full view of their native town." Perhaps—but whale ships were in the habit of shipping the greenest of crews, so most Nantucketers were probably quite used to enjoying the sight of a large vessel careening off toward the Pacific with sails luffing sloppily and sheets and halyards flying out of inexperienced hands. More than once, when the wind was onshore, the pious Islanders doubtless heard the voices of red-faced officers howling ineffectual orders at the top of their lungs wafting across the waters of Nantucket Harbor.

It wasn't only the Quaker tradition of economy that explained the practice of signing up landlubbers, though that was no doubt part of the equation. Unlike the professional seamen of merchant vessels, who were paid a fixed salary based on their rank and the expected length of the voyage, whalers received a lay, or share of the profits from the voyage. The system was derived from the earliest days of shore whaling, when all were partners and shared relatively evenly in the catch. But as the length of ships and cruises grew along with the capital necessary to undertake a voyage, owner-captains took an ever larger slice of the profits. By the 1820s the typical range might go from a $\frac{1}{16}$ share for the captain (in addition to whatever ownership stake he might have), to a rather minuscule $\frac{1}{200}$ share for ship's boys.* First Mate Chase's lay on the *Essex* was $\frac{1}{64}$.

The upshot was that while an able-bodied sailor on a merchant ship probably earned more than his bottom-rung whaling counterpart, a lucky whaling captain—particularly one who was also an investor in the ship—stood to clear far more than his salaried counterpart. Usually about one-third of the catch covered the cost of crew and officers.

As important as economics, whaling ships simply had more time than merchantmen in which to turn green hands into qualified sailors. On a cruise expected to last for years, with no set destination or fixed time of return, little premium was placed on the speed with which a new member could furl a sail or splice a rope. There would be plenty of time to learn to tie a bowline: an unlucky whaler could sail for a full year without even seeing a leviathan.

Whalers also had more officers than merchantmen and packet ships, which meant there were more experienced people around to train newcomers and handle emergencies. Whereas a merchant ship out of (or under the command of a captain from) Barnstable or Yarmouth typically carried a captain and two mates, a whaler shipped a mate and harpooner—or harpooneer, as Melville called them—for every whaleboat on the davits. The mates had to have sailed on at least one and more likely two or more earlier whaling voyages. And though it was quite possible to be promoted to the position of harpooner (boatsteerer) on one's first voyage—the primary qualifications were abundant strength coupled with a minimal sense of caution—more often that job went to persons on their second or third whaling trip. What the scoffing merchant crews said was true: whalers shipped a

---

* *Phebe*, out of Nantucket in 1835, was typical: Captain George Allen, $\frac{1}{16}$; boatsteerers, $\frac{1}{20}$; 1st mate, $\frac{1}{25}$; 2nd mate, $\frac{1}{35}$; 3rd mate, $\frac{1}{55}$; seamen, $\frac{1}{165}$; green hands, $\frac{1}{190}$; boys, $\frac{1}{200}$. The captain also usually got a bonus if the catch was especially large. Once whaling was big business, the men and boys who shipped before the mast were as likely to get ripped off by the captains and owners of whale ships as they were on any other ship.

lot of green hands. But they also promoted more rapidly and regularly than their Cape cousins.

Though it may not have been a yacht-club performance, the *Essex* ultimately did get under way. As they passed the eastern end of the island, they set the topgallants and, wrote Chase, "left the coast of America with a fine breeze, & steered for the Western Islands." Nickerson and some of the other Nantucket natives lolled about the stern, looking back to watch their homeland disappear below the horizon. The teen was feeling homesick already, and a bit scared, when he was snapped to attention by First Mate Chase's tweaking his ears. Did he think he was invited along on the *Essex* to watch the sunsets when there were ropes to be coiled and decks to be swept? "You boy, Tom, bring back your broom here and sweep clean," Nickerson later remembered Chase yelling. His voice was hoarse, whether by nature or from an excess of yelling as the *Essex* left its mooring Nickerson didn't say. "The next time I have to speak to you, your hide shall pay for it, my lad!"

It is difficult to ferret out the personal relationships among the crew from the few clues sprinkled throughout the two extended narratives and two short accounts left by survivors of the *Essex* disaster. As already mentioned, Pollard and Chase had served together on at least one and possibly two previous voyages of the *Essex*. And it's safe to assume that Seth Weeks and William Wright at least knew each other before sailing in 1819. Many decades after the disaster, when they were all old men retired from the sea, Nickerson, Chase, and Pollard were friends on Nantucket.

In the Nickerson account there is a distinct tone of sympathy for the doomed captain and one of respectful ambivalence toward Chase. On that first evening, Pollard gave a brief speech on the quarterdeck to the assembled crew "without overbearing display or ungentlemanlike language." Nickerson thought Chase, on the other hand, was a "hard Overseer," a man whose voice "assailed" a "boy of my years who had never been used to hear such language or threats before."

Whether Pollard and Chase had consciously worked out a good-cop-bad-cop strategy is unknowable, but maintaining discipline and managing intercrew relations were obviously a major part of a captain's and a first officer's job. In his gentlemanly speech, Pollard told the crew that an officer's orders were the equivalent of captain's orders, and that willful malefactors would be punished. The crew were then assigned to quarters—two-thirds in the forecastle and one-third down in steerage. They were also assigned watches, which would be rotated in order to give equal chances at sighting whales. On most boats this was accomplished by each officer choosing in turn, the way teams might be chosen in a game of pick-up basketball.

Twenty or so men sharing quarters on a cramped ship for anywhere from two to five years is a frightening prospect in the best of circumstances, and maintaining peace was of paramount importance to the captains of whaling and merchant vessels alike. With that goal in mind they issued orders and tongue-lashed offenders; supplied or denied adequate food and shore leave; split the men among various watches and messes; and then possibly rearranged them as personalities dictated. And, in some cases, officers meted out various corporal punishments. Finally, if a particular crew member proved impossible to the point of threatening the voyage, he might be left on shore. Fishing vessels from the Cape and the Islands, by contrast, being smaller and more often family operated, were by tradition less regimented.

On thousands of voyages over nearly two centuries, representing hundreds of thousands of man-years at sea, most captains' authority proved effective. But not always. At one o'clock in the morning on Christmas day, 1857, somewhere between Australia and New Zealand, five crewmen crept up to the cabin of the whaling ship *Junior*. At some signal, they simultaneously fired guns at the four sleeping officers yet did not manage to kill a single one of them; their aim may have been thrown off by the gale that was blowing outside. They did, however, succeed in lighting First Mate Nelson Provost's bed on fire.

"Oh my God, what is this?" shouted Captain Archibald Mellen. The lead mutineer, Cyrus Plummer, answered by grabbing him by the hair and yelling, "God Damn You, it is me!" which he accentuated with several mortal hatchet blows to the captain's head. His sidekick, Cornelius Burns, stabbed the third mate with a boarding knife, a long blade used for cutting blubber from the carcasses of whales. Before the wounded first and second mates could be similarly finished off, however, the attackers were called back up on deck. Apparently the mutiny wasn't a unanimous action, and their coconspirators needed help convincing the rest of the crew that Plummer would now be commanding the *Junior*.

As soon as Plummer left the officers' cabin, the first mate hid himself somewhere among the barrels and bales in the hold. The second mate, meanwhile, who was more gravely wounded, wandered up onto the deck where the mutinous rank-and-file yelled for his death. But Plummer refused to kill him and instead had him put in leg irons. He then ordered the bodies of the captain and third mate thrown overboard and set a course for Australia.

With the help of the first mate, who was fished out from his hiding place with the promise of his life and the argument that only he was capable of bringing the ship through the treacherous waters surrounding Australia, the *Junior* made land at Cape Howe on the southeast corner of the continent. There, Plummer, who couldn't write, took the bizarre step of dictating a confession into the ship's log: "This is to certify that we, Cyrus Plummer, John Hall, Richard Cartha, Cornelius Burns, and William Herbert, did, on the night of December 25th last, take the ship *Junior* and that all others in the ship are quite innocent of the deed." Then he and his fellow mutineers took two whaleboats filled with whatever they could get into them and went ashore. In the log book he added a warning that if the *Junior* stuck around too long or its crew tried to follow them, they would return to the vessel and sink her.

Exactly why Plummer thought the wounded mates might hang around for more interaction with their murderous fellow crew members is unclear. What they did instead was sail straight to Sydney and inform the local officials, who promptly rounded up eight of the mutineers, including Plummer. Special wood and iron cages were built, and they were all shipped back to New Bedford on the *Junior*.

At the subsequent trial, which was followed with intense interest in the ports of Cape Cod and the Islands, the defense argued that the men were driven to crime by the hard fare of the captain. The jury agreed, at least in part; four of the eight accused were declared innocent of all charges, three were convicted of manslaughter, and only Plummer was found guilty of murder. The judge, who made it clear he felt the jury was too lenient on the others, sentenced Plummer to die, but he was spared when President Buchanan commuted his sentence to life in prison.

Despite the sensational trial and the resultant publicity, the *Junior* affair was not the most notorious mutiny in whaling history. That dubious honor indisputably belongs to the *Globe*, which sailed out of Edgartown in December 1823. Like the *Essex*, the *Globe* was thought to be a fortunate ship: on its previous voyage it had brought home the first cargo of more than two thousand barrels of sperm oil in its hold, representing a take of approximately forty whales. It was the *Globe* that in the year before the *Essex* sailed discovered the offshore grounds. Her captain on that voyage, George Gardner, and his crew were apparently not the types to keep a fishing secret; the following year fifty other ships, including the *Essex*, headed for that area.

Also like the *Essex*, the *Globe* in 1823 was commanded by a member of an established whaling family, though this time of the Vineyard: Captain Thomas Worth. First Mate William Beetle was also from that island, as were a boatsteerer named Gilbert Smith and a handful of the crew. Crew member Anthony Hansen was a Wampanoag from Cape Cod. There were plenty of Nantucketers involved as well, both among the crew and on the list of owners, but the most important of all was a twenty-one-year-old Nantucket boatsteerer named Samuel Comstock, the ringleader of the mutineers.

It was Comstock who shortly before midnight crept down to the cabin and buried a hatchet in the skull of the sleeping captain. A fellow conspirator named William Humphries held up a lantern so he wouldn't miss. According to Comstock's younger brother George, who was also a member of the crew but was later cleared of any involvement in the mutiny, the blow "cut the top of [Worth's] head very nearly off."

Fellow mutineer Silas Payne, meanwhile, was having some difficulty completing his appointed task of sticking a boarding knife into the ribs of First Mate Beetle. He hit a bone, which only succeeded in waking Beetle from his slumbers. "What-what-what-what-what-what-what is this?!" other crew members remember the wounded man yelling. "Paine! Comstock! Don't kill me! Have I not always . . ."

Comstock had by now finished off the captain with a second hatchet blow and came to take over from Payne. "Yes, you have always been a damn rascal," he said, interrupting the wounded Beetle midsentence. "You tell lies about me out of the ship, will you! It's a damned good time for you to beg now, you are too late."

Beetle didn't go without a fight. He got his hands around Comstock's neck. The light was knocked out. Comstock lost his hatchet. There was mayhem, but only for a moment. Comstock (perhaps with some help from Payne) retrieved his hatchet and "broke skull." According to the account written later by Comstock's brother, the Vineyarder lay moaning on the pantry floor for some time before the elder Comstock finished him off.

What motivated Comstock to lead his bloody campaign is one of the enduring mysteries of the *Globe* mutiny. Captain Worth could be stern; on the day of the killings he flogged a soon-to-be mutineer named Joseph Thomas with the end of a rope while the rest of the crew watched. But he was not, apparently, a tyrant: in a deposition given to the American consul in Valparaiso, Chile, after the grisly affair had played itself out, the younger Comstock testified that the biggest complaint any of the crew had about the commander was "his not allowing enough time to eat their victuals."

Comstock's motive seems to have been a series of small personal gripes that drove him over the bloody edge. Just before putting a bullet in the back of Third Mate Nathaniel Fisher's head, Comstock reminded his victim of a wrestling match they'd had a few months before. Fisher had handily won the bout, embarrassing Comstock in front of the combined crews of the *Globe* and the *Enterprise*, a Nantucket whaler they were sailing with at the time. Comstock had thrown a wild punch, and Fisher threw him bodily to the deck, no doubt eliciting further cheers and laughter from the spectators. Comstock swore out loud right there that some day he would kill Fisher, but the latter assumed the former was either posturing or simply overheated.

The night he died, Fisher again misjudged Comstock. At the first sign of trouble, he and the *Globe's* second mate, John Lombard, barricaded themselves inside their stateroom, prompting Comstock to fire a musket through the door.

"Did I hit you?" he asked.

"Yes," came the reply. A musket ball had ripped open Fisher's jaw. The mutineers then either broke down the stateroom door or convinced the two officers to open it with promises of mercy. As soon as he was through the door, Comstock tried to run a bayonet through Lombard. As he charged, though, he slipped (on Fisher's blood, say some sources) and fell.

The first mate was over him in an instant, holding the bayonet directly over the mutineer's heart. Then, for reasons unclear, Fisher let Comstock up and gave him the gun. If Comstock promised to spare Fisher's life, as some accounts suggest, he lied. As soon as the weapon was back in his hands, he ran the blade several times through the middle of Lombard. Fisher no doubt realized his mistake, but it was too late. Comstock told him to turn around. Maybe Fisher felt the muzzle of the gun against the back of his head or heard the preliminary click of the trigger, but he died instantly when the bullet went through his brain.

Lombard, however, still wasn't dead. He begged for mercy. According to the mutineer's younger brother, "Comstock told him he was a bloody man he had a bloody hand and would be avenged." Again he drove his blade through Lombard's midriff. Lombard begged for water. "I'll give you water," said the blood-crazed harpooner, and stabbed him again.

Somewhat miraculously, this perforated officer survived until the next morning, when he again begged to be allowed to live. Comstock threw him overboard. Somehow he managed to hang on to the plank-shear, the last piece of decking on the outer edges of the ship. "Comstock," someone remembered him yelling, "you said you would save me." But the mutineer replied in cinematic bad-guy fashion by stepping on the desperate man's fingers. Lombard fell into the sea, and though he swam along behind still calling out for help, after a few minutes he was not heard again. And then, at last, he couldn't be seen either.

Comstock's only motive other than his self-described "bloody hand," his insane appetite for revenge, may have been a fantasy of setting himself up as the king of a tropical paradise. On an earlier voyage on the *Foster*, he asked that Captain Shubael Chase leave him ashore somewhere in the Pacific and was denied. Now in command of the *Globe*, Comstock ordered the crew to sail for the Kingsmill Islands. Before they got there, though, there was more killing to be done.

According to a deposition given later by one of the survivors, Comstock made the entire crew move into the cabin with him. This was a truly grisly slumber party, "where the mutineers used to sing, and carouse, and tell over the story of the murder, and what they had dreamed." Two of the perpetrators, Payne and Oliver, "could scarcely ever sleep, spoke with horror of the ghosts which appeared to them at night." But Comstock "appeared to exult in what he had done." Sure the captain had returned to him in his sleep, bloody, caved-in head and all, he told the others. But he simply told him he'd kill him all over again if he didn't get lost.

Comstock's paranoia was reserved for the living. On the second day after the uprising, one of the original conspirators was seen loading a pistol: William Humphries, an African-American sailor from Philadelphia, the man who had held the lantern for Comstock during the initial homicide. Like all the principal mutineers with the exception of Comstock, he had joined the crew of the *Globe* only a month before in Oahu. (For reasons tantalizingly unknown but probably having to do with free love, six members of the original crew of the *Globe* jumped ship there, and Captain Worth was forced to hire replacements from among the population of beachcombers who had deserted previous ships.) Now Comstock became convinced that Humphries might be harboring some regrets. Humphries replied that he had overheard two crew members planning a counter-revolution.

A trial of sorts was held with a jury of two mutineers and two crew members, after which Comstock sentenced Humphries to be hung by the neck. The noose was tied, and Comstock ordered all members of the crew to take hold of the other end of the rope. When he rang the ship's bell and they all began to run aft, Humphries "was swung to the fore yard without a kick or a groan." He did, evidently, have some regrets; his last words were, "When I was born I did not think I should ever come to this."

As it turned out, Comstock was right to worry about the loyalty of his fellow mutineers. When the *Globe* arrived at Kingsmill the local islanders stood on the beach waving their weapons at the ship until it sailed away to a vast atoll in the eastern Marshall Islands. There Comstock loaded the whaleboats and went ashore. The men made tents from sails, and Comstock commenced his reign as the king of paradise.

It lasted for two days. On the morning of February 16, 1824, fellow mutineers Silas Payne, John Oliver, and several others ambushed Comstock. It was now his turn to beg in vain for his life. "Don't shoot me, don't shoot me, I won't hurt you," he said, but no one believed him. He was shot simultaneously by four musketeers, and then, just to be sure he was dead, Payne chopped his neck almost through with an axe. His body was sewn into a sail. Then, in a bizarre moment of inspiration, they held a proper funeral for their slain leader; a chapter was read from the Bible, muskets were solemnly fired into the air, and Samuel Comstock was buried in a deep grave.

That night the six men who were left on board the *Globe*, including Comstock's younger brother, cut the anchor rope and sailed away to Valparaiso, leaving those onshore behind to fend for themselves. In Valparaiso they put the ship into the hands of the American consul, who took their depositions and sent the ship back to Edgartown under a new captain.

Back in the Marshall Islands, meanwhile, Silas Payne took up the tyranny where his dead comrade had left off, trying to extend his brutal reign to the locals. His sidekick, Oliver, "became very much attached to liquor." At least one, and possibly two, native women were badly flogged for insubordination or amusement, it's unclear which. One woman who tried to run away from Payne's tent was brought back and put in leg irons. Another local, a man, was put in chains for stealing tools.

A week after Comstock's death, a crowd of islanders surrounded the camp and began throwing stones. All but two of the Americans were killed.

It's unclear why Lay and Hussey were spared—perhaps because they were young. They were adopted by the Marshall Islanders. On December 29, 1825, a United States Navy schooner arrived to search for survivors of the mutiny. Whether by choice or under duress, both young men had been tattooed from head to toe like Queequeg, but they had otherwise been well treated. They eventually made their way back to Nantucket. Neither was ever charged or implicated in the mutiny, and both signed up for later, presumably less eventful, whaling voyages.

There was nothing extraordinary about events on the *Essex* as Nantucket slipped below the horizon to the west and then the sun, too, dropped out of sight. Later there would be a good-natured complaint about the food on board, a complaint that generated a rare outburst of ire from Captain Pollard. But that first night even the ship's fare was not yet boring.

"All were seated around our kid, or tub of Salt Meat, with Each Man his tin Cup of Tea, and holding In our hands a huge piece of Salt junk and Cake of hard biscuit," Nickerson recalled many years later. Though ships' officers ate from plates with silverware and napkins, the men and boys in the forecastle sat in a circle on the floor and tore food from the communal pot with their hands. Nevertheless, said Nickerson, "all seemed to enjoy their meal as well as though they had been seated at Table in a palace groaning under its weight of costly viands." They may, as he said they often did, have discussed politics. Or the older members of the crew may have regaled the newcomers with tales of whales now dead.

According to Nickerson, the day they set sail turned into a fine August evening off Cape Cod and the Islands. There was a decent breeze, probably from the southwest and warm. The stars came out. No one was in a hurry to go to sleep. It was "a clear and beautiful sky," Nickerson wrote, "and the hands were lounging about the Decks during the night long after the watches had been relieved."

CHAPTER 20

THE GULF STREAM

At precisely eight bells the following morning, Captain Pollard mustered all hands onto the deck to get the *Essex* ready to whale. No leviathan had yet been found; whales would not necessarily be expected to be seen for weeks or possibly months. You never really knew, though, and just because everything required for a whaling voyage was stowed on board at the time of departure didn't mean it was all where it needed to be at the moment whales were sighted. There were ropes to be spliced and coiled, harpoons to be sharpened and stowed, whaleboats to be fully rigged and outfitted.

It was common practice to leave the rigging of crow's nests—sometimes with seats, sometimes empty barrels, sometimes just hoops and stands—until the ship was under way. On many whaling vessels during the first days out, nests for two men would be put up in each mast, so there would at all times be eight or even twelve eyes constantly scanning the surface of the water for any sign of prey.

Furthermore, it was never too early to teach the new crop of sailors the basics. None of the existing accounts of the last voyage of the *Essex* mention Pollard ordering any formal lowering and rowing drills, though it would not have been uncommon for him to do so on a calm day. Nor is there any mention of the men practicing their moves on logs or blackfish, as was sometimes done on other ships.

Perhaps Pollard was one of the gentler whaling captains, content to wait until the inevitable seasickness wore off. There were apparently more than a few cases on board: "Many were rolling and tumbling about the Decks almost dead or willing to Die or be cast into the sea," wrote Nickerson, though he insisted that he was among the spared who guffawed at the suffering of their comrades. Pollard wasn't so soft, however, that he was going to take a chance on missing his prey. Seasick or no, everyone had to take his two-hour shift at the top of the mast. One lad, presumably with a stomach already displeased by the motion of the deck, looked up at the pendulant crow's nest and said something to the effect of, *No thanks.* But "a few soft words from the officers" were enough to change his mind.

There were additional incentives to go aloft; usually a generous reward of tobacco or money was promised to the first to see a whale that was captured. And for some, the elevated solitude was its own reward; "There you stand, a hundred feet above the silent decks, striding along the deep, as if the masts were gigantic stilts, while beneath you and between your legs, as it were, swim the hugest monsters of the sea," wrote Melville. "Let me make a clean breast of it here, and frankly admit that I kept but a sorry guard. With the problem of the universe revolving in me, how could I—being left completely alone at such a thought engendering altitude. . . ."

Their second morning at sea, whoever was in the crow's nest of the *Essex* called out that there was a ship on the horizon. It was the *Midas*, five days out of New Bedford, and they stayed together long enough for Pollard and his counterpart, Captain Spooner, to compare their calculated longitudes. Though more than a half century had passed since the invention of the chronometer, which finally made it possible for ships at sea to accurately calculate their east-west positions, the device and technique were not yet in general use in the private sector. Nor were most captains, Pollard included, fully proficient at taking accurate lunar observations, which was another method of determining longitude. So whenever ships spoke at sea, they compared their estimations of position as a sort of backup.

Pollard, like many of his contemporaries, was essentially making educated guesses based on how fast he thought the *Essex* had traveled since leaving Nantucket. "We had no means of ascertaining our true position as our ship was sailed by what Nautical men term 'Dead Reckoning,'" remembered Nickerson, adding, "the latter I think a very appropriate name and in this instance not misapplied."

The *Essex*, for all its arklike appearance, was a faster vessel than the *Midas*, and slowly pulled away and was again alone at sea. All was as it should be. But as the day wore on, the weather began to worsen. Heavy clouds built up to the southwest, and the sea became "very rough which caused the ship to roll and tumble heavily." The wind and swell weren't severe enough during the night, however, to cause Pollard to order the men into the masts to furl any sail. It wasn't a full-fledged storm. Not yet, anyway.

As they entered the Gulf Stream the next morning, however, a heavy rain began to fall. The topgallants, highest of the three square sails on each mast, were ordered taken in on both the fore- and mizzenmasts. But there was still plenty of canvas aloft when a violent squall caught up with the ship.

They saw the storm coming, recalled First Mate Chase, "but miscalculated altogether the strength and violence of it." At the last minute Pollard ordered the helm to turn away from the approaching squall in order to try to run before it. But the wind arrived a moment too soon and caught them "three points off the weather quarter"—near enough to broadside to cause trouble. It got hold of the remaining sails: the foresail, mainsail, and mizzensail, along with all three top sails; the main topgallant; and the foretopmast steering sail. Lightning flashed repeatedly. Thunder clapped. And in a split second, the ship essentially tipped over onto her side.

The *Essex* was "on her beam-ends," as it's called. Her deck was nearly vertical and her masts virtually parallel to the water. The tips of the yards, on which hung the square sails, were in the water on the downward side. For the inexperienced crew it was, First Mate Chase later recalled dryly, a moment of "utmost consternation and confusion."

The ship was so far over that despite the order to let all the halyards and sheets go, the sails wouldn't come down. It must have felt to the green hands like an eternity that they were lying there prone to the waves. But both Chase and Nickerson later recalled that after only a moment or two, the *Essex* "gradually came to the wind, and righted."

Not that the trouble was over. They were now facing directly into the blow with their canvas not yet fully down. "The sails were all aback, with the yards very near Square, which pressed the ship so far backward before the sails could be taken off that she was very near running under stern first," remembered Nickerson, "which as every seaman must know, is a most dangerous position for a ship to be caught in."

Storms at sea. According to Roget's thesaurus, the wind can be big, great, fresh, strong, stiff, high, howling, spanking, ill, dirty, or ugly. There can be not only squalls, but thick squalls, black squalls, white squalls, line squalls, and thunder squalls. There can be tempests, waterspouts, hurricanes, tropical storms, typhoons, williwaws, violent blows, and heavy blows. And near

Twenty-four schooners "nearly all heavily laden" and one barkentine were driven ashore in Vineyard Haven Harbor during the Portland Gale of 1898. (COURTESY OF THE MARTHA'S VINEYARD HISTORICAL SOCIETY)

the equator, or the line, as whalers and sailors alike called it, there could be raging equinoctials. It can blow half a gale or a whole gale, or a gale that "would blow the hair off a dog."

Or, once or twice a generation, there can be a storm that locals call (but the thesaurus doesn't mention) a "memorable gale." There have been many that qualify, and their effects on the landscape of Cape Cod and the Islands have already been mentioned. The first recorded hurricane, in August of 1635, took the roof off the Pilgrims' trading post in Bourne and "floated it to another place." On November 20, 1798, a memorable gale dropped six feet of snow on the Cape and left twenty-five bodies on its beaches from seven vessels that went ashore in the blizzard. In 1851 the Minot Gale—so named because it washed away Minots Ledge Light in Cohasset—raised seas eighteen feet above normal in Barnstable and broke a hole through Nauset Beach. (A thirteen-acre island off Chatham also disappeared in the storm.) In 1871 the ship *Nina* ended up inside the Provincetown Post Office. In the memorable gale of 1880, thirty-eight ships were seen in trouble on the Nantucket Shoals by the crew of the Nantucket Lightship. In November of 1898, thirty-six hours of snow and seventy-plus-mile-an-hour winds destroyed 140 ships, including the passenger steamer *Portland*, which "broke up" seven miles northeast of the Highland Light with two hundred people on board. None survived, and the storm became known as the Portland Gale.

The most memorable gale of all, the storm for which the phrase may have been coined, roared in off the ocean in 1841. Like the Halloween Gale almost exactly 150 years later, now famously remembered as "the Perfect Storm" in Sebastian Junger's remarkable book of that title, the memorable gale of 1841 was in October, and its primary victims were fishermen. From Truro alone, fifty-seven men and boys who sailed out to George's Bank in schooners to fish for cod never returned home. Of nine boats to sail from the town, seven—the *Arrival, Altair, Cincinnatus, Pomona, Prince Albert, General Harrison,* and *Dalmatia*—were lost. From Dennis, meanwhile, at least twenty fishermen drowned or otherwise disappeared. From Yarmouth, ten. There were plenty of merchant ships driven ashore in that storm as well: strewn up and down the beaches the morning after the storm were more than one hundred bodies.

The loss was obviously devastating to Truro, both emotionally and economically. The fifty-seven victims lived within two miles of each other. Three were boys not yet in their teens. The local insurance company failed. "Who lives in that house?" Thoreau remembered inquiring. "Three widows," was the reply.

The storm did not, however, claim everyone from Truro who went out in it. Captain Joshua Knowles in the *Garnet* and Matthias Rich in *Water Witch* managed to beat the memorable gale, but just barely. *Garnet* sailed out of Provincetown Harbor on October 2 and headed out to George's Bank under full sail. Overnight, as the wind stiffened, Knowles progressively took in sails, until by six o'clock the following morning only the foresail was set, and it was double-reefed to lessen its exposure to the wind. By evening that had blown "to ribbons," causing the captain to turn again to the mainsail, which also self-destructed. With only the jib left, and soundings going from fifteen fathoms to twelve to eight and then to six, they knew they were drifting into the George's deadly shoals. Knowles ordered all crew members below-decks, except for his brother Zack, who stayed above.

As immense waves broke all around them, the two brothers decided their only hope was to try to come about. If they could swing the boat off, before the wind, they might be able to make progress out of the shoals to deeper water. But just as she began to fall off, the *Garnet* was broadsided by a great wave. As the wind had done to the *Essex* twenty years before, the water put the *Garnet* on her beam ends. Captain Knowles was lashed to the helm in the traditional fashion, but Zack was immediately washed overboard in the deluge. The waves in that gale were titanic; another vessel, the

Reform, was flipped completely over, stern over bow, so that when it came up the sea-anchor line was wrapped around the bowsprit.

Somehow, Zack Knowles managed to keep hold of the mainsheet and drag himself back on board. When he got there, the foremast was broken off fifteen feet above the deck, the mainmast was unstepped, and the galley and everything else from the deck was entirely gone. The brothers furiously cut away the wrecked rigging with a hatchet, while below, the crew crawled into the hold and moved all the ballast (which had shifted) over to the windward side in an effort to right the boat. The *Garnet* was essentially a wreck, but by the end of the long night, the worst of the gale was over and they had not run aground.

In the morning light, Knowles and his crew jury-rigged a mast and used the remaining staysail for a foresail and the gaff topsail for a jib. They found a few potatoes floating around the hold and made a sorry meal. They raised a distress flag, but by day's end they had seen no sign of help. Finally, just as the sun was setting, they were picked up by the *Roscius*, a packet out of Liverpool, England, with four hundred passengers on board. After his crew was safely on the other ship, Captain Knowles chopped a hole in the bottom of the *Garnet*, sending her to the bottom. He then went aboard *Roscius* himself, where he was welcomed aboard by its captain, who, as it turned out, was also of Truro.

Matthias Rich of Truro had a bad feeling about the memorable gale before most of his fellow townsmen. At four A.M. on Sunday morning, about the time Knowles was taking in his jib for the first time, Rich decided to make a run for home. He later remembered passing the rest of the Truro fleet, "then lying comfortably to the northwest under foresail with two or three vessels carrying bob jib . . ." Only the *Pomona* and the *Bride of Dennis*, he said, appeared to think better of waiting out the storm and turned to follow his lead.

The wind was such that there was no possibility of tacking, so the three ships were either going to make it around the Cape or not. If their luck held—that is to say, if they didn't get pushed too far south—they would come in north of Race Point and thus make it safely into the bay. But at one o'clock in the afternoon, the long arm of the Cape was sighted not only under their lee, but, Rich later remembered, "well along to windward."

"Our desperate condition was at the first moment a terrible shock, but quickly recovering, I sprang on deck, called up my crew, ordered the jib set.

Under the pressure of the jib she fell off so far that the land was windward of the bowsprit. I knew we had a good sea-boat; I had tried her in a hard scratch, and knew that our race was life or death."

Rich tried to raise a reefed mainsail, "but before half-way up, our vessel lay so much on her broadside, that the halyards were lost, the sail came down by the run, and blew to pieces, the main boom and gaff going over the lee rail. We first tried to cut them away, but fearing the main top-in-liff would carry away the mainmast, got on a tackle and pulled the boom and part of the mainsail out of the water. Then righted and came up to the wind, making good headway."

Good enough, anyway, to squeak around Race Point into the relative safety of Herring Cove by 6:30 that evening. This was more than could be said for either of the ships following him. When the *Pomona* drifted keel-up into Nauset harbor several days later, all that remained of her crew were the bodies of three drowned boys found in the cabin. The *Bride of Dennis* disappeared without a trace.

It was in Truro that Thoreau noticed that the sound of the surf is not the same to all ears. When he presumed that an old, nearly blind beachcomber he found sitting by the sea must, like himself, enjoy the sound of the waves, the man rebuked him. "No, I do not like to hear the sound of the surf," he said. His son, it turned out, had been lost at sea in a storm. "I found that it would not do to speak of shipwrecks there," Thoreau wrote elsewhere, "for almost every family has lost some of its members at sea."

The experience of the unfortunate companions of the *Water Witch* shows that as harrowing and deadly as a storm at sea can be, attempting to come into harbor could often be worse. With adequate sea room a ship can turn and run before the storm, as the *Essex* tried somewhat ungracefully to do. Or, depending on the nature of the storm and the capacities of the ship, a captain may decide to head up into the wind with only minimal sail set and ride out the blow hove to. Had the 1841 storm been merely bad, or even severe, had it been anything short of memorable, in all likelihood the ships that chose to ride it out at sea would have done at least as well as those that raced for home.

Notwithstanding the occasional snug harbor, land has a habit of ripping the underbellies off of ships. Or, in the case of the shoals off of Cape Cod, a sandy bottom may not harm the hull at all, but it will hold a vessel snugly in place while the waves beat it to pieces. Plenty of ships from Cape Cod and the Islands tragically ended their business in deep water; hundreds simply disappeared. It is safe to say that in the age of sail, however, when every ship traveling between Boston or Salem and points south had to round the Cape, many more vessels found their demise in the shifting shallows between Monomoy and Race Point. Or in Nantucket Sound itself.

As early as ships began to arrive in the vicinity of Cape Cod and the Islands they began to wreck. The Cape Cod fans of Thorwald think he lost his keel around Provincetown one thousand years ago. Gaspar Cortereal's disappearance in the area in 1501 was presumably not by choice. The two French mariners redeemed by Thomas Dermer in 1614 were apparently shipwrecked on the Cape. Champlain wrecked his rudder on Nantucket shoal, and the *Mayflower* almost foundered on Pollock Rip. The Nauset Indians helped rescue survivors from the wreck of the *Sparrowhawk* in 1626. And despite all the high-tech gadgets and gewgaws available to the mariner today, the local sea floor still catches a few: in 1992, no less a ship than the *Queen Elizabeth II* ran aground in Vineyard Sound on what was purported to be a previously uncharted shoal, and her passengers ended their glamorous cruise aboard the humble New Bedford–Vineyard ferry *Schamonche*.

The exact number of ships that have wrecked on the Cape and Islands can never be known, but the various overlapping estimates published over the years give a sobering enough picture. In 1864 a report to the state legislature on the feasibility of a Cape Cod Canal counted 827 disasters to ships making their way around the peninsula in the previous seventeen years. It was, the report noted, a highly conservative estimate. Between then and the beginning of canal construction in 1909, another 900 wrecks took place on the lower Cape. Another writer counted 687 wrecks there between 1875 and 1903. In 1909 alone, there were 22 wrecks on the outer Cape and almost as many in 1911, 1912, and 1913. Between 1907 and 1917 there were 156 wrecks on the ocean side of the Cape. By one estimate, a sailing vessel caught in a northeast storm off the back side of Cape Cod had less than a 50 percent chance of making it to safety. Even absent a storm, ships could and did get into trouble: there are on average forty-five days of significant fog on Cape Cod annually.

In Asa Lombard's brief history of the Cape Cod lifesaving service, *East of Cape Cod*, is an amazing map showing the locations where "principal wrecks took place from 1850 to 1900." Each one is marked with a small dot, and there is not a place along the beach where there was not a wreck in that half century. On a similar map in Kittredge's 1930 history of the Cape, the dots representing wrecks are so numerous and dense that they look more like a depiction of the sand lying off the beach. In many places, especially at either end—Monomoy and Provincetown, where the ships were

The W. H. Marshall, *one of the thousands of ships to wreck off Cape Cod and the Islands during the nineteenth century, came ashore on Nantucket's south shore in March of 1877.* (Courtesy Nantucket Historical Association)

obviously trying to make their way around the corners—the hatch marks signifying wrecks bulge out, mimicking the bars themselves.

If a captain and crew were fortunate enough to beat their way far enough north to make it around Race Point before they got too far west into the shoals, they could look forward to hot rum in Provincetown. (There were, however, more than a few wrecks within the harbor itself.) If, on the other hand, a captain was forced to go south, passing Monomoy was only the start of his troubles. One New Bedford paper estimated, almost unbelievably, that between 1843 and 1903 there were more than two thousand wrecks on the Nantucket Shoals alone. Nor was the sailing any better in Nantucket Sound, where there are more shoals than deep water.

There wasn't much of anywhere to go in Nantucket Sound, anyway. Nantucket Harbor had the bar across its mouth; a small booklet published in 1877 by Arthur Gardner tells of five hundred wrecks on Nantucket itself. None of the harbors on the Nantucket Sound–side of the Cape were suitable for sizable vessels. The only reliable storm harbor was Holmes Hole (Vineyard Haven)—so ships traveling up from points south waited there until weather and tide looked auspicious for passage around the Cape. But even Holmes Hole faces directly into the teeth of a northeaster, so during a bad winter storm from that direction, there was only Tarpaulin Cove, well into Vineyard Sound. Not that Vineyard Sound offered particularly smooth sailing. As mentioned earlier, there were hundreds of wrecks on the Elizabeth Islands. Scores more ships met their end on Devil's Bridge, including the passenger steamer *City of Columbus*, which inexplicably struck the bar on a perfectly clear night in 1848 and left 121 people dead. Middle Ground also grabbed its share of hulls. Ships sank everywhere, and the wreckage kept right on into the twentieth century: in the ten years after the First World War, 255 sailing ships and 71 steamships wrecked in the waters off Cape Cod and the Islands.

It was always a gamble knowing when to stay on a grounded ship and when to leave. Chances were pretty good that once a ship was solidly stuck, particularly on the bars off the lower Cape, the waves were going to make short work of it. But there was always a chance of staying on board, especially if the storm appeared to be abating. There's an old adage that only cowards and fools leave a sinking ship.

The *Albert S. Butler* is a case in point. She was one of 140 vessels to get into fatal trouble during the Portland Gale of 1898 when she ran aground with a crew of seven off Peaked Hill Bars near Provincetown. Three sailors tried to get to shore in a dory; the first drowned when he mistimed his jump from the ship and landed in the water instead of the boat. The other two drowned when they capsized not long after. Meanwhile, a rescue crew arrived onshore and managed to shoot a line out to the ship with a cannon. A breeches buoy was rigged, and two of the four remaining members of the crew made a harrowing crossing to shore. The last two sailors balked at being hauled in a little basket over several hundred yards of thundering waves and were essentially left for dead by the shore crew, who could do no more for them. But a few hours later, when the ship had skidded over a few more bars and the tide had receded, the two men jumped onto dry land.

For thousands stuck in the sand or on the rocks, though, it was obvious

The motto of the United States Life Saving Service was "You have to go out but you don't have to come back." (GRANT SMITH/CORBIS)

their ships could not hold through the storm. Then the lifesaving crews onshore were the only hope. In 1786, the Massachusetts Humane Society was founded with the goal of establishing a series of shelters along the coast where a winter shipwreck victim lucky enough to make it ashore might escape the very real prospect of freezing to death. There were also volunteer lifesaving crews who valiantly did their best to rescue victims. But it wasn't until the U.S. Life Saving Service was established in the 1870s that regular patrols of the beaches to save the stranded were made.

Originally there were nine stations stretched out along the lower Cape, at Race Point, Peaked Hill Bars, Highland, Pamet River, Cahoon Hollow, Nauset, Orleans, Chatham, and Monomoy. Four times a night every night between September and June, the Life Savers walked in all weather back and forth along the beach to halfway houses between the stations, where they exchanged a small metal token with their counterpart, who had walked in the opposite direction from the next station down the beach. If they saw a ship in distress, they fired flare guns to give solace to the stranded and, if possible, to send the news back to the stations. Then they started back to get the rest of the crew. In daylight the Life Savers often knew before the doomed captain when a vessel wasn't going to make it around the bars, and hitched the horse to the boat trailer and the men to the rescue cart and started down the beach.

If there was a reasonable chance of getting the lifeboat through the surf and back—*reasonable* being an extremely relative term in this case—the surf boat was launched and a crew attempted to row out and pick up sur-vivors. The motto of the corps was "You have to go, but you don't have to come back." In situations where it was simply too rough to risk rowing, the only hope was to shoot a line through the rigging with a special cannon used for the purpose, called a Lyle gun. It was possible under the best of conditions—an offshore breeze—for twelve hundred yards of line to go out. But three to four hundred yards was the more likely distance. When the gun had been fired well, the men on the ship would pull the whip line from the beach and tie it as high as they could onto the mast of the vessel. There was a block attached to it and a tag showing how to tie it properly, though presumably most sailors knew how to secure a line.

Back onshore, every member of the rescue team had a well-rehearsed duty. Some buried a sand anchor to which the line was to be attached. Oth-ers set up the wooden stay on which the beach end of the rope was raised in an effort to get the line as high over the water as possible. Once the main line from ship to shore was secured, the buoy itself—a sort of basket capable of carrying one person—was suspended from it, and the stranded sailors hauled it out to the ship. In weekly drills, the lifesaving teams practiced until they could set up their buoy in five minutes. The best crews could do it in two.

But that was in practice. In real life, in a storm, there was much that could go wrong. When the schooner *J. H. Eells* ran aground on March 15, 1887, about 350 yards off Nauset Beach in water too rough for the surf boats, the crew of the Nauset station fired their Lyle gun eleven times. Eleven times the crew aboard the doomed ship and the crowd gathered on the shore watched the line fall short. All the stranded mariners were in the rigging of the ship, with the exception of one who lashed himself to the jibstay on the bowsprit. The ship sprang a leak and began to settle lower.

Someone suggested trying a different gun that was back at the Humane Society.

By the time the bigger cannon was brought down to the scene, the schooner was completely underwater. Only the masts and bowsprit were out. The tide was rising. The lifesavers moved the gun up onto the bluff to try to get more distance out of it, but still the line fell short by seventy-five yards. Finally Keeper Knowles of the Nauset Life Saving Station decided to load the new cannon with four times as much powder and sent the line across the rigging of the floundering ship. Everybody cheered.

Two sailors in the ship's rigging got to the rope and dragged out the heavier rope that was attached to it. But when the time came to drag out the block and the main rope, the along-shore current was too strong. The men onshore dragged it back, starting from farther up the beach; still the shipwrecked were not strong enough to pull the rope in. The man on the bowsprit, who turned out to be the captain, made no effort to come up and help. After a few hours of struggle, the line broke. Another line was fired out, and this time a third member of the crew joined in pulling the heavy line out. Still, though, the men in the rigging couldn't haul the line out to them. It got dark, and the people onshore went home to light fires.

The Life Savers stayed on the beach. By dawn it appeared that the captain had been washed off the bowsprit during the night. One of the three men left in the rigging was also dead from exposure. The sea had laid down a bit, but the surf was still too strong to launch the lifeboat; so the crowd, which had come back after breakfast to keep vigil, waited and watched. They no doubt talked of other wrecks more and less tragic, and of ships they were themselves on during frightening times, of what the captain should have done differently. Finally, a tugboat out of Boston happened by and rescued the two survivors, and everyone was able to go back about their business until the next ship piled up onshore.

CHAPTER 21

CLAY POUNDS

Of the thousands that went down over the centuries, the two most famous wrecks on the Cape were probably the pirate ship *Whidah*, which went aground off Wellfleet on March 26, 1717, and the English frigate *Somerset*, which wrecked during the Revolutionary War on the bar off Dead Man's Hollow in North Truro.

Whidah was the flagship of the pirate Samuel Bellamy, who got his start in the West Indies and is one of the stars in the current historical recasting of pirates as freedom-loving antiestablishmentarians rather than greedy cut-throats. "I am sorry they won't let you have your sloop again," Bellamy is remembered to have said to Captain Beer, whose ship was captured by the *Whidah* on its way toward the Cape and Islands from somewhere off the Carolinas. Bellamy, who was elected to the position of captain by his merry band of fellow buccaneers, had just been outvoted on the issue of whether or not to give Beer his ship back.

"Damn the sloop, we must sink her, and she might be of use to you," Bellamy went on. "Tho', damn ye, you are a sneaking Puppy, and so are all those who will submit to be governed by laws which rich men have made for their own security, for the cowardly whelps have not the courage other-wise to defend what they get back by their knavery; but damn ye alto-gether: Damn them for a pack of hen-hearted numskuls. They vilify us, the scoundrels do, when there is only this difference, they rob the poor under cover of law, forsooth, and we plunder the rich under the protection of our own courage." So join us, the pirate said to Captain Beer, "had you not better make one of us, than sneak after the asses of those villains for employment?"

But for reasons of his own, Beer remained unconvinced that it would be such a glorious thing to be a pirate king. And when he mumbled something about his conscience, Bellamy really warmed up. "I am a free Prince," he announced, "and I have as much authority to make war on the whole world, as he who has a hundred sail of ships at sea, and an army of 100,000 men in the field; and this my conscience tells me; but there is no arguing with such sniveling puppies, who allow Superiors to kick them about deck at pleasure; and pin their faith upon a pimp of a parson: a squab, who neither practices nor believes what he puts upon the chuckle-headed fools he preaches to."

In the end there was nothing to be done with Beer but put the sniveling puppy ashore at the notorious piratical haunt, Block Island, and head up around the Cape as planned. In all likelihood the *Whidah* avoided the two sounds and sailed around the outside of Martha's Vineyard and Nantucket. Two weeks later the *Whidah* had collected two more prizes off Cape Cod, including the *Mary Anne* of Dublin with a happy cargo of Madeira in the hold. The other was a sloop out of Virginia.

One story goes that it was Captain Crumpstey of the *Mary Anne* who led Bellamy to his doom. As the weather began to turn, Bellamy supposedly promised to return to Crumpstey his vessel if he led the pirate fleet—now four vessels—safely into Provincetown. Instead, according to the lore, he led them onto the bar. Whether or not it actually happened that way, at least two of the vessels ended up on the bar between Orleans and Wellfleet. Many of the pirates who were on the *Mary Anne* survived, as their shallower draft allowed them to skid over the outer bar and ground closer to the beach. Seven of these were subsequently rounded up in an Eastham grogshop, taken to Boston, and hung.

On the larger *Whidah*, only two made it to the beach, a Cape Cod Indian named John Julian and a Welsh carpenter named Thomas Davis. One hundred forty-four drowned, including Captains Bellamy and Crumpstey. Julian and Davis scaled the bluff and wandered through the storm until eventually they came to the house of Samuel Harding of Eastham, who took them in and warmed them up. Whether Harding was convinced by their insistence that they were honest sailors who had been forced into piracy by Bellamy is unknown, but at any rate citizen Harding seemed more excited than alarmed by the late-night arrival of the two drenched picaroons.

A good number of Nantucketers turned out in 1873 to help unload the cargo of coffee from the grounded Minmaneuth. (COURTESY NANTUCKET HISTORICAL ASSOCIATION)

Without telling any of his neighbors, Harding hitched up his horse and wagon and all three returned to the beach. There they managed to remove and squirrel away several wagonloads of washed-ashore loot before word got out that a pirate ship was on the beach and the rest of the town's wreckers—i.e., the rest of the town—arrived with their own wagons. It wasn't only locals who came, either; the first time a whaleboat is known to have crossed the Cape in Jeremiah's Gutter, a swampy cut between Boat Meadow

River and Town Cove in Orleans, was supposedly for the purpose of looking over the pickings after the wreck of the *Whidah.*

Call it salvage. Call it beachcombing. Call it wrecking. For a century and
a half ships came ashore on the outer beach of Cape Cod roughly every
two weeks on average—more in the winter months, fewer in the summer.
Even if it weren't a more frugal age than today, which it undoubtedly was,
and even if Cape Cod weren't a famously thrifty region, such a regular tide
of gifts from the sea was sure to transform the natural habit of removing
anything valuable into a venerable, if not entirely respectable, vocation.
Professional wreckers had their rigs ready at all times in their barns, loaded
down with crowbars, axes, knives, and anything else they might need to
break open a ship. They paced the beach; they knew the propitious winds
and the killer tides. They waited like spiders.

The pros often worked at night, sometimes almost the very night of the
wreck. They were very good at their jobs. When a brand-new fishing
schooner called the *Fortuna* went aground at Race Point in February of
1894 and scudded over the bar to the beach, two famous wreckers, Barna-
bas and Watkins, were there waiting with their horses, carts, and tools. The
crew had left the ship in lifeboats soon after it struck the bar, so the two
men were able to get right to work on the empty boat. They commenced
at around nine P.M., and by dawn "everything of value but the rigging"
was gone.

Most people pursued other careers when there wasn't a ship ashore. The
Reverend Isaiah Lewis of Wellfleet once famously dismissed his congregation in the middle of a sermon when he saw a ship in distress through the
window. His last words in the church were, according to the diary of the
Reverend Dr. William Bentley, "Start fair," and the whole congregation
rushed for the beach, stopping only long enough to retrieve their crowbars.
A similar story is told about a certain Reverend Lewis of Chatham, who
was handed a note midsermon from his wrecking partner—a ship was
aground. He called for a moment of silent prayer and slipped out the back
"and joined his partner on the beach, where, so the story goes, they made a
profitable deal to float the stranded vessel for her captain."

Such tales, though often repeated, don't exactly have the ring of gospel
truth. Nor is there any confirmed evidence of anyone on Cape Cod or
the Islands actually engaging in mooncussing, which was the potentially
murderous practice of luring ships aground by setting up false lights to con-
fuse captains into thinking they were in safer water than they actually were.

Such deceptions could be foiled by the appearance of the moon—hence the name. Of course, mooncussing wasn't something to brag about if it did occur.

The best loot to get from a wreck was money, preferably gold doubloons and pieces of eight. But cash was an extremely rare find, though the owners of a ship might pay good money to a local who knew his tides and shoals well enough to get a ship off a bar in one piece. The cargo of a merchant-man was the next best find. Then came navigational equipment. There was also a good market for used or mended fishing nets, masts, spars, deadeyes, blocks, shackles, stays, halyards, ship's wheels, chocks, cleats, and chain-plates. Finally, there was the wood itself. More than a few Cape Cod barns and houses were constructed or expanded using timber from wrecks.

The residents of Cape Cod weren't the type to let a little thing like a war for independence get in the way of the ancient law of salvage, "find-ers keepers." When the British frigate *Somerset* ran aground near the Clay Pounds on November 8, 1778, the local militia promptly rounded up nearly five hundred British survivors and marched them off toward Boston. The rest of the locals then got to work dissecting the ship, despite efforts by the Revolutionary leadership to claim the wreck as a prize of war. "From all I can learn there is wicked work at the wreck, riotous doings," scolded General Joseph Otis of the patriotic Barnstable family. "The Truro and Provincetown men have made a division of the clothing, ship's stores, hard tack and anything loose. Truro took two-thirds and Provincetown one-third. There is a plundering gang that way." A certain Colonel Doane of the American militia was sent aboard to restore order. But it didn't seem to have much effect on the outcome—Doane, it turned out, was from Wellfleet.

The political disposition of Cape Cod and the Islands during the American Revolution was decidedly mixed. Proindependence sentiment was strongest on the Cape. James Otis Jr., about whose 1761 plea against arbitrary search and seizure John Adams later said, "Then and there . . . the child Indepen-dence was born," came from Barnstable. His sister Mary Otis Warren was a leading propagandist of the cause and eventually wrote the first published history of the war. In 1774 there was a peaceful protest march some fifteen-hundred strong down the Cape to the courthouse in Barnstable to protest the king's elimination of independent jury trials in superior court.

Oddly enough, however, Barnstable did not vote for independence in

June of 1776. They weren't quite loyalist either, voting in the end only to give their representative "no instructions" on the issue. And though every other town on the Cape did vote to break with England, it was nowhere a unanimous action. Throughout the prelude to the Revolution, all over Cape Cod liberty poles went up during the day and were sawed down by pro-British factions at night. Half the town of Wellfleet moved out of Massachusetts rather than fight the king.

When hostilities finally began, the British immediately seized Provincetown as a base of operations and proceeded to enforce the ban on trade. The *Somerset* was semipermanently stationed there, and when it wasn't out looking for the French fleet, as it was the morning it went aground, it could be found looking for Yankee trading vessels or raiding various Cape Cod villages for supplies. British warships regularly gathered as well in Tarpaulin Cove on the Elizabeth Islands, from which they intercepted traffic through the sound and periodically harassed the residents of Falmouth and occasionally the Vineyard.

The resultant hard times did lead to instances of personal derring-do by local patriots: one evening in 1779 Colonel Joseph Dimmock and some twenty other Falmouth volunteers in three whaleboats rowed over to Tarpaulin and hid behind a dune overnight. At dawn they stormed and recaptured a schooner full of corn and made off with it across the sound. They were doing fine until they ran aground at Menemsha, where the British retook the ship. It wasn't over, though; another brash attack just before high tide lifted the boat, and the rebels were on their way to Woods Hole. The following year Dimmock captured a twelve-gun ship from right out of Edgartown Harbor and took it back to the Cape.

The virtual defenselessness of the Cape and Islands against the overwhelming power of the Royal Navy is often cited by local historians as a prerequisite to understanding the sometimes tepid resistance offered up by the locals. For instance, when General Charles Grey, along with four thousand troops and forty ships stationed in Newport, arrived in Vineyard Haven Harbor in 1778, the residents of that island dutifully rounded up ten thousand sheep and six hundred oxen and drove them down to the waiting ships. They also handed over the money already collected in taxes to the rebel government in Boston. Far from risking the bombardment of their town or staking out positions behind their myriad stone walls from which to take potshots at oncoming Redcoats à la Johnny Tremaine, the main complaint heard from Vineyarders after the raid was that General Grey didn't give them enough credit for cooperation.

In fairness to the Vineyarders, only the week before, Grey's force had burned much of the village and ships of New Bedford. From the hills of their north shore the Vineyarders could see the smoke. And Grey's own "Intelligence report on State of the Island of Martha's Vineyard," most likely supplied by a local loyalist, noted that of the 600 in the local militia— out of a population of 3,300—"not more than two third of that number are ever at home, being employed as Pilots, on board privateers."

On the other hand, there's the example of Falmouth, which was only marginally less vulnerable than Martha's Vineyard but nevertheless put up a stiff fight. A British force of ten ships (albeit much smaller than Grey's) rendezvoused in Tarpaulin Cove in the spring of 1779 with the intent of proceeding to Falmouth and raiding that town. On the second of April, a small landing party attempted to abscond with twelve cows that belonged to Ephraim and Manassah Swift but were chased off by the militia. The next day while one of the ship's big guns fired cannonballs, double-headed shot, bars of iron, and grapeshot into the town, ten longboats with 220 Redcoats attempted to land. The combined militias of Falmouth and Sandwich had entrenched themselves on shore, and what Kittredge described as "the only real engagement between the local militia and His Majesty's troops that occurred on Cape soil" ended as a resounding victory for the rebels when the landing party retreated again to its ships. The English tried next to get ashore at Woods Hole, but failed there, too, and finally gave up.

Kittredge also repeated an amusing anecdote about the home guard in Truro, which supposedly foiled a similar landing by the novel strategy of marching the local militia in circles around the top of a hill. From the decks of the attacking vessels it appeared that a truly large force of defenders had gathered. The attack was called off.

Defenders of Vineyard patriotism have always possessed a ready-made foil to insinuations of inadequate revolutionary spirit: "the Nation of Nantucket," as many eighteenth-century residents of that island liked to call their home. Nantucket's indifference to the complaints against the royal government appeared early on and did not go unnoticed in the more fervent cradles of liberty on the continent. In all likelihood the ersatz Indians who boarded three ships in Boston Harbor in December of 1773 and liberated them of their cargoes of tea knew full well that two of the vessels belonged to the Rotch family of Nantucket. The following May, fifty whaleboats were confiscated from the island by Continental soldiers and taken to Lake Champlain for the use of Benedict Arnold. And in 1775, the Continental Congress acted to prohibit any exports from the mainland to

Nantucket other than what the islanders themselves might consume, in order to prevent Nantucketers from transshipping supplies to the British.

By wartime, Nantucket's attitude was closer to outright loyalty to the king. When Captain Zeb Coffin tried to buy a cargo of flour in Philadelphia, wrote Kezia Coffin Fanning in her diary, "the Congress would not suffer him to bring any declaring that we were all Tories at Nantucket." In 1779 General Horatio Gates of the Continental Army wrote to the authorities in Boston urging them to prevent Sherburne, as Nantucket Town was then known, from continuing its effort to get a separate peace, commenting that "such Things are not only pernicious to the General Confederacy of the United States but traitorous." The governor of Connecticut, meanwhile, publicly suggested that any proindependence residents of Nantucket might as well move off-island, which many did during the war period. Similarly, a smaller number of loyalists from the mainland went in the other direction.

The English, for their part, reciprocated by granting the islanders special permits allowing them to hunt whales despite the general ban on fishing and commerce imposed on the rest of the rebelling colonies. Whale oil and other whale products were increasingly important to England, not only for lighting but for a variety of early industrial products and lubricants. Just as Nazi rocket scientists were solicited by the Allies after the Second World War, whenever American whaling ships were captured at sea, Nantucket crew members were offered the opportunity to join the English whale fleet.

The alternative offered was usually prison or impressment into the Royal Navy, both of which were known to be unsavory options. More than a few accepted the offer. According to a letter written in 1778 by Benjamin Franklin and John Adams—the American commissioners in France—of the roughly seventeen vessels in the English whaling fleet off Brazil, "all the officers and almost all the men . . . are Americans from Nantucket and Cape Cod in Massachusetts, excepting two or three from Rhode Island and perhaps one from Long Island."

A good part of Nantucket's response to the Revolution was no doubt a sincere result of the dominance of Quakerism on the island, with its rejection of violence as a tool of progress. And the often-noted and slightly cynical observation that Quaker religious principles meshed with local commercial goals isn't really supported by the outcome of the island's experimentation with neutrality. Both American privateers and English forces regularly attacked Nantucket vessels at sea and in port, so that by war's end the island was even more destitute than the severely depressed Cape Cod and Martha's Vineyard. By one count more than twelve hundred Nantucketers were killed or taken prisoner during the hostilities; one-quarter of the roughly eight hundred families still sticking it out on Nantucket at war's end were being held together by women whose husbands were dead.

Even Kezia Coffin—a confirmed loyalist whose contacts with both the British authorities in New York and (it was rumored) various smugglers gave her a virtual monopoly on the island during the war—was broke. At the peak of her power, she lived in a large house on Center Street that scandalized her fellow Friends with its ornament, its spinet, and its north-facing façade (everyone else sensibly faced south). More importantly, she held liens on the houses, wharves, warehouses, or other real estate of many of her neighbors. But when the worm turned, it did so with a vengeance; according to some sources, when she needed to auction off her holdings, her neighbors took turns as the only bidder to arrive. She still had her spirit, however. She had to be carried out of her repossessed house in her chair because she refused to leave. She may also have been the inventor of the harassing lawsuit; when her lawyer told her she had no chance of success, she replied that she didn't want to win but "to keep this in court as long as I live."

After the war Nantucketers moved off the island in waves. Some, like the forty families that founded Dartmouth, Nova Scotia, left because the effort to be recognized by the new American government as a neutral country failed. Some went with William Rotch, the leading ship owner of Nantucket whose cargo of tea had ended up in Boston Harbor. He sailed to England on the fourth of July, 1785, and promised Prime Minister William Pitt that he had one hundred whaling families whose loyalty to the crown was so enduring that for only two hundred pounds apiece they would move from their little island to England. Pitt offered eighty-seven pounds, and Rotch went across the channel and closed a better deal with the French in only five hours.

In the end, though, only nine families went with Rotch to Dunkirk. And by 1793, when France and England were again on the brink of war, Rotch worried that if they continued flying under the French flag they would all be caught or destroyed by the English. So he took all his ships back across the channel. The English, however, hadn't forgotten that he'd spurned their offers the first time around and promptly confiscated as many of Rotch's ships as they could catch. He got them back, but the message was fairly clear, and Rotch and company returned to Nantucket, where they found themselves unwelcomed by those who had toughed out the worst of the postwar depression on-island. Rotch eventually wound up at the mouth of the Acushnet River in Buzzards Bay, where in 1765 his father, Joseph, and a shipbuilder named Joseph Russell had started a small settlement called New Bedford.* Still other Nantucketers, like those who went to Hudson, New York, or the Ohio Valley, just wanted a fresh start.

Enough stayed behind on Nantucket, however, to get right back to work killing whales and making money. In February 1783, the ship *Bedford*, carrying a load of oil from Nantucket, became the first ship to sail up the Thames toward London flying the Stars and Stripes. The ship's captain was William Mooers. Its primary owner was none other than the decidedly nonnationalistic William Rotch.

It should be noted that plenty of individual Nantucketers did their part in the fight for liberty. Just as Grey's spies had noted about the Vineyard and was doubtless true of the Cape as well, hundreds of sailors from Nantucket went out on privateering voyages to harass English shipping. Nantucketers were well represented in John Paul Jones's various crews, and two Islanders, Henry Gardner and Jerry Evans, were reportedly among the men Jones ordered up into the yards of the *Bonhomme Richard* with a bucket of grenades during that ship's famous battle with the more heavily gunned British frigate *Serapis* off Flamborough Head, England.

The *Serapis* should have won the day. But at the last minute, when the two ships were gunwale to gunwale, blasting away at each other point-blank, and fighting was hand to hand on the decks, someone in the rigging succeeded in lighting the fuse on a grenade and lobbing it down the main hatch into part of the *Serapis*'s powder supply. The tables turned, and when the fight was over Jones was captain of the *Serapis*. But sadly, the *Bonhomme Richard*—named by Jones's French backers after his friend Ben Franklin's Poor Richard—was all but driftwood from the engagement and had to be abandoned.

Potential driftwood was about all that was left of the *Somerset* when the good citizens of the lower Cape were through with her. She didn't actually drift, though; remnants of the ship resurfaced periodically for the next century and a half.

---

*William Bradford and others originally bought the site of New Bedford in 1652, and an early settlement of Quakers there sinfully refused to support a Congregationalist minister. It was abandoned during King Philip's War.

The bones of the English warship Somerset, *wrecked during the American Revolution, resurfaced out of the sands of Provincetown in 1973, in 1925, and as shown in this picture, in 1886.* (COURTESY OF THE NICKERSON MEMORIAL COLLECTION, CAPE COD COMMUNITY COLLEGE)

The wreck of the *Somerset* by the forces of nature is an appropriate sort of monument to the role of the Cape and Islands in the Revolution. The militia were brave at Falmouth and cunning in Truro. Dimmock had his minor successes in Tarpaulin Cove, as did hundreds of privateers from all over the region in all the oceans of the world. But in the end, it was a gale, the Cape Cod beach, and a riotous crowd of crowbars that struck the single most damaging blow to the English: a flagship lost, and a crew of nearly five hundred taken prisoner. And it wasn't even a memorable gale.

Neither was the storm that knocked the *Essex* on her beam ends a generation later. That storm wasn't even half a gale. It was just a precocious squall, gone almost as soon as it began and followed, wrote First Mate Chase, with "fine weather again." The only thing memorable about it is that it happened to a doomed ship.

It's hard to read the various narratives of the *Essex* disaster without seeing in the roaring wind and rain some Melvillian premonition of things to come. It was only their second day out, after all; they were barely out of sight of Nantucket. Then came the "heavy and repeated claps of thunder."

What's more, other than a few sails virtually all the damage was concentrated in two distinct areas: the gear with which the crew of the *Essex* intended to kill whales, and that with which they intended to prepare their meals. According to Nickerson, all three whaleboats on the larboard side were either stove in or gone, along with all their harpoons, ropes, and assorted tackle. And the "cook house together with all its apparatus had been carried away and broken up."

CHAPTER 22

AWAITE PAWANA

It was time for me to get back into the kayak, back onto the changeless changing water that makes this corner of Massachusetts a cape and islands rather than just land. Makes it a seasonal Valhalla rather than a suburb, the edge of wilderness rather than the outskirts of civilization. It was May, rapidly becoming June, becoming summer on the Cape and Islands—becoming paradise.

I packed my trinkets and navigational aids and waited once more for the right day to cross Vineyard Sound. I resumed my old habit of listening hourly to the National Weather Service broadcasts: ". . . at the Buzzards Bay entrance tower the wind was out of the west at nineteen knots and the seas were four feet. . . ." Again the wind seemed to blow hard whenever I had the freedom to leave and was maddeningly calm when obligations kept me on the Vineyard. Some time during the previous winter the National Weather Service replaced all its announcers with someone I thought must be a visiting, speech-impaired scientist from Sweden. I thought this until I was told it was, in fact, the voice of a computer. That Big Brother should choose to make his debut as a forecaster of New England weather seemed oddly appropriate, and one morning when he reported in his strange, clipped way that it was windy and I could see from my window that it was not, I disregarded his disinformation and set out across the sound.

I came later to think it was a mistake to do so. Having fussed around with my gear during the predawn calm, by the time I got a few miles out into the sound the wind had begun to pick up. The water, meanwhile, which had been at nearly dead high when I made the decision to paddle, was soon flowing east with the falling tide. Just as Big Brother had predicted, seas built to around four feet. Whitecaps appeared in what seemed an unnecessarily sudden way.

I won't say that I was ever really in danger, but I was out past the Lucas Shoals in seas I didn't like the look of, seas that looked like they were going to get worse before they got better. I was probably three miles from home and three miles from Tarpaulin Cove and was making relatively slow progress due to the necessity of heading northwest into the oncoming waves. My plan for this trip was not to go west again to Cuttyhunk but to work east past Woods Hole and along the northern shore of Nantucket Sound, maybe to paddle up the Bass River to its headwaters, where Thomas Nickerson's ancestor William lived before he was run out of Yarmouth in 1641.

Instead, in the middle of the sound I turned around, thinking that if I was going to paddle three miles in rough water I'd rather be getting closer to a hot shower than the well-posted private coast of Naushon. A good-sized dump of water poured over my bow and around my sprayskirt in the process of my changing course, but otherwise the maneuver was uneventful. I told myself that my reason for chickening out was that I hadn't brought bivouac gear, and at the rate I was going I wasn't likely to make it to the motels of Woods Hole or Falmouth by dark as I had planned. Probably closer to the truth, though, was that Big Brother had said this wind was going to blow for several days. And I, now a dutifully respectful little brother, could wait.

About a quarter of the way back to the north shore of the Vineyard I saw off to my right a large marine animal. Or rather, a very large part of a large marine animal. It was black, mottled a bit with white, larger than any animal I had seen in Vineyard Sound before. It moved under its own power and then disappeared beneath the surface. It was not an ocean sunfish; I had seen many of those. And I am fairly certain it was not a leatherback turtle, though I had previously seen only one of those. Perhaps it was a large seal. I didn't see it twice, and I couldn't stay long to watch. I didn't see a whale. It was surely not whale. But neither did I think when my boat touched the home shore that the voyage was in vain. It was not, after all, a mistake to set out.

CHAPTER 23

CAPE VERDE

Pollard wanted to return to Nantucket to get more whaleboats. Only two of the original five were undamaged by the squall, meaning there weren't enough boats for all three crews to lower simultaneously once they got into whales. Nor would there be any spare boats to replace the inevitable losses to thrashing flukes and other misfortunes. But after consulting with First Mate Chase and the other officers, Pollard changed his mind and ordered a course set once more for the Azores. We can't go back to Nantucket, he told the crew, because the northeast wind would make such a trip too long.

Not everyone was convinced by his reasoning. The *Essex* went forward, Ship's Boy Nickerson wrote later, because a reputation for good fortune left a ship far more rapidly than it was earned, and Captain Pollard no doubt knew that sailors in their home port would desert an unlucky ship even faster still. So on the *Essex* went, and every time they passed a homeward-bound ship—Nickerson remembered there were many along this well-traveled stretch of water—all the green hands started to mumble about how sorry they were that they ever signed up to go whaling.

Not that there were any whales to be seen. The waters around the Azores were often productive, but though the crew of the *Essex* continued their shifts in the mastheads and were kept at work "fitting the ship and preparing all things which would be useful," they saw no prey.

At the end of August or the beginning of September, the islands of Corvo and Flores were sighted. From the distance, thought Nickerson, they

looked like "a cloud with its sides nearly perpendicular." Almost simultaneously to the cry from the masthead, however, the wind died, leaving them
within sight of land but unable to close in on it. All through the day they
waited, without so much as a zephyr to push them along, all through the
night, too.

By the next morning, Pollard had had enough. Two boats were lowered,
a barrel of oil was loaded on, and crews were selected. They rowed all
morning until the ship was hull down, meaning only her masts could be
seen. The high white cliffs of Flores seemed as far away as ever. They rowed
on until the entire ship was below the horizon. Pollard and his officers had
breakfast before leaving the *Essex*, but the crew had had nothing to eat. Still
they rowed and finally reached the port of Santa Cruz.

Once Pollard was through the formality of applying to the American
consul on the island for permission to trade—something virtually every
passing whaling captain requested—the barrels of oil were off-loaded and
tapped. One of the lesser officers, probably Obed Hendricks or another
boatsteerer, was designated "clerk for the day" and given a quart pot and a
pint cup with which to measure out the currency. Then, while the luckier
members of the rowing crews wandered around town, the clerk officially
opened for business.

It was, at times, a noisy event. There was the usual haggling over price
and quality, of course, for if "the clerk be too liberal, he will pay dear for
his whistle, and his oil cask will be empty before his boat is laden with his
trade," reported Nickerson. Some local farmers came down to the shore
with only a small bowl of potatoes, others with a whole barrel. "And then
will come perhaps a few onions or some half dozen fowls," recalled Nickerson. The onions from the Azores were huge, up to six inches in diameter,
and the potatoes, too, were big. And in a place with not much else of interest going on and even fewer ways to make a living, even persons with nothing to trade often crowded around the barrel. Many had cups of their own
with which they attempted to catch any spillage. Arguments broke out over
"who should have the first opportunity to catch the drippings, until the
clerk, worn out with their confusion, drove them away."

Whoever it was that Pollard chose as clerk of the day had a knack for
commerce. By late afternoon the whaleboats were full of provisions, and
there was still oil left over. It was a successful day's work, and Pollard ordered
the leftover oil to be given away, distributed here and there to "the poor old
women of which there were many around us asking alms." Then they all
climbed back in the boats, rowed out of the harbor, and were overjoyed to

discover the *Essex* had managed to close the distance and lay just around the first point. Pollard gave the order to set sail as soon as the boats were unloaded and back on the davits.

A similar scene took place little more than two weeks later in the Cape Verde Islands, but there the locals weren't interested in purchasing whale oil. They wanted white beans. And they weren't selling vegetables, they were peddling hogs. Pollard wasn't unprepared: he had the beans and wanted the bacon, so as soon as the barrel of legumes could be gotten ashore, business commenced. This time, a barrel and a half of beans purchased thirty hogs, which might seem like a good price except that the animals weren't likely to win any prizes at the fair. "The hogs that are taken from those islands are almost skeletons and when walking the bones seem to almost pierce through the skin," reported Nickerson.

Knowing the relative value of all manner of goods, or at least being able to estimate it, was almost as important to being a successful whaling captain as skillful navigation and finding prey. With no way to fully stock a ship in advance for such long and unpredictable voyages, captains were also by necessity small-time traders. So along with the usual whaling gear, hardtack, rum, matches, pea jackets, sea boots, sea biscuits, et cetera, there were all kinds of other things stashed away in the hold. In Tongatapu in the Tongan Islands, for instance, a log keeper named Mayhew on the whaling ship *Cadmus* out of Edgartown noted that the captain sold 120 yards of cotton cloth, 50 pounds of bread, 5 pounds of tobacco, 100 flints, and 4 muskets. In exchange, the galley was replenished with a half ton of yams, 45 hogs, 40 Dunghill fowls, 300 coconuts, wood, and water.

This ongoing need of whale ships to restock the galley during their peregrinations often forced them into obscure ports overlooked by merchant vessels with their more specific routes. It was a Nantucket captain of the certifiably old Island name of Mayhew Folger who "rediscovered" Pitcairn Island in 1808, where he found one survivor of the nine mutineers from the *Bounty*. Edouard Stackpole, in his definitive history of American whaling, *The Sea-Hunters*, made a compelling argument that another Nantucketer was the first to recognize Antarctica as a continent. According to one estimate, by 1834 more than four hundred islands in the Pacific had been (re)discovered by New England whalers, the vast majority of them from Cape Cod and the Islands. They named them after themselves, their wives, their ships, and their investors. There was once a New Nantucket in the Pacific, a Chase's Island, a Rotch's Island, and a Chatham Island. There is still a Starbuck Island and a Swain Island.

Not that the merchant mariners from Cape Cod and elsewhere didn't do their share of improvising, as Elijah Cobb's adventures in revolutionary France attest. Isaac Clark, also of Brewster, was the first to skipper an American vessel up over the top of Europe into the White Sea. His neighbor from Yarmouth, Captain Ebenezer Sears, was the first around the bottom of Africa into the Indian Ocean. John Kendrick of South Orleans (now Harwich), in command of the *Columbia* in 1787, was the first American around Cape Horn into the Pacific. After he traded ships with Robert Gray, his fellow captain in the expedition and the one who rightfully deserves most of the credit for its success, Kendrick took the forty-foot *Lady Washington* across the Pacific to Japan in 1791. He was the first American there.

The first woman of European descent to visit Japan was Abigail Jernegan of Martha's Vineyard. Jernegan's husband, Nathaniel, was captain of the *Eliza F. Mason*, which arrived in Japan shortly after Commodore Perry's 1854 "opening" of the country. Bringing one's wife along was one of the perquisites of command for the captains of both whaling and merchant vessels, and though it was not the norm to take advantage of the possibility, neither was it extraordinarily rare. In the Sea of Okhotsk off Russia, three whale ships—the *Phoenix* of Nantucket, the *Cowper* from the Vineyard, and the *Rodman* of New Bedford—sailed for a few weeks together, and all had women on board. There was even a slumber party of sorts one night when four women spent the night on the *Cowper*, with Susan Folger Fisher as their host. Another time, in the middle of the Pacific, some sources refer to a party of no fewer than nine women who managed to gather on Captain Charles Grant's ship for a Christmas gam.*

Once in a while, the women who went to sea were relatively new brides, like Hannah Rebecca Crowell of West Sandwich (now Sagamore), who married William Burgess of Brewster in 1852. He sailed away once, less than four months after their marriage, in command of the brand-new clipper ship *Whirlwind*, and was gone for more than a year. That was enough for both of them, and she went on the next voyage. The ship sailed

---

*The word *gam* originally meant a school of whales, or, as a verb, it meant whales gathering together in a school. The origin was probably *game*, as in prey. But the whalers soon applied it to themselves as well, hence a gam was a meeting of two or more ships at sea, for the purpose of trading news or passing time.

from Boston for San Francisco on February 4, 1854, and judging from her letters and journal, once she got her sea legs Rebecca Burgess adored life at sea. "It fills the mind with a sense of majesty and greatness of the Ruler of the Universe to gaze upon this mighty expanse of water," she wrote. "I can say that it is pleasanter than any scene I have witnessed on land."

She passed some of her time in writing and in visiting with the only other woman on board, a passenger. She exercised with barbells and occasionally played hymns on her accordion in concert with a crew member who also played. Mostly, though, it seems she studied the art of sailing. She practiced myriad nautical terms on her husband, to his great amusement. She modeled her own journal after the ship's log, and studied Bowditch's *American Practical Navigator*. By the time *Whirlwind* returned to New York, she could take altitudes and calculate positions and courses as accurately as her husband.

More often than young brides, however, the record is of women who had finished the hard labor of raising offspring in the general absence of their sailing husbands and accompanied their spouses on what might have been their valedictory cruises. Fisher of the *Cowper*, for instance, chose to go along with her husband, Nehemiah, in honor of their twentieth wedding anniversary. Most of their years of marriage were doubtless spent apart. She wrote with obvious pleasure of occasional afternoons when she and he would put ashore on a deserted Russian beach and the two of them would walk together gathering berries.

Likewise, when Captain Justus Doane of Chatham came out of retirement in 1853 for one last voyage around the world, he determined to take his beloved with him. He was one of the premier clipper captains, having made, among other things, a record passage from Boston to Honolulu in ninety-six days. But the second honeymoon was cut short in Calcutta, where he and she alike contracted cholera and died within a day of each other.

Many women went on only one or a few voyages, but Charity Randall of New Bedford went on every voyage with her husband John Oliver Norton of the Vineyard. "She had to," someone who knew both Nortons was quoted as saying in Emma Mayhew Whiting and Henry Beetle Hough's remarkable book *Whaling Wives*, "or he would never have come back alive."

More literally crucial was the presence of Caroline Mayhew on the *Powhatan* in 1846. When her husband, the captain, along with most of the rest of the crew were flattened by smallpox in the middle of the south

Atlantic, it fell to her to remember her lessons in navigation learned at the Dukes County Academy in West Tisbury. Fortunately for the ship, she had a good memory.

Sadly, as it turned out, young Hannah Rebecca Burgess, née Crowell, was required to perform the same duty, though not on *Whirlwind*. In the much larger *Challenger*, a 202-foot, 1,334-ton extreme clipper, she and her husband sailed again for San Francisco in 1854 and from there to Honolulu, Hong Kong, and Whampoa, the port of Canton. There, the ship was loaded with tea for the London market.

Rebecca, as she was called, fell ill during the voyage around the Cape of Good Hope to Europe and ate a dozen raw eggs per day for two solid months, which seemed to cure her. But though she was well by the time they got to London in April of 1856, her husband, William, was diagnosed there with a malady of the liver. The doctors gave him a dose of mercury, which naturally very nearly killed him, though by June he felt well enough to set out for the Chincha Islands off Peru to pick up a cargo of guano. But apparently he was not cured. Rebecca kept the ship's log for virtually the entire voyage, and by the time the ship was loaded with guano Captain Burgess was bedridden and not sure if he would survive even a voyage to Valparaiso, where there might be better medical help. When someone suggested he find a backup captain, as the first mate was not a competent navigator, he is remembered to have replied, "My wife has navigated the *Challenger* in these nineteen months and is fully capable of doing so now." A few weeks later he was dead at sea, and just as he predicted, she guided the ship safely into Valparaiso.

A few of the many books on whaling mention a woman who actually sailed before the mast as a full-fledged whaler. Her name is lost and her existence unsubstantiated, though tradition has her coming originally from Rochester, New York, and sailing out of New Bedford. She supposedly was able to hide her gender for two years and, according to some versions, was only discovered when the captain ordered her shirt removed so she could be flogged for insubordination.

Not surprisingly, perhaps, the presence of women didn't always sit smoothly with those men who were not permitted to bring their families. A mate on the *Gazelle* wrote of his captain's beloved that "she is the meanest, most hoggish and the greediest female that ever existed. Her looks is despised by everyone on board and the whistle of a gale of wind through the rigging is much more musical than the sound of her voice." Nor were the women who sailed always impressed with the quality of their husbands'

When her husband the captain died, Hannah Rebecca Burgess piloted the extreme clipper Challenger *to safety.* (COURTESY OF THE SANDWICH GLASS MUSEUM)

employees. Lucy P. Smith of Martha's Vineyard traveled on the whale ship *Nautilus* and wrote of the first mate: "Without exceptions I think him nearest to a savage of anyone I ever met. He possesses a very quick, ungovernable temper, is also very jealous, and is very ignorant of the rules of good breeding, and yet has a very high opinion of himself. At times he is very social and at other times will not answer when spoken to. If we only had decently civil officers, I should enjoy life. As it is there is but little enjoyment. All that induces me to endure it is my husband's society."

Given the jealousy with which current residents of the Cape and Islands guard what few remnants of old-time quaintness remain in the region, it is somewhat ironic that for a century and a half the region was far more worldly than it is today. With so many men and not a few women who went to sea and saw the world, the region was in some ways more cosmopolitan even than New York or Boston. As early as 1809, one writer estimated that three-quarters of the male population of Brewster were mariners, and as late as 1930 another writer claimed to know of ninety-nine captains in that town who had sailed on all seven seas. And while Brewster and Nantucket probably had the greatest numbers of ocean-going captains and officers, they were merely the first among relative equals in that category.

According to a letter from Daniel Webster to a friend of his in Dennis, the great orator once represented a client in Barnstable County who was involved in a lawsuit that somehow hinged on the relative position of the rocks and coral in Honolulu harbor.* "The counsel for the opposite party proposed to call witnesses to give information to the jury. I at once saw a smile which I thought I understood, and suggested to the judge that very probably some of the jury had seen the entrance themselves. Upon which, seven out of the twelve arose and said they were quite familiarly acquainted with it, having seen it often," Webster recalled. The same thing no doubt would have happened on Martha's Vineyard or Nantucket; on Thanksgiving day 1852, there were 145 whale ships docked in Honolulu harbor.

The effects of such an influx from Cape Cod and the Islands was not always beneficial to the long-term health of the ecology and indigenous cultures of the Pacific. Hunting seals for the Chinese market was always a much smaller business than whaling, but with ships like the *Favourite* out of Nantucket arriving in Canton in 1807 with more than 87,000 skins in the hold, it didn't take long for the seal and sea-elephant populations of the south Atlantic to collapse. Arguably even more insidious in the long run was the fact that almost everywhere merchants and whalers went, rats, pigs, goats, and missionaries were sure to follow. The impact of the first three was unquestionably to the detriment of local flora and fauna. Even today, the Park Service is trying to get the pigs out of Hawaii's national parks.

---

*Webster often visited Cape Cod and the Islands for business and bluefishing, and once caught a nine-pound cod on a fly rod.

One's opinion of the missionaries, of course, depends largely on one's perspective and one's opinion of the sometimes idyllic and sometimes quite violent lives of the various Polynesians. For the purposes and scope of this book, however, it will have to suffice to say that the missionaries at least had better intentions and more restraint than the whalers themselves. Though understandably few participants were willing to risk writing the details, there were regular orgies in Oahu and elsewhere. One sailor on Obed Starbuck's *Hero* in 1822 wrote of the ship being met by enough beautiful swimming "Wyhunas" that "every man took to himself a rib."

Farther west in northern New Zealand's Bay of Islands, the port of Kororareka (now Russell) was well known to American sailors as "the whorehouse of the Pacific." It was, in some ways, an alter ego to the Cape and Islands: Caroline and William Mayhew of Edgartown, owners of a major whaling station there, once counted 130 whale ships in the harbor; the nearby whaling waters were called the Chatham Grounds. But there was more for sale in Kororareka than sex. In 1822, the Nantucket *Inquirer* ran a story about one of the first Maori shrunken heads to appear on the island: "The skin resembles parchment, and is very curiously tattooed. The inside of the skull is perfectly clean and smooth—the teeth in a fine state of preservation, as are the eyelids, ears, lip, nose, etc.," the paper reported. Shrunken heads became such a fad on Nantucket, says the historian Philbrick, that there was "a black market in these artifacts that encouraged rival tribes to war against each other so as to acquire more heads for the illicit trade. Indeed, if a whaling captain saw a native whose facial tattoos especially appealed to him, he 'might order a head on the hoof, so to say,' and when he returned on his next voyage, the shrunken head would be waiting for him." Roughly half the Maori population succumbed to disease and head-hunting by 1839.

Caroline and William Mayhew were only two of the many Cape and Islanders who took up permanent residence in various far-flung ports. "Go where you will from Nova Scotia to the Mississippi you will find almost every where some natives of these two islands employed in seafaring occupations," Crevecoeur wrote in 1782. A generation or two later he might have included the globe.

Some relocated by choice: in the 1850s Grafton Hillman, formerly of the Vineyard, ran a mariners' hotel and a warehouse and shipyard in Paita, Peru. Others ended up halfway around the globe by accident: a young sailor named John Higgins of Brewster was wrecked off the coast of Australia in the early 1850s. He found another ship and got as far as the Caroline Islands before it, too, wrecked, leaving him as the only known survivor. Taken in by the local Polynesians, he proceeded in cinematic fashion to marry the local king's beautiful daughter. By the time one of his old neighbors in Brewster, Captain Charles Freeman, found him, Higgins had no intention of returning to Massachusetts. His ability to communicate with passing whalers made his adopted lagoon a stopping-off place for trading cocoa oil, pigs, and other goods. He gave Freeman a few letters to take back to his family, letting them know he was alive and well, which he was—until the neighboring group of islanders, perhaps jealous of the wealth earned through trading or unconvinced by the preaching, attacked his adopted village and killed him.

David Whippey, who left Nantucket on the whaling ship *Francis* in 1819, was luckier. After changing ships a few times without finding a job he considered worth keeping, he got himself discharged in the Fiji Islands, where he became something of a courtier to the powerful King Kakombau of Ambow Island. Kakombau eventually gave him his own island to administer, a tropical paradise called Ovalau.

The global reach of Cape Cod and the Islands had effects at home, too, not the least of which was the immeasurable broadening of outlook that came with a relative abundance of men and women who had seen more of the world than their own field and barn. On a superficial level, this was manifested in homes full of curiosities brought back from far corners of the earth, and not only shrunken heads. The Folger Museum on Nantucket has an entire room devoted to various Polynesian artifacts brought home by whalers. The Glass Museum in Sandwich is similarly well endowed with curiosities from China. The previously mentioned Caroline Mayhew returned home from the Bay of Islands to Edgartown with a kangaroo. The largest tree in that town—an immense pagoda on North Water Street—also crossed the Pacific in a whaling ship. Even the cobbles that today seem so intrinsic to Nantucket's aura came to the island as ships' ballast.

Of a far more lasting and positive impact than the various baubles and curios, or even the cobbles on Main Street, were the sailors recruited in far-away ports who eventually made new (though sometimes temporary) homes for themselves on Cape Cod and the Islands. In 1807 two Cantonese merchants arrived in Nantucket on the *Favourite* and took up temporary residence on the island. They returned to Nantucket again in 1814. At various times during the nineteenth century there were tiny but recognizable populations of Polynesians living on that island and on Martha's Vineyard.

But the most important group of arrivals by far were the various Portuguese-speaking sailors from the Azores, the Cape Verde Islands, and Portugal itself. The Atlantic Islands, because they were so often the first ports visited after leaving home, were also where green hands with second thoughts about a life at sea often chose to desert. If they couldn't be rounded up and returned to the ship, local sailors were hired to replace them.

Beginning in the second half of the 1700s, ships from Cape Cod and the Islands occasionally sailed to the Azores and Cape Verde with nothing but skeleton crews, expecting to fill out the roster with the qualified (and relatively inexpensive) sailors there. The welcome extended to the Portuguese by the existent Anglo-Americans, sad to report, was not always warm. (As late as the 1940s, Anglo writers wrote of "invasions" by Portuguese Americans.) But from this seed, sizable Portuguese-American communities developed on the Vineyard, on Nantucket, at Provincetown, Falmouth, Harwich, Chatham, and farther inland at New Bedford, Fall River, and Providence.

Interestingly, the Cape Verde Islands played a bit part in another long-term process of change on Cape Cod. When the *Essex* first sailed into the harbor at the island of Mayo, Nickerson recalled gaping at "large pyramidal hills (that) looked very curious to us who were strangers, as they were perfectly white and all about one height." The strange hills were locally produced salt.

Cape Cod at that time was itself a major producer of salt, which was used primarily for curing cod and other fish to be shipped down to the sugar plantations of the Caribbean. A byproduct, Glauber salt, was used by tanners to keep hides soft. In the early colonial period, small quantities of salt were made by boiling sea water over enormous quantities of wood; as much as 350 gallons of water must be evaporated to produce a bushel. But by the American Revolution, when the British blockade put a stop to salt imports, wood was too precious for such uses. Then John Sears of Dennis built his first trough. It was essentially a long wooden vat full of sea water that he covered over whenever it rained, and his neighbors called it "John Sears's Folly"—until the end of the summer, that is, when John Sears had eight bushels of salt to sell at wartime prices, and his neighbors had fish to cure. (In 1783, a bushel of salt brought a whopping eight dollars.) Sears got a shaky patent on the process, which he sold for forty dollars to Nathaniel

Freeman of Harwich, who added a windmill to pump water into the vats. By 1802, there were 136 saltworks on the Cape, producing 40,000 bushels of table salt and 182,000 bushels of Glauber salts. Then, another war broke out and raised domestic salt prices even higher.

As far as Cape Cod and the Islands were concerned, the War of 1812 was largely a repeat of the Revolution. The Royal Navy once again established itself in Provincetown and (occasionally) at Tarpaulin Cove. And once again, against a relatively passive backdrop, there were occasional daring feats, most of them at sea. Captains Matthew Mayo and Winslow Knowles of Eastham, for instance, were captured by a British schooner in 1814 while on their way back from selling a cargo of rye in Boston. Knowles went back to Boston to try to round up three hundred dollars to ransom the schooner, and Mayo was told to pilot the British schooner around the Cape. A gale came up, and Mayo was ordered to anchor in the lee of Billingsgate Island. He did, but then found an opportunity to cut the hawser down to the last few strands with his pocketknife.

When the line parted and the schooner began to drift, Mayo recommended they attempt to make for a harbor he knew of about ten miles to the leeward. The harbor turned out to be the flats of Eastham, and when the ship struck sand Mayo told his escort not to worry—the tide was rising and they would soon be off. The only problem, he said, would be if the townspeople saw a bunch of Redcoats on deck and got suspicious. The marines and sailors all dutifully went below-decks and proceeded to get into a keg of rum.

The tide was not, as Mayo had promised, coming in. It was going out. And when the vessel began to list over and the marines stumbled out of the hold, they were greeted by their erstwhile captive pilot, who had thrown all their weapons overboard—all but the two pistols he was pointing at them. Mayo then jumped overboard and waded ashore, where nearly the entire town of Eastham had collected, as usual, to see what might happen to the wreck. At dead low tide, the local militia walked out and rounded up the entire crew.

If that were how the story of bumbling Englishmen bested by plucky Patriots ended, it might sound a little too much like an episode of *Hogan's Heroes*. But according to Enoch Pratt's 1844 history of Eastham, Wellfleet, and Truro, the militia marched their captives straight to a local tavern. And from there, later that night, the English all managed to escape, steal a whaleboat, and get themselves back to the *Spencer*. Not long after, Commodore

Ragget of that ship informed Eastham that all the vessels in town, plus the saltworks and all the buildings, would be destroyed unless they came up with $1,200. They did, and were not molested by the British again during the War of 1812.

Throughout the war, Commodore Ragget made a habit of sailing into local harbors with offers not to burn the houses if the townsfolk agreed to pay ransoms. Only Orleans of the lower Cape towns refused to pay anything, and found out he wasn't bluffing. Ragget's first cannonballs landed on the beach and in the marshes, and then he ran aground trying to get closer, both of which errors must have amused the townsfolk. But not for long: Ragget sent two barges in and burned two ships lying on the flats. Falmouth, too, was bombarded, just as it had been in the Revolution. The brig *Nimrod* with eighteen guns showed up in January of 1814 and demanded a ship in the harbor. When the town refused, the cannonballs flew. But nobody was hurt, and the *Nimrod* eventually left without the prize.

For the most part, though, opposition on Cape Cod and the Islands to "Mr. Madison's War" and the resulting disruption of trade was even more widespread than loyalism had been in the Revolution. Although the English policy of impressing American sailors into their navy—the nominal reason for the hostilities—was universally hated on Cape Cod and the Islands, only Sandwich, Barnstable, Falmouth, and Orleans were openly in favor of war. On the Vineyard, too, opinion was decidedly mixed. And once again, Nantucket attempted to broker a separate deal for herself, going so far as to promise the English not to pay taxes to the United States government. As a result, two British admirals, one of them named Coffin, went to England's infamous Dartmoor Prison and singled out the Nantucket sailors to inform them that they would soon be released. But as it had a generation before, the Nation of Nantucket wound up just as destitute as her neighbors by war's end. Once again, dozens of families left the Cape and Islands for good.

Perhaps the only good local economic news was the price of salt, which had risen with the cutoff of imports. Between the cannons on the courthouse lawn in Barnstable, which were originally specified for the protection of that town's saltworks, and the various other towns willing to pay Ragget his protection money, there was very little disruption of production. What's more, whaleboats loaded with salt easily evaded the British blockade at Provincetown by crossing the Cape through Jeremiah's Gutter,

The saltworks of South Yarmouth, circa 1870. (COURTESY OF THE STURGIS PUBLIC LIBRARY, BARNSTABLE)

a small ditch between the head of Boat Meadow Creek and Town Cove in Orleans.*

By 1824 there were sixty-nine saltworks in Provincetown, fifty-four in Eastham, fifty-two in South Yarmouth, eighty in Chatham. Hundreds of windmills with canvas sails trimmed by retired mariners pumped bay brine up into vast networks of vats. According to one traveler in 1839, there were salt vats all along the shoreline south of Provincetown for twenty miles. On the Vineyard, meanwhile, saltworks were concentrated along Lagoon Pond in Vineyard Haven, with a few more scattered around up-island. (Nantucket was considered too often foggy to be competitive.) By the Civil War there were five hundred saltworks on the Cape, representing an estimated $2 million investment.

But in the second half of the century new salt mines in the American West opened, driving down prices. Wood by then was too scarce on Cape Cod and the Islands even for vat building. Worst of all, though, were the imports from overseas producers. As early as 1819, when the *Essex* dropped anchor in the harbor at Mayo to trade for pigs, Nickerson and others

---

*The same route, coincidentally, that the Macys, Starbucks, et al. used to cross the Cape on their first trip to Nantucket.

among her crew noticed several American ships in the port taking on cargoes of salt.

Captain Pollard didn't want any salt, and any qualms among his crew caused by the squall seemed to have either passed or were never significant enough to inspire mass desertions, so he wasn't looking to hire any sailors, either. One source of renewed optimism on the *Essex* was no doubt their extraordinary good fortune just before coming into port. While off the island of Mayo they saw a ship piled up on shore. It was the whaler *Archimedes*, which not long before, while under the command of George B. Coffin, had struck a rock and been intentionally run aground. Usually the sight of fellow mariners' misfortune was a sobering one, but where there are grounded whalers there are sure to be recyclable whaleboats, so Pollard and the officers of the *Essex* were "more cheerful than usual" as they took turns looking through the spyglass.

They headed in as close as was safe in order to get a better look, and two men came out from the *Archimedes* in a rowboat. The crew and captain had already returned home, the men reported. The contents of the wreck, meanwhile, now belonged to the acting American consul, Ferdinand Gardner (of Hudson, New York, but as that town was founded by Nantucket whalers, he was presumably also of the Island family of that name). Perhaps a deal could be struck with him, the men in the rowboat suggested.

Gardner only parted with one whaleboat, but Pollard was happy nonetheless. As Nickerson wrote, "in our situation even one boat was a goodly prize; and we were under many obligations to him for thus far supplying our need." It was a bit of an understatement: later, the lives of six members of the *Essex* crew—including both Nickerson and Chase—would come to depend entirely on the sturdiness of the *Archimedes*'s whaleboat.

There was one other event in Mayo that served to lighten the mood. While going ashore to trade for hogs within full sight of the entire crew, Pollard and his mates managed to capsize their whaleboat in the surf. No one was hurt, but everyone aboard was soaked to the skin, and the eyes of sailors back on the *Essex* were wet with laughter. The ship's boy could think of "nothing that a sailor would not encounter willingly where life would not be too greatly endangered if he can but turn the laugh upon his captain or officers."

Neither Chase nor Pollard mention the dunking in their own narratives of the voyage; both stick to the hardships to come. But it's probably safe to assume they managed to maintain their good humor despite the indignity. After a day and a half in Mayo, with their new whaleboat stowed and their thirty thin pigs safely aboard, the somewhat merrier crew of the *Essex* set sail again in search of the leviathan. This time their course was generally southeast, toward the Falklands, Cape Horn, and beyond that, the Pacific.

CHAPTER 24

THE HORN

D ays went by, then weeks. No whales.

Occasionally, someone in the crew of the *Essex* called out that they could see sails on the horizon. Perhaps they belonged to another whaler bound for Nantucket or Edgartown—the lucky bastards. Or bound out like themselves. Or, the ships could have been traders under the command of captains from Yarmouth or Brewster. The men and boys on the *Essex* rarely knew, though, because other than the whaler *Atlantic*, no ship passed close enough to be identified.

They sailed along with the *Atlantic* for a few days in the vicinity of the equator, and there must have been some small consolation in hearing that the other ship wasn't making much better time than the *Essex*: it was, said *Atlantic's* mate, the slowest passage he'd had to the line in thirty voyages. *Atlantic* was doing better in terms of whales, however; back in Cape Verde the crew of the *Essex* had seen three hundred barrels of oil off-loaded from the *Atlantic* and sent home in a merchant vessel.

"Nothing further transpired to break in upon the daily duties of the ship save now and then a passing squall," remembered Nickerson. When that happened the sailors were ordered up into the yards to take in the topgallant studding sails, or even the topgallants themselves. Pollard wasn't about to get laid on his beam ends by a paltry blow again. But as soon as the gusts were over, the sails were reset and they pushed south once more.

. . .

Sailing along in sight of another ship for days or even weeks at a stretch was a luxury peculiar to whalers and fishermen, ships with no destination other than a general desire to be at certain hunting grounds at a certain time of year. For the merchant captains of the Cape, on the other hand, with places to go and be, a happy voyage was a fast one. Merchant ships might pass close enough to compare their calculations of longitude, but little more (unless a favorable wind held them within sight for longer). By the 1850s, when being the first of the fleet to arrive in the gold-clogged markets of San Francisco and Australia could mean double, triple, or even quadruple profits, voyages around the horn (and around the world) became all-out races.

One such contest took place in 1853 between Captain Moses Howes of North Dennis and his distant cousin Captain Frederick Howes of Yarmouth (at one point there were twelve Captains Howes in Dennis). Moses, commanding the clipper *Competitor*, left Boston on the twenty-seventh of March. Frederick, in the *Climax*, left the same port the next day. Both ships were on their maiden voyage. Both captains piled on the sail. And fifty-four days after they left the hub, both vessels were at the horn. North Dennis still had a one-day lead on Yarmouth when the *Competitor* split her stem. Captain Moses was hoping to stretch out his lead, but he apparently pushed the ship too hard in the traditionally howling winds and enormous seas of the passage into the Pacific. He spent five long days hove to, fixing the resulting leak and pumping out the bilge. The *Climax* passed him and pushed out a four-day lead into the Pacific.

There was still a lot of sailing to be done, however. And though the *Climax* was equipped with its captain's new invention, the Howes double topsails (which would become standard on future clippers), Moses was able to close the gap. After 115 days and something in the neighborhood of fifteen thousand miles, the ships caromed into San Francisco Bay in exactly the same position they left Boston, with the *Competitor* one day ahead of the *Climax*.

Neither ship, however, approached the record for a trip between San Francisco and Boston. That honor belonged to Captain Freeman Hatch of North Eastham, who in 1853 commanded the extreme clipper *Northern Light* from one port to the other in an almost unbelievable seventy-six days.

The *Essex*, working her way south through the Atlantic toward Cape Horn, wasn't making anywhere near that kind of progress. Roughly 850 nautical miles north of the equator, the wind had lost its resolve almost entirely, leaving the ship frequently becalmed. What's more, it seemed to rain perpetually in the tropics. It poured down so hard that at times the scuppers couldn't clear the decks and the water washed over the plank-shears. The new sails mildewed. With no prey to chase and almost no wind to work, there wasn't much to break the monotony of the watch, other than meals. And the meals, which had tasted so good that first night out, were now monotonous themselves.

Every ship had a slightly different menu, depending on the relative price and availability of goods at the time of sailing or at various stops during the cruise. But such variation was more often in the details than the entrées, which almost invariably consisted of boiled salt meat of one sort or another along with some sea bread or potatoes or beans. The officers and captain usually ate together at table, though on many ships a strict tradition was enforced whereby mates only came to table after their superior officer had taken his first bite of food.

The crew's mess was somewhat more democratic: the day's meat and vegetables were all rather unceremoniously dumped into a large pan, or kid, along with some bread and taken to the forecastle. There the men would divide it up and eat it with their hands, sitting on benches or their sea chests or the deck. Unless there were whales around, or blubber to be tried out, meals were usually served on a strict schedule: 7:30 A.M., noon, and 5:00 P.M.

"The beef was saltier than Lot's wife, and had to be soaked in a 'steep-tub' overnight before it was cooked," remembered Vineyarder George Fred Tilton, who sailed on both whalers and merchantmen toward the end of the nineteenth century. "Saltpeter would eat all the fat off it, and it was pretty tough eating. The pork was all right, but we didn't get it as often. The coffee was called 'bootlet'—I suppose it was made from old boots parched and ground. It came in four or five pound packages that smelled musty before they were ever opened." The ship's tea, Tilton remembered, "looked as if it had been used, dried out and rolled up again, and where they got the molasses from, God only knows! It was the poorest to be found, black and sour, and mixed with salt water to be found, to make it go further. That is what we had to sweeten our tea and coffee with."

Whale meat, except from the youngest of victims, generally wasn't considered fit to eat by most whalers. But if, by chance, a blackfish or a dolphin were speared, Tilton recalled with his usual style, it might be stewed with dumplings "that were not afflicted with anything to make them light, but they were always eaten with avidity." Occasionally, usually not more than once a week, there was a desert of duff: flour, lard, and dried fruit boiled together in a bag and served with molasses.

The one time Nickerson remembered Captain Pollard losing his temper was when, as an act of protest, the men before the mast returned the kid without eating a bite of the food it held. "You scoundrels!" Pollard shouted, taking off his hat and stomping on it. "Have not I given you all the ship could afford? Have not I treated you like men? Have not you had plenty to eat and drink? What in hell do you want, more? Do you wish me to coax you to eat? Or shall I chew your food for you?" All the men were sheepishly standing before him during the tirade. None replied.

"I'll kill the whole bunch of you togather & then Bang up North-West and go home," he shouted. According to Nickerson, this was a favorite expression of Pollard, though no one but himself knew what it meant. As he walked back to his cabin, the crew heard him mutter, "Thirty hogs in the Isle of May, Duff every other day, butter and cheese as much as you could sway, and now you want more beef, damn you." It became known as his soliloquy.

It was bad and frustrating luck for the *Essex* that they had yet to come across any whales, but not extraordinarily so. By the nineteenth century, the industry had so successfully progressed from onshore to offshore—had, in other words, exterminated the whales from anywhere near Cape Cod and the Islands—that it was quite possible for a ship to go a full year without finding a single whale. The *Eliza Mason* under Nathaniel Jernegan of Edgartown got all the way to Hawaii in 1854 without taking a single whale. They still had nothing to show for their efforts a month later when, according to the journal of Abigail Jernegan (who, as mentioned earlier, was the first non-Asian woman known to spend a night in Japan), the ship very nearly had to be scuttled in order to put out a fire in the hold.

The problem was discovered near the bow at around 10:30 at night by the third mate, a Mr. Pease, who immediately woke Captain Jernegan. There wasn't much to see from the top deck, just a bit of smoke curling up. But where there's smoke. . . . And where there's too much smoke for anyone to go below-decks long enough to get a good look, there's real trouble. Jernegan ordered all the hatches to the affected area closed and then had his men cut a hole in the upper deck above the probable location of the blaze. Smoke poured out. With long-handled cutting spades the men then cut a hole in the deck below. Water was pumped in; steam poured out. It was a good sign. A few moments later, though, Jernegan and his mates concluded that despite the steam, more smoke was engulfing the ship. The few volunteers who offered to go down through the hole and try to open more holes in the lower deck were hauled back up nearly senseless.

By dawn, the pitch used to caulk the seams of the top deck was boiling and bubbling. When the caulking flared up, as it occasionally did, the men would rush over to stomp or douse it out. By six that morning, there were five feet eight inches of water in the hold of the ship, but still the fire was not out. Jernegan wrote in his journal, "Closed ship as tight as possible but kept water going. . . . Called all hands with determination of finding who had fired the ship. Dark times."

The crew was mustered in the middle of the ship to face the captain and his mates. Jernegan asked who set fire to the ship and got no answer. Ships occasionally caught fire from embers and sparks during the process of trying out the whale oil, but in the case of the *Eliza Mason*, there had been no blubber to cook, so it was assumed that arson was involved.

"Who fired the ship," Jernegan demanded a second time. No answer. He called for his Bible, and each member of the crew was ordered to file by the captain. He was remembered to have looked them dead in the eye as each put his hand on the Bible and said that no, he had not set fire to the ship.

Jernegan ordered his ten least-favorite crew members placed in irons, which was done. Still none confessed. The ship by now was fairly low in the water, but the smoke continued to creep out of the closed hatches. Jernegan paced the deck with a sufficient scowl, then ordered three of the chained men strung up in the rigging at such a height that their toes just brushed the deck. Standing before them he picked up a rope and carefully raveled the end of it into a cat-o'-nine-tails. Then he began to whip. Once, twice.

On the third lash one of the men cried out that he had something to say. Jernegan hit him three more times and then stopped. Three men were implicated; two of the original suspects plus a third whom Jernegan had not previously suspected. All received four hundred lashes immediately. But of course, the punishment did nothing to stop the fire. "Ship was now filled with smoke and gas," Jernegan wrote later in his journal. The smoke didn't just make men cough, but sent them into fits, which, the captain noted, "it would take 3 or 4 to hold one and was awful to witness."

There was nothing to do but continue the old strategy of closing all the hatches and pumping in water; their only hope was that the fire was still low enough in the ship that it could be flooded out without sinking the vessel. By noon the water was less than thirty inches below the lower deck. All the rest of that day and through the night the ship burned, and the men pumped in water. *Eliza Mason* settled lower and lower in the sea.

At 5:30 that evening there was still smoke coming from every hatch and around the hawse pipes. Jernegan wrote a chillingly declarative sentence in his journal: "Thought she would go." They pumped on, flooding between the decks. But a half-hour later, Jernegan reported, they "found the chain bolts hot on the starboard side." This implied that the fire had spread to both sides of the ship. Jernegan decided it was time to send his wife, Abigail, and young son, Holmes, over to the *Jirah Swift*, another whaler that had come to their assistance. "It brought tears to my eyes to look on that noble ship and think she was on fire," he wrote in his log.

Now that he knew his ship was going down, Captain Jernegan gave the arsonists a choice: they could be hung from a yardarm immediately or they could stay tied to the rigging while the rest of the crew abandoned ship. They chose to be hung. He ordered the nooses readied, and the crew stood by waiting for his order to execute. But for some reason Jernegan held off one more night.

Perhaps he smelled through the smoke a change in the weather. That night the calm gave way to a stiff breeze and a squall. The wind and slight seas "hove the ship so that the water we had put in the hold must have swashed up between the timbers of the lower deck," Jernegan wrote later. Smoke finally gave way to steam alone. The fire had burned through "the thick streak in the hold, up between the timbers, and out over the waterways between the decks." The lower deck was burned nearly through. But, amazingly, the *Eliza Mason* was still afloat, and after men from both ships pumped like hell to get the water out, she was made seaworthy again. When she returned to Martha's Vineyard, there were 1,124 barrels of whale oil and 16,800 pounds of whalebone in the hold.

While the fire was still burning, the arsonists confessed. According to Jernegan's journal, "the only reason given was that they wanted to live on some islands we were passing." Their intent, they said, was not to burn the ship to the waterline, but only to create enough of a diversion to allow them to jump ship and row away. And in Roratonga two months later, two of them did somehow escape.

Desertions were common enough on whalers, particularly those perceived as unlucky. One sailor on the *Essex*, whose name appears to have been lost, jumped ship in Peru. But it goes almost without saying that most sailors who found themselves stuck for months on unlucky ships like the *Eliza Mason* or the *Essex* (at least until it got around the horn) found more intelligent diversions than setting the boat beneath them on fire. They carved scrimshaw, of course, and the teeth of sperm whales were traditionally distributed to the men before the mast. The surface of natural sperm tooth is rough and ribbed, and a sailor could burn up a lot of hours filing and polishing just to get it ready to carve. But on the *Essex* there weren't yet any spermaceti teeth to work with.

In their free hours sailors wrote letters, played cards, mended or made clothes. They sang songs, which went in and out of favor like pop tunes today: "They had many of the latest sailor songs, which had not yet got about among our merchantmen," Richard Henry Dana Jr. remembered of some English sailors. Or danced: on Dana's ship there was "a broad-backed, thick-headed boy from Cape Cod" who could "dance the true fisherman's jig, barefooted, knocking with his heels, and slapping the decks with his bare feet, in time with the music." The mate loved this performance, said Dana, and "always stood at the steerage door, looking on, and if the boys would not dance, he hazed them around with a rope's end, much to the amusement of the men."

On more than one whaler, the keeper of the log chose to do so in rhyming verse, making the job both more interesting and time-consuming, though adequate time did not always improve the poetry. "Four months has passed since we got oil/ Our ship is going all the while/ It grieves my heart to think that we/ Have looked in vain the whales to see/ I look ahead two years to come/ I feel in hopes we shall get some," wrote one such bard in 1835. Six months later he added, "The whales is scarce our water is low/ And soon to New Zealand we must go."

Few ships became as artistically inclined as the *Alpha*, which sailed out of Nantucket in 1846. After twenty-seven months at sea the seven sailors before the mast who could read formed what in today's parlance would be called a writing workshop. We "started a sort of Coterie or literary society," wrote William Hussey Macy in a letter home to his cousin Susan Burdick, "each member of which was to bring in and read, once a week, an original composition either in verse or prose." When that got boring—"in the process of time, this became stale, as everything will"—they took up dancing. Not only the expected sailors' rounds, but also, said Macy specifically, formal cotillions. The image is rather ripe: men who had not bathed or in some cases even changed clothes in months. Men whose job was to boil animal fat in a process that produced clouds of smoke Melville described as "horrible to inhale, and inhale it you must, and not only that but you must live in it for the time. It has an unspeakable, wild, Hindoo odor about it such as may lurk in the vicinity of funeral pyres." Men like these, out there in the middle of the ocean, bowing and kissing each other's hands under the rising moon.

Finally, apparently out of desperation, the crew of the *Alpha* turned to the stage, incorporating themselves as the "Alphean Marine Theatre." They issued playbills to their shipmates. "We commenced on a small scale with dialogues, single scenes from Shakespeare, etc., etc., and gradually mounted to greater efforts. We have produced Garrick's comedy of the 'Guardian,' with the most triumphant success. Our stage is on deck (as we perform only on fine evenings) with an immense drop curtain triced to the rigging." The unexpected star was a certain Charles Bailey. He was, said Macy, an absolute marvel in drag.

None of the surviving accounts of the last voyage of the *Essex* mentions any such organized diversions. The kind of boredom that drove men to creativity typically didn't happen on whalers until well out into the Pacific. What's more, at around thirty degrees south of the equator, two-thirds of the way down the continent of South America and far out in the south Atlantic, someone in the masthead finally spotted a shoal of whales and called out to the crew below. "Here was the prospect of a chance to display our skill," remembered Nickerson, "and for the uninitiated to have some little practice." Pollard brought the *Essex* as close as practical to the whales—to within about a mile—and the order was given to lower the boats. Within minutes only three members of the crew remained on board the ship.* The rest, distributed among three whaleboats, pulled with all their might toward the prey.

Rowing a twenty-to-thirty-foot boat up to a fifty-to-eighty-foot animal in the middle of the ocean in order to stick it with a spear took some getting used to. Whales are the largest creatures ever to inhabit the planet, dwarfing even the grandest of the dinosaurs. A sixty-foot sperm whale is larger than a dozen elephants. A whale that size has a head about eleven feet tall and eight or nine wide. It is about thirty-five feet in circumference

---

*Traditionally, the "keepers" would be the cook, the cooper, and, unless he chose to lower as well, the captain; it's not clear in this instance, but Pollard probably lowered.

Leaving the ship in pursuit of a whale, circa 1900. (COURTESY NANTUCKET HISTORICAL ASSOCIATION)

at the neck. When floating near the surface, its "crown" can be as high off the water as the roof of a one-story cape house. And if such a whale engaged in pitchpoling, pushing itself up vertically, presumably to get a view of goings-on at the surface of the water, it could tower some thirty feet above a whaleboat. Conversely, when it went head down and lob-tailed, the exposed thrashing flukes were more than half as wide as a whaleboat was long.

Scientific American in 1887 estimated the strength of an eighty-foot whale at probably around 145 horsepower, and though modern, noninvasive research has shown the great leviathans to be among the most peaceful of all creatures, it's no surprise that they are inclined to fight back when threatened. Green hands were often told not to watch as they approached, which wasn't difficult, since only the man at the steering oar faced forward. The ongoing matter of honor—to outpace one's comrades in the other whaleboats and be the first to reach the whales—also helped focus the squeamish.

Whaleboats were designed primarily for speed and maneuverability. Built of half-inch-thick cedar planks laid clinker style over a frame of equally light but sturdy ribs, which were usually crafted of white oak, they were relatively wide and shallow craft. A twenty-eight-foot whaleboat might be just under six feet wide and just over two feet deep. It had a flat bottom for sharp turning and was double-ended so as to be able to travel forward or backward through the waves with equal dexterity. There were several thwarts, usually of inch-thick pine, and a removable mast that could be stepped through the most forward of these. Sailing was one of the quietest ways to approach a whale if the wind was favorable, but the men virtually always added their oar power even when the sail was set.

In a classic whaleboat, there were five oars in addition to the steering oar, each usually coded with stripes indicating its position. At the bow on the starboard side was the boatsteerer's (harpooner's) oar, with five stripes. Behind that, on the port side, was the bow oar, with four stripes; the bow oarsman was responsible for stepping and lowering the mast as need be. The midship and tub oars—numbers three and two—were longer and heavier than the oars at either end, up to sixteen feet long. The last rowing oar was called the stroke oar and was about twelve to fourteen feet long. It was typically handled by the lightest member of the crew, whose job it also was to tend the mainsail sheet. The steering oar was long enough to be recognizable without special markings. It was handled by the mate until a whale was successfully harpooned, at which point he traded places with the harpooner, for reasons that will be discussed later.

The numbers weren't simply to make sure the right-sized oar ended up in the correct oarlock. When the whales were still far off, all men pulled evenly at the oars, and the officer in the stern steered according to his own judgment if he could see the whales, or followed broad directions that came from the crow's nest if he couldn't. (Every ship had its own code of flags and sail movements to direct their whaleboats to whales, codes that were kept secret in case there were other whalers hunting in the same pod.) But once the boat closed in on its prey, when it was trying to get "wood to blackskin" so that the harpooner could stand and strike, the officer at the steering oar might whisper "Pull two," or "Stern three," and the sailor at that oar would respond immediately with a forward or reverse stroke. If he failed to respond adequately, punishment might come soon thereafter from the whale or the officer, or both.*

---

*Tilton on his first whale: "Three days out of Bermuda we raised a sperm whale, and I was the most excited and anxious boy in the world. I wanted to lower and get him and I don't suppose that anyone ever moved any faster than I did when we got the order to lower. We went on him and got fast without any fuss, but believe me, from that time on nobody wanted to get away from him any worse than I did. I thought that anyone must be perfectly crazy to attempt to kill such a thing. He only made sixty-five barrels, so you see he was a lot smaller than a great many that have been taken, but I was scared blue. When they sung out to 'haul ahead,' that is, close to the whale, I wasn't but little account, but when they said 'Stern all,' I was as good as any man in the boat."

There were many critical moments in the business of killing leviathans, but few rivaled the initial approach. Any hint of something unusual—a touch by a careless oar or the bow of the boat—and the giant beast could sink straight down and away. And although a whale's eyesight is not considered to be particularly good, they are highly sensitive to sounds. Oarlocks, usually just a pair of wooden pegs, were lined with leather to quiet them. On calm days, the oarsmen pulled when the whale spouted and stopped when he stopped. Then, as they got near the whale, they would change from oars to paddles, which were quieter still.

The usual strategy was to pull up behind and slightly to one side of a whale in order to get ahead of its flukes. By then the mate would have already ordered the harpooner to ship his oar and stand in the bow, ready to strike when ordered. The most effective place to sink the harpoon was just behind the head, and occasionally a whale would become aware of the approaching hunters and dive or tip back at just the right moment to expose the spot.

Harpoon points varied depending on the decade, the ship, and the preference of the man throwing it. In general, though, the points were steel followed by a roughly thirty-inch shank of iron into which was driven a six-foot hickory sapling, preferably with the bark still on. One-flued irons—whalers preferred the term *iron* to *harpoon*—had one barb, two-flued had two, and so on. Toggle irons pivoted so that as the whale pulled away, the tip point slid until it was perpendicular to the shaft, making it nearly impossible to pull out. Toggle irons, which were originally invented by Native American whale hunters in the American arctic, were introduced to New Englanders by an African-American manufacturer named Lewis Temple. Temple was one of about ten full-time harpoon makers living in New Bedford in the middle decades of the nineteenth century. It was a good business to be in: one of his competitors alone sold 58,517 harpoons between 1828 and 1868.

The boatsteerer always honed his own irons and then stropped them with leather until they had a razor's edge. He kept them in leather sheaths to protect their edges. When the moment arrived to throw the dart, he did his best to bury the point in the back of the whale all the way "up to the hitches," meaning two and a half feet into the blubber of the beast. There were generally two "live" harpoons attached to the whale line, one fast to the end and the other on its own short line that was looped around the main line, and if at all possible the harpooner got a second iron into the animal before it took off. But if he did not, the second harpoon was always thrown overboard, lest it get whipped around the boat by the exiting whale line.

As soon as a whale was struck, the call was *stern all* and the boat would back away from the beast. If the mast were raised, it was now quickly unstepped and hinged down. The first fifteen fathoms of the whale line were coiled separately from the rest to allow the whale to get clear of the boat before it felt any drag. After that, the rope ran through a Y at the bow of the boat into which a pin was inserted to keep it from jumping out.* It then ran between the men all the way back to the stern, where there was a "stout timber head" around which it was wrapped a couple of times to create drag. From the timber head it ran to the "tubs" in the waist of the boat.

The first reaction of a whale when struck was usually to dive. The line, which was two-thirds of an inch thick and could theoretically bear three tons, would fly out of the tubs at a terrifying rate. Friction on the timber head sometimes caused it to burst into flames, and the sailor at the stroke oar was always equipped with a bailer to douse it regularly with seawater. Rope flying out of the boat at that speed and power could and did occasionally rip a man's arms off if a hand got caught in it in an outgoing coil. That was if he was lucky; more often in that unfortunate situation the sailor was yanked out of the boat and instantly dragged several hundred feet underwater. Whalers went down so fast that sometimes the others in the boat didn't see it happen. Likewise, a knot that stuck in the Y could drag an entire boat underwater before anyone in the crew knew what was wrong. The rope probably killed as many whalers as did any other mishap; the sailor whose responsibility it was to lay the three hundred fathoms of line into the tubs in flat, concentric "Flemish" coils, which would later peel out of the wooden box in a relatively orderly way, took care to do his job well.

Usually, two hundred fathoms of rope (twelve hundred feet) would do the job, but not always. When it looked as if a whale was going to take out the whole line, another boat might come over and attach more rope. Or occasionally whalers would revert to the ancient Native American method of attaching floats, or "drugs," to the line, along with a flag so they could find the whale again once it became tired. One whale harpooned off Greenland took out six miles of line and had fifteen harpoons in it but still somehow managed to take down a whaleboat along with the miles of line.

---

*Harpooners on Nantucket sometimes wore these pins around their necks as a sort of badge of honor, and there was rumored to be a secret society of eligible women on that island who were sworn to marry only men who had killed their first leviathan.

Sperm whales are capable of diving deeper than any other mammal—to an astounding ten thousand feet, according to some modern estimates. If a whale went down and down and down, and there were no other boats close by to lend line, a whaleboat was in trouble. When it went down until it appeared the boat would be dragged under, there was no choice. The harpooner took up the axe that was always in the bow for that purpose and held it over the whale line, waiting for the last possible minute before cutting free.

After its initial dive, a whale typically rose and swam hard on the surface. The whaleboat was towed along behind in what was known, to the chagrin of whalers from Provincetown and the Vineyard, as a Nantucket sleigh ride—"the Lord only knows what Nantucket has to do with it any more than any other place," wrote a grumpy George Fred Tilton in his autobiography. During the ride, the crew all hauled on the line until the boat was alongside the whale, if possible. Initially, though, it often wasn't. When a whaleboat is flying along over the waves at ten or twelve knots, there is virtually no way even for six strong men to pull it much closer to the fifty-ton engine at the other end of the line. Many times the power of the whale pulling to free itself would mangle the harpoon beyond use, bending and twisting the iron like a paper clip. Other harpoons were pulled so hard and long that they simply stretched like Silly Putty. Once the whale slowed to about half its original speed, however, the men could haul in the line.

As the boat got near the whale, the steerer would go out wide to avoid the flukes, a whale's most useful weapon. By this time, the harpooner and the mate had usually switched places on the theory that at the beginning of a chase the job that required the most experience was in the stern, steering the boat up close enough to a whale for a harpoon to be successfully thrown. But a harpoon is only designed to attach a line to the animal, and once that was achieved the critical job became killing it. So the mate went forward and picked up the lance.

The lance was a flat, oval-shaped blade welded to a stiff iron shank of six feet. There was a short rope with which to draw it back and a socket for an additional wooden handle to make it longer. Whenever a boat was able to get close enough, the mate tried to push the lance all the way under the shoulder blade to the vitals of the whale. Then he churned it up and down to do as much internal damage as possible. It often happened—for a host of reasons ranging from awkwardly placed harpoons to tangled ropes—that the boat couldn't get that near until the whale was nearly expired. In such a situation the man in the bow would just stab at the desperate beast as many times as possible. Sometimes, using another weapon called a boat spade, they would attempt to chop at the tendons in the small of the tail so as to disable the flukes and thus the whale.

Sharks by the hundreds would sometimes gather and join in the fray, attracted by the huge plume of bloody water. Orcas, too, were known to attack wounded whales. The victim itself, meanwhile, thrashed and struggled. Right whales in particular were adept at searching with their flukes and smashing anything they could find. Gray whales were called devilfish by the whalers because a mother of that species could go into a rage and attack the boats if its young were hurt. A sperm whale typically rolled over and fought on its back, so that its huge, fifteen-foot jaw could open up into the air and smash closed again. But even when swimming right side up at its top speed of eight to twelve knots, its head rose up out of the water until the jaw was visible.

Sometimes, the whale simply won the match. Ropes parted or were chopped to save the boat from going under. Probably half the whales harpooned got away, either to die from their wounds or live to be slaughtered later. Harpoons were marked with the name of the ship and the year, and often they turned up again when a whale, once lucky, was caught successfully by another whaler. Such an iron thrown and lost in Hudson Bay by a harpooner on the *Ansel Gibbs* out of New Bedford turned up in the western Arctic a few years later when the whale was taken by another New Bedford boat. The whale ship *Milton* took a whale that had a harpoon in it that the crew estimated to be fourteen years old. In a prerun of sorts for the outrageously facetious and environmentally criminal "research whaling" still carried on by Japanese and Norwegian whalers, much of the earliest knowledge of whale migrations was discovered in this grisly manner.

Whales were also lost after they were already dead. Despite having earned the name *right* because they floated when dead and were therefore the right ones to hunt, right whales occasionally sank. Sperm whales, too, didn't always float. Occasionally in a situation like this, there was a special harpoon with massive barbs and a heavy weight that could be slid down the whale line and into the whale. With the heavier line attached, the whale might be lifted up with a ship's windlass. More often, though, sinkers were simply abandoned.

In almost all cases, it was grisly and dangerous work. Whales have tremendous hearts; a child could swim through a blue whale's aorta. When the lance found its mark, blood gushed out as if from a firehose—into the air, into the men's faces. "When we hauled alongside with our two whales," recalled one whaler, "we all looked as much like murderers as anything

"Cutting In." (COURTESY OF THE MARTHA'S VINEYARD HISTORICAL
SOCIETY)

else." Murderers sentenced to hard labor. Once a whale was dead, the
excitement ended and the real work began. Whalers had various theories
about whether it was easier to tow a dead whale by the head or the tail, but
either way, dragging a forty-five-ton carcass behind a rowboat for several
miles into the wind was inhumanly hard labor. There was no rest after
the whale was hauled in, however; any sharks that had gathered during the
killing were still at work eating away at everyone's share of the profits. The
processing began immediately.

Once gotten to the ship, a line or chain was looped around the small of
the whale's tail and run through a porthole at the bow, where it was
secured. Enough sail was then set to move the vessel at a rate that kept the
carcass alongside while the blubber was removed. A scaffold was rigged out
over the whale, not much more than a plank really, on which the mates
worked with twenty-foot-long cutting spades and chisels. There was a rail
to lean against, and they were usually tied to a fellow crewman whose job
was to haul them in if they fell. It was slippery work.

Whenever possible, the men on the scaffolding stabbed with their long-
handled spades the blood-crazed sharks below them. This was less in the
hope of actually killing one outright than of distracting its fellow binge
feeders, who would momentarily turn their frenzy in the direction of their
wounded comrade.

The first job was to get a massive blubber hook positioned in a hole cut
between the eye and the fin. Then the blubber was stripped off in a long

spiral, the men on deck hoisting the hook up with a block and tackle as the men on the scaffolding cut and filleted with their long-handled spades. When the tackle was as high as it could go, another hook was put in the blubber lower down, and the first piece was cut off with a long-handled, long-bladed boarding knife. The resulting "blanket piece," which was generally about three feet wide and twenty feet long, went down into the hold until the cutting was done and the trying began.

Sometimes, particularly if there were more than one whale alongside, the trying began immediately. The try works, usually two or more large iron kettles set in a brick furnace that in turn sat in a shallow bath of water to prevent fires, was typically located just behind the foremast. The blankets were first cut into pieces one man could lift—usually about one foot wide and three or four feet long—which were carried to a bench called the horse. There they were sliced further, not all the way through but enough so that they could flip like the leaves of a book. These pieces, which some called bibles, went into the pot. When the oil was cooked out of them, the scrap that remained was fished out and thrown into the furnace for fuel.

The smoke from all this, wrote Melville, smelled "like the left wing on the day of Judgement; it is an argument for the pit." And Crevecoeur, who visited Nantucket while there was still a good deal of trying out being done on shore, commented: "At my first landing I was much surprised at the disagreeable smell which struck me in many parts of the town; it is caused by the whale oil, and is unavoidable; the neatness peculiar to these people can neither remove or prevent it." But the smell of the boiling oil pots apparently wasn't bad enough to prevent many sailors from deep frying their allotment of hardtack for a few minutes. When the furnaces were up and running, the trying went on twenty-four hours a day until all the oil was in barrels in the hold. On many ships, the captain ordered the cook to bring up a bag of flour and make a continuous supply of donuts in the boiling oil for the tired lads.

Once the whale's body was stripped, the head, which had previously been severed and allowed to float behind the ship, was hauled aboard. The heads of smaller whales could be brought aboard in one piece. Those of large whales, however, were brought up in pieces. The lips of a right whale or other baleen whale were removed first, as they were full of oil. Then the upper jaw was brought aboard, along with its whalebone. Later, this would be broken into individual pieces—nearly six hundred in all, some of them twelve feet long—which would then be scraped smooth and hung in the rigging to dry.

"Trying Out." (COURTESY OF THE MARTHA'S VINEYARD HISTORICAL SOCIETY)

A sperm whale's lower jaw was brought aboard first, along with its teeth, which traditionally went to the crew for carving. Above a sperm whale's mouth is a mass of tough, oil-filled gristle called white-horse, which was brought aboard next, followed by a boneless layer of blubber called the junk. Last of all came the great tank—or case—filled with precious liquid spermaceti oil. In all, roughly a quarter of the oil to be gotten out of a sperm whale came from its head.

If possible, the whole tank was hoisted aboard, but when that proved impractical a man was sent over the ship's edge with a bucket. A hole was opened in the whale's head cavity, and the man began to scoop out the spermaceti. When he could reach no deeper, he sent the bucket down on a rope. When that failed, into the body cavity he went himself, "up to his armpits," one whaler recalled, "and dipped out almost 6 hogshead of clear out of her case beside 6 more of the noodle."

Killing and processing whales was obviously not a job for anyone squeamish about the bodily fluids of dead animals. "All hands strip down to a shirt, a pair of overalls rolled up to the knees, showing a pair of bare shins and sockless feet in large brogans," remembered one whaler who worked primarily in warm climates. "And in we go—grease from head to foot—day and night until the whale is all cut safely on board. It gives you a funny sensation at first to get into a deck full of blubber, with the slimy stuff around your exposed cuticle, and oil squashing out of your shoes at every step."

It's a hellish picture: the outsized slabs of fatty skin swinging overhead on great hooks; the men covered in raw gore bearing razor-sharp blades on the ends of long poles, or climbing in and out of cavernous carcasses with ladles and dippers, or feeding scraps of gristle to a roaring furnace. The cauldrons of oil bubbled as ever more bibles were added. The unspeakably foul-smelling smoke circled up and trailed away to leeward. And surrounding it all, a churning chorus of happy sharks. With repetition, though, apparently anything can be gotten used to: it was, said the same whaler who remembered the squooge of oil between his toes, "a prosy job, and nasty is no name for it."

As it turned out, there would be no greasy feet or fingers aboard the *Essex* at the end of that first whale hunt. The lowering was uneventful, and First Mate Chase's boat won the informal race from the side of the ship to the shoal of whales. They got themselves into a perfect position to strike, but bad luck still accompanied them. Nickerson, who was a member of Chase's crew and was probably rowing in the stroke position, remembered being in the boat one second and in the water the next. "As we were in the very act of harpooning a whale," he recalled fifty years later, "our boat was stoven by a whale coming up under the boat, which we had not before seen."

On many whalers, one whaleboat was always ordered to "play loose," which meant letting the others go up and strike and then coming in to help with the kill, or, as the case may be, pick up the survivors. It seems unlikely with only three boats and no oil as yet in the hold that either Captain Pollard or Second Mate Chapple's boat would have played loose, but both immediately came to the rescue of the men and fished out the pieces of the wrecked boat. The whales immediately swam to windward, the direction in which it was most difficult for sailing ships to follow.

The crew, no doubt, was not encouraged by the outcome, which must have seemed like more misfortune on an already dubious voyage. Back on board the *Essex*, it looked for a while as though they were down to only two whaleboats. Though half of Chase's boat was still in one piece, its keel was broken in two places. Eventually, though, the officers were able to effect an adequate splice, and the boat was declared at least good enough if not good as new. And even better, the more experienced among them must have thought, at least no one was hurt or killed in the incident. More than a few whalers were killed or maimed in fluke accidents.

Some sailors and ships were extraordinarily lucky: Peleg Nye, a harpooner from Hyannis Port, fell into the open mouth of a wounded sperm whale that closed its jaw over his knees. Down went the whale, with a screaming Peleg sticking out like a cigar. *To the bottom of the sea,* Peleg said after the whale had died and floated to the surface and he was fished out of its mouth and revived by his crewmates. He lived to be seventy-nine and was known, inevitably, as the "Jonah of Cape Cod."

In Obed Macy's 1835 history of Nantucket, Captain Benjamin Worth of that island is quoted as saying that he "began to follow the sea in 1783, being then fifteen years of age, and continued until 1824. During this period of forty-one years I was shipmaster twenty-nine years." Figuring an average speed of four miles per hour, he estimated that he had sailed almost 1.2 million miles. He had "assisted in obtaining 20,000 barrels of oil," which probably represented more than 350 whales. In all that time, he boasted, he never lost a man, or even had one break a limb.

Others were unlucky to the same degree that Worth was fortunate. The *Franklin* left Nantucket in 1831 and wasn't at sea more than a month before a man fell from the rigging and was laid up for two months. Then another fell and broke both legs. Another was put ashore shortly thereafter with tuberculosis. Two more men drowned when a harpooned whale dragged their boat under. Then another sailor fell from aloft and died. Another died of scurvy. He was followed by a boatsteerer who got fouled in the line attached to a harpoon, and after that by the mate, who somehow ruptured himself, developed a hernia, and died. The captain died the same day as the mate, though it's not clear why, and a few days later yet another sailor fell from the rigging. Then the scurvy struck with a vengeance, killing three more men and leaving the rest of the crew too weak to control the ship. The *Franklin* finally ran aground on the coast of Brazil.

There were a lot of ways to die at sea even if you didn't get out of your ship and row out to poke at giants. You could, as already discussed, run aground off the Cape and freeze to death in the rigging. You could fall from a spar while furling a sail and break your neck. At least one whaler was killed when a blanket piece of blubber fell on him. Almost all the diseases of the world were available to you, and there were usually no doctors on board. The cure, such as it was, often came from the captain's copy of *The Sailor's Physician*, and it wasn't necessarily a comfort. In the 1824 edition there is a lot of cold-water dousing, mercury eating, and bloodletting prescribed. "Of the application of leeches," wrote Dr. Parsons, "the manner of applying these is too well known to require a description."

Elijah Cobb, the Brewster captain who survived Paris on the Ninth Thermidore, retired from the sea the year before the *Essex* sailed on her final voyage. He'd been to the Gulf of Guinea in the *Ten Brothers* to trade fabrics and tobacco—not for slaves, though it was a prominent slaving port, but for gold, ivory, and coffee. Three of his neighbors were there as well, Captains Isaac Clark, Joseph Mayo, and David Nickerson. Fever broke out. In letters home Cobb wrote sentences like: "Esq. Clark has paid the dept [*sic*] of nature, it was my task to close his eyes . . . after a sickness of 8 days— Young Kimbal died 4 days before, Captain Nickerson was very sick on board this ship . . ." Mayo died next. David Nickerson set sail for home but died at sea. Of the captains, only Cobb made it home to the Cape, where he apparently decided he'd finally had enough of the wider world.

Death was sometimes quite ordinary. On his first voyage out, Benjamin W. Luce, a cabin boy from Martha's Vineyard, caught what his obituary called a cold and was dead six days later. Captain Roswell Coon, originally of Nantucket, then of the Vineyard, took his wife, Harriet Cleveland, and five-year-old son, John Calvin, on the *Barnstable* in 1852. By the time they got to Honolulu, Harriet was seven months pregnant; she stayed in the islands and gave birth to little Grace Ann while he went north for the Arctic season. By December they were again together and at sea, but there is a gravestone in Edgartown cemetery that reads GRACE ANN, DAUGHTER OF R.M. AND HARRIET COON: BORN AT THE SANDWICH ISLANDS, AUGUST 9, 1853. DIED MAY 1, 1855, AT SEA IN LAT 40 DEG S. LON 78 DEG W.

It's worth noting that First Mate Owen Chase of the *Essex*, in his story written immediately after returning to Nantucket, doesn't mention the seemingly ominous incident of a boat being smashed on the very first lowering of the voyage. And when he does describe a strikingly similar occurrence a few months later, after the ship was around the horn and into the Pacific and had several hundred barrels of oil in her hold, he curiously puts himself in the bow holding the harpoon rather than at the stern, where he was far more likely to have been. "I was in the boat myself," he wrote, "with five others, and was standing in the fore part, with the harpoon in my hand, well braced, expecting every instant to catch sight of one of the shoal which we were in, that I might strike; but judge of my astonishment and dismay, at finding myself suddenly thrown up in the air, my companions scattered about me, and the boat fast filling with water. A whale had come up directly under her, and with one dash of his tail, had stove her bottom in, and strewed us in every direction around her."

Nickerson, when writing about that second staving, put Chase in the stern: "the mate called his harpooner to throw his dart, when as quick as thought, the whale turned to come up under the boat, capsizing her, smashing in one side, and throwing us into the sea."

It may be that the difference in accounts is simply an honest difference of memory, in which case Chase is more likely to be accurate than Nickerson, as he wrote much closer to the actual events. Nickerson, furthermore, was writing after the publication of *Moby-Dick* (which was a dismal failure at the time) and at the request of a pulpy novelist. He may have seen the dramatic value of the first staving more clearly than First Mate Chase did.

On the other hand, Chase, with the audience to himself, may have moved himself from stern to bow because even though lower in rank than first mate, throwing the harpoon was the more glamorous occupation. More to the point, it was the job of the officer in the stern to keep the boat from getting smashed to bits while approaching whales. And though everyone on Nantucket knew that even the best among them periodically lost their whaleboats to flailing flukes, Owen Chase could not have relished the prospect of describing all the times the boat under his command had to be collected in pieces by the other whaleboats, even if no one got hurt, as was the case in both incidents.

As was the case as well the third time First Mate Chase's boat was smacked by a whale. It was only four days later, and Nickerson was again in the crew. This time they were actually on to a whale when it busted a hole through the planking with its tail. They were able to chop the line to the whale and plug the hole with their shirts, and by bailing and rowing furiously, they made their way back to the *Essex*.

It was by far the least of the three incidents in terms of damage to the whaleboat. But Nickerson and Chase agree that it was also, in hindsight, the beginning of their ordeal.

CHAPTER 25

HOME!

On April 16, 1820, the first mate of the *Essex* became a father, though he didn't know it at the time. In all likelihood Owen Chase didn't even know his bride Peggy Gardner was pregnant. It had taken the *Essex* a painfully long five weeks to beat westward around the bottom of South America, but finally, near the first of the year, they passed into the Pacific. During the first half of January they stopped briefly at St. Mary's Island, where, Chase wrote later, "our object in going in there was merely to get the news." But as they were one of the more recent ships around the horn, the news they sought was not of home but of the whaling season farther out.

Not long after, they gammed three other Nantucket whalers south of Valparaiso, where Nickerson remembered "delivering what letters we had for them." But these ships, too, could not have known that Owen Chase's wife was expecting. And by April, when she went into labor, the *Essex* was again alone at sea, cruising for whales somewhere off the coast of Chile. Back on Nantucket, Peggy Gardner Chase named her new daughter Phebe Ann.

Home! For all the romantic, adventurous, lonely lives that various Cape and Islanders led on the oceans of the world during the age of sail, the truth was that far more lives were lived and ended quite mundanely back at home. Children grew up in the absence of fathers. Sisters married. Mothers and grandmothers died or didn't die; either way their sons and brothers couldn't know until a lucky gam brought a letter. For the majority of the men at sea, news from Brewster, Wellfleet, Nantucket, Edgartown, or anywhere else on Cape Cod and the Islands was usually more exciting than a twelve-knot sleigh ride behind a bull sperm.

"It was amusing to watch those of our lads who [had] been disappointed and found no letters for them," wrote Nickerson about the moments after the *Essex* finally did receive news from home. This was early in the summer of 1820, after nearly a year at sea, and they had gammed the whaling ship *Aurora*, which had on board not only plenty of letters but some newspapers as well. "They would follow us around the decks, and whilst we were reading our letters would seat themselves beside us, as though our letters could be of service to them or convey news from their own friends."

Letters sent to sailors were typically addressed in the manner of one from Edgartown that read, simply, "Capt. Nathan M. Jernegan, Ship Splendid, Pacific Ocean," and every captain that left home port carried a bag of such optimistic correspondence. From ship to ship, officer to officer, gam to gam, the packets passed, until at last they usually found their way into the hands of the intended recipients. The letters the men and boys on the *Essex* received from the *Aurora* had been in transit for five months. So once again, though he may have received a letter from Peggy saying she was expecting, Owen Chase still would not have known with certainty that the dangerous business of giving birth had been successfully completed.

Letters were sent back to the Cape and Islands in the same way; slow, late, filled either with small observations to pass the time or with unwanted news of the worst kind. It was a strange, bisected sort of life that wasn't any easier for those left behind than for those at sea. "Oh Peter, lonesome are the wakeful midnight hours that my thoughts are on you and my own situation," wrote Susan Cromwell of Holmes Hole (Vineyard Haven) to her whaling-captain husband on the first day of 1854. She was raising two children and pregnant with a third, though neither she nor he yet knew it. "But we are separated," she wrote in another letter two weeks later, "and nothing that we can write will ever bring us together, nothing but time and the goodness of God can ever suffer us to enjoy our selves together again. I hope with a pleasing anticipation of seeing you in one year from next spring. Do write me long letters. Good night my Dear Husband. How I want you with me. Past 9 O'clock."

Different people developed different strategies regarding news from either home or sea, and letters were not always torn open immediately. This may at times have been in order to savor the experience. But not always. A letter, particularly if it didn't come from one's spouse, often meant the worst: "Captain Luce read today (for the first time) the letters he received from home when at Talcahuano, and by them learned that his wife was dead," wrote the third mate of the bark *Emily*. Luce had kept the letters for twenty days before opening them.

And many years later, long after the ordeal of the *Essex*, Owen Chase did receive a letter at sea informing him that his wife back home in Nantucket had given birth to a child. This wasn't the same ship, or wife, and Chase was by then a captain. But he wasn't exactly overcome with joy to read the news. The baby, it seems, was born more than sixteen months after he had gone to sea.

Home! For better or worse it had a way of carrying on. Letters no doubt went to the Pacific with news of the great fires that consumed various home towns. Nantucket burned badly in 1838. The heart of downtown Vineyard Haven burned in 1883. But the worst conflagration of all was probably the Nantucket fire of 1846. It hadn't rained in weeks, and the fire, which began at night in a hat store about an hour before midnight, spread rapidly from roof to roof. It melted iron safes and sent rivers of burning whale oil out over the water so that the harbor, too, was aflame. Some houses were dynamited in an effort to create a fire-break; others were looted by rowdies. When the smoke finally cleared, 360 buildings on roughly 36 acres, including the Athenaeum, the Episcopal church, and almost the entire waterfront, were gone.

But the vast majority of the letters did not contain bombshells of any kind. Maybe someone mentioned the groundbreaking for the new glass factory in Sandwich in 1824, or the first elms planted on Nantucket's Main Street by Charles and Henry Coffin in 1851. Or that in 1865, the selectmen of Orleans decided to banish a local troubled youth to an island in the middle of Pleasant Bay after he had chopped off the foot of Joe Newton's horse for no apparent reason. Mention may have been made as well of the various illustrious speakers on the lecture circuit: Emerson, Harriet Beecher Stowe, Frederick Douglass. Someone may have relayed that Thoreau, when he spoke at the Nantucket Atheneum in 1854, began his remarks with the announcement, "I wish to give you a strong dose of myself. You have sent for me, and will pay me, and you shall *have* me, even if I bore you beyond all precedent." Mostly, though, letters were full of the usual but important news of children growing up and getting married, or falling down and breaking fingers. Of relatives going into or out of business. Of proto-industrial American life.

Every available detail of life back on Cape Cod and the Islands was immensely valuable to those at sea, and what the folks at home didn't see fit to add to letters could sometimes be gleaned from old copies of the local newspapers that were passed hand to hand like sacred texts. "There is nothing in a strange land like a newspaper from home," wrote Richard Henry Dana Jr. "It is almost equal to *clairvoyance*. The names of the streets, with the things advertised, is almost as good as seeing the signs." When the crew of the *Essex* were done with their personal mail, they turned voraciously to the few newspapers the *Aurora* passed along. "Many of us set up all our next watch below to overhaul them," remembered Nickerson. "And although they did not contain any very important news, yet to us the whole was interesting, and I learned the contents so well by heart, that I could have repeated them six months afterwards."

Despite their global seafaring, the towns of Cape Cod and the Islands, like most of America, were at heart far more insular and self-sufficient than they are today. In the earliest days of European settlement, the only mill was at Plymouth, and for a few years grain had to be taken there or else ground by hand in the manner of the Native Americans. The first gristmill on the Cape was built around 1640 by Thomas Dexter, one of the original ten settlers in Sandwich. In the century that followed, all over Cape Cod and the Islands, virtually everywhere that there was even a modest flow of water, a dam was built and a mill of some sort constructed. By the early 1800s there were eight grain mills in Sandwich, along with three tanneries, a cotton mill, and a nail factory. In 1825, the famous glass works began operation and by 1850 the men and women who labored there were producing a half million pounds of glass per week, primarily from sand imported from Florida and the Jersey shore.

All over the Cape and Islands, "rivers" that nowhere else in New England would qualify even as brooks became centers of local industry. The Coonamesset River, Mashpee River, Cotuit River, Little River, Marstons Mills River, and the Tiasquam River were all put to work grinding grain or cleaning wool. West Brewster became known for a time as Factory Village for the five mills along the banks of the never-mighty Stony Brook. On Chilmark's Roaring Brook—which is not wider than a sea kayak is long, and is not navigable by even a white-water kayak—there was a grain mill, a china clay mill, and a sizable brick mill.

"The least channel where water runs, or may run," Thoreau noticed, "is important, and is dignified with a name." Often the names were neither native nor creative. In Chilmark, for instance, there was a paint mill at Paint Mill Brook, the outlet of which can be hard to find even if you know exactly where to look (the clays of Gay Head were a source of pigment). And there was a fulling mill on Fulling Mill Brook, which isn't much bigger.

By modern standards, the environmental impact of these industries may seem minor, but it did not go unnoticed or unmourned at the time. In 1806 there was a heated battle over the dam on the Coonamesset River in Falmouth because it blocked the migration of the alewives. One man died when the prodevelopment faction attempted to make a point by firing a cannon full of fish, but not in vain; the herring run was sacrificed in the name of progress.

There was at least one attempt to build a tidal mill at Wellfleet in 1790, but more often where there wasn't sufficient flowing water—which was most of the Cape and Vineyard and virtually all of Nantucket—locals turned to the ubiquitous wind. As mentioned earlier, hundreds of relatively simple windmills were constructed all over the Cape to pump seawater into salt vats. But there were also many large and beautiful wind machines scattered around the region designed to grind corn, clean wool, or perform other tasks.

Windmills were so complicated to build and maintain that there was always a good market for used mills; Kittredge estimated that more than half the mills on the Cape were moved at least once. Considerable art and skill was required to run them as well, but scaling out on long yards to trim and furl sails came rather naturally to millers who had likely spent most of their late teens and early twenties out of sight of land.* Orleans was still wind-grinding grist in 1892.

There were tanneries in many towns, and blacksmiths in almost all. Once the wood supply ran out, many communities turned to peat from local swamps for fuel. Some bogs, like Iron Ore Swamp on the Vineyard's North Road, are repositories of iron leached from the surrounding glacial till. Peat from these was sent to foundries like the Pocasset Iron Works and turned into, among other things, cannonballs for the guns of Old Ironsides.† Clays,

---

*"It was a game among kids to hang onto the blades of windmills and ride them up. At least one, a girl named Hepsibeth, did a full three sixty, rising fifty feet into the air while the boys below yelled, Hold On Hepsi."
†Old Ironsides, incidentally, was built by a Vineyard man, Chilmark's George Claghorn.

While the men were at sea the women, like the Barnstable cranberry harvesters shown here, kept the home economy going. (COURTESY OF THE STURGIS PUBLIC LIBRARY, BARNSTABLE)

too, were mined, most notably at Sandwich and at Gay Head, where ships from Boston docked a half mile offshore to be loaded by ferries.

Despite the declining productivity of local soils, agriculture remained an important part of the economy of much of Cape Cod and the Islands throughout the period. Interestingly, as grain and grazing declined during the second half of the nineteenth century, two crops that rose to local prominence were former staples of the traditional Wampanoag and Nauset diet. In the early 1800s someone in North Dennis observed that when sand blew in on a wild cranberry patch, the plants produced far more fruit, but it wasn't until 1846 or '47 that the first real cranberry farms opened at Pleasant Lake in Harwich. The center of strawberry farming, meanwhile, was Falmouth: in 1919 seventy-three train cars of strawberries, mostly raised by the Portuguese-American community, were shipped from Falmouth to Boston.

But the largest part of the economy, even for those who stayed on shore, was always somehow connected to the sea. Cheek by jowl with the salt vats were miles of racks on which cod, herring, mackerel, and other fish were dried for export to Europe and the West Indies. There were ninety fish warehouses in Provincetown alone in 1840. There were boatyards in all the larger port towns, along with sailmakers, chandlers, ropewalks, and the like. Due to the limits of its wood supply, most builders on Cape Cod and the Islands were restricted to constructing relatively smaller vessels, like brigs and schooners. But one generation of one family, the Shivericks of East Dennis, managed to compete with the great yards of Maine. Between 1850 and 1862 they built and launched eight world-class clippers: *Revenue, Hippogriffe, Belle of the West, Kit Carson, Wild Hunter, Webfoot, Christopher Hall,* and the *Ellen Sears.*

The epitome of the ocean-based home economy was Nantucket, center of the whale industry and by 1830 the third richest municipality in the state (after Boston and Salem). By 1832, reported Philbrick, the island had one shipyard, five boat shops, seventeen oil factories, nineteen spermaceti candle factories and two candle-box factories, ten ropewalks, twenty-two barrel makers, one brass foundry, ten blacksmith/harpoon shops, four spar shops, two bakeries specializing in ship's bread, two block factories, four sail lofts, three rigging lofts, numerous general provisioners, a rum distillery, four banks, several insurance companies, and sixty grog shops. With a year-round population approaching ten thousand (as compared with seventy-five hundred today) Nantucket was, said Daniel Webster, an "unknown city by the Ocean."

But for all the worldly connections and commercial bustle of the Cape and Islands during the maritime period, the region remained essentially a place of small towns. The total population of the Cape in 1800 was around twenty thousand; by 1860 it had risen to thirty-six thousand. There were the good things about small towns: almost always a cousin or uncle could provide a berth on a boat for any local boy in search of an opportunity; almost always a sister or an aunt could help raise children left fatherless or motherless; there was safety and community. There were other effects of smallness, though. During the earliest decades Provincetown periodically lost its entire population during slump years. In Chilmark, on the Vineyard, there was so little influx of new blood that a recessive gene for deafness gradually worked its way through the population of intermarried cousins. There were so many deaf people up-island on the Vineyard by the middle of the nineteenth century that the townspeople had developed their own sign language. Virtually everyone, hearing and deaf, could speak it. Alexander Graham Bell came to the island to study the phenomenon but was unable to isolate its cause.

Even Nantucket, big and rich as it was, vacillated between outward achievement and depressing insularity bordering on cultural bankruptcy. Power and wealth were so concentrated on the island that Ralph Waldo Emerson estimated that fifty people owned 70 percent of all the property, and John James Audubon, who visited in 1840, remarked that most of the residents "know little more than the value of dollars."

The island produced extraordinary women like Maria Mitchell, who was the first person to discover a comet with a telescope and the first woman elected to the American Academy of Arts and Sciences. But it also, according to Crevecoeur, was a place where a significant proportion of the female population relieved their loneliness and boredom by using opium. And judging from the numbers of opium bottles found in the wreckage from the Great Fire of 1846, it was a habit that lasted for generations.

For better or worse, home was still home. And though the men and boys on the *Essex* and a thousand other ships memorized the newspapers and reread their letters until the paper wore out, they could not go back until the hold was full. Oil or cargo, it didn't matter which, but you didn't go home empty. And though it had been a long time coming, the *Essex* was finally making slow but relatively steady progress toward that goal. Before speaking the *Aurora* off the coast of Peru, they had spent the season cruising the coast of Chile, where they took eight sperm whales and added roughly 250 barrels of oil to the hold. Though Chase and Nickerson gave slightly different estimates of the catch at various points on the voyage, they agree that this was not a particularly good take for the season. After meeting the *Aurora*, however, they did better, adding another 500 or so barrels to the hold along the coast of Peru. It was rough going, though, given the nature of the seas, and Nickerson remembered the whaleboats often being repaired not from damage done by whales but because they were smashed against the side of the *Essex* while being lowered or raised.

They stopped at several of the usual whalers' spots along the South American coast. When some of the men began complaining of swollen gums and blotchy skin—the first signs of scurvy—Pollard headed for the island of Más Afuera, which was for several decades a famous sealing ground until the seals were exterminated. By 1820 there was little left on the island but feral goats, which the men of the *Essex* were unable to catch. They were able, however, to catch some fish and restock their wood and water supply. Pollard also put in briefly at Talcahuano in order to paint the ship and give the crew a little well-deserved shore leave.

It had been five months since they were last at anchor in an actual town. Each man was issued a dollar advance, for which the captain told them he would deduct a dollar fifty from their eventual pay. Much of it was spent before noon at the fandango, where, Nickerson remembered, the young women playing guitars "looked more to getting Jack's money than to the Notes of [their] music."

At Arica, the officers attended a party on board the London whaling ship *Mary*, and the crew left behind on the *Essex* watched longingly while laughing women were hauled to the top of the mast in a chair rigged for the occasion. They saw drained flasks flying over the rails until "in a short time the empty bottles could be seen in a string for half a mile on the sea . . . the tide having taken them along like a row of Indians marching single file." And they saw Father Sideacco, the jolly priest of the town, without whom "no party could be complete," capsize while rowing back ashore and disappear until he was found under his overturned boat, holding on for dear life and breathing in the hollow of air.

At the end of the season, just before heading out to the offshore grounds, they went tortoise hunting in the Galapagos Islands. It was something of a standard stop for New England whalers: "These turtle are a most delicious food, and average in weight generally about one hundred pounds, but many of them weigh upwards of eight hundred," said Chase. "They are strewed over the deck, thrown under foot, or packed away in the hold, as it suits convenience." The best thing about them from the point of view of a whaler was that as long as the climate didn't get too cold tortoises could live for a year without any food or fresh water, though Nickerson remembered that after a few months they would often wander the decks tasting everything they could reach.

They were simple enough to catch. The crew roamed around the rocky, dry islands, and whenever they found a terrapin they flipped it over on its back and quickly jammed rocks between its shell and knees so as to prevent it retracting its legs. Then, specially made canvas straps were tied to each foot, and the animal was hoisted up backpack style and carried to the ship. It was back-breaking work over slippery ground, and many animals were dropped or thrown down in anger, their shells breaking, spoiling them for either the sailors' purposes or their own.

One man—Nickerson doesn't say which—got lost on his way back to the ship and, in the 110 degree heat, slit his tortoise's neck and drank the blood as it oozed out. And Thomas Chapple, apparently as a joke, lit Charles Island on fire. "Judging from the extent of desolate ground," said Nickerson after another visit to the islands years later, "there must have been thousands upon thousands of terrapin, birds, lizards, and snakes destroyed. And it probably burned until the rainy season set in."

There weren't as many tortoises to be had as in previous years: they got only three hundred from Hood's Island and another sixty from nearby Charles Island.* "Very Scarce" is how Nickerson described the situation. "Very scarce," like the Wampanoag around Patuxet after the plague. Or like the furs the Pilgrims sold to pay off their European backers. Scarce like good soil and wood back home, like the alewives from the Coonamesset and the oysters from Chatham. Like whales from the coastal waters of Cape Cod, then from the Islands, and the Gulf Stream and the Brazil Ground and everywhere else between Nantucket and where they were now. Scarce like the seals of Más Afuera and every other remote rock around the horn and beyond. But it was a glorious new age of global commerce: seal skins to China, tea to England, oil to everywhere. It was open markets and free trade. Scarcity was business as usual in the global oil business.

They were engaged in "an exterminating warfare against those leviathans of the deep," said Chase. "The whales have been driven, like the beasts of the forest, before the march of civilization, into remote and more unfrequented seas, until now, they are followed by the enterprise & perseverance of our seamen, even to the distant coasts of Japan."

The crew of the *Essex* hoisted their meager three hundred giant reptiles up on deck—including one that weighed six hundred pounds, took six men to carry, and became known to the crew as "the commodore." At daybreak on the morning of October 23, the *Essex* sailed west from the islands that later inspired Darwin into the heart of the Pacific Ocean, with Thomas Chapple's conflagration still visible back on shore.

Then, almost exactly one month later, entirely out of the deep blue a giant bull sperm smashed in and destroyed not just a whaleboat but the *Essex* herself.

---

*Again, Chase and Nickerson disagree on the number of tortoises: Chase reported 360 total, Nickerson 280.

CHAPTER 26

INTO THE BLUE

It is hard to imagine now that at first it was anything but too horrific to believe. At eight o'clock on the "extremely fine and clear" morning of November 20, the lookouts in the masthead had called out, "There she blows." The ship was put about, and they sailed down toward the spouts. They were in whales! The crew was in a grand mood, boatsteerer Thomas Chapple later remembered. With 750 barrels of oil already in the hold and a shoal of sperm whales in sight, it was no longer inconceivable that "they should soon complete their cargo."

Only hours later, instead of chasing profits, they were rowing after the few scrawny hogs that swam away from the barely floating hulk of their ship.

The hunt began normally enough. When the *Essex* got within about a half mile of the whales, Captain Pollard ordered her "brought to the wind, and the main-top-sail hove aback." This was to hold her general position while the whaleboats went after their prey. All three lowered immediately. Pollard commanded one. Chase, with Nickerson in his crew, was in charge of the second. And Matthew Joy or Thomas Chapple ran the third.

When they got to where the whales had been, they were nowhere to be seen. This wasn't particularly unusual—sperm whales regularly dive for around forty-five minutes—so the hunters sat in their boats and waited for the great mammals to come back up. "Presently one rose," Chase remembered, "and spouted a short distance ahead of my boat; I made all speed toward it, came up with, and struck it; feeling the harpoon in him, he threw himself, in an agony, over towards the boat, (which at that time was up alongside of him,) and giving a severe blow with his tail, struck the boat near the edge of the water, amidships, and stove a hole in her."

As previously mentioned, this was the third time Chase had his boat stove in. Somebody grabbed the boat's hatchet and chopped the line attached to the harpoon—no one wants a Nantucket sleigh ride with a hole in his boat. The whale was, by now, peeling the rope out of the tub at high speed. The men stuffed their coats in the hole, and Chase ordered one man to bail as fast as he could while the rest rowed back to the ship. Both Pollard and Chapple, meanwhile, succeeded in getting themselves attached to whales.

Back on the *Essex*, Chase ordered young Nickerson to take the helm of the ship and steer down toward where the other boats were fighting their whales. He and the others, meanwhile, brought the broken boat up on deck and decided they could repair it faster than they could get the ship's fourth boat untied and lowered. They were just beginning to nail a piece of canvas over the hole as a short-term repair when the whale appeared to the wind-ward side.

Nickerson recalled that he saw the leviathan first and called out to Chase, which would make a certain amount of sense, because he was at the helm. Chase, somewhat typically, claimed he saw it first and called out to Nickerson. And Pollard, whom Nickerson, Chase, and Chapple all agree was off in his whaleboat attached to a whale at the time, claimed he saw the whale first, "rushing with great swiftness through the water, right toward the ship."

It is Chase, however, who gave the most detail:

> I observed a very large spermaceti whale, as well as I could judge, about eighty-five feet in length; he broke water about twenty rods off our weather-bow, and was lying quietly, with his head in a direction for the ship. He spouted two or three times, and then disappeared. In less than two or three seconds he came up again, about the length of the ship off, and made directly for us, at the rate of about three knots. The ship was then going with about the same velocity. His appearance and attitude gave us at first no alarm; but while I stood watching his movements, and observing him but a ship's length off, coming down for us with great celerity, I involuntarily ordered the boy at the helm to put it hard up; intending to sheer off and avoid him.

Nickerson remembered hearing the command: "On his seeing the whale, he instantly gave me an order to put the helm hard up." Then he remembered a chorus of shouts. Then he remembered a crash. "He came down upon us with full speed, and struck the ship with his head, just forward of the fore chains," remembered Chase, which "gave us such an appalling and tremendous jar, as nearly threw us on our faces. The ship brought up as suddenly and violently as if she had struck a rock, and trembled for a few seconds like a leaf. We looked at each other with perfect amazement, deprived almost of the power of speech."

Not just momentarily, either. "Many minutes elapsed before we were able to realize the dreadful accident," said Chase. During this time the whale passed beneath the ship and came up on the leeward side. It was ostensibly in somewhat of a daze itself, though one survivor, possibly William Wright of Barnstable,* remembered it trying in vain to get hold of some piece of the ship with its jaws.

The men on board couldn't stand around gaping for too long, because it was soon clear that they were taking on water. Chase ordered the pumps rigged, and the men began pumping furiously. But water was coming in faster than they were getting it out, and Chase "perceived the head of the ship to be gradually settling down in the water." The whale, meanwhile, came to and swam off to windward.

Nickerson remembered that while the whale was resting beside the *Essex* there was some talk of getting a lance and killing it, but Chase decided against it when he noticed the leviathan's tail lying directly under the ship's rudder. Once again, this is a detail Chase left out of his version of the story, and once again, there are several ways to interpret the difference. In Chase's opinion, the *Essex* was already damaged beyond repair—"by this time the ship had settled down a considerable distance in the water, and I gave her up as lost"—and he turned all his efforts to getting the two whaleboats ready to be used as lifeboats, should that become necessary.

---

*It may also have been Chapple or Weeks, as the detail comes from interviews taken on board the *Surrey*, which ultimately rescued those three. I chose Wright based on the assumption that when the *Essex* crew divided themselves into the three surviving whaleboats, they most likely maintained roughly the same crews they were accustomed to using when chasing whales. If this was true—and it's at least slightly supported by the fact that Chase's list of the lifeboat crews has Nickerson in the first mate's boat—then only William Wright would have been on the *Essex* at the time of the attack. Chapple was in his own boat attached to a whale, and Weeks was in Pollard's boat.

Nickerson, on the other hand, thought the ship was still salvageable. It's hard to know exactly what to make of his opinion. At the time of the events, he was far less experienced than Chase; at the time he wrote his version, however, he was a retired captain himself. Also, unlike Chase, who was in command at the critical moment, as ship's boy Nickerson could never be held accountable for any decisions made on the *Essex*.

Not that Nickerson meant to suggest that Chase should have done differently. When he wrote, "could we have fore seen all that so soon followed, [Chase] would probably have chosen the lesser evil and have saved the ship by killing the whale even at the expense of losing the rudder," Nickerson, with his fifty years of hindsight, was only ruminating on what might have happened had different decisions been made. What so soon followed was even less likely than what had just occurred. Chase had ordered the signals raised to call the other whaleboats back to the ship when he saw the big whale, "apparently in convulsions," about a quarter-mile downwind. "He was enveloped in the foam of the sea, that his continual and violent thrashing about in the water had created around him, and I could distinctly see him smite his jaws together, as if distracted with rage and fury."

Chase went back to work "getting all things ready to embark in [the whaleboats] if there should be no other resource left." Then the men again began to yell. "I turned around, & saw him about one hundred rods directly ahead of us, coming down with twice his ordinary speed," Chase recalled. It was suddenly clear that the first collision was not the "dreadful accident" Chase originally thought it had been. "To me at that moment, it appeared with tenfold fury and vengeance in his aspect. The surf flew in all directions about him, and his course towards us was marked by a white foam of a rod in width, which he made with the continual violent thrashing of his tail; his head was about half out of water, and in that way he came upon and again struck the ship."

Chase ordered Nickerson to bring the ship hard up in a last-minute attempt to avoid the collision, but again to no avail. "I should judge the speed of the ship to have been at this time about three knots, and that of the whale about six. He struck her to windward, directly under the cathead, and completely stove in her bows. He passed off to leeward, and we saw no more of him." The force of the blow pushed the ship backward "a considerable distance," according to Chapple. And one of William Wright's rescuers remembered being told that all the men on deck were knocked down, and that the stern was pushed under to such a degree that "the water came dashing in the cabin windows."

Mere speechlessness was now supplanted by profound shock. "Our situation at this juncture can be more readily imagined than described," wrote Chase. "The misfortune befell us at a moment when we least dreamt of any accident; and from the pleasing anticipations we had formed, of realizing the certain profits of our labour, we were dejected by a sudden, most mysterious, and overwhelming calamity." This time, though, there were no long minutes of stupefaction. The ship was now most definitely sinking, and rapidly. When they tried to get to the pumps, reported Nickerson,* the water was already over the lower deck.

"We were more than a thousand miles from the nearest land," wrote Chase, "and with nothing but a light open boat as the resource of safety for myself and companions. I ordered the men to cease pumping, and every one to provide for himself; seizing a hatchet at the same time, I cut away the lashing of the spare boat, which lay bottom up, across two spars directly over the quarter deck. . . ."

With those thousand watery miles no doubt on his mind, William Bond, one of the men who had joined the ship from Boston, waded into the flooding cabin and managed to save two quadrants and two copies of Bowditch's *Practical Navigator*. He went down again and returned with the captain and first mate's trunks. Chase, meanwhile, had collected two compasses from the binnacle.

All of this, along with whatever else the other men had managed to collect, was thrown into the one serviceable whaleboat. Bond tried to wade down to the cabin a third time, but by then it was already too flooded, and he came back empty-handed.

As the *Essex* began to list over onto her beam ends, they shoved the whaleboat over the plank shear and jumped aboard. When they were two boat lengths away from the ship, she "fell over to windward, and settled down in the water." It had all taken ten minutes.

Now was the second occasion for motionless bewilderment. "What an association of ideas flashed across our minds on the instant," wrote Nickerson. "Here lay our beautiful ship, a floating and dismal wreck,—which but a few minutes before appeared in all her glory, the pride and boat of her Captain and officers, and almost idolized by her crew." The sketch he later

---

*Yet another point of difference between Nickerson and Chase: Nickerson wrote that this was the first time they tried to get to the pumps.

included in his memoir of the voyage shows the *Essex* with sails up on all three masts and listing heavily to port.

"We looked upon each other, as if to gather some consolatory sensation from an interchange of sentiments," wrote Chase. "But every countenance was marked with the paleness of despair. Not a word was spoken for several minutes by any one of us; all appeared to be bound in a spell of stupid consternation."

In all likelihood, no one on the *Essex* had ever heard of or imagined a whale destroying a ship. To be sure, certain whales periodically gained reputations as fighters. In 1832 the whaling ship *Hector* encountered one that didn't wait to be attacked before destroying the whaleboats. First it smashed the mate's boat with its tail. Next it took the captain's twenty-eight foot boat in its jaw, lifted it entirely out of the water, and shook it to pieces. As was the case with a lot of fighting whales, this one turned its fury on the boat rather than the men in the water and was soon chasing after a bobbing water keg like a bass after a popping plug.

The whale was not, however, quite as distracted by the keg as the mate who lowered in a new boat thought he was. The crew pulled like hell to get away from the whale, which chased them for half a mile with its jaw on the surface snapping away; more than once the crew barely escaped the nutcracker. Finally it made the mistake of rolling over to catch a breath while within reach of the boat, and the mate drove home his lance. Later, while cutting the blubber, they found harpoons from the whaling ship *Barclay* of Nantucket, whose mate was killed by the same whale not long before.

Old sperm bulls, in particular, were thought to be the most likely fighters, especially if they had been attacked before and had escaped serious injury. These whales often traveled alone or in pairs, and the most famous one was called Mocha Dick. (He was not actually white, and was finally killed by whalers.) But even Mocha Dick went after whaleboats, not whale ships. But the *Essex* was not, as many accounts suggest, the only known instance of a whale ship attacked by its prey. The *Ann Alexander* sank in the offshore grounds on August 20, 1850, after being attacked by a whale that had already destroyed two of her whaleboats.* The crew were rescued after

---

*A whale taken five months later by the *Rebecca Sims* was found to have harpoons from the *Ann Alexander* in it, along with pieces of ship's timber embedded in its head. It had put up no fight when it was finally captured.

two days in their whaleboats by the ship *Nantucket*. That same year the *Parker Cook* out of Provincetown was struck twice by a whale that had already smashed one of the ship's whaleboats. The *Pocahontas* out of Vineyard Haven was attacked by a whale and limped into Rio de Janeiro leaking 250 strokes of the pump per hour. The bark *Kathleen* was sunk by a whale in the Atlantic on March 7, 1902. Other ships, like the Nantucket whaler *Union*, collided with whales at night and sank. And there were ships like the *Lady Adams* that disappeared without a trace or clue as to their fate.

According to the various accounts, it wasn't Pollard himself but a member of his whaleboat crew who first looked back from where they were fighting a whale and noticed that the *Essex* was gone. "Oh my God, where's the ship?" Obed Hendricks supposedly shouted.* (Nickerson's version has him saying, "Look, what ails the ship, she is upsetting.") Almost immediately everyone was shouting and scanning the horizon. A similar moment of shock occurred in Chapple's boat at around the same time, and both immediately detached themselves from their whales and rowed the roughly two miles back to the scene of the disaster.

Pollard's boat got there first. "He stopped about a boat's length off, but had no power to utter a single syllable," Chase remembered. "He was so completely overpowered with the spectacle before him, that he sat down in his boat, pale and speechless. I could scarcely recognize his countenance, he appeared to be so much altered, awed, and overcome, with the oppression of his feelings. . . ." When finally he could speak, it was only to ask, "My God, Mr. Chase, what is the matter?"

"We have been stove by a whale."

The *Essex* by now was all the way over on her beam ends, and only the buoyancy of the 750 barrels of oil was keeping the ship from foundering entirely. Pollard ordered the crew to begin cutting away the masts from the ship, which he hoped would right her to a degree that they could get on board and try to salvage some food and water. Using only the three small hatchets from their whaleboats, the men worked for close to forty-five minutes. Once loose from the weight of the masts and rigging, the ship did come two-thirds of the way back up to an even keel.

---

*Again, the identification of Hendricks as the speaker here depends on the assumption that the lifeboat crews were the same as the whaling crews; Chase identifies the quote as from "the boatsteerer in Pollard's boat."

It was now close to noon, so while the men chopped through the deck above where they thought the food was stored, Pollard rowed a bit away from the wreck to take a reading. The men on board found six hundred pounds of hard ship's bread and a half dozen tortoises. They also found as much fresh water as they thought they could carry—sixty-five gallons per boat—a musket and powder, a couple of woodworking tools, two pounds of boat nails, and two pigs that came swimming out of the wreckage. Pollard, meanwhile, found that they were just south of the equator at a longitude of 119 degrees west: roughly a thousand miles from the nearest land.

They spent that night tied in a line to the carcass of their ship, taking turns on watch to make sure that no spars or other wreckage washed up against the boats. "Such a night it was to us!" remembered Chase. "So full of feverish and distracting inquietude, that we were deprived entirely of rest." At times he, and no doubt others, found himself weeping.

The next morning they wandered around the wreck "in a sort of vacant idleness" for hours, dazed, confused, not yet really grasping the magnitude of their situation. Finally, though, apparently more by common agreement than any direct orders from Pollard, they got to work making additional sails for their whaleboats. Each boat was rigged with two masts to carry a flying jib and two spritsails; the spritsails were made so that two reefs could be taken in them in case of heavy blows.

The wind picked up during the day, and the sea eventually grew quite rough. Water came over the gunwales of the whaleboats as they worked. In hindsight, though, the sloppy seas were probably a good thing, as it convinced them to make additional alterations to their boats. Using cedar from the wreck, they built up their gunwales an additional six inches. Had they not done so, Chase thought they would not have survived some of the storms to come. At noon they found that in the preceding twenty-four hours they had drifted almost fifty miles farther from land.

Still, it was hard to leave: "Our thoughts, indeed, hung about the ship, wrecked and sunken as she was, and we could scarcely discard from our minds the idea of her continuing protection." But after another night spent tied to her remains, the *Essex* began to break up. No new supplies had been found despite numerous searches. The barrels in the hold were beginning to break open, and all around the wreckage lay a slick of their hard-earned sperm oil.

The moment came to leave her. "It has appeared to me often since to have been, in the abstract, an extreme weakness and folly, on our parts, to have looked upon our shattered and sunken vessel with such an excessive fondness and regret," wrote Chase, "but it seemed as if in abandoning her we had parted with all hope, & were bending our course away from her, rather by some dictate of despair."

None of the men was hungry, but all drank as much as they could of the fresh water, as they had found more than they could bring away with them. Six went with Chase in the worst of the three boats—"she was old and patched up, having been stove a number of times, during the cruise." Seven went in Pollard's boat and seven in Chapple's boat. And at 12:30, after one last noon observation of the sun and one last futile climb to the top of the broken-off foremast to scan for other ships and a promise to try to stay close together, they set off for the coast of South America, some two thousand miles away.* Nickerson recalled some men calling out farewells to the wreck, and others who could not stop looking back. In Chase's boat, from the very beginning one man had to bail almost constantly.

The wisdom of the navigation decisions of Pollard and his officers after the wreck of the *Essex* is one of the more scrutinized facets of the story, most notably by Thomas Heffernan of the Melville Society in his remarkably detailed exegesis on the Chase narrative, *Stove by a Whale*. The debate usually focuses on whether and what they could or should have known of various closer destinations, like Hawaii or Pitcairn Island, and whether the reasons they decided against sailing to the closer locations they did know of, most notably Tahiti and the Marquesas, were justified. The answers will never really be known, depending as they do on such factors as what version of Bowditch's *Practical Navigator* they had, which islands not in their *Navigator* they nevertheless knew of, and whose version of the story one is inclined to believe.

According to the *Navigator*s that were most likely rescued from the ship's cabin by William Bond, the nearest land was the Marquesas at roughly fourteen hundred miles, followed by the Society Islands. But Chase wrote that "these islands we were entirely ignorant of," and that "if inhabited, we presumed they were by savages, from whom we had as much to fear, as from the elements, or even death itself."

During the course of the nineteenth century there were isolated instances of trouble between mariners from Cape Cod and the Islands and

---

*According to research by Thomas Heffernan, there were at least three other whaling ships in the area: *Governor Strong*, *Thomas*, and the *Globe* (of the famous mutiny described earlier). *Balaena*, *Persia*, and *Golconda* of New Bedford and the *Coquette* of London were also probably working the offshore ground. But none were seen.

natives of the Pacific. Two years after the *Essex* sank, the *Syren* was attacked by a group of Palau Islanders who came aboard to trade. In the melee two crew members were killed, and several others, including Captain Frederick Coffin of Nantucket, were wounded. According to at least one version of the story, the ship was only retaken when a stash of tacks was thrown down on the deck from the rigging, causing all the barefooted attackers to jump overboard.

A similar battle in the Marshall Islands in 1835 resulted in the deaths of at least nine crew members and an unknown number of Polynesians. More than thirty Marshall Islanders came aboard the Falmouth whaling ship *Awashonks,** ostensibly to trade, and then picked up the ship's cutting spades and lances and attacked the crew. Captain Prince Coffin was nearly beheaded in the first moments of the attack, and Mates Gardner and Swain were also killed. A stalemate ensued, in which a handful of Cape and Islanders holed up below periodically poked their guns out and fired ineffectually at the invaders, who virtually controlled the deck. According to one version, the tide turned in favor of the Americans only when Third Mate Silas Jones ignited an open barrel of gunpowder below a spot where he concluded a significant number of the enemy was collected. The roof of the cabin was gone, but so were all the Marshall Islanders who had been standing on top of it. Two months later, the *Awashonks* reached Honolulu.

In 1825 the *Oeno* of Nantucket wrecked on a reef near Turtle Island in the Fiji group. The castaways were taken in by the first group of islanders they met, but a few days later a band from another island attacked, and all but one were killed. This was young William Cary, the ship's cooper, who hid out in a crevice of a rock for three days, surviving on a single coconut. When he finally came out of hiding, he was immediately captured. He remembered turning his head away so that he wouldn't have to see the deadly blows coming his way. But the visiting marauders had returned to their own island, and he was adopted by the friendlier locals.

After several weeks, a more powerful monarch, King Toka of Lakemba, took Cary away from the Turtle Islanders, and for the next year or so the American lived relatively well, if not quite happily, as a favored member of Toka's entourage. He helped entertain visiting dignitaries and accompanied Toka on state visits to nearby islands, including a four-day voyage made in twenty canoes to visit the far more powerful King Kakombau of Ambow Island. Each night along the way they spent at a different island, and as they

---

*The *Awashonks* was built in Woods Hole and named for a long-dead Wampanoag queen.

finally neared their destination, an emissary from Kakombau came out in a large canoe to escort them in to Ambow.

Cary was sitting with Toka in his royal canoe when Kakombau's deputy paddled up. There was a period of silence while the head man from Ambow studied the prisoner. Cary didn't know what to think: in this year he had encountered two friendly groups of Fijians and one hostile group. Finally, though, Kakombau's emissary stood up and said, in perfect English, "How are you, William Cary?"

"Don't you remember a David Whippey?" he went on when Cary merely stared back at him, dumbfounded. Finally, though, Cary answered that yes, he had once had a playmate back in Nantucket by that name. The native, who was not a native, grinned. "I am that David Whippey," he said. As mentioned in an earlier chapter, Whippey had left Nantucket seven years before and, after reaching the Fijis, never looked back. Cary did eventually go back to Nantucket, but not until he had spent another six years working and wandering the Pacific.

Generally speaking, though, the fears of Polynesian violence expressed by Owen Chase were not based on much in the way of first- or even secondhand knowledge. All of the above-mentioned incidents of violence took place after the *Essex* disaster, and if the officers of the *Essex* knew that Captain Cook had been killed by the Hawaiians forty years before, they presumably also knew that he had been treated quite well by the Tahitians. They may or may not have known of relatively regular visits to the Hawaiian Islands for sandalwood as early as the 1790s by John Kendrick and other Cape Cod captains involved in the Northwest fur trade. (Chase reported that Pollard was worried it was hurricane season in Hawaii.) It is hard to imagine that they had not heard of their fellow Nantucketer Mayhew Folger's 1808 discovery of the *Bounty* mutineers on Pitcairn Island, but, as will become apparent, they clearly didn't know where Pitcairn was located.

As for whalers like themselves, the first two whale ships to visit the Hawaiian Islands—*Equator* of Nantucket and *Balaena* of New Bedford— had only gotten there a month after the *Essex* left Nantucket. The whaling ships *Syren* and *Maro* had only discovered the "on Japan" whaling ground six months before the *Essex* sank. Within a decade, Hawaii, Tahiti, and the Marquesas would all be well known to whalers, but in 1820, from the perspective of three open boats with limited food and water, the islands of the mid–Pacific Ocean were terrifying.

At least, that is, according to Chase. It should come as little surprise by now that the Chase and Nickerson narratives give significantly different accounts of the decision to sail south to get out of the trade winds, and then east for South America. Both agree that there was a conference of the ship's officers, during which various options were discussed. Chase's account gives the impression that there was unanimity regarding the dangers of sailing west. He also noted specifically that they had managed to rescue no charts, only the *Navigator*. Though helpful, Bowditch's book was notoriously inaccurate; comfort may have been taken in the knowledge that South America was a big target.

Nickerson, on the other hand, remembered Pollard wanting to make for the Society Islands, but that he was overridden by Chase and the other officers, who "urged the probability of a speedy passage to the coast of chili [*sic*]." It was, Nickerson thought, the fatal error, which could only be explained by "gross ignorance or a great oversight somewhere." In ten days of sailing or less, he calculated, the survivors could have "been landed safely, probably without the loss of a single individual." For what it's worth, on a later voyage Pollard told some missionaries, "We knew that we were at no great distance from Tahiti, but were so ignorant of the state and temper of the inhabitants, that we feared we should be devoured by cannibals if we cast ourselves on their mercy."

CHAPTER 27

SOUTH PACIFIC

So south and east they directed their boats. They calculated that they had sixty days of provisions, assuming they could survive on a half a pint of water and a pound of bread a day. They calculated additionally that they had fifty-seven days of sailing before reaching the coast of South America, assuming the weather went their way.* Their fondest hope was that they would be rescued by another ship long before they found out if their calculations and assumptions were on or off the mark. But no one dared to assume such luck. There was nothing now to do but wait and react. And pray.

After three days at sea, the whaleboat carrying both Chase and Nickerson began to take on water more rapidly than could be bailed out. They had been sailing under reefed sails almost from the outset, with waves periodically breaking over the sides of the boats. And though at times the wind seemed to moderate a bit and schools of dolphins chased along beside them, at night the wind always seemed to rise to a gale. With the wind still howling, they tore up the floor of their leaking boat and saw that one of the planks near the bow had pulled away from the frame about six inches below the water line. There was no way to fix it from within.

---

*Twenty-seven days to get far enough south to escape the trade winds, then thirty more to reach the coast.

They came about immediately. Because the leak was on the leeward side, the new tack brought the bad board nearly to the surface. When everyone moved to the new leeward side, the hole heeled out of the water just enough for one of the crew to reach out and bang in a few nails. The fix worked far better than they could have hoped, but the effect was not celebratory. It was too early in the voyage for this kind of thing to start happening. It hadn't even been a serious gale.

"When it is recollected to what a slight vessel we had committed ourselves," wrote Chase, "our means of safety alone consisting in her capacity and endurance for many weeks, in all probability, yet to come, it will not be considered strange that this little accident should not only have damped our spirits considerably, but have thrown a great gloominess over the natural prospects of our deliverance." The gloom, recalled Nickerson, was "not easily effaced." Only the hymns sung at dusk by Richard Peterson, the sixty-year-old New Yorker, eased their troubled hearts, at least temporarily.

On the sixth night at sea—after a day of good progress and another fighting a contrary wind—Pollard's boat was attacked by a large shark. It was too dark to see well, but it seemed to be about twelve to sixteen feet long and followed the boat for a while before attempting to take a good-sized bite out of the bow. Just as the whale had, it struck not once but twice before finally being driven off by a few pokes in the side with a spritpole.* Water poured into the vessel. "I have been attacked by an unknown fish, and he has stove my boat," Pollard yelled to Chase, and they frantically began transferring provisions from the damaged boat into the others.

All through the night they bailed and wondered. "The night was spissy darkness itself," Chase remembered, "the sky was completely overcast, and it seemed to us as if fate was wholly relentless, in pursuing us with such a cruel complication of disasters." They worried through the dark that the shark was still around. But in the morning they were able to repair the boat from the inside by pushing the broken planks roughly back into place and nailing a few thin strips of cedar crosswise along the inside. The wind was in their favor, and they started on again.

Chase did his best during these days to keep a rudimentary log on a bit of paper that had been rescued from his sea chest, but couldn't write much for the continuous heaving and spraying. Similarly, they attempted to take a navigational reading each noon, but with no hourglass or logline they gave

---

*Used to raise and lower the sails.

up on dead-reckoning their longitude. There were nearly constant minor repairs to the boats, which seemed to leak more and more each day.

The worst effect of the rough weather by far was that a good portion of their bread supply in both Pollard's and Chase's boats had been soaked with brine. It was still edible after careful drying, but the saltiness made their allotted half-pint of water painfully more inadequate than it already was. "Our extreme sufferings here first commenced," wrote Chase. They knew the bread was at fault, but there was nothing to be done other than eat it. To save it for the end would be to let it spoil. To discard it was even more out of the question; the intermittent bad weather and contrary winds caused their intended southeast course to turn slightly southwest. Worse than behind schedule, they were actually farther from their destination than when they began. There was a moment of hope the day after the shark attack when they were again surrounded by dolphins, and someone in Chase's boat had the idea of trolling a fly made of a small piece of white cloth tied to one of the few fishing hooks that had been in Chase's chest. The animals never hit the lure, however, though they "continued playing around us, nearly all day, mocking both our miseries and our efforts."

On the eighth day at sea Chase suggested they eat one of their two tortoises. "I need not say, that the proposition was hailed with the utmost enthusiasm," he wrote later, and Nickerson remembered that "all seemed quite impatient of an opportunity to drink the warm blood as it came oozing from the wound." They cooked it, entrails and all, in its own shell and were cheerful for the first time in many days. They were even more cheerful three days later when they finished the last of the damaged sea bread. According to their best estimates, they had now traveled nearly five hundred miles from the wreck.

The work of keeping the boats afloat was continuous. Because it had been stove so many times, Chase's boat, in particular, was "Old and Crazy." Nickerson wrote that none back home would have trusted it to go ten miles, and that Chase "lets no opportunity pass whereby he can add a nail by way of strengthening." Most of the repairs were relatively minor, but one time Benjamin Lawrence had to tie a rope around his waist and go under the boat while holding his breath to work on the plank next to the keel.

Other than the repairs and the daily prayer meetings led by Richard Peterson, there was little to occupy their minds but calculations of if and how and under what circumstances they might survive. Or fail to survive. These calculations began to change as days went by and they fell further behind schedule. One of their greatest worries at first was that the boats would be separated during the night or during a storm. It even happened a few times, though they were always able to find each other by raising lanterns up their masts or, once, firing a pistol. Toward the end of the second week, however, Chase noticed that their early certainty that the survivors from any boat lost would be welcomed aboard the remaining two was starting to waver.

"As our situation became more straightened and desperate, our conversation on this subject took a different turn," he remembered. Everyone agreed that additional passengers would only "weaken the chances of a final deliverance for some, and might be the only means of consigning every soul of us to a horrid death of starvation." But no one liked the thought of being forced to "unconcernedly witness their [fellow crew members'] struggles in death, perhaps beat them from our boats, with weapons, back into the ocean."

What's more, they wasted hours at a time looking for each other when they got separated; hours better spent racing toward land. "There is no question but that an immediate separation, therefore, was the most politic measure that could be adopted, and that every boat should take its own separate chance," Chase concluded. They couldn't do it, though. "Desperate instinct," Chase said, "bound us together." So on they went.

After eighteen days in the open boats a gale came up from east-southeast that caused them first to reef their sails, then haul them down, and finally even unstep their masts and attempt to lay to and ride the storm out. The only comfort in that night may have been the torrential rain. They tried for a while to collect some to drink by spreading a sail, but as with every other time it rained the half-bucket they collected was too salty from spray and from the saturated sails themselves. So they lay low in the tossing boats, either attempting to look upward at the lightning-filled sky or keeping their eyes tightly shut as they did their best to "await the fate of sailors as became men." And though everyone, no doubt, tried opening his mouth to catch a drink—and though Chapple, for one, thought the rain gave them some relief—when the storm finally abated everyone was desperately thirsty. After twenty-two days in the open boats some of the men attempted to drink their own urine.

Hunger caught up with thirst. A few flying fish came into the boat once and were devoured whole and live. They ate their last tortoise. Some harvested a few tiny clams off the bottom of the boats, but found themselves too weak to get back over the gunnels without help. Chase now kept all the rations and remaining water in his sea chest and made sure to drape himself over it when he slept. He kept his pistol loaded at all times. In their respective boats, Pollard and Joy presumably took similar precautions.

On the twentieth of December, after exactly one month in the open boats, William Wright woke up and saw land.

"It appeared at first a low, white, beach, & lay like a basking paradise before our longing eyes," said Chase. "It is not within the scope of human calculation, by a mere listener to the story, to divine what the feelings of our hearts were on this occasion. . . ." The island looked to be about six miles long by three, with steep and rugged cliffs, and after consulting their *Practical Navigator*, they concluded it must be an island called Ducie and that they had therefore made even less progress east toward South America than they had previously supposed. In fact, it wasn't Ducie at all but a fellow member of the Pitcairn Island group now known as Henderson Island. They had sailed seventeen hundred miles (as the crow flies). Not that the sufferers in their leaky whaleboats really cared about the name or the distance: it was land! And even better, as far as they could tell from cruising up and down the coast a bit, it was uninhabited. As Nickerson recalled, "each man seemed to greet it as a final end to his long confinement and sufferings."

As it turned out, there was a good reason other than remoteness that Henderson Island was (and still is) uninhabited. Chase and two others went ashore first, wading in from the boats with loaded guns in case hostile natives lay in wait in the bushes. They were so weak from the passage that this in itself left them winded, and they rested for a few moments on the beach before splitting up to look for water. They found none. It was like a cruel joke.

Chase managed to kill one fish in the shallows by braining it with the butt of his gun, and "in less than ten minutes, the whole was consumed, bones, and skin, and scales, and all." But, he said, "there was no indication of the least moisture to be found." Pollard and Chase discussed their options, and the first mate seems to have been of a mind to keep going rather than waste provisions poking around a dry island. Then suddenly, one of the other men called out that he had found fresh water.

Three drops of it, to be exact: "He had found a place in a rock some distance off, from which the water exuded in small drops, at intervals of about five minutes; that he had, by applying his lips to the rock, obtained a few of them, which only served to whet his appetite, and from which nothing like the least satisfaction had proceeded." It was promising enough, though, to convince them to spend the night on Henderson Island. Surely they would find water in the morning.

They did not. Their lips by then were cracked and swollen, and no one could really speak much. "A sort of glutinous saliva collected in the mouth, disagreeable to the taste, and intolerable beyond expression," Chase wrote. They fanned out in every direction, climbing as high and far on the sharp rocks as their weakened and shoeless state allowed. They found birds, "of a beautiful figure and plumage," and tame enough from lack of exposure to people to be simply taken by hand from their nests in crevices on the mountainside. They found eggs and crabs and peppergrass. That afternoon, remembered Nickerson, "every one seated himself upon the beautiful green grass and perhaps no banquet was ever enjoyed with greater gusto or gave such universal satisfaction."

If they did not find water after one more day, Pollard announced, they would set off again. The next morning, at dead low tide, Chase was back at the rock that dripped once every few minutes, trying in vain to dig a well. Others were up in the rocky hills, stumbling from bush to bush looking for water. Chase remembered flailing away at the ground with two other men, digging a relatively deep hole and staring into it for long moments, hoping to see water collect at its bottom. None did, though, and he fell back in exhausted despair. He remembered sitting there in gloom and then looking back the quarter mile along the beach to their pathetic camp, where a number of his comrades were carrying something like a keg. A Keg? A KEG!

Chase was the last to get to the spot, a small bubbling spring that only appeared for an hour or so at low tide. Every one else had had their fill, or were waiting a bit before drinking more. "When I arrived at the spot, whither I had hastened as fast as my weak legs would carry me, I found my companions had all taken their fill, and with an extreme degree of forbearance, I then satisfied myself, by drinking in small quantities, and at intervals of two or three minutes apart. Many had, notwithstanding the remonstrances of prudence, and, in some cases, force, laid down and thoughtlessly swallowed large quantities of it, until they could drink no more. The effect of this was, however, neither so sudden nor bad as we had imagined; it only served to make them a little stupid and indolent for the remainder of the day." They were drunk on water.

It took the crew of the *Essex* two more days to eat virtually everything edible on the island. On Christmas, after a full day of foraging, some had not collected enough even for one meal. "Every accessible part of the mountain, contiguous to us, or within the reach of our weak enterprise, was already ransacked for birds' eggs and grass, and was rifled of all that they contained," wrote Chase. The birds they did see had gotten wise to the ways of humans and began to "forsake the land." Talk of living on the island until a ship chanced by faded.

Not among everyone, however. When the patched-up whaleboats pushed off from the beach on December 27, the two Barnstable boys, Seth Weeks and William Wright, decided to stay behind. So did the Englishman Thomas Chapple, who felt he was too weak to survive the voyage. No one objected, as it would lighten the boats and they were forfeiting their provisions. But somewhat oddly, none of the three came to see the boats off, and Chase had to walk down the beach to where they were working on their thatch hut to say good-bye. A few tears were shed, and promises made to write to each other's relatives should anyone survive. Pollard also put some letters in a tin box and nailed them to a tree, in case no one lived. The last thing Chase remembered doing was collecting a load of firewood and a flat rock for each boat, in case they caught a fish or had other reason to cook.

What was unfortunately not in their *Practical Navigator* was Pitcairn Island, where the children of the *Bounty* mutineers were at that moment surviving reasonably well. Pitcairn lies only one hundred miles from Henderson Island and would figure thirty years later in another great open-boat crossing by sailors from Cape Cod and the Islands. On March 5, 1858, when the clipper ship *Wild Wave* under Captain Josiah Knowles of Brewster wrecked in the middle of the night on a reef off Oeno Island,* he and six others left most of the survivors camped on that speck of sand and sailed in one of the ship's longboats twenty miles south to Pitcairn with the intention of borrowing a larger boat from the *Bounty* colony. There was some bad weather to be weathered, and when they did get to Pitcairn all they found were signs saying that everyone had moved to Norfolk Island, a few abandoned houses, and a copy of *Jane Eyre*. Some of the men cried.

There wasn't much more to be done. Knowles buried the eighteen thousand dollars in gold he had rescued from the *Wild Wave* and slept on top of it. They hunted goats—"nineteen goat meals this week," Knowles wrote in his diary. After a month they apparently concluded that it was better to die at sea than spend the rest of their days eating goat meat and rereading *Jane Eyre*, and they began to build a boat big enough to get them to Tahiti, which was fifteen hundred miles away. They worked for months, using what tools they could find around the abandoned village to cut and

---

*Oeno was in the wrong place on Knowles's chart.

hew trees. For nails they burned houses and sifted through the ashes. For one mast they appropriated the town flagpole. They picked apart what old rope they could find to make oakum for caulking and built a ropewalk to twist new lines for their vessel. They made sea salt and laid in a supply of goat meat, collected twelve hundred oranges, and rounded up a small flock of chickens.

By the third week of July the six of them had built and launched a thirty-foot schooner that Knowles named the *John Adams*. Leaving three sailors behind, he and two others sailed off to the Marquesas. When they got there, however, the natives didn't strike Knowles as friendly enough, and he had all but decided to sail on for Hawaii, another three thousand miles away, when they happened upon the American sloop-of-war *Vandalia*. The *John Adams* was soon sold to a local missionary, and everyone on Pitcairn and Oeno was rescued.

But the crew of the *Essex* didn't know about Pitcairn and set their sights instead for Easter Island. "All we knew," wrote Chase, "was that it existed as laid down in the books." That, and the belief that it couldn't be any more barren than the island they were leaving. They figured it was about 850 miles away and hoped to make it there in eight to ten days.

They did not succeed. After nine days of sailing, Chase and Pollard concluded that they had been pushed too far south to have any hope of reaching Easter. Their best chance now, they concluded, was to sail for Más Afuera, where a lifetime ago they had stopped in the *Essex* to get wood. It was, they figured, twenty-five hundred miles away. Also that day, the last of the food collected on the island was eaten, and they were back to living on bread alone.

Day ten since leaving Henderson Island passed. Day eleven passed. Day twelve. On the thirteenth day, Second Mate Matthew Joy asked to be moved from his boat into the captain's, as he felt quite ill. Day fourteen passed. On day fifteen, Joy asked to be moved back to his own boat, where he died quietly. On day sixteen, they sewed him into his clothes, said a prayer, and committed him to the deep. Joy had always been sickly, even before the whale attack, they told themselves. But still, it was impossible to ignore that they were now only sixteen in the boats instead of seventeen. Impossible to ignore, in other words, that they were beginning to die.

The next night, the boat carrying Chase and Nickerson became separated from the other two in a gale. "I turned my head back, as I was in the habit of doing every minute, and neither of the others were to be seen," Chase remembered. He put about and hove to for an hour, hoping the others would catch up, but they did not. Nor did they appear in the morning. The gloom brought on by Joy's death now deepened, reported Chase: "we had lost the cheering of each other's faces." It was, echoed Nickerson, a "despondency which could not be easily shaken off."

They took a reading and calculated that they had only come nine hundred miles from Henderson Island. Rations were cut to an ounce of bread and a quarter-pint of water per day.

The eighteenth day passed.

Around the nineteenth day at sea, Nickerson noticed that "our bodies already debilitated seem no longer able or willing to act in concert with the mind." This, thought both Chase and Nickerson, is what induced one of their comrades, probably Peterson, to attempt to get more bread while Chase was sleeping.* Chase drew his gun and almost killed him, but relented. The sun, both Nickerson and Chase remembered, was merciless, and they were almost too weak to trim the sails or sit at the steering oar. For hours on end they all lay in the bottom of the boat under a sail and let the boat drift through the baking hours.

Joy's old boat, now under the command of Obed Hendricks and still in company with Pollard's boat, ran out of food. Pollard shared some from his own boat.

The twentieth day passed, but that night a large shark attacked Chase's steering oar. They tried to fight back with one of the lances that had once been used to kill whales but were too weak to even pierce the fish's skin. It attacked again, its huge jaws coming out of the water toward the boat's stern post, before finally swimming off.

The next morning they were equally incapable of getting a harpoon through the skin of one of the porpoises that played around them. And when two days after that a shoal of sperm whales surrounded them, they merely lay in the bottom of their boat in trepidation, listening to the now "terrible noise of whale-spouts near us." When their old prey at last moved off, they were, according to Nickerson, "overjoyed." Chase spent some time that day talking about religion with Richard Peterson, the sixty-year-old New Yorker who led them every day in prayer and whose hymn singing in stronger days had comforted them, but in the aftermath of the whales, most just "lay quietly and slept soundly." Peterson made Chase promise to write to his wife if he were to die there in the boat.

---

*The only clues as to his identity are that he was one of the two African Americans in their boat and that he was described as a "good old man."

The twenty-fourth day at sea passed.

On the twenty-fifth day Peterson refused to eat his allotted ounce of bread. He lay between the seats hardly moving, as he had for most of the past three days. Chase, Nickerson, and no doubt Benjamin Lawrence and Isaac Cole all tried to change his mind, tried to cheer him up and get him to eat. But he was ready to die, he said. And then, at four o'clock, he did, leaving only four alive in Chase's boat. On the twenty-sixth day they buried Peterson at sea. In Pollard's boat that day, the last of the food ran out.

The twenty-seventh day under the sun passed.

On the twenty-eighth day after leaving Henderson Island, Charles Shorter died in the whaleboat now under the command of Obed Hendricks. His body, however, would not immediately be committed to the deep. Two months had passed since the whale had struck and Pollard and Chase had first decided to make for South America rather than risk being eaten by the unknown Marquesas Islanders, and they were now at the point where, Pollard wrote, "We had no other alternative." They all no doubt said a prayer. And then someone took up a knife. Someone else built a small fire on the ballast sand at the bottom of the boat in order that the meat they were able to cut from Shorter's body could be "roasted to dryness."

It is not entirely clear from the accounts who died when and who, exactly, ate whom. The problem stems from the fact that Nickerson and Chase—the primary sources—were both in the boat separated by now from the other two. Chase wrote that Pollard told him Shorter died on the twenty-eighth day at sea, and that Lawson Thomas died two days later. Nickerson, however, said Pollard told him that Thomas had died first, ten days earlier. Further confusing matters, both Chase and Nickerson leave open the slight possibility that those in Pollard's boat didn't partake of the first body, whichever that was. Regular rations did last a bit longer in Pollard's boat, but given that Hendricks and Pollard were trying their best to keep their two boats as close to each other as possible, it seems unlikely that one crew would have taken such a drastic measure without the other. At any rate, both accounts concur that by the time the third man died, everyone in both boats was hungry enough to take and eat of the body.

The thirty-first day passed.

Isaiah Shepherd died in Hendricks's boat on the thirty-second day at sea, and his remains were shared by the crews of both boats. By now all three boats were so far south of their intended course that instead of suffering from the heat, they were constantly cold. When they tacked in order to head northeast toward warmer latitudes, the effort left everyone so exhausted that for more than an hour no one could even sit up to steer. Chase recalled that everyone was covered with boils and sores.

Sam Reed died in Pollard's boat on the thirty-third day at sea, and his flesh "constituted the only food of the survivors whilst it lasted," which turned out to be only three days. The night Reed died, Pollard and Hendricks's boats separated. Hendricks and West, the only two still alive in that boat, were never seen again. There doesn't appear to have been a storm; they were just too weak to keep track of each other through the dark hours. The thirty-fourth day passed, as did the thirty-fifth. And on the thirty-sixth day, Pollard, Coffin, Ramsdell, and Ray ate the very last of Reed. It was the last day of January, 1821.

"What could we do?" Pollard later said to some Christian evangelists in explanation for the actions of the next day. "We looked at each other with horrid thoughts in our minds, but we held our tongues. I am sure that we loved one another as brothers all the time; and yet our looks told plainly what must be done."

Ramsdell suggested they draw lots. It is important, he said, that at least one of us survive to tell our friends and family what we have endured and what became of us. Pollard said *No, but feel free to eat me when I die.*

What twenty-year-old Barzillai Ray thought of the idea is not known, but Owen Coffin was remembered to have spoken up in favor of drawing lots. Like Ramsdell, he was seventeen years old. Back on the *Essex*, he was Pollard's cabin boy, a job he may or may not have gotten because he was also Pollard's cousin. When they tore up pieces of paper and put them in a hat, Owen Coffin was unlucky.

Pollard immediately either offered to trade places or to call the plan off. "My lad, my lad," he remembered himself saying, "If you don't like your lot I'll shoot the first man that touches you." Nickerson reported that Coffin "cheerfully accepted his fate at this moment." Chase chose the word "submitted," and recalled that Coffin did so with "great fortitude and resignation." Captain Pollard recalled his "poor emaciated" cousin pausing a moment or two, "then, quietly laying his head down upon the gunwale of the boat, he said only 'I like it as well as any other.'" He thought of his mother, and asked that they go to her if they survived and tell her he was thinking of her and his family.

They drew lots again to see who should pull the trigger. Most of the evidence suggests that it was Ramsdell who now received the unfortunate draw: both Nickerson and Chase imply that Pollard told them this was so. But, in a letter written in 1876, Nickerson wrote that Ramsdell told him that it was in fact Pollard who lost the second draw, and that the captain at first refused, saying he could never do it, but ultimately relented. But there's no question that one of them put the pistol to Coffin's head and pulled the trigger.

The thirty-eighth day passed without any sign of sails or land. And the thirty-ninth, fortieth, forty-first, and forty-second. Nothing.

Curiously, though Nickerson gave a detailed reckoning of the cannibalism and sacrificial homicide on Pollard's and Hendricks's boats, he forgot to mention that he himself and the others in Owen Chase's boat were reduced to similar extremes. Isaac Cole began to lose his mind around the forty-third day at sea, first announcing that he had given up hope and then, after a brief pep rally from Chase and the others, crawling up to the bow, hoisting the jib, and shouting that he would live, he would live! The next morning, however, he began to rant and rave at a new level. He demanded a napkin, among other things, then collapsed, and six hours later died in "the most horrid and frightful convulsions." Nickerson reported only that "in the morning we committed his body to the deep in the most solemn manner. Never yet had man died more deeply lamented than did this man by his remaining friends."

Chase, however, was more forthcoming with the details. They "set to work as fast as we were able to prepare it so as to prevent its spoiling. We separated his limbs from his body, and cut all the flesh from the bones; after which, we opened the body, took out the heart, and then closed it again— sewed it up as decently as we could, and committed it to the sea. We now commenced to satisfy the immediate cravings of nature from the heart, which we eagerly devoured, and then [ate] sparingly of a few pieces of the flesh; after which, we hung up the remainder, cut in thin strips about the boat, to dry in the sun: we made a fire and roasted some of it, to serve us during the next day. In this manner did we dispose of our fellow-sufferer."

And so they sailed on through the forty-fourth day at sea in a boat festooned with drying strips of flesh, just as they had once sailed in the *Essex* surrounded by drying slabs of whalebone. But on the forty-fifth day the sun-dried meat turned green, so they relit their fire and cooked it all.

The forty-sixth day passed. Barzillai Ray died in Pollard's boat on the forty-seventh day: Pollard and Ramsdell lit the fire. The forty-eighth day passed. The forty-ninth day passed. The fiftieth passed.

On the fifty-first day, Nickerson, Chase, and Lawrence ate the last remains of Isaac Cole. On the fifty-second day at sea in the open boats they began again to take rations from their final two cakes of bread. At their usual ration of one ounce per day, there were three days' worth left. They had three hundred miles, they figured, to go.

Then there were two days of bread left. Chase saw a heavy cloud on the horizon, which he took to be a sign of land. Their limbs now were swollen and painful. They were feverish. For days on end they thought only about the wind: "We tremblingly and fearfully awaited its progress, and the dreadful development of our destiny." But the cloud gave Chase great new energy and hope. It must be Más Afuera, he said to the other two. We should be there in less than two days. Nevertheless, before dawn the next morning, Thomas Nickerson gave up hope.

"After having bailed the boat," Chase remembered, Nickerson "laid down, drew a piece of canvass over him and cried out that he then wished to die immediately. I saw that he had given up." Chase tried all of his by-now well-honed arguments. It was a "great weakness and even wickedness to abandon a reliance upon the Almighty while the least hope, and a breath of life remained." He told him again and again that they were so close to land . . . that by tomorrow at the latest. . . . To no avail.

Chase was almost certain now that Nickerson would die: "The coldness of death was fast gathering upon him: there was a sudden and unaccountable earnestness in his manner that alarmed me, and made me fear that I myself might unexpectedly be overtaken by a like weakness, or dizziness of nature." Nickerson stopped talking altogether. Chase went back to sleep. It was the fifty-fourth day since leaving Henderson Island, the ninetieth since leaving the *Essex*.

"There's a sail!" Chase remembered hearing Benjamin Lawrence yell a few hours later, and he remembered clearly that "the only sensation I felt at the moment was that of a violent and unaccountable impulse to fly directly towards her." Nickerson revived at the news as well. The ship was seven miles off, but they caught up. It was the English brig *Indian*, and her captain, William Crozier, wept when he saw the condition of the three men his sailors hauled on board. A few days later in Valparaiso they were transferred to the United States frigate *Constellation*, whose captain, Commodore Ridgely, wrote that "bones [were] working through their skins . . . & the whole surface of their bodies one entire ulcer—was truly distressing . . ."

For Pollard and Ramsdell, however, now roughly three hundred miles to the south, the day was not much different from the fifty-three that preceded it. The fifty-fifth day passed. And the fifty-sixth, and -seventh, and -eighth. But finally, on the fifty-ninth day at sea, they, too, saw a sail and were rescued by the whaling ship *Dauphin* of Nantucket, whose captain's name was Coffin. According to Ridgely's journal, they were unable to move when found, and were "sucking the bones of their dead Mess mates, which they were loth to part with."

Commodore Ridgely quickly arranged for a ship heading out to Australia to look for the three who stayed behind on Henderson Island. The ship *Surrey* went first to Ducie, which was where Pollard and Chase erroneously thought they had been, but the captain fortuitously went on to Henderson after finding no signs of recent human activity on Ducie. The fresh water supply had turned out to be unreliable, and Chapple, Weeks, and Wright discovered no other food sources. They had found a cave with eight human skeletons seated side by side on the ground—presumably earlier, even-more-unfortunate castaways. It wasn't a discovery likely to raise their hopes. But though they were so weak that Captain Raine of the *Surrey* thought they wouldn't have survived another month on the island, all three were alive enough to come stumbling out of the woods on April 9 at the sound of the ship's gun firing.

It was over.

CHAPTER 28

OUT OF THE BLUE

Of course, for Chase, Pollard, Nickerson, and the other survivors of the *Essex*, it was never really over. Pollard still had to walk up through the crowd of spectators gathered on the wharves and streets of Nantucket, and that was nothing compared to his promise to Owen Coffin that he would personally go to the boy's mother and tell her his fate. That he would go to this woman, his own aunt, and say . . . what could he say? But he did go, quite soon after returning home. "On his arrival he bore the awful message to the mother as her son desired," Nickerson wrote in a letter long after, "but she became almost frantic with the thought, and I have heard that she never could become reconciled to the capt's presence."

Others were more understanding. As soon as Pollard was recovered from his weakness, the owners of the *Two Brothers*, the ship on which he had returned from Valparaiso, offered him a command, and he sailed to the Pacific with Nickerson again in his crew. A fellow captain who met Pollard during this voyage noticed that he kept an unusually large store of vegetables in a net attached to his cabin ceiling but that he was otherwise "cheerful and modest" about his previous hardship. Before the hold was half full of oil, however, *Two Brothers* wrecked on a reef in the Hawaiian Islands, and Pollard and Nickerson again found themselves in whaleboats "with 4 oars & each a sail, one quadrant one compass two *Practical Navigators* no clothes but those we stood in, neither water nor provisions except two small pigs." But they were rescued this time after only a few days.

Toward the end of his life, Essex survivor Owen Chase went "insane," squirreling food away in the recesses of his Nantucket home. (COURTESY NANTUCKET HISTORICAL ASSOCIATION)

Pollard resigned himself to his misfortunes: "Now I am utterly ruined," he said, "no owner will ever trust me with a whaler again, for all will say I am an unlucky man." He never went to sea again, and became a night watchman back on Nantucket. "To me [Pollard was] the most impressive man, tho' wholly unassuming, even humble—that I ever encountered," Melville wrote in his copy of Chase's narrative after meeting him many years later. "To the islanders he was nobody."

Chase was far luckier at sea than Pollard, making several extremely successful whaling voyages in the 1830s and early 1840s. But Chase, too, carried the *Essex* ordeal with him. When his first wife died two weeks after giving birth to their third child, in 1824, he married the widow of Matthew Joy, who had died in the whaleboats.* As he grew older he became obsessed with food. "He was constantly storing away things . . . going to stores and ordering many groceries, he would store them in the cellar against an imagined need," his grandson later remembered. "His

---

*This was not the wife who had a baby sixteen months after Chase went to sea; that was his third wife, Eunice Chadwick, whom he divorced immediately upon returning to Nantucket, despite the fact that she had taken care of all his previous children while he was away.

Thomas Nickerson's account of his ordeal in the middle of the Pacific was lost in a Connecticut attic for nearly a century. (COURTESY NANTUCKET HISTORICAL ASSOCIATION)

mind was reverting to the days in the boat when they were so terribly in need of food."

"Owen is insane (will eventually be carried to the insane hospital)," wrote one of his cousins to another in 1868, the year before Chase died at the age of seventy-three. "He called me cousin Susan (taking me for sister Worth) held my hand and sobbed like a child, saying 'Oh my head, my head' it was pitiful to see the strong man bowed, then his personal appearance so changed, didn't allow himself decent clothing, fear's he shall come to want." According to his obituary, the headaches started soon after the *Essex* disaster.

After the wreck of the *Two Brothers*, Nickerson went back to sea. He spent most of his career, however, working as a shipping broker in Brooklyn, New York, and retired back to Nantucket, where he operated an inn in the 1870s. Compared to Chase and Pollard, and from the tone of his narrative, he appears to have been relatively unscathed by the ordeal. Nonetheless, as already mentioned, he was unable even fifty years later to write openly about eating human flesh. Less is known of the lives of Benjamin Lawrence, Charles Ramsdell, Seth Weeks, William Wright, and Thomas Chapple, though there is evidence that the first three also commanded vessels. But it's likely the disaster was never entirely over for any of them, not even after they were dead, it seems.* Nearly one hundred years after the return of the survivors, one of Benjamin Lawrence's daughters was asked for details of her father's ordeal. "Miss Molly," she is remembered to have replied, "we do not mention this in Nantucket."

Likewise, it's no simple thing to pinpoint when an era ends, or even begins to end. The return of the *Essex* survivors was not, in itself, either cause or effect of the impending decline of maritime culture on Cape Cod and the Islands. By most measures, in the 1820s the full glory of the age of sail was still to come. The recession that followed the War of 1812 was a memory; the great Pacific whaling grounds were just beginning to be opened and denuded, and the western Arctic grounds were yet to be discovered; the clippers that the sideburned Cape Cod captains raced around the world at midcentury were not yet on the drawing boards.

But where does one begin and end describing the life of a great wave, which only rises and crests most gloriously just before crashing and receding into the next oncoming ripple? The goriest days of global whaling were still to come, but already in 1823, the year after the *Essex* survivors returned, New Bedford surpassed Nantucket as a whaling port. In 1874, for the first time in nearly two hundred years, there were no whaling vessels sailing from Nantucket.†

The sandbar at the mouth of Nantucket Harbor, which Congress consistently refused to do anything about, no doubt contributed to the island's decline. Writers who stress the role of Quaker solidarity and semi-communal ownership of the land in the rise of Nantucket naturally see seeds of the island's downfall in the gradual turn away from both in the nineteenth century. In 1852, a tinkerer in Waltham, Massachusetts, figured out how to refine Pennsylvania "earth oil" into a lamp oil that was better and cheaper than whale. Even Owen Chase knew that whaling was a

---

*Ramsdell may or may not have become a captain, though in Nickerson's obituary he's mentioned as one: "Notwithstanding the terrible sufferings through which they passed, these five men all continued to follow the sea, all rose to the command of vessels, and all lived to a good old age." Benjamin Lawrence, twenty-one at the time of the *Essex* wreck, became a captain as well and then retired from the sea and bought a little farm at 'Sconset. Weeks and Wright may have crewed out on New Bedford boats. Weeks may have been a captain. Captain Charles Ramsdell died in 1866, Owen Chase died in 1869, Pollard in 1870, and Captain Benjamin Lawrence in 1879. Nickerson died in 1883, Weeks in 1888. William Wright went back to sea and was lost in a hurricane in the West Indies.

†As virtually all whaling voyages lasted two to five years, the number of ships that cleared each year represented only a fraction of the total fleet. For instance, in 1857, the total whaling fleet for Nantucket was 41 ships, versus 329 ships for New Bedford.

doomed industry based on the overharvesting of a class of animals that are slow to reproduce.

But there was a deeper reason for the decline of Nantucket, and though the high-flying island fell hardest, it was not alone. The last whale ship sailed from Barnstable in 1846, from Truro in 1852, from Falmouth in 1859, Sandwich in 1862, Wellfleet in 1867. Only Provincetown and New Bedford continued whaling into the twentieth century. Nor was the decline limited to whaling. The great Shiverick shipyard didn't survive the post–Civil War depression and became a guano storage plant. All across Cape Cod and the Islands the nautical glory of the first half of the nineteenth century slipped away in the second.

The decline ultimately had less to do with local conditions than with changes off-island and off-Cape. The United States was becoming a continental colonizer rather than a colony of seaports, a process that was only accelerated by the disruption of trade during the War of 1812 and the forced removal of Native Americans from the Ohio Valley, where more than a few Cape and Islanders went following that war. Simultaneously, the nation was becoming a major consumer of whale products rather than primarily an exporter: whale oil was the first industrial revolution's lubricant, whalebone its plastic. New Bedford rose not only because it had a fine, deep-water port, but because that port was squarely on the mainland. It had a railroad spur in a nation that was looking west. Nantucket and Martha's Vineyard remained, naturally, islands off the coast. And though Cape Cod had trains—rails reached Wellfleet in 1869, the same year they crossed the continent—with the exception of Provincetown, the peninsula's harbors weren't adequate for large vessels.

Even fishing declined in the second half of the nineteenth century—or rather, changed and became concentrated locally in Provincetown and to a lesser degree in Wellfleet and Chatham. Part of the reason was competition from the Great Lakes and the increased demand for fresh fish that favored fleets closer to Boston or New York. But the main cause of decline was a version of the same cycle that has dogged the fishing industry ever since. Growing markets led to overfishing and the decline of stocks close to home. The need to go farther out for new species led to bigger boats. The need for bigger boats squeezed out the viability of smaller ports and poorer family operations. Bigger boats also required bigger catches to justify the bigger investments. Bigger catches came with new technologies—purse seines replaced hand lines, trawlers replaced seines—which more often than not required fewer laborers. This meant fewer jobs for the children of fish-

Drying cod and other groundfish in Provincetown, circa 1900. (COURTESY OF THE SOCIETY FOR THE PRESERVATION OF NEW ENGLAND ANTIQUITIES)

ermen. Bigger catches also eventually meant declining catches, which started the whole cycle over.

Yarmouth, which was never a major fishing port but generally supported at least twenty or thirty cod or mackerel vessels in the first half of the century, was completely out of the business by 1863: "The last of the fishing fleet have been sold," the local paper ruefully reported that year. Even Wellfleet, which had one hundred or more schooners in its mackerel fleet at the end of the Civil War, was down to less than twenty-five by 1889.

With the ships and fishing vessels went the ropewalks, the sail lofts, the chandlers, the carpenters. With the whales went the barrel makers, the candle makers, the candle box makers, the harpoonsmiths, the ambergris kings, and the whalebone merchants. With the salt cod went more barrel makers, the rest of the salt makers. With the sailors went the grog shops.

Even the harvest of wrecks ultimately tapered down to a mere trickle. The transition to steam power in the final decades of the nineteenth century meant fewer ships were caught trying to beat around the Cape. But the real change happened with the opening of the Cape Cod Canal, first envisioned in 1676. Every coastal vessel that traveled directly from Cape Cod Bay to Buzzards Bay was one that didn't have to duck into Provincetown Harbor to wait out a bad blow. Or, if it was past the hook, didn't have to worry about the Peaked Hill Bar or the Nantucket Shoals, didn't have to wonder if it could make it into Edgartown or Vineyard Haven. Ironically, though it made the Cape technically an island, the canal helped cut Cape Cod and the Islands off from what remained of the seafaring economy.

The California Gold Rush of 1849 and the Civil War in the 1860s also contributed importantly to the downward spiral. A few Cape and Islanders were able to make quick killings in California; Isaac Keith's machine shop in Bourne did a good business making mining tools to be shipped west, laying the groundwork for its later expansion into a sizable railroad-car company. Captain Henry Cleveland of the Vineyard heard of the gold rush while in Valparaiso and immediately off-loaded all his whaling gear and headed up to Panama, where he picked up three hundred would-be prospectors paying $200 each for cabins and $150 each for steerage. Gold rush profits helped fund the golden age of clippers.

But the rush also hit hard at small towns where farms were failing or whaling was on the decline. Companies with names like the Cape Cod and Sandwich Mining and Trading Company and the Dukes County Mining Company organized vessels to take prospectors out to the gold fields. Nowhere was hit harder than Nantucket; some even took down their houses and shipped them out to the latest promised land. Not surprisingly, it didn't always pan out. Like a lot of other captains who took their ships into San Francisco, Henry Cleveland soon found that his entire crew had deserted for the gold fields. By 1850, the local papers were printing letters from Cape-Codders-cum-Californians telling of how many perfectly good large ships lay abandoned in San Francisco Bay.

Then came the Civil War, with its dead boys and economic disruption. The United States government bought twenty-four whalers off the docks at New Bedford, loaded them with stone from walls all over Buzzards Bay, and then sent them to the mouth of Charleston Harbor to be sunk.* The Confederate states' government, meanwhile, did its best to destroy the rest of New England's whaling ships wherever it found them. The Confederate warship *Shenandoah* alone rounded up virtually the entire Arctic fleet in 1865, taking twenty-four ships in all.

The population of Nantucket in 1840 was nearly ten thousand; by 1870 it was at slightly above four thousand and falling. The population of Truro fell by half, to less than a thousand, between the beginning of the Civil War

---

*Ironically, the man selected to be the commodore by the assembled crews of the fleet of seventeen was Rodney French, one of the very few whalers in the history of the industry to be convicted of moonlighting as a slaver, and who later became mayor of New Bedford.

With the decline of whaling, offshore fishing, and agriculture, inshore fishing and shellfishing grew in importance. (COURTESY OF THE MARTHA'S VINEYARD HISTORICAL SOCIETY)

and 1883. A dozen families from that town took their houses with them to wherever they moved. The population of the Cape as a whole in that same period dropped from thirty-six thousand to twenty-seven thousand, and kept falling.

There were scattered efforts to get on the industrial train. On Nantucket, optimistic entrepreneurs failed in their attempts to start hat factories, shoe factories, a silk industry. But with no real rivers on the Cape and Islands and no easy way to fuel steam engines now that all the wood had been burned to make glass and bricks and saltworks and fish flakes, there was little chance for much success. Even in the relatively industrial towns of Sandwich and Bourne, home to the famous glass works* and the Keith (railroad) Car Company, the population dropped. After steadily growing for more than two centuries, the official population (which notably didn't take into account the decline of the Wampanoag) of the two towns fell by 30 percent between the outbreak of the Civil War and the turn of the century, to 3,105 persons.

Not that the Cape and Islanders who remained lived lives removed from the sea. Inshore fishing, lobstering, and shellfishing grew in importance as

---

*In 1887 the workers unionized and went on strike. At issue was eighty-seven cents owed by the company to a glassblower. The company refused to pay, so the men refused to work. The company owners said they would close down the factory if the workers weren't back on the job on the first day of 1888. The strikers stayed away. The plant never reopened.

deep-water pursuits waned. And Provincetown and Chatham remained viable ports for as long as fish remained on George's Bank. In the warmer waters of the Islands, harpooning swordfish was profitable until that species, too, was harvested beyond its sustainable limit.

The residents of Cape Cod, Martha's Vineyard, and Nantucket continued to play leading roles in the whaling industry even after it moved to Buzzards Bay (and, ultimately, to San Francisco). In 1902, a Gay Head Indian named Amos Smally became the only whaler known to have killed a giant white sperm whale. And just as the various Nickersons and Knowleses and others of Harwich and Brewster went up to Boston or Salem to take command of their clippers or down to New York to assume the helms of their London packets, so the New Bedford whaling fleet was overwhelmingly owned and commanded by various Coffins, Folgers, Swains, Jernegans, and Chases. At one point Jonathan Bourne of Sandwich owned twenty-four New Bedford whaling vessels, more than anyone else. And at the close of the century, near the end of New Bedford's greasy whale-killing spree, when eight whaling ships got caught in the ice in the Arctic Circle, it was the Vineyarder George Fred Tilton who offered to borrow a dogsled and cross seventeen hundred miles of frozen Alaska to get help.

This was not the first, or even the second, time a group of whaling ships had stayed too late above the Bering Strait. In the fall of 1871, thirty-four whalers and one trading ship got caught in the ice with more than twelve hundred people on board. That time the local Indians came out in great numbers in late August and warned the whalers that this was going to be their last chance to leave. But there were whales around, and every other year the ships had managed to get out in September, so the New Englanders simply smiled at the Alaskans with their quaint superstitions and kept on killing whales, boiling oil, and waiting for the wind to change around to the northeast and blow the ice away.

The natives, it turned out, knew their ice. After the *Comet* and *Roman* were crushed, followed by the old Falmouth veteran *Awashonks*, the captains had had enough. At noon on September 14, everyone climbed into two hundred whaleboats and headed through the blizzard down an eighty-mile-long lead in the ice to where seven whaling ships waited in open water. It took sixty hours, with one stop for a bonfire and coffee, but everyone ultimately made it. A year later, when another fleet returned to the Arctic, all but one of the stranded vessels had been destroyed. A few years later, several hundred sailors made a similar escape from twelve ships caught in the ice; fifty-three who elected to stay behind died.

Tilton was the third mate of the steam and sailing bark *Belvedere* in 1898 when it got caught. This time the ships hadn't tarried, starting south at the last of August, as was usual. But the ice came early. *Belvedere* almost got out in time, Tilton later wrote, but twice turned back to pick up other crews that were forced to jump out onto the ice when their vessels were crunched by pack ice blowing onshore. Four other ships were stranded even farther back.

"We were a pretty full ship," Tilton remembered. "Our own regular crew numbered forty-five men, we had rescued fifty-three from the *Orca* and forty-nine from the *Freeman*, so that there was a considerable gang to provide for and no safety for us if we stayed aboard the ship. Any day or hour a shift of wind might start the ice to piling, so we decided to go ashore and build a camp. The best place we knew was on the Sea Horse Islands, and we knew, too, that if we could get the ship in behind them, there was a chance that we might save her."

The Sea Horse Islands were about three miles away, and a crew went to work sledding provisions there. Others took down the yards, spars, and anything else that could be removed from the ship, while still another gang chopped out a canal through which they were finally able to work the now-lightened ship to the relative safety of the island's lee. After a minor drama involving one sailor hoarding supplies, whatever could be salvaged from the other wrecks was also collected. Nevertheless, when everything and everyone was moved seventy miles away to the little whaling station at Point Barrow, the captains calculated that there was barely enough food to provide two scant meals a day for the eight ships' crews. Tilton, figuring half the men would probably get weak and die, now made an outrageous offer. He would walk out to get help.

With a dog team purchased from the local natives and fifteen days' provisions loaded on a sled rigged with a mast and sail, Tilton and two Siberian natives set off on October 23. The men behind cheered until they were out of earshot. Over the next few weeks Tilton and his men lost their ax, their tent blew to shreds, and their food ran out. Some days they were completely snowed in. Others they traveled all day around openings in the ice without progressing more than a few miles closer to their goal.

They scaled mountains so steep they had to unload the sled entirely and haul everything up by ropes, dogs included. Then they sledded down the other side at break-neck speed, with only their sail as a brake and no clear idea of what lay ahead. Once they spent two days going up a mountain only to find a "solid bulkhead that we couldn't go around or climb over," and spent two more days backtracking to the beach. Another time, they had no choice but to saw off an ice floe and hope the wind would push them across the open water in front of them rather than out to sea. At occasional native villages they traded cartridges for seals, and once ate from a dead and not-exactly-fresh whale.

Finally, almost a month later, they left their dogs in a snow cave; the animals wouldn't travel in a blizzard. The three men roped themselves together and stumbled ahead through a whiteout to the whaling station at Point Hope. "As we went along I would stop and dig through the snow once in a while. If I struck soil I knew I was too far inland, and if I struck ice, too far offshore, and altered my course accordingly. That's the way we worked along from daylight until dark." Occasional wind squalls left them lying flat on the ground, and once Tilton had to force his companions to get back up and keep going. Eventually, though, they walked right into a house without seeing it.

"I knew it was a house, though, and felt my way along the side, looking for the entrance," Tilton remembered. "It was a tunnel, built Eskimo style, and I ducked into it. I crawled over a dog and found the door, and as I did a Norwegian by the name of Anderson, who had started the station, opened it, and says, 'For God's sake, where did you come from?' " When the snow ended, Tilton retrieved his dogs; one had blown off a cliff and died, but the rest were fine.

They had come six hundred miles, and the Siberians refused to go farther. Tilton hired a native Alaskan couple—"Tickey was a good man, and his wife (Canuanar) was twice the man he was"—to accompany him on the remaining eleven hundred miles of his journey. It was a longer variation on the first month's adventures, with higher mountains, deeper snow, and the addition of their being forced to eat some of the dogs. When they finally reached the shore of the Shelikof strait—between mainland Alaska and Kodiak Island—the trading company that they had hoped to get a boat from was gone.

There was nothing left but "one old discarded dory that wouldn't hold pumpkins." Tilton took apart the sleds, drilled holes in the dory planks, and threaded the sinew lashings from the sleds into the planks and pulled them as tight as he could. "After that I tore up the only suit of underwear that I had on earth and one of my deerskin suits, and caulked her with the rags." At dawn on the seventeenth of March, they started off across the thirty-

The last whale ship to sail out of New Bedford, the bark Wanderer, *ran aground on Cuttyhunk in 1924.* (COURTESY OF THE MARTHA'S VINEYARD HISTORICAL SOCIETY)

seven-mile strait, "and from the time we shoved her overboard until we landed on Kodiak—two hours before sunset, I never left the oars, and Tickey and Canuanar never left the bailers. Talk about a basket. . . ." There, he found a boat and a skipper to take him to Valdez, where he caught a ship for Portland.

As it turned out, Tilton's seventeen-hundred-mile trek had little impact on the outcome of the disaster of 1898. The crews left behind at Point Barrow found enough caribou to survive, so the resupply ship sent at Tilton's direction primarily allowed the ships that were still intact to hunt through the next season rather than rush back south.

By the time they had chased and killed their way from "all around" the *Mayflower* in Provincetown Harbor to the western Arctic waters that were only unfrozen for a few months a year, the whalers were running out of blubber to hunt. The New Bedford *Mercury* commented of Tilton that had he been a professional explorer "the world would have proclaimed this marvelous achievement, and he would have been celebrated in books," but he "made nothing of it and reshipped for another whaling voyage."

In the end, though, the whaling voyages dried up, and Tilton wound up pretty well celebrated in the host of nostalgic books about the age of sail. He spent most of his later years back in Chilmark, racing horses with his neighbors or trying somewhat halfheartedly to make a go at trapping fish. His final glory, however, was as captain of the whaling bark *Charles W. Morgan*. The *Charles W. Morgan* was the last whaler to sail out of Provincetown. But by the time Tilton took her helm, she was permanently tied to a dock in New Bedford. There "Cap'n George Fred" regaled the growing numbers of visiting tourists with tales of the old days of sail.

CHAPTER 29

THE GREAT BEACH

I pay a lot of taxes in the town of Chatham, and that is private property you're on." It had taken me the better part of a week to paddle from the north shore of the Vineyard to the town landing at Little Mill Pond at the back of Chatham's Stage Harbor. I was on my way to the national seashore, to the Great Beach, and other than a malicious wind that forced me to abandon my kayak for a few days in Mashpee, I had had no trouble to speak of on the journey thus far.

Now, though, after what my GPS told me was 49.8 miles and was probably more like 60 with all the zigs and zags and excursions up into the Bass River and elsewhere, I had pulled my boat up on the wrong side of the public landing sign. I had gone so far as to leave it overnight next to a canoe five feet to the west of the sign rather than with the collected dories to the east of the sign, and as a consequence, the man speaking to me was in a state of rather extreme and, it seemed later, somewhat pathetic agitation.

"Don't worry about him," said a friendly clammer who was loading a bushel of littlenecks into his pickup truck, which was to the east of the sign. "I've been listening to that for twenty years."

"I'm more worried about his heart," I said, partly in jest.

"Don't worry about that, either," said a second clammer who was out on the pier. The two men laughed. My sister and I—she had joined me in Chatham for the last few miles' paddle out to the great and public national seashore—had to laugh a bit, too.

In the interest of full disclosure, I should point out before someone else does that the beach from which I am fortunate enough to set out on most of my voyages is not open to the public. In Massachusetts and Maine, alone among American coastal states, the rights of shoreline-property owners extend not just to the usual high water line, but all the way down to low water. With the exception of the Elizabeth Islands, the Vineyard probably has the most restricted beaches of the region.* Nantucket admirably has an islandwide policy of open access to the beaches, but even there, some feel the need to post signs reminding walkers that wandering the water's edge is a traditional privilege extended by the owners of the sand and not, by any means, to be considered a human right.

It was as much to protect beaches of the lower Cape *for* the people as it was to save them *from* the people that the Cape Cod National Seashore was established in 1961. Setting aside forty miles of beach and more than forty thousand acres of coastal landscape elicited the usual gnashing of teeth by local rights advocates and others with an intent to subdivide and conquer. Former Speaker of the House Tip O'Neill was burned in effigy by the Wellfleet Chamber of Commerce, but steadfastly supported the park effort. Senator Leverett Saltonstall of Massachusetts worked out a deal allowing existing houses within the proposed park to remain in private hands, which divided local fury enough to allow good sense to prevail. The most important factor in the creation of the first national seashore, however, was that the summer White House at that time was located in Hyannis Port, and its resident was convinced of the importance of saving Thoreau's Great Beach.

It's interesting to me that the southern coast of Cape Cod is fringed with well-preserved wildernesses, private to the west and public to the east. Between lies the whole wild gamut of human development, most but not all of it of the summer variety. After crossing again from my home beach to Tarpaulin Cove and visiting again the lonely graves of Judith Game and J.G., I paddled along the empty wooded shore of Naushon Island. With its horses-only policy and strictly limited access, Naushon is probably less humanized than much of the national seashore, which in places can look like a *Consumer Reports* testing facility for off-road motor vehicles.

---

*When my editor made the mistake of coming ashore at West Chop in a stiff wind in order to make an adjustment to his wood-and-canvas kayak, a college kid in a "security" T-shirt appeared instantly and said, "I'm sorry, but it's my job to tell you if you are not off this beach within ten minutes we'll have to inform the police." As a point of law, however, both the Chatham and West Chop man were in error; the commonwealth's constitution reserves the right of access to all shores for purposes of fishing and navigation.

Heading east I paddled along below handsome shingle-style houses of the sort that Kittredge referred to as "looming horrors of the Victorian epoch," and past small cottages on stilts that looked imported from the Outer Banks of the Carolinas. In bright sun I beached at a thoroughly funky motel in Falmouth, smack on the water, where vacationers were enjoying a midmorning smoke in the shade of small concrete balconies while watching the youngest sailors of the Falmouth Yacht Club navigate their tiny sailboats back through the jetties at the harbor's mouth. A cigarette boat went out of the harbor in a cloud of blue smoke. A woman baited hooks for her children to throw into the edge of the channel while her husband drove up the road to the Food Buoy for eggs and bacon on rolls.

Farther along I passed public beaches packed with umbrellas at their entrances and devoid of people at their fringes. And open stretches of conservation land that seemed almost miraculously beautiful given the distressingly high proportion of that coast that is artificially hardened with rock imported from elsewhere. Miles of humble and wholesome houses are perched side by side above granite seawalls and similarly misguided rock groins that supposedly guard remnant crescents of sand below but really ensure that no proper beach will again form. It was midsummer on the warm coast of Massachusetts. There were jet skis, sailboats, parasails, fishermen, and even a few other kayakers. Swimmers swam, lifeguards whistled, and I glided by it all at a pace that eventually felt surprisingly effortless.

At one fifty-foot stretch next to a crowded public strand, someone had painted in yard-high letters PRIVATE BEACH on the seawall, and a man and a woman sat alone in lawn chairs between two granite groins like a pair of satisfied potentates. At another private stretch of beach, the lovely and unmarred section belonging to the massive resort of New Seabury, the managers kindly let me stash my kayak with their Hobie Cats for two days while the wind blew better than twenty knots.

Somewhere off the coast of Centerville the last knobs of the Vineyard disappeared below the horizon. I had planned to paddle into Hyannis Port to see if I could make out the houses that were not houses but are, in fact, "the compound," until the sound of sirens wafting from Hyannis itself convinced me to bypass the Cape's big city and head straight for the nonfunctional lighthouse at Gammon Point. The momentary appearance and then scurrying dive of a sea turtle the size of a pizza (I think it was a young green, *Chelonia mydas*) confirmed to me that I had made the right decision. I passed the unfortunate mouth of little Herring River in West Harwich, with its historic windmill on one bank and a building the Soviet Board of

Architectural Review would have rejected as too large and soulless on the other bank. The first sculpted knobs of Monomoy National Wildlife Refuge appeared above the horizon. With Monomoy in sight, the national seashore was within reach. I rested that night in Chatham.

The next morning I was determined that I had not paddled fifty-nine miles in order to let an unhappy man spoil my mood, so like Champlain in Stage Harbor four centuries ago, my sister and I merely sped up our efforts to stow our gear and shove off. We left the angry taxpayer of Chatham and his friendly clam-seeking neighbors behind and paddled back out of Little Mill Pond, into Mill Pond, down the Mitchell River under the bridge, into Stage Harbor, and then out of Stage Harbor. We turned east there and skimmed our boats along between the northernmost tip of Monomoy Island and the elbow of the Cape, across the blue-green channel and the yellow-green flats. At last we arrived at the edge, the outmost outermost, where, like Thoreau, like Edna St. Vincent Millay, like Henry Beston and John Hay, like four million visitors a year, we "put all America behind us."

Then we went a little farther. A dozen large seals gamboling around in the surf that was breaking over an offshore bar about seventy yards out to sea dared us to haul our boats over the barrier beach and come out—which we did. They came close to have a better look at us, then dove and reappeared a bit farther out, daring us to come a bit farther—which we did. Again and again we followed.

At last, though, it was wise to turn around. We faced west, with all America before us and seals behind, and paddled back to shore.

CHAPTER 30

OAK BLUFFS

In the 1880s, the same decade during which the last survivors of the *Essex* died of old age on Nantucket and Cape Cod, a real-estate speculator on Martha's Vineyard bought the public parks of Oak Bluffs. Charles Abbott let it be known immediately that he would be happy to sell Ocean Park, Hartford Park, Waban, Penacook, Niantic, Hiawatha, Naushon, Nasha-wena, and Petaluma Parks to the abutters. Or to Cottage City itself, as the town was then officially called. But if no one was willing to come up with the 800 percent profit he felt he deserved for having recognized the devel-opment potential of the land in question, and come up with it quickly, he fully intended to subdivide and sell to summer people.

The town had no need to be nervous, Abbott promised in a letter circu-lated to his new neighbors. The parks would be most tastefully developed. He planned to "restrict all purchasers to the erection of such buildings as shall be ornament to the excellent neighborhood in which the land in question lies." The town, however, was quite alarmed. It wasn't a lot of acreage relative to the island as a whole, but it was almost all the open space in the dense little village—it was as if someone had managed to get the deed to the Boston Common and lay it out with house lots.

Not that the selectmen of Cottage City had any problem per se with the idea of people buying chunks of land, carving them up, and then packing them with houses for summer people. Tourism and subdivision are often described as arriving unbidden on the Cape and Islands, but more often than not the principal promoters in the early days were wealthy and respected local whaling and merchant families. The very parks in question had been created less than two decades before by a pioneer crop of speculative developers led by Captains Norton, Darrow, and Collins, all of Edgartown.

The thought that money might be made from visitors to the region was firmly rooted long before the demise of the seafaring economy. Seaports by their nature are equipped to minister to the needs of transients—every town had at least one tavern and inn during the seventeenth and eighteenth centuries. Crevecoeur in 1763 was arguably a tourist. Genteel hunters and fishermen like Daniel Webster recreated regularly on the Cape and Islands in the first half of the 1800s. Nathaniel Hawthorne inaugurated the literary tradition in the region when he summered on the Vineyard in 1830. Wealthy Nantucketers maintained summer places for themselves across their island in Siasconset as early as the 1790s, and in 1835 Obed Macy wrote of that fishing village that "as a summer resort, no place in the United States presents greater attractions for the invalid."

When Thoreau first arrived on the Cape in 1849 his intention was to write a travel article for *Putnam's Magazine* about a place that he claimed in the grand tradition of all travel writers was "wholly unknown to the fashionable world." But when he got to Provincetown he found there was already a hotel there that was "too high for us." The arrival of the railroad* played a predictable role in the process, not only because it made travel to Cape Cod (and thus to the Islands) so much easier than the old stagecoach or packet schooner, which it indisputably did, but also because the Old Colony Railroad was a tireless promoter of travel to the region. Cape Cod, one brochure promised, not only had plenty of good hotels but was also "dotted with fine old towns, which haven't yet been spoiled by too many fashionable notions."

From the beginning, the Cape and Islands were promoted as more relaxed and less status-oriented than the swank contemporary resorts like Saratoga. Cape Cod, Nantucket, and Martha's Vineyard were nostalgic places, in other words, where simpler pleasures were still appreciated and modern life was forgotten. Macy wrote proudly that Siasconset "is not, indeed, the focus of fashionable life," but was a place instead where "useless forms and ceremonies are laid aside." And *Harper's* magazine in an 1868 travel article wrote that "these thousands of people who frequent Martha's

---

*At Sandwich in 1848, at Hyannis in 1854, at Yarmouth in 1865, at Wellfleet in 1869, and at Provincetown in 1873.

Vineyard at this season have more and fresher pleasures than those who summer at Newport or Long Branch. . . ."

This wasn't just a marketing slogan. On the Vineyard, in particular, the early promoters of land schemes like Oak Bluffs were also in large measure responding to a phenomenon they played no part in creating; the thousands mentioned by *Harper's* (and dozens of other articles in *Atlantic Monthly*, the New York *Times*, and elsewhere) had not traveled to the island seeking real-estate opportunities, or even an earthly paradise. They came to Martha's Vineyard for salvation.

Given the region's long history as a landing place for separatists, Quakers, infant dunkers, and other spiritual malcontents (notably few of whom found the sale and resale of Wampanoag and Nauset land incompatible with their spiritual missions), it is appropriate that some of the deepest roots of the tradition of spending a few summer weeks on Cape Cod and the Islands lay in a religious revival. Revivals were periodic occurrences in the region, as they were elsewhere in young America. Throughout the Great Awakening of the first half of the 1700s, "new lights" battled "old lights" on Cape Cod and the Islands. And on through the century Baptists baptized, Quakers quaked, and a few Presbyterians got very excited.

There were stranger groups as well. One sect called the Come-Outers appeared in the years before the Civil War in Barnstable and were known for walking along the tops of fences instead of on the sidewalks with the ordinary sinners. Their God also apparently told them to carry on conversations in sung couplets, often to the tune of "Old Dan Tucker." Not long after, many in Pocasset became disillusioned with a popular cult when one of its leaders dreamed, like Abraham, that God had told him to kill his child, which, unlike Abraham, he and his wife proceeded to do.

It was the Methodists, who arrived on Cape Cod and the Islands near the end of the 1700s, that transformed the standard outdoor sermon from something a preacher resorted to when no church was available into a nascent summer industry. The first Methodist camp meeting on the Cape was a week of nearly round-the-clock prayer meetings and evangelizing at Wellfleet during the summer of 1819.* The flock at that point was mostly local, though Kezia Fanning, a woman who wrote in her journal about virtually everything that happened on Nantucket, noted on August 8 that the

---

*The first Methodists on the Vineyard were probably two ex-slaves from Virginia, both of whom were lay preachers and who arrived in 1787. The very first camp meetings held by Methodists took place in the Ohio River Valley in 1799.

Methodists of that island had all gone across the sound. Furthermore, that first year the circuit riders were preaching pretty much to the converted. The spirit was nonetheless sufficiently moved that the organizers vowed to pitch the tents and spread the sleeping straw again the following summer. After a few years the camp moved to Truro, and then in 1828 to a ten-acre site in Eastham.

Camp meetings were eventually held at Yarmouth and Hyannis as well, but "Millennium Grove," as the Eastham property became known, was the largest on the Cape. As many as five thousand worshipers spent their days listening to more than 150 ordained and lay exhorters who preached in relays, or in dozens of smaller prayer and study groups.

It wasn't all hellfire and brimstone; it was steamers and cherrystones, too, along with a healthy supply of redemption. "A man is appointed to clear out the pump a week beforehand, while the ministers are clearing their throats," wrote Thoreau, "but, probably, the latter do not always deliver as pure a stream as the former. I saw the heaps of clam-shells left under the tables, where they had feasted in previous summers, and supposed, of course, that that was the work of the unconverted, or the back-sliders and scoffers. It looked as if a camp-meeting must be a singular combination of a prayer-meeting and a picnic."

As big and festive as the camp meeting at Eastham was, the revivals on Martha's Vineyard were eventually even bigger. A famous Methodist prose-lytizer, "Reformation John," held a camp meeting at the West Chop Light-house in 1827, but the phenomenon only took off on the island after the Edgartown Methodists held a camp meeting in 1835 in "a grove of enor-mous oaks" that were located in a sheep pasture up behind East Chop. The location was chosen in the hope that it would grow to attract worshipers from Nantucket and the south shore of the Cape.

Grow it did. There were nine communal tents at the first meeting in 1835. As hoped, the second year saw delegations from Falmouth, Nan-tucket, South Yarmouth, and Sandwich, along with New Bedford and a handful of other continental locales. By 1842, forty tents housed a congre-gation of nearly twelve hundred that doubled on "Big Sunday." By 1851 there were 100 tents in the grove, and by 1857 there were 250.

They weren't filled with just poor sinners, either. Among the twelve thousand or so who came to the Wesleyan Grove in 1859 were various New England governors and bank presidents. What's more, unlike most resorts of the period, African Americans were welcome. That year, just one of the

Worshipers gathered by the thousands for "Big Sunday" at the campground in Oak Bluffs, circa 1865. (COURTESY OF THE MARTHA'S VINEYARD HISTORICAL SOCIETY)

several boats stopping on the Vineyard, the *Eagle's Wing*, brought fifteen thousand people to the island during the month of August. On Big Sunday alone in 1860 there were twelve thousand of the faithful in the grove attending thirty-six simultaneous prayer meetings.

It was the kind of spiritual recharge for which people came back year after year. The camp meeting was more than religion; it was a celebration, a reunion. It was also, increasingly, a vacation. As the years went by, on both Cape Cod and Martha's Vineyard repeat repenters began to fold up their tents and transubstantiate them into wood. Because of the layout of the campground, the resulting cottages were not much larger in footprint than the tents that preceded them, though they had a second floor with a small balcony. Local carpenters worked through the winter creating ornate and unique trim that, along with the nearly universal use of gothic and Romanesque arched windows, gives the tiny buildings their signature fairy-land look.

Festive and otherworldly as the campground is, it's probably fortunate that its wacky gingerbread did not become the dominant style for summer homes in the region. Far more important architectural influences were the simple colonial lines of the little capes and the convoluted Victorian roofs of the rambling shingle houses. On the other hand, architectural historian Ellen Weiss has argued that the campground, with its curving, tree-lined streets full of essentially equal and yet personalized houses, was one of the seeds from which grew the "American romantic suburb."

Whether or not that arguably dubious honor belongs in fact to the Vineyard is for others to debate. What can be said unequivocally is that the money pouring into Wesleyan Grove in the decades after the Civil War was a great bellows that fanned the earlier efforts to promote regional tourism into a hyperspeculative land boom. How could it be otherwise when the New York *Times* called the campground an "Eden," and the New York *Express* predicted that the thirty-five acres on which it sat would within the decade be worth $3 million?

It wasn't, therefore, by accident that the first piece of land that Captains Norton, Darrow, and Collins of Edgartown wished to develop when they formed the Oak Bluffs Land and Wharf Company in 1866 was the seventy-five-acre pasture that lay directly between the Methodist campground and the sea (and included the beach). By 1872 the whaling captains had built at Oak Bluffs a massive 125-room hotel—called the Sea View—some 225 feet long and more than 100 high. There was (and still is) a flying horses carousel. One could rent a boat or a bathhouse, or a croquet set—everyone was crazy for croquet. Or a house: during the peak week, for the right amount of money, some owners were more than happy to move back into a tent and let some more fortunate sinner rent the cottage. Investors from Worcester built a vast skating rink, where visitors, redeemed and otherwise, skated to a dance version of "Nearer My God to Thee."

It all added up to a social phenomenon of the first order. The Providence *Journal* ran a regular Oak Bluffs column on its front page. The directors of the camp meeting themselves, in a letter to the U.S. Postal Service, requested that the mail come by steamer rather than under sail because, they said, their revival was "probably the largest of the kind in the country; and in connection with the great Oak Bluffs Company annually draws a

African-American vacationers at Oak Bluffs in the 1880s. (COURTESY OF THE MARTHA'S VINEYARD HISTORICAL SOCIETY)

larger number of people together than Newport, Saratoga, or any other place of summer resort this side of the Atlantic."

During the last week in August of 1874 the president of the United States arrived on the Vineyard and was mobbed by cheering throngs as he made his way down Clinton Avenue in the campground. Accompanying President and Mrs. Grant were the vice president and the governor of Massachusetts. After a brief stay the Grants went over to Nantucket and the Cape before returning to Wesleyan Grove for "a mighty Love Feast" at the tabernacle.

Money to invest takes notice of money being made: on the Vineyard alone there were soon proposed developments called Ocean View, Bay View, Sea View, Grovedale, and Lookout Mountain. There were Sunset Heights, Ocean Heights, Lagoon Heights, the Vineyard Highlands, and even Oklahoma. East Chop was to be Bellevue Heights, West Chop was to be carved into West Point Grove and Cedar Bluff. The publisher of the Vineyard *Gazette* placed his bets on a scheme called the Chappaquiddick Land Company, which was expected to produce thousands of houses on that island. On Nantucket, meanwhile, wrote Alexander Starbuck with typical humor and ersatz sympathy, "Several schemes [were] devised to interest those unfortunate people who were forced to dwell on the mainland, in Nantucket real estate." As on the Vineyard, most of the schemes involved major, almost Floridian, subdivisions: two thousand lots at Madaket, seventeen hundred lots at Nauticon, et cetera.

In some places, like the Surfside Land Company's holdings on Nantucket and "Katama the Lovely" on the Vineyard, large Victorian hotels were built specifically to entice real-estate buyers. Using a method now time-tested, if not necessarily time-honored, potential buyers were offered free lodging if they would submit to a tour of the subdivision. By the 1880s, there were some seventy-five grand wooden hotels on the Cape, most facing the warm waters of the two sounds and Buzzards Bay, and many with house lots for sale nearby. Up and down the Cape—at places with native names like the Chequesset in Wellfleet, the Chequaquet at Craigville, the Cotocheset at Wianno, the Quissett, the Menauhant, Waquoit, Sippewisset, Nobscusset—guests stayed and paid by the week or the month, or even the season. Old Colony ran a "Dude Train" with drinks and cigars for the working dads who came down on weekends to join their families.

The boom of the 1870s gave way inevitably to the bust that followed. Long lists of properties available in lieu of unpaid taxes appeared in local papers all over. It got so bad that at Nantucket's Miacomet Park, 2,300 lots were advertised as free to anyone who bought a pound of a certain brand of tea. Only forty took the bait, none of whom apparently built houses on their thirtieth-of-an-acre site. The big hotels burned, often suspiciously: the owner of the still-standing Wesley House in Oak Bluffs went to jail briefly after confessing to having lit a candle set in a pile of oily rags in a closet of his hotel.

Even the directors of the successful Oak Bluffs Land and Wharf Company were ultimately forced to liquidate their holdings. The great Sea View Hotel and the nearby wharf, boardwalk, and beach houses were sold in

The Oak Bluffs Roquet Club in 1875. (Courtesy of the Martha's Vineyard Historical Society)

1878 in an effort to reduce corporate debt. As many of the remaining lots as possible were auctioned off a few years later, leaving little on the company's asset sheet other than the streets and the parks. These were offered to the new town, at first for free, then for $7,500, payable over twenty-five years with no interest. But the town balked, which was when Charles Abbott stepped in and paid the asking price outright.

Abbott was an off-islander with a strong belief in the rights of individual property owners. As a lawyer, he had an abiding faith in the civil lawsuit, with which he attempted to cow the town into giving up its efforts to prevent him from subdividing the parks. In the long legal struggle and bitter war of words in the local paper, arguments by now familiar to conservation battles up and down Cape Cod and the Islands were hauled out and tested. The town fought righteously in the name of the little people, and in the name of history and tradition, for the preservation of the community's character. Abbott's lawyers, meanwhile, claimed that it was in fact their poor client whose personal and civil rights were being trampled by a cabal of wealthy and hypocritical residents. In the end, though, after two trips to the Massachusetts Supreme Judicial Court, Abbott was routed by a decision written largely by Justice Oliver Wendell Holmes. Cottage City managed to wallow through the slump with its parks intact.

And the profits and the losses were the first boom. Though not, of course, the last. The land bubble of the 1870s ushered in an era of speculative development on Cape Cod and the Islands that for more than a century and a quarter has waxed and waned, been tastefully executed and egregiously botched, been heralded as progress or condemned as doom. Not since the ten men of Saugus got permission from William Bradford in 1637 to head down to the Cape, get some land from the Wampanoag, and found the town of Sandwich has there been such a sustained period of surveying, dividing, buying, selling, clearing, and building on Cape Cod and the Islands.

As with the first coming of the English, this one began manageably enough from the perspective of those already there. Summer people were useful additions once the sea had given up its marketable treasures and the nation had moved landward. They wore funny clothes, spoke odd dialects, were occasionally boorish, and stayed beyond their welcome. But the seasonal strangers could always be counted on to bring with them useful trinkets—primarily cash—and then leave. "So the Cape-Codder feels no qualms about nailing up roadside apple stands for the automobilists, or about filling his spare rooms with transients," wrote Kittredge at the end of his 1930 history of the peninsula.

Sixty-five years later, the "automobilists" very nearly rioted on Route 28 when traffic to the ferry terminal in Woods Hole ground down to gridlock. There are no apple stands along the Mid-Cape Highway, which runs divided like an interstate along the crest of the Cape Cod moraine and yet, as John Hay said, "does not seem to be entirely adequate to take the massing thousands onward." The population of Cape Cod on a given day in August now runs to something over half a million people, and the Park Service figures 5 million visits are made to Cape Cod National Seashore annually. The August population of the Vineyard is estimated to be over 100,000. The Nantucket Office of Planning and Economic Development, meanwhile, won't even try to guess the population in August, what with day trippers and guest houses and hide-a-beds. They do know, however, that more than 400,000 people visit the island during the course of a year.

Of arguably greater impact on the region was the fact that by the time Kittredge wrote his history, the strangers could no longer be counted on to go back home at the end of the season. The long post–Civil War decline in population on Cape Cod and the Islands reversed itself after the First World War, and by the 1930s the Cape's year-round population was growing faster than in any other county in Massachusetts. Barnstable County's growth led the state in the '40s, '50s, '60s, and '70s as well. In two decades, the 1950s* and the 1970s, the population growth rate on Cape Cod was over 50 per-

---

*Much of the year-round population growth in Bourne, Sandwich, and Falmouth in the years immediately following World War II was the result of the various installations now known as the Massachusetts Military Reservation, which provided 20 percent of the Cape's year-round jobs.

Brant Point in the 1880s. The vast Nantucketer Hotel can be seen in the distance (center). Today, large summer houses have replaced the grand wooden hotels of the Nantucket shoreline. (COURTESY NANTUCKET HISTORICAL ASSOCIATION)

cent. Today, with 210,000 year-round residents, the Cape is home to nearly eight times as many people as it was a single human lifetime ago.

Not until the 1980s did Cape Cod's rate of population growth fall to second place in the state: Martha's Vineyard (Dukes County) grew by 30 percent in those years as compared to the Cape's dizzying enough 26 percent growth rate. The Vineyard now has a year-round population of roughly fifteen thousand. In the 1990s it was Nantucket's turn to hold the dubious honor. The faraway island added roughly two thousand people to its 1990 population of just over six thousand souls, putting it within reach of its historical high of ten thousand during the 1830s.

On the upper Cape, at least, the emergence of the year-round suburban community has changed the place even more than the summer hordes. Sprawl of the sort that has engulfed miles of Route 28 on either end of almost every town between Bourne and Orleans, and which shows signs of appearing on the outskirts of Vineyard Haven, Edgartown, and even Nantucket and little North Tisbury, does not thrive on a three-month season. Summer people don't need indoor ice rinks, indoor tennis centers, indoor swimming pools. But these things have come or are coming to the Cape and Islands. And they will make year-round life better, or at least easier, which will bring more year-round residents, who will doubtless be resented by those who came before and built the good schools and hockey rinks for their children.

Most of the building to accommodate the massing thousands has taken place at the expense of whatever ecological recovery the land had made in the long period when the locals turned their attention away from agriculture and toward the sea. By 1950, 70 percent of the Cape had reverted again to forest—second- or third-growth oak and maple, yes, but open and essentially untamed. Since that time, though, nearly one hundred square miles of woodland—an area roughly equal to the entire Vineyard—has been reconverted to residential or commercial uses. The portion of the Cape that is wooded is again below 50 percent. In the last forty-five years on Martha's Vineyard, the amount of land developed for residential or other nonagricultural uses has risen from less than 3 percent to roughly 50 percent. As recently as 1987, only 13 percent of the land on Nantucket was considered "developed"; today the figure is over 30 percent.

Even the most pressing problem facing the Cape is suburban-sounding: great plumes of poisoned groundwater seeping out from the massive Superfund site called the Massachusetts Military Reservation, the predictable outcome of decades of the federal government's craven dumping of solvents and jet fuel onto porous land.

The age of subdivision that began in earnest at Oak Bluffs in the 1860s may be entering its terminal phases, however. A century and a quarter is, after all, a long time. Roughly the same amount of time elapsed between the earliest European visits to Wampanoag and Nauset country and the permanent arrival of the English in Provincetown Harbor in 1620. It took another century for the various Nickersons, Chases, Mayhews, Starbucks, Macys, and Athearns to fully appropriate, deforest, and exhaust the local soils and turn to the sea. A century and a quarter passed between the arrival of Ichabod Paddock on Nantucket—to teach the locals how to whale—and the 1820s, when the cannibal-fearing survivors of the *Essex* returned and Nantucket was surpassed by New Bedford as a whaling port. Or between the opening of the Pacific to American whaling and the end of American whaling in the Arctic.

Since the mid-1980s, the term *build-out* has crept into the vocabulary of various planning and environmental organizations on Cape Cod and the Islands. It is a theoretical point in the not-too-distant future when all the legally developable land will either be built upon or conserved. In 1997, two highly publicized reports predicted that build-out would occur on Martha's Vineyard in 2005 and on Nantucket in 2037. The report's authors hoped their findings would spur an increase in the rate at which open land is set aside for conservation, but whether they succeeded is unclear. All that can be said with certainty is that there is a definite feeling in Cape Cod and the Islands that the spoils are being divided for what may be the last time.

With the stakes and prices going ever higher—the average price of a house on Nantucket is currently over $600,000—there is real fear among the current residents that their children may not be able to afford to stay on the island or in the towns of their grandparents, or great-grandparents, or great-great-grandparents. There is a fear on the Islands in particular that everyone in between the super-wealthy summer resident and the people who clip their private golf holes for them might be squeezed out.

Occasionally there is talk of the need to create affordable housing, and occasionally there is even action on that front. But it seems unlikely in the extreme—somewhere beyond a build-down or a new glacier—that there will ever be the equivalent of the Mashpee or Gay Head Indian reservation for the remnants of the old English families of Cape Cod and the Islands, or for the later arrivals from the Azores, Cape Verde, Portugal, Finland, and Norway in the eighteenth and nineteenth centuries. Or the middle-class African Americans who began summering in Oak Bluffs in the late nineteenth and early twentieth centuries. Or for the formerly suburban hippies who came from the mainland in the 1960s and '70s.

It's natural for those who have witnessed the Nantucket or Cape or Vineyard they once knew mutate into something else to blame the attention-grabbing influence of the famous Kennedys. Or the Clintons. Or the well-known writers and artists. Or the Nantucket Nectars "juice guys," the Provincetown drag queens, or the Black Dog T-shirt sellers. Or the Orvis fly fishing school, or the Wall Street bonus machine. Or the day trippers, or the Steamship Authority. Just as it's natural for those in any town anywhere, on any coast or by any river, to find something or someone to blame for the goodness of a place squandered.

Nostalgia cannot function properly if newcomers come for the same reason as the Old Comers. If the new are just like the old, nostalgia is no longer an act of possession or connection with the past. It is something uncomfortably close to hypocrisy. Or worse, to snobbery, which is the last resort of snobs. And so it was that William Bradford felt compelled to editorialize in 1644 about the motives of those who went down to the Cape: "It was not for want or necessity so much that they removed as for the enriching of themselves." Likewise, the Methodists of Wesleyan Grove in the 1870s felt the need to respond to the first new subdivision next door by building a seemingly uncharitable eight-foot fence around the entire campground. "O, how changed!" wrote their self-appointed historian, Hebron

Vincent, a century and a quarter ago. "Instead of a few hundreds of poor, humble followers of the Master, who came here to worship, dwelling in rough tents, we have now, it is true a remnant of these, but mostly those of fashion, and many of wealth."

And David Halberstam, writing in *Town & Country* magazine at the end of the millennium, is certain that Nantucket was "still very much a middle-class island" when he personally chose to buy a house there in 1969, but he is "not sure that the new people are brought to the island by the old and abiding pleasures that drew us."

There is sweet seduction in nostalgia, and in impending loss, and in the certainty that we live in a time that is different from all other times—a time that is already approaching some kind of an end, and not just for us. This is particularly true when summer is involved, as if it is the nature of the season, which, after all, officially commences only when the days begin to shorten. "Summer afternoon—summer afternoon; to me those have always been the two most beautiful words in the English language," said Henry James to Edith Wharton.

John Updike, for one, was wary of his nostalgia. "These are summer memories, mostly August memories; for that's the kind of resident I was," he wrote in *Hugging the Shore*. "And a danger exists of confusing the Vineyard with my children's childhood, which time has swallowed, or with Paradise, from which we have been debarred by well-known angels."

Almost alone among the many writers on Cape Cod and the Islands, Thoreau seems invulnerable to the emotion. In Chatham, he watched a sloop dragging for anchors. "It is a singular employment, at which men are regularly hired and paid for their industry, to hunt to-day in pleasant weather for anchors which have been lost,—the sunken faith and hope of mariners, to which they trusted in vain," he wrote.

> If the roadsteads of the spiritual ocean could be thus dragged, what rusty flukes of hope deceived and parted chain-cables of faith might again be windlassed aboard! Enough to sink the finder's craft, or stock new navies to the end of time. The bottom of the sea is strewn with anchors, some deeper and some shallower, and alternately covered and uncovered by the sand, perchance with a small length of iron cable still attached,—to which where is the other end? So many unconcluded tales to be continued another time. So, if we had diving-bells adapted to the spiritual deeps, we should see anchors with their cables attached, as thick as eels in vinegar, all wriggling vainly toward their holding-ground. But that

is not treasure for us which another man has lost; rather it is for us to seek what no other man has found or can find,—not be Chatham men, dragging for anchors.

But Thoreau was an uncommon individual; a landlubber who nonetheless knew that if your anchor will not hold you must cut it loose and go to sea. For the rest of us, though, or perhaps in honesty I should only say for me, erosion and slippage and subdivision feed the quiet desperation. The flood tide of humanity from the continent, which brought me here, only put me halfway up the shore. And it is still rising.

There may be giddy joy in waking from a nap on the beach to find that the water has come all the way up and has wet the towel and is licking at your feet. Any five-year-old can tell you that. Five-year-olds don't look back, however, to see how close the waves have come to the dunes and bluffs behind, trying to remember if they came this close before. But I do.

CHAPTER 31

SCORTON CREEK

There is an end to every road, I suppose, and in a salt marsh on a falling tide it's apt to be a smelly one. I paddled into the great marshes of Barnstable Harbor with the laughable idea—taken directly from a topographic map—of poking all the way through a winding slough called the Scorton Creek to Scorton Harbor over in Sandwich. I knew beforehand that it was an unlikely proposition; Scorton Creek is only a foot wide and sharply winding when it passes under West Main Street (Route 6) at the town line. My kayak, on the other hand, is seventeen feet long, two feet wide in the middle, and inflexible. But as a guiding principle, Scorton Creek served my purpose: according to the best estimates of my global positioning system and myself, it got me six winding miles up into the grass, up into the mud. Up, finally, to my knees in the muck trying to see over enough grass to figure out where in creation I was. Maps will tempt you to madness.

At the moment the prickly mud oozed over the tops of my water shoes and down around my ankles I was glad not to be one of those earliest Europeans attracted down to the Cape by the chance to harvest salt hay from this expanse. I wondered who among them it was that thought of putting snowshoes on the horses and people. Who among them said it would never work, and who ate his words when the wagons of hay rolled home.

One thing that wasn't difficult to imagine from the middle of the marsh was why they did it: free hay! If not as far as the eye could see, more than far enough for a town of one hundred intent on taking over a continent. The marshes here and in Pleasant Bay present square mile after square mile of dense waving grass, there for the taking. Until the bugs arrive. And until you take a wrong step and sink deep enough to know that this is land that isn't quite land. The hay was free—it was probably the one local resource not much used by the earlier peoples. But the getting of it must have been miserable work.

My personal goal wasn't to reenact the Pilgrim harvest. When I shoved off early one morning from the public boat launch at Blish Point, I wanted merely to see the mud and the grass and whatever I could of who or what was living there on that particular September day.

The tide rose as planned, nearing its peak, making for good progress along the occasionally rocky shore toward a place the topo map told me is called Calves Pasture Point. There is a gray shingled house there, where the harbor stops and the marsh proper begins. An American flag fluttered on the pole in the yard that morning, in the sun, in the light breeze. And the whole place looked like boiled lobsters and steamed clams, burgers and hot dogs.

It looked like an Edward Hopper painting, or a memory, or a dream. The high season was over, though the air and water were still warm with it; there was no one on the lawn with a steaming cup of coffee looking out over the marsh. I turned sideways and drifted past with the tide, looking at that house for as long as I wanted to, thinking of a single weekend of my own long gone, before turning again and paddling on up what I thought was Broad Sound but I think now was more likely Brickyard Creek. I turned once, and backtracked, before turning again and paddling in deeper. One is nearly always turning in a salt marsh: because the tide flows both in and out through a land of nearly uniform erodability, the curves approach mathematical perfection. The house and flag disappeared behind the first curve. But the grass, which I could not see over, went on forever.

Salt marshes grow on Cape Cod and the Islands wherever barrier beaches and tidal shallows conspire to make land that is too wet and salty for terrestrial plants and too dry for true sea weeds. Like the dunes and spits of Long Point, it is new land in the making out of the remnants of old land destroyed. The same currents and waves that tear down the moraine and pile up the barrier sands carry lighter sediments around the points and hooks into quiet waters like these, where they settle out. From about halfway down the low-tide line out to a depth of about ten feet, eel grass grows, breaking the current further and helping to trap even more sediment, until the land rises to a point where it becomes at last too dry for the eel grass. Where the eelgrass gives way, various grasses of the Spartina family carry on the work of catching muck. Spartina, like mangroves, has a remarkable ability to filter fresh water from salt and pump oxygen down from its leaves into its waterlogged roots.

Particle by particle, tide by tide, year by century, the land rises and the grass rises with it: marsh grass roots can go ten feet down, presumably to where the individual plant started when land and sea were lower. The peat soil of Barnstable Marsh is more than twenty feet deep in places, and samples from the bottom have been carbon dated at more than thirty-six hundred years old. "A salt marsh sanctions space and a rooted integrity," wrote the naturalist John Hay, who lives in Brewster and founded the Cape Cod Museum of Natural History. "The centuries pass, and its patience deepens."

There are cycles within cycles, and the building of marshes is not simple. Life arranges itself here depending on tolerance for salt and water and air, which in turn are affected by the familiar daily rise and fall of tide caused by the gravitational pulls of both moon and sun. And by the twice-monthly spring tides, when both celestial orbs align in a state of "syzygy" at the time of the full and new moons to produce high tides that are higher and lows that are lower. And by the twice-monthly neaps, when sun and moon pull against each other. There is also the monthly perigee tide, when the moon is at its closest to the earth. There are times when the perigee and the syzygy work together to create perigean spring tides that can be 40 percent higher than average.

On top of this is an annual cycle that produces greater tides at solstices and equinoxes, and an eighteen-month cycle called proxigee when the moon actually speeds up temporarily, thus accelerating the tides. An 18.6-year tidal cycle caused by variations in the declination of both sun and moon may account for long-term alternation between grasses of different salt tolerance in the marsh.

There are likely to be other tidal cycles yet to be deciphered. And cycles of wind and barometric pressure, which can also increase or depress tides. Long-term patterns of precipitation and dryness change the salinity in the upper marsh with implications for the species that grow there. Temperature, too, has its effect on life in the marshes. Cape Cod Bay faces the cold Labrador current coming down the coast from the north and has, on average, water that is ten degrees colder than the Gulf Stream–dominated waters to the south of the Cape. According to the National Park Service, the biota of Cape Cod Bay is more like that of the Bay of Fundy than it is like that of Buzzards Bay, only a dozen miles away. That of Buzzards and the two sounds is more like Virginia's than it is like the water just across the moraine on the north shore of the Cape.

And of course there are storms, which notably and frighteningly erase portions of lower marshes in a single afternoon but may also be the primary way for sediment to get past the baffles of the front-line plants and up into the upper marsh. In the upper Chesapeake Bay, for instance, one study found that more than half the sediment laid down between 1905 and 1975 came from only two natural "disasters": the flood of 1936 and Hurricane Agnes of 1972. Sometimes a storm will close a marsh off from the sea, and it will turn fresh; other storms reopen ponds, turning them brackish.

I paddled in, and in some more, until I was completely content there somewhere near the middle of the Great Marsh of Barnstable. Whereupon I had lunch in the company of a long-legged bird. Distant company, for she would not let me get too close before whistling sharply and moving on around the bend. At best I am a mediocre identifier of birds, but I believe it was a greater yellowlegs. Her fine long legs, at any rate, were that color, and she was larger than my books say the more common lesser yellowlegs are likely to be. It would be good to be a better birder: more than 360 species of birds have been identified on Cape Cod and the Islands. Shorebirds that migrate between the hemispheres regularly spend time here on their way up to the Arctic, and even more often on their way down to South America. Songbirds blown east by storms during their spring and fall migrations along the Atlantic flyway sometimes grab onto these last bits of land: a friend who is a very good birder once identified thirty-one different warblers in his Chilmark driveway on a single spring morning. Southern species like the glossy ibis are occasionally blown here by hurricanes, as are even stranger birds from Europe and Africa. Migrating hawks regularly pass over the region, and their fans gather with binoculars at the top of the cliffs in Aquinnah on fall mornings to wish them well.

As many birds as there now are, though, there were once many more. A century ago most people who looked closely at the winged creatures of Cape Cod and the Islands did so over the barrels of guns. The old hay grounds became killing fields. Until the migratory bird treaties put a partial end to the practice in 1916, birds like both varieties of yellowlegs were shot by the thousands in this and other local marshes for pleasure and for market. The yellowlegs "is not the equal of Wilson's Snipe or Woodcock in an Epicurean sense," claimed one text on the birds of Massachusetts, "but in autumn it often becomes very fat and toothsome."

Hunters in the marshes of Yarmouth and elsewhere supplied the tables of Boston and beyond with birds of all sizes. (COURTESY OF THE SOCIETY FOR THE PRESERVATION OF NEW ENGLAND ANTIQUITIES)

A more popular target than the yellowlegs was the Eskimo curlew, a cinnamon-colored bird about the size of a Cornish game hen with a dark stripe through the eye and greenish legs. They bred in Alaska, flew across Canada to Labrador and Newfoundland in "millions that darkened the sky," where they fattened up for the long flight south to Patagonia and Argentina. They often stopped along the way at Cape Cod and the Islands.

Fall was not a quiet time in the marshes then. Market hunters, who were running out of the once-even-more-plentiful passenger pigeon, followed the Eskimo curlews from state to state. They shot and netted them by the wagonload on the western prairies during their spring migration north, and then went to New England to wait for them in the fall. Eskimo curlews often traveled with golden plovers, and a harvest of eight thousand of those two species was a good day on Cape Cod during the 1870s. But the last Eskimo curlew ever seen in New England was shot in East Orleans on September 5, 1913. On a good day a skilled birder might identify a golden plover here in the Great Marsh or one of the other estuaries of the region, but the Eskimo curlew is extinct.

By the time yellowlegs and I had finished lunch, the tide in Barnstable Harbor had turned. When it got low enough to leave me paddling through miniature canyons with mud walls four or more feet tall, with the tough grass waving another eighteen inches or more above that, I turned around too, and began to flow back out of the marsh.

Along the way, channels much smaller than the one I was navigating periodically went off toward my left or my right, offering tantalizing views but always bending away before giving a hint of where they headed. I poked up one or two, but ended up backing out. Others higher up were already dry, like hanging valleys, and I wondered if any of them were dug not by tides but by people. Once the free hay was no longer desired and the feathered multitudes were plucked, roasted, and gone, the marshes were given over to the heirs of the Pilgrim mosquito haters so scorned by Bradford three centuries before. More than two thousand miles of ditches were dug in the salt marshes by the Cape Cod Mosquito Control (and marsh destruction) Project in an effort to dry them out. "The cost is great, but the profit greater," wrote one giddy observer in 1964; "mosquito control projects on Cape Cod have been accompanied by a 50 percent rise in the tourist trade."

The loudest contemporary outcry against the ditching came from those who favored more "modern methods," like poison. First it was kerosene sprayed by hand in Wellfleet and elsewhere. Then, starting in the late 1940s and continuing into the '60s, great clouds of DDT were dropped from airplanes on wetlands all over Cape Cod and the Islands. Only a few of the Elizabeth Islands were spared. The osprey and some of the other unintended victims of the undaunted hubris of the pesticide industry have recovered somewhat in decades since the publication of *Silent Spring*. But the Fowler's toads of little Muskeget Island, which in the thousands of years since the water cut them off from the rest of toad society had developed into a variety unique to that island, were entirely wiped out, as were all the more common and once plentiful toads on Nantucket and Cuttyhunk. Toads, it is worth noting, spend their nights and days eating pesky insects.

There were places in the canyons of the marsh where corners of land had calved off into the creek and lay akimbo, with the grass still growing at a forty-five degree angle. There were places where the entire thickness of the walls appeared to be built entirely of the shells of ribbed mussels; the living resting on the solid remains of a hundred or a thousand previous generations. People who study bivalve fecal matter think it, too, may affect the rate of soil accretion and the plant population of certain marshes.

In the 1960s and '70s, science and popular wisdom fortunately displaced most of the mosquito killers with a new image of the salt marshes as the vast exporters of nutrients at the very bottom of the inshore food chain. To its credit, in 1963 Massachusetts became the first state to protect its coastal wetlands. The production of detritus, microscopic or merely tiny bits of rotting vegetation, is the foundation of the marsh's immense popularity among diatoms and immature fish. And among insects and crustaceans, and birds.

But here again, there are cycles within. More science in the '80s and '90s has replaced the food chain with a more ecologically sophisticated web, in which sometimes marshes export and sometimes they import. Sometimes they hold nitrogen, sometimes they release it.

"It is clear that generalizations about the role of all salt marshes as either sources or sinks of material cannot be sustained," one recent text on salt-marsh ecology inconclusively concluded on the subject of rot. The newer thinking doesn't make the marsh any less important—the world still relies on, among other things, a healthy supply of detritus—it only makes us still humbler when we talk about what we know of a leaf of grass. "Those who pride themselves on cramming a thousand years into a minute," said Hay of the salt marsh, "cannot be aware of its unending reliability."

When I ceased paddling and allowed my kayak to drift like a bright yellow piece of detritus, I could hear water on all sides seeping and dripping and sucking out of the four-thousand-acre sponge. Some of the serenity of midday on the marsh was oozing out of me, as well, whether because I was tired or because I was gearing up to land again on a solid shore, I don't know.

But I was glad finally to see and pass the house with the flag again, to paddle past the few clammers out on the flats, and to arrive at the ramp at Blish Point. I was glad that the tide, which had brought me in, had washed me out again.

NOTES

In the opening pages of *The Great Beach*, John Hay humbly wrote that "anyone writing another book about Cape Cod could be accused of temerity in the face of such predecessors as the three Henrys—Thoreau, Beston, and Kittredge." Hay then proceeded to add to the library of regional literature some of the loveliest pages ever published. So it is with far greater temerity that yet another book is offered up. The more so because its subject matter includes Nantucket, where *Moby-Dick* still seems to tell more about the island than any other book, even though it neither takes place on Nantucket nor had its author been there at the time he wrote it— and it is a work of fiction to boot. And this book includes Martha's Vineyard, where no single author stands above the rest as Thoreau does for the Cape and Melville does for Nantucket, but where shelves full of good writing and solid scholarship more than make up the difference.

As in any general historical work, this book is largely a retelling and reorganizing of tales others have told before. And while all the sources I consulted were helpful in some way, and many of them are mentioned in detail below, a handful of general sources were important enough to my efforts that they deserve special acknowledgment: *Cape Cod, Its People and Their History*, by Henry C. Kittredge, 1930–68, 2d edition, with a post epilogue by John Hay, 1930 (Hyannis, Mass.: Parnassus Imprints edition, 1987); *Shipmasters of Cape Cod*, also by Kittredge, 1935 (Hyannis, Mass.: Parnassus Imprints, 1987); *Cape Cod and Plymouth Colony in the Seventeenth Century*, by H. Roger King (New York: University Press of America, 1994); *Sandwich, A Cape Cod Town*, by R. A. Lovell Jr. (Sandwich, Mass.: Town of Sandwich Massachusetts Archives and Historical Center, 1996); *A History of Chatham, Massachusetts*, by William C. Smith, 1916–17 (Chatham, Mass.: Chatham Historical Society, 1981); *The History of Nantucket: County, Island, and Town*, by

Alexander Starbuck, 1924 (Bowie, Md.: Heritage Books, 1998); *The History of Nantucket*, by Obed Macy, 1835 (I used a facsimile reprint of the 1880 edition from Higginson Press); *Away Off Shore: Nantucket Island and Its People, 1602–1890*, by Nathaniel Philbrick (Nantucket, Mass.: Mill Hill Press, 1994); *The History of Martha's Vineyard, Dukes County, Massachusetts*, 3 vols., by Charles Edward Banks, M.D., 1911 (Edgartown, Mass.: Dukes County Historical Society, 1966); *Martha's Vineyard, Summer Resort 1835–1935*, by Henry Beetle Hough (Rutland, Vt.: Tuttle Publishing Co., 1936); a variety of articles in the *Dukes County Intelligencer*, mostly by Arthur Railton (Edgartown, Mass.: Martha's Vineyard Historical Society); *The Sea-Hunters*, by Edouard A. Stackpole (Westport Conn.: Greenwood Press, 1953); *Indian New England Before the Mayflower*, by Howard S. Russell (Hanover, N.H.: University Press of New England, 1980); and *Prologue to New England: The Forgotten Century of the Explorers*, by Henry F. Howe (New York: Farrar & Rinehart, 1943).

In the specific notes below, as above, I've put the original date of publication immediately following the title. If I used a reprint or a later edition, that information follows in the parentheses. After the first reference to a source, only the author's last name is listed. Also, though I eventually read most of the sources that other writers referred to in their works, out of courtesy to earlier researchers I have attempted to credit quotes to the source where I originally found them.

Chapter 1 The underlying source for all the many retellings of Epenow's story are Ferdinando Gorges's various memoirs, which I found principally in a collection of Gorges's writings called *Sir Ferdinando Gorges and his Province of Maine . . .* , James P. Baxter, ed. (Boston: Burt Franklin, 1890). *The Complete Works of John Smith* (Chapel Hill: University of North Carolina Press, 1986) and *Captain John Smith: A Select Edition of His Writings*, Karen Ordahl Kupperman, ed. (Chapel Hill: University of North Carolina Press, 1988) were also useful. The essential facts of the story are laid out most clearly in part one of Arthur Railton's series on the English and Indians on Martha's Vineyard that ran in *Dukes County Intelligencer* in May 1990, in *Capawack alias Martha's Vineyard*, by Warner Foote Gookin (Edgartown, Mass.: Dukes County Historical Society, 1947), and in Howe.

"The principal inhabitants . . ." and Gorges quotes that follow—Baxter, pp. 19–25.

"in search for a mine of Gold . . ."—Smith, quoted in Banks, vol. 1, p. 69.

"when they will not give a doit . . ."—*The Tempest*, William Shakespeare, Act II, scene 2.

"a war now new . . ."—quoted in *New England Frontier, Puritans and Indians 1620–1675*, 1965, by Alden T. Vaughan (Tulsa: University of Oklahoma Press, 3d edition, 1995), p. 16.

Chapter 2 The primary sources for all versions of Gosnold's voyage are two short narratives written by members of the expedition. I used the 1966 Readex Microprint facsimile version of John Brereton's *A Briefe and true Relation of the Discoverie of the North Part of Virginia . . .* , which was first published in 1602. Gabriel Archer's *Relation*, I found (among other places) in *Early History of Naushon Island*, by Amelia

Forbes Emerson, 1935 (Boston: Howland and Co., 2d edition, 1981). Also of great use was *A Voyage of Discovery to the Southern Parts of Norumbega*, by Warner F. Gookin (Edgartown, Mass.: Dukes County Historical Society, 1950). In this and several chapters to follow, Howe provides an indispensable overview of the pre-1620 contact between Europe and New England, supplemented by *Sailors' Narratives of Voyages along the New England Coast, 1524–1624*, George Parker Winship, ed. (Boston: Houghton Mifflin, 1905), and *The English New England Voyages, 1602–1608*, David and Alison Quinn, eds. (London: Hakluyt Society, 1986).

"About twelve of the clock . . ." and other Brereton quotes to follow—from Brereton, pp. 4–12.

"M. Cortereal 1511 V. Dei Dux Ind"—Howe, p. 8.

"800 sayle"—*Description of New England*, by John Smith, quoted in Howe, p. 248. One of the best accounts of precolonial fishing voyages to the New World can be found in *Cod, A Biography of the Fish That Changed the World*, by Mark Kurlansky (New York: Walker & Co., 1997).

"The Coast is very full of people"—this and the other quotes from Archer's account of the voyage are from Emerson, pp. 31–40.

"Now when a group of Indians . . ."—Howe, p. 66.

Chapter 3 "Noe-pe"—Banks, p. 32. Banks remains after nearly a century the baseline source for Vineyard history, but critiques of his scholarship can be found in almost every historical book on the subject, particularly Gookin, *Capawack*.

"Bay of Currents"—This particular interpretation of the Norse Sagas, one of many, comes from *The Story of Cuttyhunk*, by Louise T. Haskell (New Bedford, Mass.: Reynolds, 1953), p. 7.

Chapter 4 The most useful books on the economy and ecology of New England before the permanent arrival of the English are *Indian New England before the Mayflower*, by Howard S. Russell (Hanover, N.H.: University Press of New England, 1980) and *Changes in the Land*, by William Cronon (New York: Hill and Wang, 1983). Also helpful were *Native Roots*, by Jack Weatherford (New York: Fawcett Columbine, 1991), *Manitou and Providence*, by Neal Salisbury (New York: Oxford University Press, 1982), *The Invasion Within*, by James Axtell (New York: Oxford University Press, 1985), *The State of Native America*, M. Annette Jaimes, ed. (Boston: South End Press, 1992), *The Wampanoag*, by Laurie Weinstein-Farson (New York: Chelsea House, 1989), and *Abram's Eyes*, by Nathaniel Philbrick (Nantucket, Mass.: Mill Hill, 1998). The miscellaneous quotes from Archer and Brereton narratives come from the two sources previously mentioned.

"What could they see . . ."—The unpublished manuscript of *Of Plymouth Plantation*, William Bradford's now-classic account of the first three decades of English colonization in New England, was stolen from Boston's Old South Church during the American Revolution. In 1855 it turned up in the library of the Bishop of London, and was first published in 1856. The dog-eared paperback edition I used was published by Random House in 1981. The specific quote appears on p. 70.

"the proper time of year to be a summer visitor"—Hough, p. 9.

"strawberries, red and white"—Brereton, p. 3.

"open plains as much as twenty or thirty leagues . . ."—Russell, p. 8.

"faire, big, strawberries" and "very pleasant and agreeable"—Russell, pp. 9–10.

"not a tree in the same"—quoted in Cronon, p. 25.

"They use not to winter and summer in one place"—*New English Canaan*, 1632, by Thomas Morton, quoted in Cronon, p. 49.

"There is no underwood . . ."—*New England Prospect*, 1634, by William Wood, quoted in Banks, p. 31.

"Indian burning promoted the increase . . ."—Cronon, p. 51.

"There has been no timeless wilderness . . ."—Cronon, p. 11.

"Any notion, however . . ."—Russell, p. 125.

"The men employ their time . . ."—*Good Newes from New England*, 1624, by Edward Winslow (Bedford, Mass.: Applewood Books), p. 63.

"The hunter's legs . . ."—Russell, p. 100.

"detailed to an inquiring anthropologist . . ."—Russell, p. 76.

"which all their remedies . . ."—Russell, p. 35.

"Their dwellings are separate . . ."—quoted in Howe, p. 133.

"shows you all along large corn fields . . ."—Smith (Kupperman, ed.), pp. 235–36.

Chapter 5 At the risk of diminishing sales, I'm obliged to say that if one could read only one book on Cape Cod, it had better be Thoreau's *Cape Cod*. Mine is a 1951 Norton edition with an introduction by Henry Beston.

"Though once there were more whales . . ."—Thoreau, pp. 183–84.

For the demise of fishing, see Kurlansky and *Song for the Blue Ocean*, by Carl Safina (New York: Henry Holt, 1998).

"Daggett family of Cedar Tree Neck . . ."—*It Began with a Whale*, by John Tobey Daggett (Somerville, Mass.: Fleming & Son, 1963).

"the great south west God . . ."—Salisbury, pp. 34–36, and Russell, pp. 46–47.

"One Allen of the Vineyard . . ."—Philbrick, *Away Off Shore*, p. 137.

"Here's what Cape Cod doesn't have . . ."—from "Cape Cod: the Real Thing," by Peter Smith, *Travel and Leisure Family*, Spring/Summer 1999.

"Tarpaulin Light is a tiny . . ."—in addition to Emerson, *Lighthouses of Cape Cod, Martha's Vineyard, Nantucket*, by Admont G. Clark (Hyannis, Mass.: Parnassus Imprints, 1992) was helpful.

"The dead do not reign here alone"—*A Thousand-Mile Walk to the Gulf*, by John Muir (Boston: Houghton Mifflin, 1916), p. 69.

Chapter 6 "Christian colonies on that continent . . ."—Gorges, p. 20.

"whitish sandy cliffe" and "a colonial refuge for oppressed English papists"—Howe, pp. 84–85.

"to discover an Isle supposed to be about Cape Cod" and other John Smith quotes that follow—quoted in Howe, p. 184.

"caused them to dance again better than before"—Howe, p. 103.

"In [his] homely Musicke . . ."—Quinn and Quinn, p. 220.

"Cap Blanc"—*Cape Cod and the Old Colony*, by Albert Perry Brigham (New York: Putnam's Sons, 1921), p. 6.

"It was almost low tide . . ." and other Champlain quotes that follow—Howe, pp. 116–43.

"the Salvages say there is no channel"—Smith (Kupperman, ed.), p. 236.

"At Capawe . . ."—Howe, p. 185.

Chapter 7 More has been written about the natural world of the Cape and Islands than probably any other regional subject, with the possible exception of whaling. Foremost are Henry Beston's *Outermost House* (New York: Doubleday, 1928) and virtually anything by John Hay, but particularly for me, *The Run* (Boston: Beacon Press, 1959), *The Great Beach* (New York: W. W. Norton, 1963), and *The Way to the Salt Marsh* (Hanover, N.H.: University Press of New England, 1998). Robert Finch (*Common Ground*, New York: W. W. Norton, 1994) and Wyman Richardson (*The House at Nauset Marsh*, New York: W. W. Norton, 1947) are good additions, as is the poetry of Mary Oliver, which I first encountered in Robert Finch's fine anthology of Cape Cod literature, *A Place Apart* (New York: W. W. Norton, 1993).

For technical information on the natural processes at work and the geological background of the Cape and Islands, the starting place was *These Fragile Outposts*, by Barbara Blau Chamberlain (Garden City, N.Y.: Natural History Press, 1964), *A Geologist's View of Cape Cod*, by Arthur N. Strahler (Hyannis, Mass.: Parnassus Imprints, 1988), and *Cape Cod: Its Natural and Cultural History*, by Robert Finch (Washington, D.C.: National Park Service). *The Beaches Are Moving*, by Wallace Kaufman and Orrin H. Pilkey (Durham, N.C.: Duke University Press, 1995), *Against the Tide*, by Cornelia Dean (New York: Columbia University Press, 1999), and *This Broken Archipelago*, by James D. Lazell Jr. (New York: Times Books, 1976) were also helpful. Finally, *Blue Rooms*, by John Jerome (New York: Henry Holt, 1995) is not about the ocean, it is about water, and it was helpful to me.

"stolen cliff materials"—Chamberlain, p. 264. Much of the discussion of the Aquinnah cliffs draws on the work of Chamberlain.

"mosaically interlocked . . ."—Chamberlain, p. 32.

"Ktaadn . . ."—*The Maine Woods*, by Henry David Thoreau (New York: Penguin, 1988), p. 94.

"the bared and bended arm . . ."—Thoreau (all the remaining Thoreau quotes in this and the following chapters are from *Cape Cod*), p. 14.

"The Elizabeth Islands offer the condiments of existence . . ."—Genio Scott, as quoted in *Profiles in Saltwater Angling*, by George Reiger (Englewood Cliffs, N.J.: Prentice Hall, 1973), p. 60.

Chapter 8 (See the introduction to the notes for Chapter 4.)

"commonly called by our Dutch captains . . ."—Howe, p. 225.

"to take whales . . ."—Smith (Kupperman, ed.), p. 220.

"Here are no hard Landlords . . ."—Howe, p. 248.

"One Thomas Hunt . . ."—Smith (Kupperman, ed.), p. 221.

"twenty seven of these poore . . ."—Howe, p. 274.

"deceived the people . . ."—*Mourt's Relation*, 1622, author unknown (Bedford, Mass.: Applewood Books, 1966), p. 52.

"nurture them in the Popish Religion"—quoted in Howe, p. 275.

"two small bones . . ."—Russell, p. 112.

"and never left watching and dogging . . ."—Bradford, p. 92.

"the country was in a manner left void . . ."—Howe, p. 280.

"This spring also . . ."—Bradford, p. 302.

"thousands of men have lived . . ."—*Mourt's Relation*, p. 63.

"many, yea, most . . ."—*Mourt's Relation*, p. 80.

"They found [Massasoit's] place . . ."—Bradford, p. 97.

"they died on heapes . . ."—from *The New English Canaan*, 1632, by Thomas Morton, quoted in Howe, p. 282.

"About four years ago . . ."—*Mourt's Relation*, p. 51.

"ancient Plantations . . ." and other Dermer quotes that follow—Howe, pp. 285–87.

"all [Dermer's] men slain . . ."—Bradford, p. 92.

Chapter 9 In addition to many of the works already mentioned (particularly those in the introduction to the notes to Chapter 4), a number of other sources were particularly useful for the chapters covering the initial English arrival and settlement of the Cape and Islands. *Three Visitors to Early Plymouth*, Sydney James, ed. (Bedford, Mass.: Applewood Books, 1963), is a fascinating anthology of letters written by visitors to the colony in the years between 1620 and 1627. Likewise, *The Puritans in America*, Alan Heimert and Andrew Delbanco, eds. (Cambridge, Mass.: Harvard University Press, 1985), *A Little Commonwealth*, by John Demos (New York: Oxford University Press, 1970), and *Everyday Life in Early America*, by David Freeman Hawke (New York: Harper & Row, 1988), were particularly good for background, and *Land Ho! 1620*, by W. Sears Nickerson (Lansing, Mich.: Michigan State University Press, 1997), for information about the voyage of the *Mayflower* herself. Also of great service was the four-part series on "The English and the Indians on Martha's Vineyard," by Arthur Railton, that ran in the *Dukes County Intelligencer* in 1992. *Quaker Nantucket*, by Robert Leach and Peter Gow (Nantucket, Mass.: Mill Hill, 1997), and *Thomas Mayhew, Patriarch to Indians*, 1932, by Lloyd C. Hare (New York: AMS Press, 1969), were also useful.

"flaying some alive . . ."—Bradford, pp. 27–28.

"special instrument . . ."—Bradford, p. 89.

"unacquainted with the Bible"—quoted in Francis Murphy's introduction to Bradford, p. viii.

"No Bishop, No King . . ." and "I will harry them out . . ."—Heimert and Delbanco, p. 4.

"were hunted and persecuted . . ." and the rest of the quotes on the debate among separatists—Bradford, pp. 9–28.

"already delayed . . ."—Bradford, p. 51.

"To speak the truth . . ."—Bradford, p. 46.

"If ever we make a plantation"—Bradford, p. 64.

"like Gideon's Army . . ."—Bradford, p. 60.

"some of those vast and unpeopled countries . . ."—Bradford, p. 24.

"a proud and very profane . . ."—Bradford, p. 66.

"They were not a little joyful"—Bradford, p. 56.

"a good harbor and pleasant bay . . ."—*Mourt's Relation*, p. 16.

"fell upon their knees . . ."—Bradford, p. 57.

"My forefathers didn't come over . . ."—*Bartlett's Familiar Quotations* (Boston: Little, Brown, 1992), p. 638.

Chapter 10 (See the introduction to the notes to Chapter 7.)

"This air struggles . . ."—Chamberlain, p. 257.

"No joy but lacks salt . . ."—from the poem "To Earthward," by Robert Frost.

"seemed ungracious to refuse . . ."—Thoreau, p. 117.

Chapter 11 (See the introduction to the notes to Chapters 4 and 9.)

"Some did it necessarily . . ."—*Mourt's Relation*, p. 24.

"The willingness of the persons . . ."—*Mourt's Relation*, p. 19.

"five or six people with a dog . . ." and quotes in the story that follows—*Mourt's Relation*, pp. 20–22.

"The corn and beans they brought away . . ."—Bradford, p. 74.

"We thought it best herein to gratify his kindness . . ."—Bradford, p. 25.

"resolved to dig it up" and quotes that follow—*Mourt's Relation*, pp. 27–31.

Chapter 12 "scarce any of us were free . . ." and quotes that follow—*Mourt's Relation*, pp. 27–43.

"at least it was the best . . ."—Bradford, p. 79.

"scarce fifty"—Bradford, p. 85.

"so general a disease . . ."—Bradford, p. 105.

"a small can of beer"—Bradford, p. 86.

"returning with three great seals . . ."—*Mourt's Relation*, p. 44.

"very fair sunshiny days" and quotes about arrival of Samoset, Squanto, and Massasoit that follow—*Mourt's Relation*, pp. 47–57.

Chapter 13 "make satisfaction . . ." and quotes about visit to Massasoit that follow—*Mourt's Relation*, pp. 60–67.

"savage and brutish men . . ."—Bradford, p. 26.

"the profanest"—Bradford, p. 259.

"with much lightning and thunder . . ." and quotes that follow—*Mourt's Relation*, pp. 69–71.

Chapter 14 "to revenge the supposed death . . ." and quotes that follow—*Mourt's Relation*, pp. 74–79.

"they had many gratulations from divers sachems . . ."—Bradford, p. 99.

"Appanow"—from *New England's Memorial*, by Thomas Morton, 1669, quoted in Dwight B. Heath's footnotes to *Mourt's Relation*, p. 83.

"an Indian of Tisquantum's family" and quotes that follow—Winslow, pp. 11–15.

"famine began now to pinch . . ."—Bradford, p. 121.

"I know your weakness . . ."—Bradford, p. 102.

"meddled with the maids"—Bradford, p. 185.

"crazed in his brain"—Bradford, p. 233.

"We would wish such to keep at home . . ."—Bradford, p. 159.

"And instead of an Ancient [flag] . . ."—letter from Emmanuel Altham to Sir Edward Altham, September 1623, in James ed., p. 31.

"swamps and other desert places . . ."—Winslow, p. 52.

"No sooner was the boat discharged . . ."—Bradford, p. 135.

"otherwise, had it been in their own custody . . ."—Bradford, pp. 121–22.

"The chief places aimed at . . ."—Winslow, pp. 21–22.

"In this place Squanto fell sick . . ."—Bradford, p. 126.

Chapter 15 The story of Thomas Granger and the related quotes—from Bradford's chapter "Wickedness Breaks Forth," pp. 351–58.

"never felt the sweetness . . ."—Bradford, p. 197.

"And yet in other regards this benefit . . ."—Bradford, p. 281.

"acting in association with the Old Comers"—King, p. 45.

"Fye fye! . . ."—King, p. 75.

"drunkards, liars, and swearers"—King, p. 149.

"neck and heels"—King, p. 93.

"But some will say . . ."—Heimert and Delbanco, p. 43.

"No part or parcel . . ."—from the Records of the Court of Plymouth, quoted in *A Pilgrim Returns to Cape Cod*, by Edward Rowe Snow (Boston: Yankee Press, 1946), p. 293.

"This then is a sufficient reason . . ."—Heimert and Delbanco, p. 44.

"When the committee from Plymouth . . ."—Thoreau, p. 52.

"It was the historian, not the Puritan . . ."—Vaughan, p. 62.

"fairly according to the rank . . ."—King, p. 71.

"As it is with waters . . ." and following quotes on the Granger case—Bradford, pp. 352–57.

"And others still, as they conceived . . ."—Bradford, p. 283.

"Stay and make a pause . . ."—Bradford, p. 69.

"It was not for want or necessity . . ."—Bradford, p. 369.

"This I fear will be . . ."—Bradford, p. 283.

Chapter 16 "far-away island"—one of the various definitions of the meaning of Nantucket, notably in *Nantucket, the Far-Away Island,* by William O. Stevens (New York: Dodd, Mead, 1945).

"whose length is half the circumference . . ."—Kaufman and Pilkey, p. 68.

Chapter 17 The library of books about the age of sail and the era of whaling is large and continually growing. Significant sections of the general works already mentioned, particularly the various histories of Nantucket—Macy, Starbuck, Philbrick—and Kittredge's history of Cape Cod, are devoted to the activities of Cape and Islanders at sea.

On whales and whaling: Above all else there is, of course, Herman Melville's novel *Moby-Dick*. Of the myriad nonfiction works on whaling, the most generally useful is *The Sea-Hunters: The New England Whalemen during Two Centuries 1635–1835*, by Edouard A. Stackpole (Westport, Conn.: Greenwood Press, 1953); *The Story of the New England Whalers*, by John R. Spears (New York: Macmillan, 1908), is highly readable, though, like many books of that vintage, it is poorly referenced. The same is true of the 1926 book *The Yankee Whaler*, by Clifford W. Ashley (New York: Dover, 1991), and A. Hyatt Verrill's *The Real Story of the Whaler* (New York: Appleton, 1916). *Whaling Wives*, by Emma Mayhew Whiting and Henry Beetle Hough (Cambridge, Mass.: Riverside, 1952), is the most readable of several accounts of women who went to sea on whale ships. In the often poorly written memoir genre, my personal favorites are *The Cruise of the Chachalot*, by Frank T. Bullen (New York: Appleton, 1904), *Pursuing the Whale*, by John A. Cook (Cambridge, Mass.: Riverside, 1924), and *Cap'n George Fred*, by George Fred Tilton (New York: Doubleday, 1928). For the story of the *Essex* there are the narratives by Chase, Chapple, Pollard, and Nickerson. The first three are collected in *Narratives of the Wreck of the Whale-Ship* Essex, 1935, by Owen Chase et al. (New York: Dover, 1989). The last was published with an excellent afterword by Edouard Stackpole under the title *The Loss of the Ship "Essex" Sunk by a Whale* (Nantucket Historical Association, 1984). Indispensable as well was *Stove by a Whale: Owen Chase and the* Essex, by Thomas Farel Heffernan (Hanover, N.H.: University Press of New England/Wesleyan, 1990).

As for the thousands from Cape Cod and the Islands who went to sea but not for whales, the counterpart to *Moby-Dick* is probably Richard Henry Dana's *Two Years before the Mast*, 1840 (New York: Penguin, 1981). The problem with Dana is that though he gives a most readable account of a young New Englander's life at sea, his is not really a book about Cape Cod or the Islands. For that there are two classic works by Kittredge: *Shipmasters of Cape Cod*, 1935 (Hyannis, Mass.: Parnassus Imprints, 1998), and *Mooncussers of Cape Cod* (Boston: Houghton Mifflin, 1937). Also useful was *East of Cape Cod*, by Asa Cobb Paine Lombard Jr. (New Bedford, Mass.: Reynolds-DeWalt, 1976), and *Blue Water Men and Other Cape Codders*, by Katherine Crosby (New York: Macmillan, 1947). There are some relevant sections as well in *The Maritime History of Massachusetts*, 1921, by Samuel Eliot Morrison (Boston: Northeastern University Press, 1961), *Greyhounds of the Sea*, by Carl Cutler (New York: Putnam, 1930), and *Pirates of the New England Coast*, 1923, by George Francis Dow (New York: Argosy-Antiquarian, 1968).

"plot was there to take Whales"—Smith (Kupperman, ed.), p. 220.

"every day we saw whales . . ."—*Mourt's Relation*, p. 16.

"They had to be farmers or starve"—Kittredge, *Cape Cod*, p. 71.

"Here they have neither wolves . . ."—*Letters from Nantucket and Martha's Vineyard*, 1782, by J. Hector St. John de Crevecoeur (Bedford, Mass.: Applewood Books, 1986), p. 32.

"so goodly a land . . ."—*Mourt's Relation*, p. 15.

"rich forests of oak and pine"—Chamberlain, p. 163. (There is some disagreement among scholars as to how significant the forests of Nantucket were, given its outlying location and the burning practices of the natives.)

"Vineyard men"—quoted in Philbrick (unless otherwise noted, all Philbrick references, including this one, are to *Away Off Shore*), p. 33.

"and were they to stay at home . . ."—Crevecoeur, p. 71.

"east of Tisbury"—quoted in Chamberlain, p. 165.

"Tethered in the desert . . ."—Thoreau, p. 137.

"now beaver and peltry fail us"—Stackpole, p. 18.

"whale bots or the like"—Stackpole, p. 21.

"anyone who could hold an oar . . ."—Philbrick, p. 70.

Chapter 18 "considered fully competent . . ."—Nickerson, p. 12.

"she submitted to the Power of Truth . . ."—Starbuck, p. 521.

"The scandal pitted not only Quaker . . ."—Philbrick, p. 150.

"The reading of this wondrous story . . ."—Melville's annotations to his copy of Chase's narrative, as reproduced in Appendix A of Heffernan, p. 191.

"All was anarchy & confusion . . ." and additional quotes of Cobb that follow—from his memoir, *Elijah Cobb, A Cape Cod Skipper*, by Elijah Cobb (New Haven: Yale University Press, 1925), p. 27ff.

"After discharging my cargo . . ."—Cobb, p. 59.

"very much like the picture I have seen of Noah's Ark . . ."—Nickerson, p. 12.

"A 'spouter' we knew her to be . . ."—Dana, p. 281.

"heavy, bluf-bowed and stubby . . ."—Stevens, p. 33.

"the character and standing . . ."—Chase et al., p. 17.

"any compensation save the privilege . . ."—Nickerson, p. 12.

"in all respects a sound, substantial . . ."—Chase et al., p. 20.

"and seventy two ninety fifths"—Heffernan, p. 10.

Chapter 19 "that all were overjoyed to hear . . ." and Nickerson quotes that follow—Nickerson, pp. 12–13.

"left the coast of America . . ."—Chase et al., p. 20.

"You boy, Tom . . ."—Nickerson, p. 13.

"Oh my God, what is this?"—quoted in Spears, pp. 342–43.

"cut the top of [Worth's] head very nearly off . . ."—deposition of George Comstock, at Valparaiso, June 9, 1824. Consular Dispatches, Valparaiso, Vol. I., quoted in Stackpole, pp. 416–18.

"where the mutineers used to sing . . ."—from the account of crew member William Lay, quoted in Stackpole, p. 425.

"was swung to the fore yard . . ."—Stackpole, p. 419.

"became very much attached to liquor"—from the account of crew member Cyrus Hussey, quoted in Stackpole, p. 425.

"all were seated around our kid . . ."—Nickerson, p. 14.

Chapter 20 "Many were rolling and tumbling . . ."—Nickerson, p. 14.

"There you stand, a hundred feet above . . ."—Melville, pp. 152 and 155.

"We had no means of ascertaining our true position . . ."—Nickerson, p. 22.

"very rough which caused the ship to roll . . ." and quotes on the squall to follow—Nickerson, p. 15.

"but miscalculated altogether the strength . . ." and quotes on the squall to follow—Chase et al., p. 20.

"would blow the hair off a dog"—Tilton, p. 164. In addition to the generous sections on gales and weather in many of the texts already mentioned, I benefited as well from *Cape Cod Maritime Disasters*, by William P. Quinn (Orleans, Mass.: Lower Cape Publishing, 1990), and *Disaster on Devil's Bridge*, by George A. Hough Jr. (Mystic, Conn.: Marine Historical Association, 1963).

"floated it to another place"—Bradford, p. 313.

"Who lives in that house?"—Thoreau, p. 158.

"then lying comfortably to the northwest . . ." and quotes from Rich that follow—quoted in Snow, pp. 117–18.

"No, I do not like to hear the sound . . ."—Thoreau, p. 158.

"You have to go, but you don't have to come back"—Lombard, pp. 75–76.

Chapter 21 "I am sorry they won't let you have your sloop again" and other quotes that follow—Dow and Edmonds, pp. 121–22.

"everything of value but the rigging"—Lombard, p. 146.

"Start fair"—Kittredge (*Mooncussers of Cape Cod*), p. 35.

"From all I can learn . . ."—Kittredge (*Mooncussers*), p. 44.

"Then and there . . ."—*Oxford Companion to American History*, by Thomas H. Johnson (New York: Oxford University Press, 1966), p. 604.

"Intelligence report on State of the Island . . ."—from "Grey's Raid: The Island's Biggest Historical Event," by Arthur R. Railton, *Dukes County Intelligencer* (Martha's Vineyard Historical Society, February 1997), p. 115.

"the only real engagement . . ."—Kittredge (*Cape Cod*), p. 125.

"the Nation of Nantucket"—Philbrick, p. 138.

"the Congress would not suffer him . . ."—Stackpole, p. 70.

"such Things are not only pernicious . . ."—Starbuck, p. 213.

"all the officers . . ."—Spears, p. 92.

"to keep this in court . . ."—Stevens, p. 101.

"fine weather again"—Chase et al., p. 21.

"cook house together . . ."—Nickerson, p. 15.

Chapter 23 "a cloud with its sides nearly perpendicular" and quotes that follow—Nickerson, pp. 18–19.

"it fills the mind with a sense of majesty . . ."—from the journal of Hannah Rebecca Burgess, quoted in *The Challenge of Hannah Rebecca*, by Martha Hassell (Sandwich Historical Society, 1986), p. 17.

"She had to . . ."—Whiting and Hough, p. 34.

"My wife has navigated . . ."—Hassell, p. 55.

"she is the meanest, most hoggish . . ."—Whiting and Hough, p. 8.

"Without exceptions I think him . . ."—Whiting and Hough, p. 7.

"The counsel for the opposite party . . ."—Kittredge (*Shipmasters*), p. 6.

"every man took to himself a rib"—Philbrick, p. 173.

"the whorehouse of the Pacific"—"Partners in History: The Bay of Islands and Martha's Vineyard," by Joan Druett, *Dukes County Intelligencer*, November 1991. Druett's *Petticoat Whalers* (Auckland, New Zealand: Collins, 1991) gives a more detailed picture of the sordid life of American whalers in New Zealand.

"The skin resembles parchment . . ."—Nantucket *Inquirer*, October 29, 1822, quoted at length in the endnotes of Philbrick, p. 256.

"a black market in these artifacts . . ."—Philbrick, p. 185.

"Go where you will . . ."—Crevecoeur, p. 61.

"large pyramidal hills . . ."—Nickerson, p. 21. *The Saltworks of Historic Cape Cod*, by William P. Quinn (Hyannis, Mass.: Parnassus Imprints, 1993), was helpful in the discussion that follows.

"more cheerful than usual"—Nickerson, p. 20.

Chapter 24 "nothing further transpired . . ."—Nickerson, p. 20.

"The beef was saltier than Lot's wife . . ."—Tilton, pp. 51–52.

"You scoundrels . . ."—Nickerson, p. 26.

"Closed ship as tight as possible . . ." and quotes about the fire that follow—from the journal of Nathaniel Jernegan, quoted in Mayhew and Hough, p. 48ff.

"They had many . . ."—Dana, p. 347.

"a broad-backed, thick-headed boy . . ."—Dana, pp. 251–56.

"Four months has passed . . ."—Mayhew and Hough, p. 12.

"started a sort of Coterie . . ."—Stevens, p. 37.

"here was the prospect of a chance . . ."—Nickerson, p. 22.

"*Scientific American* . . ."—quoted in Spears, p. 172. Of much more modern use on the biology of whales is *The Book of Whales*, by Richard Ellis (New York: Knopf, 1985), and *Among Whales*, by Roger Payne (New York: Scribner's, 1995).

"When we hauled alongside . . ."—Spears, p. 264.

"like the left wing on the day of Judgement . . ."—Melville, p. 418.

"At my first landing . . ."—Crevecoeur, p. 22.

"up to his armpits . . ."—Philbrick, p. 113.

"All hands strip down . . ."—Spears, p. 280.

"As we were in the very act . . ."—Nickerson, p. 22.

"Jonah of Cape Cod"—Snow, p. 332.

"began to follow the sea . . ."—Macy, p. 214.

"Of the application of leeches . . ."—*The Sailor's Physician*, by Usher Parsons, M.D. (Providence, R.I.: Barnum Field, 1824), p. 135.

"Esq. Clark has paid the dept [*sic*] of nature, it was my task to close his eyes . . ." —Cobb, p. 93.

"I was in the boat myself . . ."—Chase et al., p. 23.

Chapter 25 "our object . . ."—Chase et al., p. 22.

"delivering what letters we had for them"—Nickerson, p. 28.

"It was amusing . . ." and additional quotes on news from home—Nickerson, pp. 34–35.

"Capt. Nathan M. Jernegan . . ."—Mayhew and Hough, p. 2.

"Oh Peter, lonesome . . ."—from the letters of Susan Cromwell to Captain Peter Cromwell, in the collection of the Martha's Vineyard Historical Society.

"Captain Luce read today . . ."—Mayhew and Hough, p. 2.

"I wish to give you a strong dose . . ."—Nantucket *Inquirer*, January 1, 1855.

"There is nothing . . ."—Dana, p. 332.

"The least channel . . ."—Thoreau, p. 45.

"unknown city . . ."—quoted by Philbrick, p. 9.

There were other effects of smallness—the best source on hereditary deafness in Chilmark is *Everyone Spoke Sign Language*, by Nora Ellen Groce (Cambridge, Mass.: Harvard University Press, 1985).

"know little more than the value . . ."—quoted in Philbrick, p. 193.

"looked more to getting Jack's money . . ."—Nickerson, p. 30.

"in a short time . . ."—Nickerson, p. 36.

"These turtle are a most delicious . . ."—Chase et al., p. 22.

"Judging from the extent . . ."—Nickerson, p. 42.

"an exterminating warfare . . ."—Chase et al., pp. 19–20.

Chapter 26 "extremely fine and clear," and additional quotes of Owen Chase describing the attack by whale and the long voyage in the open boats—Chase et al., pp. 24–72.

"rushing with great swiftness . . ."—Pollard's brief account of the disaster appears in Chase et al., pp. 85–88.

"On his seeing . . ." and additional quotes of Nickerson describing the attack and the long voyage in the open boats appear on pp. 45–72 of his narrative.

"How are you, William Cary"—Stackpole, p. 301, and Stevens, p. 67.

Chapter 27 See the notes to the previous chapter regarding quotes from the various narratives of the *Essex* disaster.

"nineteen goat meals this week"—quoted in Kittredge (*Shipmasters*), p. 230.

"bones [were] working through their skins . . ."—journal of Commodore Ridgely, as quoted in Heffernan, pp. 99–100.

Chapter 28 "On his arrival . . ."—letter from Thomas Nickerson to Leon Lewis, October 1876, reprinted as Appendix C of Nickerson, p. 86.

"with 4 oars . . ."—Heffernan, p. 149.

"Now I am utterly ruined . . ."—Chase et al., p. 88.

"To me [Pollard was] the most impressive . . ."—Melville's annotations to his copy of Chase's Narrative, Appendix A of Heffernan, p. 194.

"He was constantly storing away things . . ."—quoted in Stackpole's afterword to Nickerson, p. 80.

"Owen is insane . . ."—quoted in Heffernan, p. 143.

"Miss Molly, we do not mention this . . ."—quoted in Stackpole's afterword to Nickerson, p. 78.

"The last of the fishing fleet . . ."—Kittredge, *Cape Cod*, p. 197.

"We were a pretty full ship . . ."—Tilton, p. 176ff. Also of great use regarding whaling in the Arctic is *Whales, Ice, & Men*, by John R. Brockstoce (New Bedford, Mass.: University of Washington/New Bedford Whaling Museum, 1986).

"solid bulkhead . . ."—Tilton, p. 193.

"As we went along . . ."—Tilton, pp. 196–98.

"one old discarded dory . . ."—Tilton, p. 215.

"the world would have proclaimed this . . ."—quoted in Spears, p. 398.

Chapter 29 "looming horrors . . ."—Kittredge, *Cape Cod*, p. 79.

"put all America behind us"—"A man may stand there and put all America behind him" is the last line of Thoreau's *Cape Cod*, p. 238.

Chapter 30 There are relatively few historical books on the rise of the tourist economy on Cape Cod and the Islands. In addition to some of the books already mentioned—particularly John Hay's "postepilogue" to Kittredge's *Cape Cod* and Henry Beetle Hough's *Martha's Vineyard, Summer Resort*, Robert Finch's anthology of regional literature, and several relevant chapters of *Three Centuries of the Cape Cod County*—two other books were useful enough to mention specifically: *City in the Woods*, by Ellen Weiss (Boston: Northeastern University Press, 1998), is a fascinating architectural history of the town of Oak Bluffs; and *Cape Cod Railroads*, by Robert Farson (Yarmouthport, Mass.: Cape Cod Historical Publications, 1993), is exactly what it sounds like.

"restrict all purchasers . . ."—quoted in Hough, p. 174.

"as a summer resort . . ."—Macy, p. 251.

"wholly unknown to the fashionable world"—Thoreau, p. 237.

"too high for us"—quoted in "Tourism and the Economy: Inns of the First Two Centuries," by John Braginton Smith, in *Three Centuries of the Cape Cod County*, p. 195.

"dotted with fine old towns . . ."—J. Smith, *Three Centuries*, p. 196.

"is not, indeed, the focus . . ."—Macy, p. 251.

"these thousands of people who frequent . . ."—quoted in Hough, p. 66.

"A man is appointed to clear . . ."—Thoreau, p. 57.

"a grove of enormous oaks"—Hough, p. 33.

"American romantic suburb"—Weiss, p. 38.

"Eden"—various New York *Times* stories on early Oak Bluffs are quoted in Weiss, pp. 50–52. The New York *Express* is quoted at length in Hough, pp. 53–54.

"probably the largest of the kind . . ."—quoted in Hough, p. 83. Grant's visit is covered in Hough, p. 113ff.

"Several schemes [were] devised . . ."—Starbuck, p. 633.

"So the Cape-Codder feels no qualms . . ."—Kittredge, *Cape Cod*, p. 306.

"does not seem to be entirely adequate . . ."—Kittredge, *Cape Cod*, p. 310.

"It was not for want or necessity . . ."—Bradford, p. 369.

"O, how changed . . ."—quoted in Hough, p. 71.

"still very much a middle-class island . . ."—from "Nantucket on My Mind," by David Halberstam, *Town & Country*, July 1999, pp. 76 and 126.

"These are summer memories . . ."—from *Hugging the Shore*, by John Updike, excerpted in *Cape Cod Stories*, John Miller and Tim Smith, eds. (San Francisco: Chronicle Press, 1996), p. 141.

"It is a singular employment . . ."—Thoreau, pp. 160 and 161.

Chapter 31 In addition to the books mentioned in the introduction to the notes for Chapter 7, I made additional use in this chapter of *Saltmarsh Ecology*, by Paul Adam (Cambridge, England: Cambridge University Press, 1990); *Birds of Massachusetts and Other New England States*, by Edward Howe Forbush (Boston: Commonwealth of Massachusetts, 1925); *Wilson's American Ornithology*, by T. M. Brewer (New York: H. S. Samuels, 1853); *The Land Birds and Game Birds of New England*, by H. D. Minot (Boston: Houghton Mifflin, 1903); and my trusty *Peterson Field Guide*.

"A salt marsh sanctions space . . ."—*The Way to the Salt Marsh*, by John Hay (Hanover, N.H.: University Press of New England, 1998), p. 246.

"is not the equal of Wilson's Snipe . . ."—Forbush, p. 438.

"millions that darkened the sky"—Forbush, p. 458.

"The cost is great . . ."—Chamberlain, p. 220. For the effects of DDT on local amphibians and reptiles, see Lazell.

"It is clear that generalizations . . ."—Adam, p. 349.

"Those who pride themselves . . ."—Hay, p. 246.

INDEX